Warwickshire County Council

Ken 3/20			

This item is to be returned or renewed before the latest date above. It may be borrowed for a further period if not in demand. **To renew your books:**

- **Phone the 24/7 Renewal Line 01926 499273 or**
- **Visit www.warwickshire.gov.uk/libraries**

Discover ● Imagine ● Learn ● *with libraries*

THE WORLD
BENEATH THEIR FEET

THE WORLD BENEATH THEIR FEET

The British, the Americans, the Nazis
and the Mountaineering Race to
Summit the Himalayas

SCOTT ELLSWORTH

JOHN MURRAY

First published in the United States of America in 2020 by Little, Brown and Company
First published in Great Britain in 2020 by John Murray (Publishers)
An Hachette UK company

1

Copyright © Scott Allen Ellsworth 2020

A CIP catalogue record for this title is available from the British Library

Hardback ISBN 978-1-473-64962-0
Trade Paperback ISBN 978-1-529-30719-1
eBook ISBN 978-1-473-64963-7

Typeset in Adobe Jenson Pro

Printed and bound in Great Britain by Clays Ltd, Elcograf S.p.A.

John Murray policy is to use papers that are natural, renewable and recyclable
products and made from wood grown in sustainable forests. The logging
and manufacturing processes are expected to conform to the
environmental regulations of the country of origin.

John Murray (Publishers)
Carmelite House
50 Victoria Embankment
London EC4Y 0DZ

www.johnmurraypress.co.uk

For
John Roper Ellsworth
and
William Upfield Ellsworth

Contents

Contents

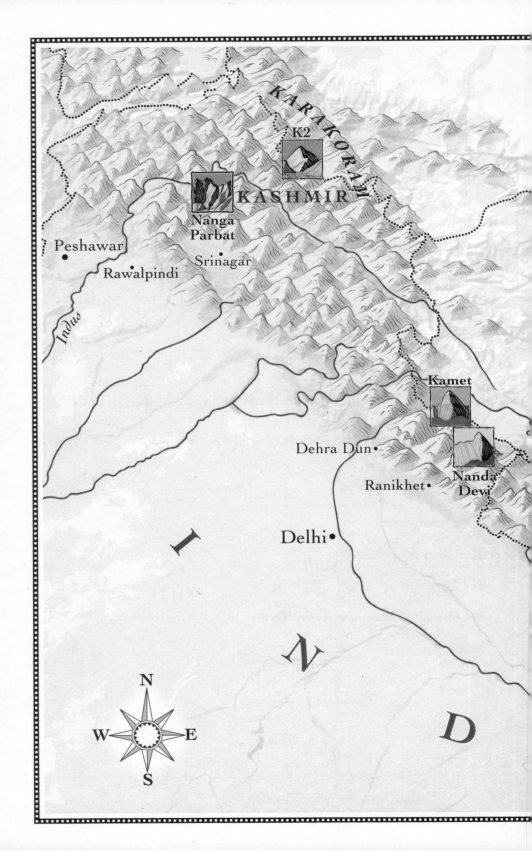

HIMALAYAS
1931 – 1953

0   MILES   200

0   KM   200

TIBET

Minya Konka

Lhasa

Brahmaputra

NEPAL

Everest   **Kanchenjunga**

BHUTAN

SIKKIM

Darjeeling

Purnea

Brahmaputra

Ganges

I N D I A

A Note to the Reader

This is a book about a period of time, not so long ago, when significant portions of the Earth were still cloaked in mystery. Long before the invention of the internet or cell phone technology, it was also an age when real-life heroes went about their work far from the glare of the twenty-four-hour news cycle, and were often cut off from the rest of the world for weeks, if not months, at a time.

The individuals who populate this story were a complicated lot. Some were principled, steadfast, and tenacious. Others were devious and cowardly. A handful were brilliant, others foolhardy. Like you, however, most of them were avid readers. On the highest mountains on the planet, where every additional ounce might determine the difference between victory and defeat, they brought along dog-eared copies of *Wuthering Heights*, *Pride and Prejudice*, and *The Oxford Book of Greek Verse* in their rucksacks. Two thousand feet below the summit of Mount Everest, inside a tiny tent pitched along a murderous ridge, a British climber named Eric Shipton tried to read, by flickering candlelight, Thorton Wilder's *The Bridge of San Luis Rey* , a novel which questioned the meaning of life in the face of the sudden and deadly collapse of an ancient rope bridge in eighteenth century Peru.

Many people believed that mountain climbers, as a whole, were mad.

Some undoubtedly were.

One dark, drizzly evening, while I was doing research for this book, I found myself walking along the back streets of Darjeeling, a mystical hill town perched along the edge of the eastern Himalayas. With the help of a local guide, I was trying to locate the former home of a legendary Sherpa, named Angtsering, who had worked on mountaineering expeditions back in the 1930s. While the old man was deceased, I had heard that his daughters still had a box of his climbing paraphernalia. Such materials, I'd reasoned, might help me to tell the story of the forgotten men and women who, decades earlier, had set out to climb the highest and deadliest mountains on Earth.

Finally, the guide and I found the house, a low-slung affair, painted a bright aqua with red gutters and windows trimmed in white. His elderly daughters met us at the door, dressed in long, coatlike sweaters and floor-length, patterned dresses. Clearly nervous, and uncertain of exactly what we wanted, they nevertheless invited us in and out of the rain. But as soon as the conversation turned to their father, their eyes brightened, cups of hot tea suddenly materialized, and from a battered wooden box came out old photographs and copper medals and newspaper clippings yellowed with time. Sitting in the sisters' snug living room, for a couple of brief, magical hours we were transported to another age, a time when awe and wonder lived on mountaintops, and the world was still fresh and new. I hope you will find some of that in these pages as well.

THE WORLD
BENEATH THEIR FEET

The Last Place on Earth

During the darkening decade of the 1930s, as the winds of war began to gather in the chanceries and defense ministries of central Europe and the Far East, and dictators began to trace lines on maps with their fingers, there was a race like no other. It had no fixed starting point, no single finish line, no referees, and no written rules. And while it would ultimately involve men and women from ten nations, capture front-page headlines around the globe, and claim dozens of lives, its most remarkable feature was that this was a race to a place that no human being had ever been before.

In truth, there weren't many such places left.

For the world had already grown perilously small. The North and South Poles had already been conquered. Explorers and scientists, armed with quinine, Colt .32-caliber automatic pistols, and gabardine jackets from Abercrombie & Fitch, had hacked their way into the highlands of New Guinea, uncovered a lost city in Peru, and gazed with awe and wonder upon Alaska's Valley of Ten Thousand Smokes. A Frenchman had driven a modified Citröen automobile two thousand miles across the Sahara Desert, while a sixteen-year-old ranch hand in New Mexico, mistaking a plume of bats for a funnel of smoke, discovered the most magnificent cave system on Earth.

Even former President Teddy Roosevelt, overweight and nursing an infected leg, had, in 1913 and 1914, ridden a dugout canoe hundreds of miles down the piranha-infested Rio da Dúvida—the River of Doubt—into the far reaches of the Amazon basin. And one long day in June 1928, a former Kansas tomboy turned *Cosmopolitan*

Scott Ellsworth

editor had flown in a Fokker Trimotor from Newfoundland to Wales, becoming the first woman to cross the Atlantic in an airplane. When she returned home to the United States, Amelia Earhart was given a ticker-tape parade on Broadway and a private audience with President Coolidge in the White House. Even the remotest island in the vast Pacific Ocean had, at one time or another, felt the scrape of a boat keel against its shoreline. There was no place on earth, it seemed, that was beyond the reach of humankind.

Except for one.

Stretching for more than two thousand miles from the Hindu Kush of eastern Afghanistan to the far reaches of western China, the Himalayas are the tallest and mightiest mountain range on the planet. But the tops of its highest peaks, some fourteen in number, all of which stand more than eight thousand meters, or 26,246 feet, high, had never felt the weight of a human being. Mount Everest, of course, was the best known, but the others, like K2, Annapurna, and Kangchenjunga, were equally majestic and foreboding. The southern face of Nanga Parbat, along the edge of Kashmir, shot up nearly ten thousand vertical feet—roughly the height of ten Empire State Buildings stacked end to end. Twice as high as the Alps or the Rockies, these were true geographical monsters, behemoths of rock and ice so large that they created their own weather systems.

Here was a landform so vast and impenetrable that it had altered the very course of human history, keeping Hinduism out of China, Genghis Khan out of India, and turning the fabled Silk Road to the north, bringing spices and Chinese silks to ancient Greece, and Roman coins and sturdy Russian ponies to the imperial court of the Han dynasty. But despite centuries of off-and-on exploration, from the wanderings of Marco Polo to the Great Trigonometrical Survey, the Himalayas had not given up her secrets easily. By the closing years of the nineteenth century, much of the range had still not been adequately mapped, and not a single one of its highest peaks had been climbed. Subsequent efforts, in the first decades of the twentieth century, to climb to the top of Everest, Kangchenjunga,

K2, and Annapurna, all ended in failure. The roof of the world was still untouched.

By the beginning of the 1930s, however, enough had been learned about the extreme challenges that the Himalayas posed that a new generation of mountain climbers, armed with new ideas, new equipment, and new techniques, concluded that the summits of the world's highest mountains were, in fact, within reach. So they decided to find out.

The men—and women—who tried to do so aren't household names today. Indeed, many of them had been considered to be failures during their lifetimes, misfits and odd ducks who never settled down, never got real jobs, never joined the ranks of everyday society. Some had spent their twenties bumming about the Alps with baguettes and Baedekers in their rucksacks, climbing vertical granite spires in shorts and street shoes—and they are the spiritual ancestors of today's dirtbag rock climbers and rope bums. Others were accomplished professionals who, despite the pressures of their careers, found ways to keep climbing as a part of their lives. Altogether, they encompassed cockeyed dreamers and sober realists, college graduates and illiterates, pacifists and combat veterans, a beekeeper, a large number of physicians, a Wyoming cowboy, and a New York playboy.

By contemporary standards, the equipment they used was shockingly primitive. Today, the climbers who queue up to climb Mount Everest are armed with personal avalanche beacons, real-time satellite weather reports, carbon-steel ice tools, and state-of-the-art oxygen systems. They pull on thousand-dollar insulated boots with silicone soles and moisture-wicking uppers, and they sleep in laboratory-rated down-filled sleeping bags on closed-cell foam pads. And while the specter of death still haunts the great peaks of the Himalayas— witness the long lines of climbers hoping to summit Everest, a tragedy waiting to happen—twenty-first-century climbers can monitor their pulse rates on their Apple Watches, and fuel their bodies with energy bars and isotonic sports gels. After the climbing is done, they can download YouTube videos of themselves that they shot with GoPro cameras on the summit, and post them on Facebook, Instagram, and Snapchat.

The climbers of the Great Race had none of these things.

They wore cotton parkas and scratchy woolen sweaters, and they climbed five miles into the sky wearing leather hobnailed boots while carrying wood-handled ice axes and heavy coils of manila rope. They slept in drafty canvas tents and tried to cook their meals on fickle kerosene-fueled stoves. They drank brandy and smoked cigarettes, read Doestoevsky and Dickens at 24,000 feet, and they gutted out restless nights only to discover, in the dim light of dawn, that a foot of snow had sifted on top of their sleeping bags during the night. They had virtually no decent maps, few detailed photographs, and little idea as to what lay above them.

Except, of course, for the possibility of their own demise.

For these were killer mountains. Here were avalanches so massive that blocks of ice the size of two-story houses could suddenly come crashing down. Rockfall was a near constant danger, while weakened cornices and unstable wind slab were far from uncommon. On the great peaks of the Himalayas there were murderous winds and blinding whiteouts, while temperatures could plunge downward toward life-threatening levels in a matter of minutes. And while no one in the 1930s fully understood this yet, once climbers reached a certain altitude, their bodies began to break down. On the roof of the world, death was never far.

Today that is still true. For despite the advancements in climbing equipment over the past three-quarters of a century, fatalities are far from uncommon on the highest mountains on earth. According to one estimate, one out of every four climbers trying to summit K2 has died. On Annapurna, the number is one in three. On Everest, so many bodies of climbers remain on the upper reaches that they are used as route markers.

There are new dangers as well, especially in the Karakoram, the westernmost of the great Himalayan ranges. On the morning of

The World Beneath Their Feet

June 22, 2013, a group of sixteen armed militants, shouting "God is great," ambushed a group of Chinese, American, and European climbers at their base camp on Nanga Parbat. Chen Honglu, a climber with dual American and Chinese citizenship, tackled one of the militants as they entered camp. He was killed immediately. The other climbers had their hands tied and, according to a Pakistani who survived the ambush, were told to turn their faces away. Then they were shot to death.

Afterwards, the killers had breakfast.

Viewed from today's perspective, the Himalayan climbers of the 1930s have a David-versus-Goliath quality about them, and rightly so. But that is not the whole of their story. Because these forgotten mountaineers didn't just push the limits of what the human body could endure, and extend the reach of humankind to the very edge of the sky. In their triumphs and in their failures, they also stirred the aspirations and imaginations of millions of ordinary citizens.

In its heart center, the saga of the Great Himalayan Race is a story about dreamers and dreams, hard work and determination, and of never, ever giving up. For as they scraped up against the stars, these overlooked heroes remind us of what mere human beings, armed with courage, tenacity, training, experience, and resolve, can accomplish in the face of seemingly insurmountable odds. In an age of pessimism and division, their story is one of teamwork and common purpose, lofty goals and earthbound solutions. But theirs is also a story of good and evil, of treachery and heroism, and a world changing beneath their feet—all to the incessant drumbeat of the approach of the most destructive war in human history.

This is a book about mountains.

But it is also a book about the men and women who dared to match them.

It begins in London on a late spring morning.

Book One

Fifteen minutes of dicey, fatiguing crampon work brought me safely to the bottom of the incline, where I easily located my pack, and another ten minutes after that I was in camp myself. I lunged into my tent with my crampons still on, zipped the door tight, and sprawled across the frost-covered floor too tired to even sit upright. For the first time I had a sense of how wasted I really was: I was more exhausted than I'd ever been in my life. But I was safe. Andy was safe. The others would be coming into camp soon. We'd fucking done it. We'd climbed Everest. It had been a little sketchy there for a while, but in the end everything had turned out great.

It would be many hours before I learned that everything had not in fact turned out great—that nineteen men and women were stranded up on the mountain by the storm, caught in a desperate struggle for their lives.

— **Jon Krakauer**, *Into Thin Air*
Describing events on
Mount Everest, May 10, 1996

CHAPTER ONE

Ice Axes and Dinner Jackets

R ain had hammered London off and on all week long.

It drummed the soot off the windows of the Houses of Parliament and soaked through the leather-soled shoes worn by shop clerks and secretaries hustling to work on the wet sidewalks. Along Oxford Street, the double-deckers lumbered back and forth like giant mechanical bugs, with their windshield wipers keeping a steady three-two time, while over at Regent's Park, the zookeepers once again had to leave the artificial sunlamps switched on in the nearly deserted aviaries. Even the pickpockets at Piccadilly Circus drifted away, looking for more promising territory somewhere indoors. But finally, on Monday morning, May 25, 1931, the sun reappeared, drying the pavement, opening windows in both gloomy flats and posh townhouses, and flooding the whispering gallery at St. Paul's with shafts of golden sunlight. Overnight, despite the exhaust and all the rank and pungent smells of the world's second-largest metropolis, the air suddenly seemed different. Summer, it appeared, would be coming to London this year after all.

One of the articles in the *Times* that morning was what the newspaper's composition editors in their offices on Queen Victoria Street, bent over their page mock-ups the night before, would have generously called filler—short news items that found their way into print largely because they perfectly fit into an otherwise blank bit of space left over after the most important articles were laid out. The particular item in question, buried on page 9, was a three-paragraph story titled "Kanchenjunga."

The gist of the article was that on that very day in Munich, a group of nine German and Austrian mountain climbers would be leaving for India, where they hoped to climb, for the first time ever, to the top of the third-highest mountain on earth. "The novel feature of this new venture," the unsigned story read, "is that the attempt to ascend Kanchenjunga will be made in August-September, that is, during the monsoon." The brief news item concluded by adding that "dispatches describing the establishment of camps and ice caves up the spurs of Kanchenjunga and the assault on the summit will appear in the *Times.*"

Few Londoners, of course, even saw the story. Most of the city's other newspapers ignored it, as did the news presenters at the BBC. And even for those readers of the *Times* who paused long enough to give it a quick glance over a piece of toast and a cup of tea in the kitchen, or those crammed shoulder to shoulder in the Tube on their morning commute, a brief dispatch about what a group of German mountain climbers were *hoping* to accomplish would have caused barely a ripple. Even for those-in-the-know, namely, readers who possessed at least a smattering of knowledge about mountaineering, the undated story in the *Times* wouldn't have elicited much more than a few throat clearings or stifled yawns.

And for good reason.

Because for nearly a century, the English had dominated the world of mountaineering. Though they hailed from an island nation where the highest point, a thirty-two-hundred-foot rounded bump in the Lake District called Scafell Pike, could be walked up and down on an October afternoon, mountain climbers from England were widely regarded as the world's finest, a globe-trotting race of determined daredevils who, if they didn't invent mountaineering, at least ushered it into the modern age. During one frantic decade back in the 1850s and 1860s, when thirty-six formidable peaks in the Alps were successfully climbed for the first time, British mountaineers were responsible for *thirty-one*. It was an Englishman, and not a Swiss or a German or an Italian, who was the first to stand on the summit of the Matterhorn. And while other nations also produced feats of climbing excellence, none could match the overall record laid down by the British.

Nor was that all. British climbers were the first to regularly use ice axes, the sturdy T-shaped tools with a spike at the bottom and a pick and adze at the top, that would come to symbolize mountaineering. It was a London rope-maker who manufactured the world's first mountaineering rope, and it was climbers from Great Britain who designed the first expedition tents. In an age where most of the world's population either lived far from mountains or avoided them altogether, Oxford and Cambridge men, dressed in High Street woolens and lugging tins of tea from Fortnum & Mason in their rucksacks, could be regularly found scrambling along some ice-choked ridge in the middle of nowhere, miles from the nearest human settlement. Whether or not mad dogs and Englishmen could stay out of the noonday sun was debatable. But Englishmen—and Englishwomen—simply couldn't keep out of the hills.

The spiritual home of all of this activity, however, was neither in the Alps nor the Lake District, Ben Nevis nor Mount Snowdon. Instead it could be found in an elegantly understated eighteenth-century London townhouse at No. 23 Savile Row, perched along the eastern edge of Mayfair. The Alpine Club, which occupied the building's second and third floors, was not simply the oldest mountaineering society on earth. It was also one of the most exclusive organizations in all of Great Britain. But what distinguished the club wasn't merely that its members were the products of proper, upper-class breeding, many with home addresses in Belgravia and strings of honorifics following their names. There were plenty of clubs in London that boasted similarly exclusive rosters.

Rather, the members of the Alpine Club had also inched their way up vertigo-inducing granite walls in Chamonix, battled bandits and howling winds in the Caucasus, and willed themselves to the top of some icy, unnamed summit in the Andes, their food gone and their fingers turning blue. Admission to the Alpine Club was strictly determined by its members, and while a select few hardy outsiders were roundly and enthusiastically welcomed at black-tie dinners and other club functions, full membership could not be bought. It could only be earned, the hard way, on some of the most dangerous terrain on earth.

But there was something else that bound the few hundred members of the Alpine Club together, and that was an approach to life that went beyond a comfortable bank balance, a respectable wife and obedient children, and whisky and cigars in the bar at Claridge's. Some had drunk deeply from the mystical wellsprings of Romanticism, with its exultation of both nature and the individual, and its parade of heroes, like Lord Byron and Shelley, who found fulfillment far from London's madding crowds. Others drew inspiration from national heroes old and new, from Shakespeare's Henry V going "once more unto the breach," from Lord Nelson turning the tide of battle at Trafalgar, or from George Gordon, the hero of Khartoum, calmly facing the razor-sharp scimitars of 50,000 Dervish troops. Many members of the Alpine Club found the mountains to be an intoxicant like no other, a place where every facet of one's being—physical, mental, and spiritual—was stretched to the limit.

But all of them believed, in one way or another, that life was to be *lived*. And for Great Britain's globe-trotting mountain climbers, be it for King and Country or just for themselves, that meant testing themselves against the most daunting peaks on the planet. And once you had done so—overcoming the terror that kept your feet and hands from moving along an ice-pocked ridge hundreds of yards above what could easily become your very own rock-strewn grave, or surviving a whiteout blizzard at 14,000 feet—you were changed forever. And when the climbing years were done, you rekindled those feelings with other members of your tribe over *truite meunière*, *pommes parisienne*, and bottles of Pouilly-Fuissé at the annual Alpine Club dinners.

Or, at least, those who returned did.

The World Beneath Their Feet

Because the mortal dangers in mountain climbing were far from hypothetical. On the very first ascent of the Matterhorn, three British climbers and one French alpine guide fell to their deaths when the youngest member of their party slipped and a rope broke. In the decades that followed, dozens of others also perished from loose rock and unstable footing, sudden falls and bad luck. Henry Fox, an experienced climber and early Alpine Club star, disappeared in the Caucasus Mountains, while Alfred Mummery, perhaps the greatest British climber of his era, was crushed to death in an avalanche in 1895. Humphrey Owen Jones and Muriel Gwendolyn Edwards died, on their honeymoon, when their guide stumbled and yanked them off a small peak near Mont Blanc. And on June 8, 1924, George Mallory and Sandy Irvine set off to try and reach the summit of Mount Everest—never to be seen again.

That last one stung. A lot.

For not only was Mallory a beloved member of the Alpine Club, but he was a vibrant, pulsating life force all his own. Charming, funny, and wildly handsome, he caused more than a few women, and a handful of men, to literally swoon. "Heavens!" wrote the English poet Lytton Strachey of Mallory, "he's six foot high, with the body of Praxiteles, and a face—of incredible—the mystery of Botticelli, the refinement and delicacy of a Chinese print." An occasional interloper among the Bloomsbury Set, the London-based cluster of writers and artists who cocked their eyebrows at conventional society, Mallory was also a part-time lecturer at Cambridge. But his true calling was mountaineering. Not only did he play a leading role in three Everest expeditions, but it was Mallory who, when asked why he sought to climb the world's highest peak, came up with the answer used by climbers ever since: "Because it's there." Fearless, self-effacing, and possessing a suitably upper-class background, he was a model representative of British mountaineering.

But Mallory's death also struck a chord deep in the nation's soul. For some, he called to mind another fallen hero, polar explorer Robert Falcon Scott, and his star-crossed attempt to reach the

South Pole some twelve years earlier. For others, Mallory and Irvine reminded them of their own brothers and sons and husbands whose lives had been cut short in the Great War. And while newspapermen, Anglican priests, and school headmasters penned encomiums to the two deceased climbers, it was the memorial service held in London in their honor that revealed the true measure of their worth. For among the hundreds of mourners who filled the sanctuary of St. Paul's on that crisp October Monday was no less than His Majesty, King George V. Never before had any mountain climber—anytime, anywhere—received such attention.

At No. 23 Savile Row, meanwhile, it did not take long for wheels to start turning. For while the loss of Mallory and Irvine was deeply felt, the real question was: When could the next Everest expedition be mounted? Within days of the memorial service at St. Paul's, Alpine Club speakers were dispatched across the countryside to drum up public support for such an undertaking. But an even bigger opportunity cropped up later that year—and with it, an even bigger set of problems. To help finance Mallory's final expedition, arrangements had been made with an ex-soldier and adventurer with the formidable name of John Baptist Lucius Noel to make a documentary film about the 1924 Everest expedition. The plan, of course, had been that the motion picture would triumphantly document the first successful scaling of the mountain. But when the expedition failed, and Mallory and Irvine disappeared, expectations for the film were dashed.

Undeterred, Noel instead created an extravaganza. When *The Epic of Everest* premiered in London in 1924, two weeks before Christmas, the filmmaker and impresario had transformed the Scala Theatre near Bedford Square into a miniature Tibet, complete with dazzling hand-painted backdrops of the Himalayas and a mesmerizing live performance by seven Tibetan monks, who danced and chanted to the raucous accompaniment of trumpets, cymbals, bells, and drums, the latter played with drumsticks made from human thigh bones. And the film itself, with some scenes shot at as high as 23,000 feet, was absolutely mesmerizing. No one had ever seen anything like it. Noel's gambit paid off. *The Epic of Everest* was a box-office smash, one that played to packed houses in Great Britain, Germany, the United States, and Canada.

But not in Tibet.

In Lhasa, the conservative religious authorities were outraged, both by the dancing monks and by scenes in the film that depicted the Tibetan people as childish, dirty, and lice-ridden. In response, they cut off all access to Everest. No British mountain climbers would be allowed near the mountain in 1925. When a request was formulated one year later to allow for a new expedition to Mount Everest, the British diplomatic officer in Lhasa didn't even bother to forward it to the Tibetan authorities. Instead of a triumph, *The Epic of Everest* turned out to be a disaster. The climbers at the Alpine Club would just have to sit tight until, hopefully, the government in Tibet cooled off, and the door to Everest swung open once again.

For five years, they waited.

The rains returned in September.

The London summer of 1931 had been balmy and blustery. An earthquake off Dogger Bank had rattled teacups as far north as Manchester and sent dogs scurrying beneath beds in Birmingham. Gandhi arrived in London on September 12, 1931, to attend the Second Indian Round-Table Conference, only to be pointedly told to call off civil disobedience protests against the Raj. The next day, a British airplane, powered by twin Rolls Royce engines, won the annual Schneider Trophy for the second year in a row, logging a world-record speed of more than 340 miles per hour. And in London, the English composer Edward Elgar and the London Philharmonic celebrated the opening of a brand-new recording studio in a century-old mansion located at No. 3 Abbey Road.

Over on Savile Row, however, autumn delivered a much different kind of tidings. At the Alpine Club, members were transfixed by a series of sensational firsthand reports published in the *Times* about the German expedition to Kangchenjunga. On September 26, the newspaper reported that the climbers from Munich had fought their way above 23,000 feet on what was then believed to be the second highest mountain on the planet. "The greatest technical and other difficulties are behind us," wrote the leader of the expedition. "A strong body of six climbers and four porters with a fortnight's provisions are ready in the highest camps to attack the summit of Kanchenjunga."

The news struck like a hammer. While the London climbing establishment was stuck in a kind of purgatory, waiting to see if they'd eventually get another crack at Everest, a group of German mountaineers had placed themselves into position to be the first humans—ever—to climb to the top of one of the great Himalayan giants. In their own similar quest, the British now had company. What they did not yet realize was just how truly formidable that company was.

CHAPTER TWO

A Wind from the East

They came home by the thousands.

Some walked, others nicked rides in lorries or in the wooden beds of horse-drawn hay wagons. But most traveled by rail. You could see them, crowded into boxcars and filling the passenger carriages, or standing, shoulder to shoulder, in the graylit terminals in the big cities, or lining the platforms of the train stations in the little country towns. Some, missing a foot or an entire leg, were on crutches. Others, their faces half-wrapped in gauze bandages, were now blind. Most were scarred, many carried bits of shrapnel inside them, and few would ever sleep soundly again. But all through the spring and summer of 1919 they came, wave after wave, rattling across the great iron bridges that spanned the Rhine, or trudging along dirt roads, the dappled sunlight falling across their now threadbare, blue-gray uniforms. The proud Imperial German Army that had gone off to fight for the Fatherland in the heady autumn of 1914 now returned home—ill, hungry, and broken.

And with them, like a blight, came a blackened harvest of alienation and resentment. You could see it in the haunted faces of the men who lingered in unemployment offices and darkened the corners of penny-a-dance bars, or stood on street corners in Berlin and Düsseldorf rattling coins in a tin cup. One could hear it in the awkward silences that invaded the bedroom and hovered over the dinner table, or glimpse it in an empty pew at the neighborhood church. For these were men who no longer fit into their old prewar skins, men for whom too many of the old truths had died in the stench and mud of the trenches. Their old world, with its pomp and ceremony and banners snapping in the wind, was, like their youth, gone forever.

The last of the German soldiers to return home were the former POWs. Loaded onto troop trains and channel barges, they had been taken, under guard, to prisoner-of-war camps as far away as Scotland and the Isle of Man, where they built roads, harvested crops, busted rock at quarries, and manufactured bricks and cement. Not released until more than a year after the fighting had stopped, they received no parades or official thank-you delegations when they finally made their way back to Germany. Instead, they were the last of the walking dead, the final human bill for the shattered dreams of 1914.

Among them was a shadow named Paul Bauer.

In later years, he would deliver speeches in packed lecture halls, after which his admirers, young and old, would refer to him deferentially as Herr Bauer and seek his precise and controlled signature in their copies of his books. Film crews would follow him and, once, beneath a blood-orange California sun, his name would shimmer in Olympic glory. But Paul Bauer was also a magician and an image maker, one who kept a tight rein on his private life, revealing little of his background and hiding his defeats in tight-lipped silence. Nevertheless, bits and pieces can be pried loose from old records and long-buried documents. And unlike the carefully managed profile that he presented to the world, Bauer lived a life where triumph was tainted by shadow.

Originally from Kusel, a drowsy Palatine market town not far from the French border, Bauer had been on a bicycle trip in northern Italy during the fateful summer of 1914. Nearing Lake Constance, along the Swiss border, on the way back home, he'd noticed the official placards, hastily pasted onto telephone poles and post office walls, announcing a stunning succession of events—the murder of the Archduke Ferdinand, Austria declaring war on Serbia, Russian mobilization, French mobilization, the threat of imminent hostilities. When the war finally came, Bauer enlisted in the 18th Bavarian Infantry Regiment and was quickly delivered to the Western Front. Three months later, near the Ypres Canal in Belgium, he was wounded by shrapnel. He spent his eighteenth birthday in a hospital bed.

We know that his unit, with Bauer back in the ranks, later fought in the Battle of the Somme in 1916, where nearly a half million Englishmen fell like autumn leaves, and the heat from artillery barrages was so intense that it turned tree trunks into charcoal. Bauer's regiment was "one of the best German units," wrote an American intelligence officer. "It always fought well, showing great energy in the offensive and preserving a great tenacity in the defensive." And for two and a half years, the 18th fought a brutal and unrelenting seesaw campaign against the British. Hundreds of its soldiers were cut down by machine-gun fire or atomized by artillery shells. Others fell to shell shock or trench foot, or had been the unlucky souls whose last cigarette had caught the eye of an English sniper. Then, at Messines, where British sappers blew through the German lines with a series of earth-shaking mine explosions, Bauer was taken prisoner.

The record on Paul Bauer then grows dim.

We know that he was sent to a prisoner-of-war camp in England. But we don't know in which camp, or camps, he was held, nor for exactly how long. These records appear to have vanished. But in subsequent writings, both by Bauer and by those who knew him, we do know that he saw a good bit of England during his time as a POW. And we also know that he was deeply impressed by—and jealous of—what he'd seen. Moreover, this envy would not quickly pass, but would haunt him for years.

We also know that when Bauer was finally released and allowed to return to Germany, his homecoming was—for him—particularly bitter. "In November 1919, in a station building on the Rhine guarded by colored French soldiers," he later wrote, "I was summarily commanded to remove the uniform which I had worn for five years, and in incredibly shabby 'civvies' issued by the Government, a skull-cap on my head and carrying my entire possessions in a sack on my back, I made my way home."

He did not stay long. Finding his hometown occupied by foreign troops, Bauer drifted to Munich, an old man at twenty-three. "We had fought for our people and many of my friends had followed the classic example and laid down their lives," he would later claim. "But now we found that the love of Fatherland, heroism, and self-sacrifice were looked down upon and denigrated."

"We were strangers," he added, "outcasts in our own country."

A little more than a year after Paul Bauer had moved to Munich, during the spring of 1921, hydrologists at the Bogenhausen gauging station on the east side of town took note of the fact that the levels of the Isar River, whose clear waters ran right through the center of the city, were higher than they'd been in decades. Heavy snows had blanketed the Alps all winter, and with the arrival of warmer weather came the annual spring runoff, this time to historic levels. Yet despite what was happening with the Isar, one did not have to look far for change. For on the sidewalks and in the cafés and beer halls of the ancient Bavarian capital, the ground had already begun to shift.

The Jews felt it first. In early 1921, the Orthodox synagogue on Herzog-Rudolf-Strasse was vandalized when unknown persons painted black swastikas on its front facade, while members of a local Hebrew club were ambushed and beaten up by a gang of right-wing thugs. At the University of Munich, Albert Einstein, the scientist whose theory of relativity had rocked the scientific world—the "Jew physicist" was what the anti-Semitic rags called him—was prevented from speaking on campus. Non-Jews were targeted as well. Lectures by Max Weber, the esteemed sociologist, were shouted down by rowdy students who disdained his liberal politics. And across town, posters began to appear inviting local citizens to come and hear the dynamic speaker who was the head of the brand-new National Socialist political party, or Nazis, as they were soon called. "Fellow

Germans are welcome," the announcements promised, adding, "Jews will not be admitted."

Others fared even worse. In October 1920, a servant girl named Marie Sandmeier went missing after she reported to the authorities the existence of an illegal cache of arms at her former employer's house. Her lifeless body was later found hanging from a tree in Forstenrieder Park, next to a sign that read, "You lousy bitch. You have betrayed your Fatherland." Around the same time, a local waiter also threatened to reveal the presence of another illegal stockpile of guns. "Instead," a historian later wrote, "he got a trip to the bottom of the Isar with stones tied to his legs and eleven holes in his head."

On the streets of Munich, darkness was already falling.

Paul Bauer, meanwhile, pushed ahead. He had joined the Freikorps, an anticommunist paramilitary group that waged street battles against local communists and, it was said, he even directed the shelling of a left-leaning working-class neighborhood. And while Bauer soon came to admire Nazi leader Adolf Hitler—"he who must not be impugned"—he apparently held back, at least for now, from any further involvement in Munich's rapidly changing political scene. To begin, he was simply too busy.

Determined to get ahead, Bauer had enrolled in the University of Munich, the city's 450-year-old institution of higher learning, and taken up the study of law. While the city hummed about him, with its noisy beer halls and cafés, Bauer stayed the course, burning the midnight oil while burying his head in dense volumes of statutes and case law. But his anger remained, especially against what he called the "November criminals"—the Berlin politicians who, to his way of thinking, had sold out Germany at the end of the war. Caught between academics and bitterness, Bauer needed a release. And, in time, he found one.

"My refuge," he later wrote, "was the mountains."

Rising like a Wagnerian stage set due south of Munich, the Bavarian Alps—glittering white in the winter, and cool and enchanting in the summer—were a mere two-and-a-half-hour train ride from the city center. "I began to go out into the mountains on my own," he recalled, armed with little more than a groundcloth, a bedroll, and a Bavarian Army Ordnance Map. "I followed my own paths—alone." The effect was transformative. Here, among the high, windswept ridges and jagged peaks was a world without compromise and chicanery. Here, beside the hard limestone cliffs was a land of both gleaming promises and rock-hard truths, a place for an ex-soldier to test his mettle.

"I thanked my lucky stars," he added, "and gloried in my health and strength."

In time, however, Bauer began to seek harder routes—scree-covered ledges where a misstep could lead to a broken back, ice-covered ridges as steep as a mansard roof, tight spots where unprotected solo climbing was little more than an invitation to suicide. "Gradually," he later wrote, "I began to seek the company of others again."

In reality, he didn't have much of a choice. But as it turned out, his timing could not have been better.

For in the years just before, and right after, the Great War, a new generation of German and Austrian climbers had suddenly found their footing. Unafraid to try out new ideas and novel techniques, these German-speaking mountaineers brought an energy to climbing the likes of which had not been felt in a half century. In the eastern Alps of Austria and Germany, modern rock climbing would first take shape. With Munich as its spiritual capital, nothing short of a climbing revolution would take place. The evidence was everywhere.

You could find it in the standing-room-only mountain huts in the Tyrol, where, on weekends and summer weekdays, thousands of novice mountaineers spread out their sleeping bags. You could hear it the jangle of early gear racks and the crunch of boots on sun-hardened snow. You could see it in the corner movie houses in Berlin and Frankfurt, where a new kind of motion picture, the *Bergfilm*, awed audiences with stunning, on-location mountain scenery and the fresh new faces of the actors—including a sultry, twenty-four-year-old former dancer named Leni Riefenstahl. And you could find it in the growing membership rolls of climbing and hiking clubs. Unlike the Alpine Club in Great Britain, whose membership rarely rose more than a couple of hundred, the Deutscher und Österreichischer Alpenverein boasted more than two-hundred *thousand* members. "There is a Sektion of the D.O.A.V. in every important town in Germany," wrote one astonished English traveler. "This life and all that implies has become for them as much a part of their existence as the business of earning bread."

Equally impressive were the climbers themselves. For along with their enthusiasm, the new generation of German-speaking climbers also brought with them an unparalleled openness to new ideas. In 1910, an Austrian mountain guide teamed up with a Münster blacksmith to create a new one-piece piton, the metal spike that climbers would hammer into rock walls for protection. At about the same time, a climber in Munich introduced the first true mountaineering carabiners, the oval-shaped metal connectors that would soon be used to clip ropes to pitons. Other innovations followed after the war, including ice axes with shortened staffs for climbing near vertical ice- and snow-covered slopes.

The rush of change was breathtaking. Armed with these new tools and techniques, and with a growing confidence in themselves, this new generation of German-speaking climbers began to tackle routes long thought to be impossible. And one by one, they notched a succession of the hardest rock climbs ever accomplished—the east face of the Campanile Basso, the south face of the Schüsselkarspitze, the west face of the Predigtstuhl, and the north face of the Seekarlspitze. Then, one Friday in the late summer of 1925, the northwestern face of Monte Civetta, a three-thousand-foot vertical wall in the Dolomites that had defeated mountaineers for decades, fell in fifteen hours to a two-man team led by a twenty-five-year-old Munich locksmith. Like vertical ballet dancers, the Germans and their Austrian cousins had taken climbing to a whole new level.

These accomplishments had also come with a price—broken ribs and shattered patellae, torn-off fingernails and scraped-up elbows, backs drenched with cold sweat and stomachs hollowed out by a gripping fear. The German-speaking alpinists had become the best rock climbers in the world. But they had also fought for and earned their preeminence every inch along the way. One adoring Italian mountaineering writer called the new style *alpinismo acrobatico*.

The British were less charitable. At the tradition-minded Alpine Club in London, where pitons and other forms of artificial aids were viewed by many with disdain, the new style was derided as unsportsmanlike. One Alpine Club member called it "dangle and whack" climbing. Others were more concise: it just wasn't "cricket."

Paul Bauer saw something different.

Mountaineering, for him, was never just about reaching a summit, or finding one's way up a particularly challenging route. Instead, it was also a way to reclaim the honor of Germany, the honor that had not been lost in the trenches but in the treachery of the Treaty of Versailles. "As a result of the war and the bitter aftermath, an unusually determined but unexacting generation had arisen in Germany," Bauer wrote. "In many a weary climb and many a night under canvas we had wrung from nature her inmost secrets, and had learnt to master the mountains under every condition, in wind and storm, snow and darkness." Now it was time to bring those efforts beyond the Alps. "We felt an obligation to penetrate beyond the narrow confines of our native land," he added, "Our whole being urged us on to join the struggle." In 1926, Bauer decided where German climbers needed to go next.

Stretching across the waist of land that separated the Black Sea from the Caspian Sea, the Caucasus Mountains were both a geological and a geographical marvel. To the north lay the tail end of the great Russian granary, a thousand miles of collective wheat farms and whitewashed villages that stretched all the way to Moscow. To the south was a jumble of semiautonomous republics, Communist in name only, a land of cotton and apricots, quince and pomegranates, ancient mosques and morning calls to prayer. The mountains themselves were remote, foreboding, avalanche-prone, and breathtakingly beautiful. Their lower reaches, covered in pine and oak, beech and walnut, were still infested with bands of armed thieves. But the Caucasus were also the highest mountain range in Europe. And that, for Paul Bauer, made them irresistible.

"It took us two years of writing applications, filling out forms, and so on before we could finally get permission from the Russians," he recalled. But on July 4, 1928, Bauer received word that their visas were ready to be picked up at the Soviet embassy in Berlin. The climbers then spent nearly a week in Moscow, gathering up all of the forms, permissions, and governmental introductions—*bumashki* was what the Russians called them—that they would need to present to the local officials. Then, after a three-day train ride from Moscow, they arrived in Nalchik, a sleepy provincial capital at the foot of the Caucasus range. After more *bumashki*, followed by glasses of vodka, they finally rode out on horseback toward the head of the Bezengi Valley, where the glaciers ended and the mountains began.

All the hard work and preparations paid off. Despite having to contend with electrical storms, black ice, a whiteout, and a group of local herdsmen who took far too keen an interest in their Leica cameras, the expedition was a success. Bauer's steady leadership and meticulous planning paid dividends, and the climbers worked well together. And even though Bauer was curiously circumspect, later on, as to which peaks were actually summitted, both he and his team had gained valuable experience mountaineering on truly foreign soil.

But there had also been one jarring note. For no matter where the Germans climbed in the Caucasus, the British had been there first. Once they even stumbled upon an old British climbing camp, which they recognized by the piles of rusted-out tins of English provisions. And on Dych Tau, the second-highest peak in the Caucasus, Bauer himself kept referring back to an 1888 account of its first ascent by the brilliant English climber, Alfred Mummery. Bauer's party may have been breaking new ground for German climbers, but they were still haunted by British ghosts.

On the long train journey home, past the endless villages drowsing in the August heat, there was talk among the other members of the expedition of how much more climbing they could do upon a return to the Caucasus. But Bauer's mind was already directed elsewhere. "It has become quite clear to me," he wrote shortly after arriving back in Germany, "that in 1929 we must go to the Himalayas."

But Bauer wasn't just looking for higher mountains.

"On the basis of my experience of war—I fought against the English as an infantryman from October 1914 to June 1917, and then was in English captivity until November 1919," Bauer later wrote, "I have certain indications that it is very likely for the English always to fall into certain mistakes." He wasn't just out to go to the Himalayas. He was out to beat the British at their own game. After all, he added, "I knew the English well." Paul Bauer had put down his rifle and picked up his ice axe.

Kangchenjunga was a seductress.

Once thought to be the highest mountain in the world, at 29,169 it was only 860 feet shorter than Mount Everest. A massive complex of five distinct summits, Kangchenjunga—literally, "the Five Treasures of the High Snow" in Tibetan—was ringed by soaring ridgelines, colossal moraines, and more than a dozen glaciers. Part of the mountain lay in Nepal, while the rest was in the "princely state" of Sikkim, a small but politically sensitive thumbnail of British India that separated Nepal from Bhutan, and Tibet from eastern India. One of the most massive mountains in the Himalayas, Kangchenjunga also seemed to offer a large number of potential routes to the top. And from the veranda of the Planters Club in Darjeeling, where retired British Army officers, civil officials, and owners of tea plantations went for gossip and liquid refreshments, one could sit, on a fall afternoon, and climb the mountain with one's eyes, working one's way up one ridge or another, moving quickly past couloirs and avalanche chutes, until finally pulling oneself up onto the summit. Never before or since had a great Himalayan peak presented such a compelling visual siren call.

And the climbers came. The Swiss had tried to climb it. So, too, had a mixture of French, Italian, and British gentlemen explorers. Even Aleister Crowley, the English occultist whom the tabloids had called "the wickedest man on earth," had given it a go. But Kangchenjunga had defeated them all. The local Nepalese believed that the God of the mountain kept humans away from the summit. Now, it would be Bauer's turn.

Climbing a great Himalayan peak in those days was a series of choreographed advances and retreats, a kind of perpetual motion machine that, if the odds were in your favor, would carry you successively higher and higher up the sides of the mountain until you reached the summit. The key to a successful expedition was a series of camps, beginning with Base Camp and followed by Camp One, Camp Two, Camp Three, and so on. The camps themselves were often little more than a collection of one or two or three tents, each of which was often supplied with sleeping bags, a stove, fuel, and some food. But the camps were not just where the climbers and Sherpas would sleep each night. They also served as supply dumps, infirmaries, and potentially life-saving refuges from the unpredictable and often dangerous mountain weather. They were the necessary stepping stones as an expedition moved its way higher and higher.

Usually, it would be the strongest and most experienced climbers who would lead the way up a mountain. In consultation with the expedition's leaders, they would find the safest and fastest route upwards, cutting steps with their ice axes, and avoiding as best they could the most obvious places of danger. Once they had traveled the distance that a climber or a porter carrying a full load could reasonably ascend in a day, a new camp would be established. And as each successive camp was set up, there followed a continual flow of motion, as the lead climbers pushed upward, while the porters and the other climbers kept bringing more supplies higher and higher up the mountain, then going back down to collect more loads.

But as an expedition gained altitude and the oxygen became thinner, everything grew exponentially more difficult and upward progress became slower and slower. Climbers would sometimes have to take three or more breaths between every step, while even the simplest of chores, like removing one's boots and crawling into a sleeping bag, were exhausting. Headaches and nausea were increasingly common, stomach troubles flourished, appetites diminished, breathing became more labored, and sleep grew restless. And the higher the climbers went, the distance between camps shortened dramatically, as it now took much more time, and more effort, to cover the same amount of ground.

September 16, 1931.

For an instant, it was there.

Through a fleeting hole in the clouds, the summit of Kangchen-junga came silently into view. All that they had worked for, fought for, and died for, lay before them. Gazing up wordlessly, with ice crystals dancing in the air around them and the brilliant North Indian sunlight glinting off the metal rims of their glacier glasses, the six Germans and Austrians and the three Sherpas were within days of doing something that no human being had ever done before, namely to climb to the top of an *Achttausender*—a mountain at least eight thousand meters high. Standing outside their tents at Camp Ten in the rapidly shifting morning light, with the blue hills of Tibet laid out below them like a herdsman's carpet, they were almost at the end of their path to glory. "We were nearer to heaven," one of the climbers later wrote, "than to earth."

By mid-September 1931, Bauer's climbers had overcome every obstacle that Kangchenjunga had thrown their way. The first had been the weather. According to the records maintained by the Meteorological Department of the government of India, the summer of 1931 was the hottest in the Sikkim in more than a century. Crops withered, communal wells and streams dried up, and in Darjeeling alone more than a thousand people died of typhus and other heat-related illnesses. Up on Kangchenjunga, the climbers battled sleet and even rain, treacherous footing, and the near-constant threat of avalanches, which boomed off the slopes like artillery rounds.

Other problems soon emerged as well. One of the climbers came down with malaria, another with thyroid problems, while a third suffered from sciatica. Tensions were rising, and Bauer became convinced that some of the porters were stealing food. Then, on August 9, tragedy struck. While working their way up an ice gully, either Hermann Schaller, a young Viennese climber, or Pasang, a Sherpa, slipped. Roped together, the two men fell over seventeen hundred feet to their deaths. After their bodies were recovered, Schaller and Pasang were buried beneath a huge stone cairn. "We had built them a tomb that no prince on earth could hope to have," Bauer wrote, "such as only comrades can raise to one who has fallen in a good fight."

Then they got back to work.

Within days, the prospects for the expedition had brightened. The higher that Bauer and the others climbed on Kangchenjunga, the better their footing became. Spirits rose and even the weather improved. Following Bauer's lead back in the Alps, rather than use tents they'd also begun to dig snow caves at some of their camps. Some of the men had even fashioned the interiors like the insides of Gothic cathedrals, with arched doorways and ribbed ceilings. Moreover, the men were holding up. When Bauer climbed into his sleeping bag on August 29, he did so wearily—but also with a strong dose of optimism. "We roll ourselves clumsily into our sacks," he wrote, "and go to sleep with the certainty that the chief obstacles in our way to Kangchenjunga will be overcome in a few days."

But two weeks later, when they had their fleeting view of the summit through a hole in the clouds, they were far less certain. Fighting their way up the highest reaches of Kangchenjunga, both the climbers and Sherpas were now dangerously fatigued. In order to increase their chances of success, Bauer divided them into two teams and pushed for an expedited run to the summit. The larger of the two parties would establish Camp Eleven and hollow out an ice cave there, while a second group would leapfrog on ahead, route-finding and looking for suitable spots where the next two camps, Twelve and Thirteen, could be established. Food and supplies would then be ferried to the higher camps from which the final summit push would be made. "It is so close," one of the climbers wrote on September 17, "that we are practically certain of reaching it."

Bauer was the first to turn back. On September 16, as he left Camp Ten, the pace of his climbing had become so slow that another climber, Peter Aufschnaiter, convinced him to return to Camp Nine—alone. "It was obvious to me," Bauer later wrote, "that my heart was giving out." Ketar, a porter, developed snow blindness. Hans Hartmann, perhaps the strongest climber of them all, gave in to fatigue and lack of oxygen. Peter Aufschnaiter, throttled by coughing, thirst, and fatigue, washed out as well. Still, there were three climbers left. And despite being wracked with pain and near exhaustion, on September 18 they set out to, first, establish Camp Twelve, and then push on to the summit. From what they could tell, they had only one real obstacle to overcome, one final rock wall that separated them from the summit plateau.

Instead, they discovered a nightmare. A towering, unstable mass of wind slab, deep cracks, and fluted ice flanks, it was a dead man's wall. Whoever tried to climb it, no matter how determined or brave, would fall to their death in a matter of minutes. "We sat for a long time looking at the wretched sight," one of the men later wrote. "But it was of no use. We had to turn back." The news struck Bauer like a hammer blow. Once again, Kangchenjunga was victorious.

On the way back down the mountain, at Camp Six, the climbers were greeted with letters from home, their first in months. There was also a heavy wooden crate that had been sent by the Himalayan Club. Inside was a bronze plaque commemorating the life of Hermann Schaller, which they placed on his grave. Then, as the clear autumn air started to move in, they started the long march back to Darjeeling, Calcutta, and home.

At the Alpine Club in London, meanwhile, the wheels had started to turn.

Despite the fact that Paul Bauer and his climbers had not made it to the summit of Kangchenjunga, there was no longer any question that these new German climbers were a deeply impressive and talented lot, clearly up to the task at making a serious, sustained run at a Himalayan giant. And while, for the moment, the Foreign Office had managed to keep any other nation from gaining access to Mount Everest, that might not always be the case.

There was no time to waste.

The Mount Everest Committee, a joint creation of the Alpine Club and the Royal Geographical Society that was responsible for overseeing British expeditions to the world's highest mountain, stirred back to life. Feelers were also sent out to the Foreign Office asking for a new proposal to be presented to the Tibetan government, requesting permission to launch a new Everest expedition. As it turned out, luck was on the side of the British climbers. The Tibetan army had recently sparred with the forces of a Chinese warlord—and had been badly mauled. In Lhasa, government officials wanted Enfield rifles, water-cooled machine guns, and other weapons of war, which the British would happily supply. In return, the Tibetans would allow for a new Mount Everest expedition, set for 1933. And this time, nothing would be held back.

CHAPTER THREE

Everest, 1933

London. Friday, January 20, 1933.

Liverpool Street Station was a madhouse. Surrounded by a mob of family, friends, and well-wishers, the climbers had planned to slip discreetly into their carriages on the train to the Tilbury docks. But once the bright flashes of the newspapermen's cameras lit up the red brick walls and iron rafters of the Victorian-era railway terminal, waves of excitement raced through the station. Bobbies and baggage handlers shouted encouragement, while schoolchildren, bank assistants, and shop clerks stood in wide-eyed wonder. It wasn't every day, mind you, that one laid eyes on the best of the best, the heroic Englishmen who would soon be standing on the top of Mount Everest. It wasn't every day that one saw history in the making. A bystander, seized by patriotic fervor, even presented expedition member Colin G. Crawford, a seasoned Himalayan mountaineer who had climbed with Mallory back in '24, with an umbrella. The weather, the gift giver explained, might get bad in Tibet.

Despite the chaotic sendoff, the 1933 British Mount Everest Expedition was the largest, most highly organized, and best-equipped mountaineering campaign in human history. A crack team of twelve climbers, including an Olympic pentathlete, an Arctic explorer, and veterans of previous Himalayan climbs, had been carefully selected by the Mount Everest Committee. More than £5,000, a hefty sum in the early 1930s, had been raised outright, while the remaining eight to ten thousand pounds necessary to fund the expedition had been covered through the sale of exclusive news and photographic rights to the *Daily Telegraph*, future lectures, and with a book contract for an official history. Even His Majesty had chipped in. "The King knows that expeditions of this nature require careful and costly preparation," wrote the Keeper of the Privy Purse, Colonel Sir Frederick Ponsonby, to the chair of the Mount Everest Committee, "and desires me to send you the enclosed cheque for £100 which he wishes to give toward the expenses."

His majesty was correct. Provisioning the expedition was an enormous task, one that had taken months to complete. In the end, more than twenty-one and a half tons of supplies had been purchased or collected, inventoried, weighed, and carefully packed into more than eleven hundred three-ply wooden crates, which were then shipped by sea to India. Each box, furthermore, had been numbered and painted with a special colored band, whose color would indicate whether the contents were to be used, for example, on the long march across Tibet, in one of the high camps, or on the summit attempt. And the scope and variety of provisions was mind-boggling—tins of sardines, Heinz beans, Brand's meat essences, biscuits, jams and jellies, butter, canned milk, coffee, tea, cocoa, Ovaltine, maple sugar, chocolate, Horlick's malt tablets. Physicians at the Lister Institute were consulted to make certain that the daily diets contained the proper amounts of vitamins, while each climber was also allotted a supply of "Christmas boxes," each of which was filled with hand-picked delicacies from Fortnum & Mason. Another crate held a precious supply of Johnnie Walker whisky. For the Sherpas and Bhotias who would serve as porters, there was tinned pemmican and bags and bags of *tsampa*— roasted barley flour that they would eat mixed with water or tea.

Even more care was dedicated to the clothing and equipment that both the climbers and porters would employ. New tents were specially designed for the expedition, including lightweight models made of airplane canvas for the summit assault, and, for lower elevations, one that was a cross between an arctic tent and a yurt. "It had eight curved struts, jointed in the middle to make easy porterage, a sewn-in groundsheet, which was supplemented later by a separate groundsheet made by the Hurricane Smock Company, lace-up doors, two mica windows, and ventilating cowl which could be turned in any direction according to the wind," read an official description, while one climber described it as looking "like a plum-pudding without the sprig of holly." Inside the tents, the climbers would sleep in two eiderdown sleeping bags, one inside the other, and fitted with a third outer shell made from jaconet, a type of treated cotton fabric.

Few items are more important to climbers than their boots, and here a great effort was made to provide the members of the expedition with the best ones possible. Robert Lawrie, a twenty-eight-year-old Lancashire climber and renowned bootmaker, designed a new model that, to fend off frostbite, featured "two thicknesses of stout leather, with an intervening layer of asbestos sheeting," blocked toes, and an internal layer of heavy felt. Contracted to produce seventy pairs for the Mount Everest expedition, Lawrie personally set most of the nails—the wedge and cross-shaped bits of metal that were hammered onto the leather soles of boots for added traction—himself. So successful were Lawrie's boots that he was able to take his earnings and move his shop to London.

But the most striking innovations were the wind-proof suits designed for the expedition. "One has yet to find the man brave enough to appear publicly in England in this dress," one of the climbers noted, "but of its utilitarian value, indeed of its necessity, there can be no question; for the winds of Mount Everest pass through woolen tweeds as if they did not exist." Two versions were created, one made from a densely woven cotton gabardine known as Grenfell cloth, named for a British missionary who worked in Newfoundland, the other a kind of Jacquard. "These suits have hoods fitting loosely round the face, elastic inner cuffs, and tapes to tie round the ankles, all designed to keep the wearers as warm as possible," the *Times* reported. And the suits themselves drew crowds of curious onlookers when they were put on display in a Regent Street shop window a few weeks before Christmas 1932.

The World Beneath Their Feet

Indeed, as interest in the expedition continued to grow, experts from a wide variety of fields were called in to help create the best equipment possible. J. D. Magore Cardell, a renowned eye specialist and fellow of the Royal College of Surgeons, teamed up with a London optician to create a new type of glacier goggles, fitted with an orange-tinted glass designed to ward off the most debilitating effects of ultra-violet rays at high altitude. And in the few cases where English manufacturers did not produce equipment of superior quality, the leadership of the expedition looked elsewhere, as in the case of crampons, which were purchased in Austria.

Little had been left to chance. In London, the climbers pored over scores of topographic maps, expedition logs, and telescopic photographs of Everest, analyzing and debating the best route to the summit, while the supply officers, many of them old India hands, meticulously worked out a detailed schedule for the assault on the mountain. And unlike the teams on Mallory's expeditions, the climbers of 1933 had an additional ace in the hole. Telegraph operators at the Royal Meteorological Station in Alipore would send daily weather reports to Base Camp, providing the climbers with the most accurate, up-to-date forecasts available, including the progress, a thousand miles to the south, of the summer monsoon. Never had a mountaineering expedition been so well equipped, so expertly outfitted, and so well planned. "No one, I think," climber Eric Shipton later wrote, "doubted for a moment that we would succeed."

The orphaned son of a tea planter, as a child Eric Shipton wouldn't have made anyone's most-likely-to-succeed list. Dyslexic and a flop at organized sports, he daydreamed in class and was absolutely petrified of speaking in public. At Beaumont House, a grim boarding school in Hertfordshire, his most noticeable accomplishments were that he'd received more beatings from the headmaster than any other student, save one, in recent memory, and that, on a dare, he would slurp down the contents of a fellow student's inkwell, the metallic-tasting India ink staining his teeth and gums a bright purple. Shipton's mother was so worried about her only son that, in the fall of 1922, shortly after his fifteenth birthday, she enrolled him in Pyt House, a kind of school of last refuge for young men who were either learning disabled, or too dense, too lazy, or too uninterested to succeed in the classroom. And while academic success still eluded him, he found something far more important. While rummaging around the school library one day, he discovered a copy of *Travels Amongst the Great Andes of the Equator*, Edward Whymper's gripping account of his 1880 first ascent of Chimborazo, a hulking, 20,000-foot volcano in Ecuador that had been long thought to be the highest mountain on earth.

That was all it took.

By the time he'd turned eighteen, Shipton had gone climbing in Norway and Switzerland, Italy and the Lake District. Trained in the French Alps, in part, by Nea Barnard, perhaps the most accomplished female English climber of the 1920s and 1930s, he blossomed into a superb mountaineer, one whose steady, rhythmic gate on steep snowy slopes was a wonder to behold. And when, miraculously, Shipton was offered a chance to enter Cambridge, he turned it down. Climbing was all that he wanted to do.

But it was in East Africa that Shipton's abilities as a climber fully emerged. Emigrating to Kenya, where he hoped to make a go of it as a coffee planter, he instead made the second ascent of Mount Kenya, the second-highest mountain on the continent, and the first of one of its twin summits. Not only did this feat earn front-page coverage in the *East Africa Standard*, the principal English-speaking newspaper in Nairobi, but this and other climbing feats on Mount Kenya and in the mysterious, fog-shrouded Ruwenzori Mountains of Uganda earned him considerable coverage in the *Alpine Journal*, the gold-standard mountaineering publication put out by the Alpine Club in London. So impressive were his African climbs that Frank Smythe, soon to be the best-known British mountaineer, invited Shipton, sight unseen, to join a small expedition to the Himalayas. And on June 21, 1931, Shipton joined Smythe on the summit of Kamet, a 25,000-foot peak along the India–Tibet border that then became the highest mountain ever successfully climbed all the way to the top. It was a noteworthy accomplishment. A little over a year later, Shipton was invited to join the 1933 Mount Everest expedition.

In truth, Eric Shipton was even more grateful to be a part of the show than he let on. For despite his mountaineering achievements in Africa and the Alps, when the telegram arrived in Kenya inviting him to join the expedition, the words "subject medical approval" had filled him with dread. "I had been aware of an irregular heart-beat which had led me to believe that something was amiss," he recalled, "though like Darwin before he joined the *Beagle*, I was too scared to have it examined." Desperate for some answers, he went to a doctor in Nairobi. "Under his stethoscope," he added, "my heart performed a wildly erratic syncopation; the doctor's worried frown seemed to confirm my fears, and I fainted. He said nothing to reassure me and declined to sign a certificate of physical fitness." Desperately wanting to take part in the Mount Everest expedition, Shipton was also sick with worry that, because of his heart condition, he would be kept off the expedition.

Even worse news awaited him in London. "I was appalled to learn that all members of the Everest party were required to undergo the R.A.F. medical test, then regarded as the most searching of all," he wrote. Famous for washing out hundreds of hopeful pilots-to-be, the Royal Air Force doctors put their subjects through a grueling series of physical challenges, including holding their breath for a full two minutes. "Panic stricken," Shipton remembered, "I divulged my dread secret to my mother's doctor, who, to my intense relief told me that my irregular heart-beat was due to dyspeptic flatulence, and signified nothing." Shipton sailed through the RAF tests—that is, until the examiners discovered that he had an enlarged spleen, caused by his exposure to malaria, which he denied ever having. "This was a little difficult to explain," he added, "however, it was evidently not regarded as a hindrance to climbing Everest."

Leadership of the expedition was bestowed upon Hugh Ruttledge. A forty-eight-year-old career civil servant in the British Raj, his mountaineering experience had been limited to a handful of guided climbs in the Alps, two failed attempts at a decent-sized Himalayan peak, plus a significant amount of rigorous hiking along the India–Tibet border. A fan of polo, big-game hunting, and pig-sticking—a form of hunting wild boars with spears while on horseback—Ruttledge had also made a *parikrama*, a Hindu ritual circumambulation around Mount Kailash, a 21,000--foot Tibetan peak said to be the home of Shiva. But for the members of the Mount Everest Committee, Ruttledge was a safe choice, an able administrator who would avoid unnecessary drama and keep things running on time. "A decent man," came one assessment. For their part, the climbers ended up liking him.

Frank Smythe, already a well-known British mountaineer, meanwhile, nearly missed the expedition altogether. On November 17, 1932, while being driven from a lecture on some icy roads outside of Bolton, near Manchester, a car coming in the opposite direction lost control and smashed into his vehicle head-on. Smythe, whose knees and nose got horribly banged up, was knocked out. "I remember recovering consciousness," he later recalled, "stretching out each limb and saying to myself, Good! I can go to Everest"—despite being both concussed and soaked in gasoline. After spending two weeks in the Royal Manchester Infirmary, Smythe was released.

Two months later, near the end of January, the 1933 Mount Everest Expedition was on the move. On the twenty-seventh, seven of the climbers steamed out of Marseille on the *Cormorin*, bound for Bombay. Three members of the expedition were already in India, while two others, a transportation officer billeted to the Sudan, and a physician assigned to the Hospital Mission of the Jews in Palestine, set out on their own. The final two members, including Frank Smythe and Dr. Raymond Greene—older brother of the novelist Graham Greene—set out on the *Viceroy of India*, the crown jewel of the Peninsular and Oriental Steamship Line, in early February. For the long voyage to India, Smythe, never one to be unprepared, packed a dinner jacket, studs, dress shirts, dress socks, evening shoes, a monocle, and a pair of carpet slippers.

For Eric Shipton, on board the *Cormorin* with most of the other climbers, there were more pressing matters. "We had two main occupations on the voyage out," he later recalled. The first was to try and learn a Nepali dialect spoken by the Sherpas. "I am afraid we were reluctant and most inept pupils," he added. Percy Wyn-Harris, with whom Shipton had climbed Mount Kenya and who was on the expedition as well, didn't even bother trying to learn Nepali at all, but ended up speaking to the Sherpas in Swahili, "which certainly seemed to be as effective as anything else."

Far more important, however, was their second task, a daily and nearly monthlong discussion of how Everest could best be climbed. For Everest wasn't just the world's highest mountain. It was also a puzzle. In their efforts to solve it, however, the Mount Everest Committee soon had some unexpected company.

All across Great Britain, news of the expedition found a willing and attentive audience. To a nation that had lost the races to both the North and South Poles and was now in the grips of an economic depression, the 1933 Mount Everest Expedition was a much-needed tonic. In classrooms and pubs, newspaper offices and BBC sound booths, it was the kind of national enterprise that stirred the British imagination and lifted British hearts.

One of them belonged to a former Drury Lane chorus girl named Fanny Radmall. The eighth daughter of a London draper, she had concluded at an early age that her roadmap to happiness lay not in Sunday-school lessons and sewing circles, but in silk stockings and stage lights. At age sixteen she married her first husband, a middle-aged brewery millionaire, who promptly bought her a townhouse in Paris. Eight years later, when he died, she inherited a fortune. Three more marriages followed, the last to a shipping magnate who once gave her a four-foot-long black pearl necklace worth fifty thousand pounds. By the middle of the 1920s, Lady Houston, as she was now called, was reputedly the wealthiest woman in Great Britain, a dedicated nudist who, when appearing at social functions, draped herself in diamonds and furs. Once, in a squabble over back taxes, she personally presented Winston Churchill, then the Chancellor of the Exchequer, with a check for one and a half million pounds.

"Do I get a kiss?" she asked.

"No," he growled back. "You get a cup of tea."

She was also fiercely independent in both thought and deed. Deeply patriotic, Lady Houston had been so moved by the care given by English nurses to wounded soldiers during the World War that she built them a rest home. She had so delighted in the nerve of the suffragettes—the militant British feminists who, among other things, chained themselves to the railings at Buckingham Palace in their campaign to win the right to vote for British women—that she purchased one hundred lime-green South American parrots and had them taught to screech, "Votes for Women!" And when she found out that the Labour government, under Prime Minister Ramsay MacDonald, whom she detested, wouldn't finance a British entry for the 1931 Schneider Trophy, an international air race, Lady Houston indignantly contributed to a campaign to cover the needed shortfall. One year later, when she heard that the Dalai Lama had opened up access to Mount Everest for another British expedition, Lady Houston struck again, this time with what would be known as the Houston-Mount Everest Expedition.

Her initial plan called for landing an airplane on the summit or, barring that, having one fly close enough that a weighted Union Jack could be dropped on top of the highest mountain in the world. Over time, however, more practical minds prevailed, and a plan was devised whereby two planes would fly over the summit of Mount Everest, making a detailed photo survey in route. This would be a worthy feat on its own terms, one that would help put the British at the forefront of high-altitude aviation. By early February 1933, two Westland P.V.3 biplanes, each powered by a supercharged Pegasus engine, had been partially disassembled, packed into huge wooden crates, and lowered into the hold of a Karachi-bound freighter.

Their flight crews, on the other hand, set out for India in three lightweight Gipsy Moth airplanes on a route that would carry them across France, "down the long shin-bone of Italy to Catania in the big toe of Sicily, then across the Mediterranean at its narrowest point to Tunis, and thence past Cairo, Baghdad, and Persia to the Indus river and the mudflats of Karachi." An adventure in its own right, the journey turned out to be a heady mixture of petty headaches, genuine danger, and awestruck wonder. Members of the crew were arrested and briefly detained by Fascist police in Italy when they mistakenly flew over restricted airspace, and they were caught by a blinding sandstorm in Iraq. They found Jerusalem to be "grey and grim," while Baghdad was not the fairytale city of *A Thousand and One Arabian Nights*, but "a dejected-looking collection of modern hovels and mud houses feeding on the dole of past greatness." But they also gaped in awe at the timeless desert between Tunis and Cairo, "where the outlines of several lost cities can be seen from the air along the coast, as also the great irrigation cisterns built by the Romans," and they marveled at the bazaars and polyglot humanity of Damascus, a city "so old that nobody will ever know its age."

In Karachi, the two big Westlands were reassembled and taken for test flights. Then it was on to Delhi and, by the end of March 1933, to a minor administrative outpost near the Nepalese border. From there, at a little-used army airstrip set among fields of jute and sugar cane and the ruins of former indigo factories, the air crews would attempt their unprecedented flight. Two hundred miles to the northeast, meanwhile, the earthbound British climbers were making their own journey and writing their own story, one with a fairytale beginning all its own.

Some called it the City in the Clouds.

Rising up more than six thousand feet above the dusty Bengal plains, and perched precariously along the edge of a dauntingly steep ridge, Darjeeling had the feel of a way station placed midway between heaven and earth. During the crystal-clear days of winter, when the locals huddled around smoky cookstoves and firepots, the majestic southeastern face of Kangchenjunga rose up in all of its icy glory, beckoning the faithful and utterly dominating the skyline. But during the late spring and early fall, clouds would fill the valley below, giving Darjeeling the feel of an island in the sky.

And in many ways, it *was* an island. Founded as a seasonal retreat for colonial administrators and army officers seeking to escape the blazing heat of Indian summers, the British transformed the remote hill station, accessible by a fifty-mile small-gauge railroad, into a slice of home. Cotswold cottages and Tudor mansions sprouted along the hillsides, complete with rose gardens in the back and Wedgwood teapots and soup tureens nestled in mahogany china cabinets. Parishioners at St. Andrews Anglican Church could read from the Book of Common Prayer beneath a stained-glass window of Saint George, while the quarter-hours were tolled off by the Victorian bell tower at the center of town. More English than Indian, Darjeeling was a wonder all its own, one that had attracted notable visitors the likes of Rudyard Kipling and Mark Twain.

But Darjeeling was a Nepali town as well. When British planters ventured that the lush, dripping, and often cloud-covered hills nearby might be a good place to grow tea, they hit the jackpot. Needing pickers to harvest the crop, they turned to nearby Nepal, and, in time, many of the newcomers drifted to Darjeeling, where they worked for the British residents, opened their own shops and businesses, and raised families. Among the Nepali to come to Darjeeling were the Sherpas. Ethnically Tibetan, they were farmers and yak herders who lived in villages, some as high as ten thousand feet, on the lower slopes of Mount Everest, Kangchenjunga, and the other peaks of the eastern Himalayas. Exceedingly adept at performing hard manual labor at high elevations, Sherpas were actively sought by the leaders of European mountaineering expeditions to serve as high-altitude porters. And as the word leaked out among the Sherpa communities in Nepal that good wages could be earned by lugging heavy boxes and daypacks up the slopes of the Himalayas for the British, the Germans, and others, members of the Sherpa enclave on the backside of Darjeeling began to utter quiet prayers in the smoky air of a nearby Buddhist monastery and keep their ears peeled for news of another expedition. In early 1933, their prayers were answered.

Setting up their headquarters in Darjeeling at the Planters Club, a combination guesthouse, restaurant, bar, and social club, at the end of February, Hugh Ruttledge and the other members of the expedition dove right into the process of interviewing, examining, and hiring porters for the expedition. "We went for the wiry, active, clean-bred type, reasonably intelligent," Ruttledge wrote. "Instinct is not a bad guide in these matters." Sherpas were definitely preferred. "Many of them come to Darjeeling, ten days' march, seeking work in tea plantations, or as porters or rickshaw coolies," he added. "They are fine, free movers on a hillside, and have the bold, open manner of a true Hillman." But others were hired as well, especially Bhotias, another group of ethnic Tibetans, who lived in the Chumbi valley along the border with Bhutan. In the end, the expedition hired nearly ninety porters, among them a handful of "Everest men" who had worked on Mallory's climbs.

Nor was that all. Some three hundred donkeys and yaks were contracted as pack animals, as well as more than a dozen horses to be ridden by the climbers, it was said, in order to conserve their energy for the mountain itself. A solemn blessing ceremony was held at a local Buddhist temple, where each of the Sherpa and Bhotia porters was presented with a white silk prayer scarf, which was draped around his neck, to ward off evil spirits and to protect him on the long journey to, and upon, the mountain. Then they were off.

The first leg, at least, wouldn't be the hardest.

It was merely a three-hundred-mile walk.

*   *   *

At the beginning, the 1933 Mount Everest Expedition followed what amounted to a familiar script, one that had been honed by their predecessors during the 1920s. Many decisions, such as which route to take and where to pitch camp in this area or that, had, in fact, already been made for them, and were the result of the practical experiences of previous British mountaineering expeditions. But the key determining factor on how they would approach the mountain had little or nothing to do with mountaineering at all.

Everest was a divided mountain. Its summit lay along the border between Nepal and Tibet, with the northern face of the mountain falling into Tibetan territory, while the southern side lay in Nepal. In practical terms, the shortest route to Everest from India would have been through Nepal. But by 1933, the borders of the Kingdom of Nepal had been closed to outsiders for nearly a quarter of a century. "Nepal remains closed," wrote one British observer, "because its Rajput aristocracy is none too enthusiastic about the blessings of Western penetration or of an industrial civilization." And while the authorities in Tibet were also deeply suspicious of outsiders, and routinely barred Europeans from visiting, the British had managed to win some occasional concessions from the Tibetans, at least as far as Everest went.

As a result, in order to try climbing Everest, British climbers had to approach the mountain from its northern, or Tibetan, side. To accomplish this, the British expeditions of the 1920s had to march, on foot, in a huge counterclockwise arc, from Darjeeling and through the Chumbi Valley, along the wind-whipped plains past the ancient fortress at Kampa Dzong, up the shadowed valley leading to the Rongbuk monastery, and finally to Base Camp itself. The 1933 Mount Everest Expedition would have to do the same. In the end, the trek from Darjeeling to Base Camp took forty-six days.

For the most part, it went well. Despite the late-winter weather, both the men and the animals held up as hoped—though not without some cost. "A month's winter marching across the bitter uplands of Tibet," wrote J. L. Longland, one of the climbers, "landed us in mid-April with a crop of sore throats and skinned faces." And there were tensions simmering within the ranks of the Sherpas, who chafed at more than what they felt were inadequate pay and rations. "The expedition organizers barely treated us like humans," Ang Tharkay, one of the Sherpas, said later. "The latrines that had been built were reserved exclusively for the 'Sahibs.' We had to relieve ourselves some distance away."

But for Eric Shipton, and some of the others who had not been in Tibet before, the journey had been one through a land of infinite wonder. They had passed through arid hills and forests of Scotch firs, rose trees, and juniper, as well as dust-blown plateaus and swollen rivers. Of spending one night near Tang La, a pass that was higher than the tallest of the Alps, one climber wrote that "as darkness came on, it seemed that the cold up there must be as that of interstellar space." The stars over Tibet, another wrote, were "brilliant points of electric blue fire," viewed through an atmosphere of startling clarity. There were sunburnt days and frigid, winterblown nights. On the treeless Phari plain, the expedition felt both the full force of the Tibetan wind, and the immense loneliness of the landscape. "Here was Tibet proper," Frank Smythe wrote, "and a bleak and inhospitable land it seemed, brown and desolate, unmoving and unchanging, except for the slow march of the sun and cloud in the steadfast blue of the moistureless sky."

But there was some surprising tenderness as well. Forbidden from shooting any birds or animals while in Tibet, the climbers were as amazed by the different kinds of avian life—magpies, linnets, and finches, Brahminy ducks, bar-headed geese, and crazily crowned hoopoes—as they were by the birds' curiosity and lack of fear of humans. "It is an never-ending joy to find the birds of Tibet so tame," Hugh Ruttledge wrote. "The place is a paradise for the ornithologist." Even wild goats would approach them without fear. And on many of the high passes, they found "a little forest of prayer flags," Frank Smythe recalled, "with their stiff, dry rustling." Here was a land of harsh but surprising beauty, he continued, of "yellowish hills splashed with reddish crags," glittering stars, and mornings "as dark as an English November day."

Human contacts, though less frequent, were equally fascinating—the wild-eyed mule-train drivers, hauling loads of wool to Indian markets, or the Tibetan high officials, wearing traditional robes and Western sunglasses. At Tatsang, they met Buddhist nuns who had donned dreadlocked wigs made from yak hair. At Kampa Dzong, they passed by a six-hundred-year-old fortress whose architecture could have easily been featured in a Cubist design book. They saw poverty and plenty, smallpox and superstition, generosity and cruelty. In a village called Pipitang, they came upon a bleeding man lying in a courtyard. "He asked for medical treatment, and the bystanders, who included many women, explained with amusement that he was a murderer who had just received 150 lashes by way of inducing him to confess," Ruttledge wrote. In another cluster of homes, the village madman took off all of his clothes in front of the visitors, despite the wind and cold. "The Tibetans are a tough people," Ruttledge added," in every sense of the word."

The expedition also wrestled with a few problems of their own. Some clothing and several pair of high-altitude boots were stolen, while one of the porters, drunk on *chang*—a Tibetan barley beer—burned a hole in a tent. More troubling was the discovery that the assistant transport officer was color-blind and, as a result, couldn't distinguish the carefully colored bands that differentiated boxes of supplies used for the trek across Tibet from those to be reserved for the actual climb. On another occasion, climber Wyn-Harris opened a crate of supplies only to discover, to his disgust, that it was packed entirely with "a whole load of a patent well-known nerve tonic," which had undoubtedly been donated in exchange for some free advertising. "I fed it to the yaks," he later recalled. "It didn't seem to do *them* any harm."

By early April, the expedition had crossed into the Shekar district and now, heading straight toward Everest, entered the Rongbuk valley. "The valley narrowed as the hills closed in," Ruttledge wrote, "and a powerful south wind drove into our faces. Grass disappeared. Boulder and scree, snow, blue ice and precipice would be our scenery for the next three months." On the sixteenth, they arrived at the remote and mysterious Rongbuk monastery, with its huge *chorten*, a bell-shaped reliquary, less than a dozen miles from the summit of Everest. Home to more than three hundred Buddhist monks, nuns, and assorted hermits, and occupied twelve months of the year, the monastery was, at 16,000 feet, one of the highest inhabited places in the world. But for Hugh Ruttledge, the most important job at Rongbuk was to get the head lama to bless the expedition, something that would have great meaning for the Sherpa and Bhotia porters. "It was important to secure this for our men," Ruttledge later wrote.

In truth, this was a somewhat delicate matter. "Mountaineering as a sport is incomprehensible to a Tibetan administrator," Ruttledge had written about a run-in with a Tibetan trade agent, while many everyday Nepalese and Tibetans believed that both gods and a race of snow giants lived on top of the highest peaks of the Himalayas. And on the top of Everest, it was said, was a solid gold temple. Nevertheless, the head lama, a down-to-earth and genial man, was happy to honor the British request. "The porters were paraded in their best," Ruttledge wrote, "and each man was given a rupee for an offering" before being blessed. The head lama also had the British members recite the mantra "*Om mani padme hum*"—and he broke into a light chuckle when Frank Smythe mangled the pronunciation. But the blessing was a clear success, and both the porters and the climbers were in high spirits.

The next day, the expedition set off on the last four miles to Base Camp. "It was Easter Monday, April 17th," Ruttledge wrote. "The long march was over."

Towering over them was the stuff of dreams. And nightmares.

Their real work was about to begin.

Viewed head on, the north face of Mount Everest was an awesome, sobering, bone-chilling sight, one that fully captured both the indifferent majesty of the mountain, and the scope of the challenge which lay before them. The front face of the pyramid-shaped mountain itself, much of which remained uncovered with snow for most of the year, revealing striking bands of brown, yellow, and green rock near its upper reaches, was clearly too steep to allow for a frontal assault. The only way up, the first British explorers had concluded, would be to somehow gain access to the ridges on either side, either the steep right shoulder or, more promisingly, the longer but more gradual ridge rising on the left. But where to begin?

Flowing down from the base of the north face, the Rongbuk Glacier, despite its many crevasses and incredible ice towers, was the most direct route to the mountain itself. But the glacier ended— or, rather began—flush against the steep north face, and offered no practical route up. During the 1921 Mount Everest reconnaissance expedition, however, a small party of climbers and porters discovered that an arm of this mighty river of ice, which they designated as the East Rongbuk Glacier, had a fortuitous feature at the end, which they named the North Col. It was a saddle, or connecting ridge, which ran from Changtse, a 24,000-foot peak that stood between the Rongbuk and East Rongbuk Glaciers, and a spur on Everest itself. It was a huge breakthrough. And while they had neither the time nor the supplies to make a run for the summit, the 1921 climbers had discovered a way up the mountain.

Ideally, the route went like this: from the head of East Rongbuk Glacier, a party of climbers could ascend the North Col, traverse it onto Everest itself, and then follow a short spur to the Northeast Ridge. From there they could mount the North Ridge proper, the long, gently sloping left shoulder of the mountain. Then they could work their way along the horizontal yellow and green bands of rock and past what looked like two prominent rises, which they named the First and Second Steps. After that, the climbing did not appear to be overly difficult on the way to the summit pyramid and, finally, onto the summit itself.

In fact, the British had already tried it. Twice.

The World Beneath Their Feet

In 1922, they'd set up their Camp Four at nearly 23,000 feet, just below the crest of the North Col. They had then planned on pitching just one more camp—Camp Five—at nearly 26,000 feet, but had to settle for a site that was a thousand feet lower. "This proved to be the deciding factor," the German-Swiss climber Günter Dyhrenfurth later observed, "For as is now well known, it is quite outside the realm of practical politics to attempt a difference in altitude from 25,000 to 29,160 feet—nearly 4,200 feet—in the space of a single day." Still, they gave it a try, and eventually made it to almost 27,000 feet—a new altitude record—before they had to turn back. Tragedy struck on the way down, when an avalanche took the lives of seven Sherpas.

Two years later, in 1924, the British were back. This time, however, they added a Camp Six. Situated at 26,715 feet, it would be the jumping off spot for two runs at the summit. During the first attempt, climbers Edward Norton and Howard Somerville made it past the yellow slabs, before Somerville, whose throat was in a perilous state, had to stop. Norton then went on alone for an hour, moving past the First and Second Steps, and eventually onto what would be called the Great Couloir, a steep gorge that led directly to the summit pyramid. But the couloir was filled with knee-high powder snow, and the footing was not remotely safe, especially for a solitary climber. At 28,124 feet—less than nine hundred feet from the summit—Norton turned back. No human being had ever climbed higher. Four days later, Mallory and Irvine made the second summit attempt, never to be seen alive again.

This would also be the route that the 1933 expedition would take.

But before they would do so, two questions had to be addressed.

The first was whether to take oxygen or not. To begin, the very idea was still anathema to some members of the Alpine Club who, as with pitons and other climbing "aids," didn't find the use of oxygen to be properly sporting. Some physiologists had maintained that the human body could not survive without supplemental oxygen at such great heights, though Norton's astonishing climb without it quieted that corner. There was no real doubt that oxygen could help a climber better at higher altitudes, but was this advantage enough to offset the considerable weight of the oxygen tanks and attendant apparatus, which could weigh as much as thirty-five pounds? "The question," Ruttledge later wrote, "was open." In the end, the 1933 expedition planned not to use supplemental oxygen, though just in case acclimatization proved problematic beyond the North Col, they carried along a stripped-down oxygen kit that weighed less than thirteen pounds.

The other question was less easy to answer. It was clear from the experiences of the 1922 and 1924 expeditions that Camp Six needed to be established higher if they were to have a decent shot or two at a successful summit attempt. But how high should Camp Six be? Should there also be a Camp Seven? Here, much would depend on the weather, and how many clear days of climbing they could get in before the summer monsoon set in. But there were a host of human factors as well. Could any porters be coaxed to take loads up to a Camp Seven? Would any of the climbers be in good enough shape to try for the summit? "The final pyramid, though by no means easy, seemed practicable," Ruttledge had concluded. "The problem was to reach it across the frightful slabs of the couloir walls." And to do so quickly.

But there was also one other factor at play.

Every year, near the end of May and the beginning of June, the weather in India would change dramatically, as a great gray blanket of clouds would move in from the Arabian Sea and Indian Ocean, drenching the subcontinent in rains that would last until October. Known as the *monsoon*, from an Arabic word that had been picked up by Dutch and Portuguese sailors, it was caused, scientists believed, by the difference in air pressure when the Indian landmass heated up, and then drew in moisture-laden clouds from the sea. But whatever its causes, the monsoon came and went like clockwork, with mainly minor variations, year in and year out.

And once it arrived—or "broke," as it was then said—the effects

of the monsoon on Himalayan mountaineering were of great conse-
quence. For when the monsoon clouds hit the wall of the Himalayas,
which stopped their northward movement, they dumped massive
amounts of snow on the peaks, making climbing virtually impossible.
As a result, the best time to climb a Himalayan peak, many believed,
was during the slender window of time between the end of the
Himalayan winter and the onset of the monsoon. Hugh Ruttledge,
the leader of the 1933 expedition, knew this, of course, and he had
gambled that by getting an early start out of Darjeeling and by not
rushing the long march across the Sikkim and Tibet, that the climbers and porters would have time to properly acclimatize themselves
to the higher altitudes, and would arrive at the mountain in good
physical shape.

The campaign, however, got off to a sluggish start.

Even though Base Camp had been established on April 17, two
full weeks went by before Camp Three was established along the East
Rongbuk Glacier. Part of the delay was due to late-winter storms and
wind that made work impossible. "Our advance was very slow," Eric
Shipton wrote, "and as we set out day after day I began to wonder
if we should ever reach the Col." And once they got to the base of
the North Col, the climbers found that they needed to do extensive
step-cutting and set fixed ropes in order to make a path that the
heavily-laden porters could follow. It was exhausting work. "We took
turns of about twenty minutes each at cutting the steps," Shipton
recalled. "Even that seemed an eternity and it was a great relief to
be told that time was up." Another two weeks passed before the
expedition was able to set up Camp Four, on an ice ledge some two
hundred feet below the crest of the North Col. Then came another
four days of storms. "We could do nothing," Shipton recalled, "but
lie in our sleeping bags."

On May 20, a party of climbers and porters set out to establish
Camp Five, the first real camp on Everest proper, but was forced
back by high winds. Heated arguments followed, no doubt fueled by

both fatigue and the effects of altitude. "Nerves were already frayed," Shipton recalled, "and we were all liable to lose our tempers at the slightest provocation." But an even more pressing reason soon added to the pressure to get to a point where a summit bid could be made. "Wireless messages received at the Base Camp spoke of an exceptionally early monsoon in Ceylon and its rapid spread over India," Shipton wrote. "Obviously the critical moment had arrived."

Two days later, on Monday, May 22, a party of climbers and porters, led by Percy Wyn-Harris and Lawrence Wager, were finally able to establish Camp Five, at 25,700 feet, on solid ground but on a wind-exposed location along the crest of the ridge. Spirits had risen, and the plan was to establish Camp Six the next day, followed by a summit attempt by Wyn-Harris and Wager. But Tuesday blew in on the tails of a ferocious wind, and plans for setting up Camp Six had to be scrapped. When Frank Smythe and Eric Shipton arrived at Camp Five that afternoon, they switched places with Wyn-Harris and Wager, who moved back down the mountain. Smythe and Shipton would now be the lead summit team. But once again, fate would intervene, this time in a blizzard that began that night.

The storm raged all the next day as well. Snow as fine as cake flour sifted through the tent fabric, covering everything inside the tent, and at one point the wind blew so hard that one of the guy ropes snapped. Smythe went outside to fix it, and even though he was only out for a couple of minutes, Shipton recalled, "when he returned we spent hours rubbing and thumping his limbs to restore the circulation." That evening the snow stopped and the winds ceased, and with that came a huge dose of renewed optimism. "We opened the tent flap and looked out," Shipton wrote. "Such cloud as there was, was far below us. The magnificence of the view penetrated even my jaded brain. The summit, greatly foreshortened, seemed close above us." In fact it looked so close that the two climbers discussed whether they should forego establishing a Camp Six altogether, and make a run at the summit from there.

The next morning, Thursday, May 25, a gale roared across the ridge. Not only would there be no upward progress, but the Sherpas who were also at Camp Five had reached a crisis stage. Frostbitten, exhausted, and out of food, the climbers had no choice but to retreat. Abandoning Camp Five, Smythe, Shipton, and the porters started back down to Camp Four. But that was not the end of the expedition's troubles, and what happened, or did not happen, over the course of the next two days would be debated for years to come. The next day, Friday, May 26, Ruttledge determined that a new camp, which was dubbed Four-A, needed to be built to relieve the congestion in Camp Four. On the following day, there was no upward progress, either. It was not until Sunday, May 28—"a beautiful morning," Ruttledge wrote—that the assault on the summit began again.

It all happened rather quickly.

On Sunday, May 28, Camp Five was reoccupied. One day later, four climbers, including Wyn-Harris and Wager, and eight Sherpas and Bhotias established Camp Six at 27,400 feet along the North Ridge. They were half way up the yellow band of rock, and some six hundred feet higher than the highest camp of Mallory's 1924 expedition. Yet it was far from a perfect campsite. "It was a sinister spot, glacial and desolate," Ang Tharkay, one of the Sherpas, later recalled. "It was a narrow cornice dominated by a large, rocky ridge. There was just enough room for three or four men." In fact, it barely could hold two, and those turned out to be Wyn-Harris and Wager, who stayed the night while the others headed down the mountain. The summit, one of the departing climbers noted, "now seemed so close, perhaps 1,600 feet higher and half a mile away." The next morning, Tuesday, May 30, Wyn-Harris and Wager would try and reach it.

But first they spent what Wyn-Harris later called a "very unpleasant Everest night." Despite the fact that both slept poorly and that neither man was hungry, they both managed to eat a dinner of canned chicken broth, tinned loganberries, biscuits, and condensed milk. But a more worrisome problem involved the "Tommy cookers" that they were supplied with. Unlike the Primus stoves that mountaineers used everywhere, these were essentially cans of solid fuel that were equipped with a metal ring on which one could place a small saucepan. Not only did they produce less heat, but it took nearly a half an hour to melt enough snow to get even one cup of warm water. As a result, both Wyn-Harris and Wager were dehydrated at a moment when they would need every bit of strength that they could muster.

Further down the mountain, however, the excitement was palpable. Despite the by now utter squalor of the camps, which were filled with dirty, exhausted, frostbitten, and hacking and coughing climbers and porters, the knowledge that two set of climbers—Wyn-Harris and Wager, followed by Frank Smythe and Eric Shipton—would be making summit attempts, raised everyone's spirits. E. O. Shebbeare, the transport officer on both the 1924 and 1933 expeditions, scribbled a letter to a friend from Camp Three, noting that they had two pairs of "absolutely first-class climbers in better condition and far more thoroughly acclimatized than have ever been on Everest before." Moreover, he added, "We may have climbed the mountain already."

Wyn-Harris and Wager got off early the next morning. "We started off from the tent at 5:40 a.m. and, although the wind was not particularly hard, we both felt extremely cold and felt the beginning of frost bite in our toes," Wyn-Harris later recalled. But an hour later, it became clear that Wager was also having some additional trouble, probably heart-related. "He began to find that the harder he moved the more he had to breathe," Wyn-Harris wrote. "It worried me extremely as I had always known Wager at Cambridge as being very tough." Their first objective was to pass over the First and Second Steps, but before they reached the First Step, Wyn-Harris made a surprising discovery. He nearly stumbled over an ice axe. "The thing that practically astonished me," he later wrote, "was that the steel of the ice axe was all absolutely bright and the wood was if it had been cleaned with sand paper." He realized immediately that it must have belonged to either Mallory or Irvine.

The World Beneath Their Feet

It was then, however, that Wyn-Harris made what he later described as a pivotal mistake. Rather than stay along the top of the ridge toward the First and Second Steps, he and Wager moved laterally along a band of rock until he realized that they could not re-ascend the ridge. The only way up now would be through a great gulley, filled with snow, that ran down from the summit. "Lawrence and I crossed the gulley on to the far side," Wyn-Harris recalled, "It remains one of the most horrific movements I have ever made in climbing. It was choked with powdered snow which was frozen in small particles and, when you put a foot on it, poured down the gulley like granulated sugar." Above them was loose rock lying on perilously angled slabs. It was hopeless. Though they were less than one thousand feet from the summit, Wyn-Harris and Wager were done. Not only was it already getting late, but they would need to descend all the way to Camp Five before nightfall.

Now it would be up to the second team.

Frank Smythe and Eric Shipton made it to Camp Six on Tuesday, May 30. "The climbing was difficult," Smythe wrote, "far more difficult than we had anticipated." Not only had they been forced to cut steps in a snow slope for some one hundred feet, but Shipton was clearly struggling. "I felt far from well," he recalled. And while the small tent that marked Camp Six was a welcome sight, the accommodations were less than ideal. "That night and the one that followed were by far the worst that I spent on the mountain," Shipton wrote. Because of the sloping ground that the tent was pitched on, Smythe kept rolling on top of Shipton all night long. "From sheer self-preservation, to prevent myself from being suffocated, I had to kick him with my knee or jab him with my elbow," he added. "I did not sleep at all and I do not think Smythe fared much better."

Both men were up ahead of dawn. But shortly before first light, Smythe wrote, "A gust of wind tugged at the tent. It was succeeded by another and stronger gust. By dawn a gale was blowing." There would be no attempt at the summit on Wednesday, May 31. Smythe, for one, was glad. Utterly fatigued, he was in desperate need of a day of rest. Shipton, on the other hand, was far less pleased, and worried how another day of physical deterioration would affect their chances. But the day off had practical consequences as well. Although they still had food for four or even five days, they were now down to only a two-day supply of fuel. "Food is useless at 27,400 feet without fuel," Smythe wrote. Not only were all of their food stocks frozen, needing to be thawed out in order to be consumed, but their altitude-induced lack of appetite, no doubt augmented by a mounting dislike of having to solely consume tinned provisions, was something they had to be on guard against. "Oh, for a few dozen eggs," Shipton said more than once.

Yet despite the cramped quarters and unappealing rations, their spirits were up. During the late afternoon, the storm went away, and the walls of the tent were suddenly bathed in light. Looking outside, the clouds were breaking up. "The wind was still volleying across Everest, raising spirals of loose snow," Smythe wrote. "In between the flying rags of mist the sky was green, not the warm green of grass and trees, but a cruel feline green utterly unmerciful. Yet the sight of it rekindled hope." Shipton, on the other hand, focused on the summit of Mount Everest, clearly visible—and barely more than a quarter mile away. "It looked ridiculously close," Shipton wrote.

The next day they would find out.

Thursday, June 1, 1933.

Both men were up by 3:00 a.m. They took turns melting snow for two tepid cups of café au lait, while thawing out their boots with a combination of candle flame and the much-maligned Tommy cookers. It took forever. Then, contorting themselves in the tiny tent, while muttering curses in the cold, damp air, and stopping to catch their breath, they got dressed. "We donned every stitch of clothing we possessed," Smythe recalled. Shipton wore seven sweaters, two pairs of woolen trousers, four or five pairs of socks, one pair of heavy wool mittens, a set of sheepskin gauntlets, his wind-proof suit, and a balaclava helmet. "I felt about as suitably equipped for delicate rock climbing," Shipton wrote, "as a fully rigged deep-sea diver for dancing a tango." Smythe went him even better. "I wore a Shetland vest, a thick flannel shirt, a heavy camel hair sweater, six light Shetland pullovers, two pairs of long Shetland pants, a pair of flannel trousers, and over all a silk-lined 'Grenfell' cloth suit." He, too, wore a Shetland balaclava, four pairs of socks, and two pairs of gloves. For food, each climber stuffed a square of Kendal Mint Cake—a white, chocolate bar-like confection prized by British mountaineers—into their pockets.

The whole operation had taken four and a half hours.

At seven thirty, they were finally ready to go.

"It was a fine morning," Smythe wrote, "though bitterly cold." The first bit, a shallow gully, filled with snow, that cut across about one hundred feet of the Yellow Band, would not have been at all difficult in the Alps. But at more than 27,000 feet, every step was taxing, and the two climbers had to stop and lean on their ice axes every couple of minutes in order to try and catch their breaths. "Yet, I was going better than I had expected," Frank Smythe wrote. "But, unhappily this was not the case with Eric. He was going steadily, but very slowly, and it was more than ever plain that there was something wrong with him." Despite being plagued with a stomach ache and feeling "as weak as a kitten," Shipton plowed on. But after about two hours, just below the First Step, Smythe heard a loud, exasperated sigh behind him. "Turning, I saw that Eric had stopped and was leaning heavily on his ice axe," Smythe wrote. "Next moment he sank down into a sitting position." Shipton had reached the end of his tether. After a brief parley, it was decided that Shipton would return to the tent at Camp Six, while Smythe would carry on, alone, towards the summit.

"Progress was slow, though steady," Smythe recorded, "and as I advanced and saw the final pyramid appear across the band of rocks beneath which I was traversing, there came to me for the first time that day a thrill of excitement and hope. I was going well now." But a huge problem lay just ahead. The Great Couloir was filled with snow and was, Smythe felt, "a savage place," probably unclimbable. But there was also a subsidiary couloir which offered the possibility of a way forward. Beyond it, Smythe felt, the hardest parts should be behind him. "I could see the face of the final pyramid and it did not look difficult," he remembered. "Energy alone would be required to surmount it." Frank Smythe was little more than a thousand feet from standing on top of the world.

First he would have to cross the dreaded slabs. These were plates of limestone, angled like tiles on a roof, that had bedeviled the Everest climbers of the 1920s. Worse yet, they were covered with "the worse kind of snow, soft like flour, loose like granulated sugar, and incapable of holding the feet in position." Nonetheless, Smythe pushed on, slowly and carefully. By eleven o'clock, he had maybe made it fifty feet up the slabs. But there was still another three hundred feet to go. "The summit was just in view over the rock band," he wrote, "but an aeon of weariness separated me from it." Smythe stopped to regard the incredible view before him. "The Rongbuk Valley stretched northward toward the golden hills of Tibet, and I could make out the Rongbuk Monastery, a minute cluster of buildings, yet distinct in every detail through the brilliantly clear atmosphere," he recalled. "There was nothing visible to challenge my elevation. The earth was so far beneath; it seemed impossible I should ever regain it." It was, he later mused, "a god's view."

But Frank Smythe was no god. There was no way that he could make it all the way up the slabs, climb the summit pyramid, and make it safely back to Camp Six by nightfall. "For exhausted men benighted on Everest," he'd observed, "there is only one ending." It was time to stop. But the decision, however reasonable, stung like a whip. "I cannot enlarge on the bitterness of defeat," he later wrote. "The last 1,000 feet of Everest are not for mere flesh and blood. Whoever reaches the summit, if he does it without artificial aid, will have to rise godlike above his own frailties." Smythe turned around and started his descent.

He wasn't traveling alone.

Or, at least, that's what Smythe believed. Since he and Shipton had parted, he'd felt very strongly that there was another climber moving along beside him, something that he had felt once before after taking a bad fall in the Dolomites. "This 'presence' was strong and friendly," he would write. "In its company I could not feel lonely, neither could I come to any harm. It was always there to sustain me on my solitary climb up the snow-covered slabs." So strongly did Smythe believe that this mysterious third climber was accompanying him that once, when he reached into his pocket to grab a piece of Kendal Mint Cake, he broke the square in two and turned to give the other half to his companion. Perhaps the Tibetans were right. Maybe there were gods on Mount Everest after all.

That was not the sole otherwordly episode that Frank Smythe experienced that day. As he slowly worked his way down toward the First Step, he found himself "on a series of narrow outward-sloping ledges separated by abrupt little walls." Some of the ledges were wider than the others, and one of these he paused to take a short break. "Once while doing so I was startled to see two dark objects silhouetted against the clear sky just over the NE shoulder of Everest," he scribbled in pencil in his climbing diary, now held in the archives of the Alpine Club, "They were almost like kites attached by some invisible line to the earth." One was kettle-shaped with a spout, while the other was more barrel-like, with some short legs. "I was so astonished that I rubbed my eyes. When looking again, they were still there."

Incredulous at what he was looking at, Smythe tried to determine if they were some kind of optical illusion. "First of all I looked away," he wrote. "The objects did not follow my vision, but when my gaze returned to the North-East Shoulder they were still hovering there." He stared at his watch, but when he looked up again, the odd, kite-like shapes remained. "I looked away again, and by way of a more exacting mental test identified by name a number of peaks, valleys and glaciers. I found no difficulty in Cho Oyu, Gyachung Kang, Pumori, and the Rongbuk Glacier, but when I again looked back the objects were in the same position." Finally, after about a quarter of an hour, a sudden mist—"the advance guard of bad weather"—blew in, and momentarily obscured the mysterious objects. "It lasted but a few seconds but when it passed the objects were no longer there. I breathed a sigh of relief."

The rapidly gathering mists, however, were a real concern. Not only could they herald the coming of bad weather, but they also cut down on visibility, something that Smythe could not afford to lose. "Try as I could," he wrote in his climbing diary, "I could see no signs of the tent among that vast expanse of yellow slabs." Finally, Camp Six appeared out of the gloom. "At this moment a curious thing occurred. The moment that the tent came into view something seemed to snap and I realized that my companion who all this time on the descent had seemed very close departed. For a moment I felt strangely alone." The feeling did not last. He found Shipton inside the tent and told him what had happened. Smythe did not, however, have the energy to make it down to Camp Five that day. Shipton, wanting to make sure that Smythe got a decent night's sleep, then descended to Camp Five alone.

"The weather meanwhile was thickening up and by the time Shipton left," Smythe wrote in his diary, "snow was falling." Smythe used half of the remaining fuel to cook supper, and then bundled himself into the two sets of sleeping bags. "It did not occur to me that I was spending the night higher than any other human being; I was purely animal in my desire for warmth and comfort."

He slept for twelve hours.

The next morning, Smythe found the last tin of fuel, melted enough snow for a cup of lukewarm water, and forced down a café au lait. Outside, another blizzard was brewing. There was no time for any kind of reconnaissance. "Collecting my few possessions together," he later wrote, "I crawled outside and hooked together the flaps of the tent." Then he started to head down the shelf leading toward Camp Five and the Northeast Ridge.

Ruttledge had the members of the expedition back at Base Camp by June 7. One week later, another run was made at the mountain, but it was called off a week after that. The monsoon had settled in, and the weather was impossible. Many in the party wanted to remain in Tibet until after the monsoon was over, and try again in the fall, but the Mount Everest Committee, back in London, ruled that out. By the end of July, the climbers were all back in Darjeeling.

Meanwhile, Lady Houston's wish had come true. On April 3, 1933, the two specially equipped Westland airplanes flew successfully over the summit of Mount Everest, and returned safely to the dusty airstrip outside of Purnea. While the photographs of the mountain did not prove to be of quite the scientific value that had been hoped for, Houston's renewed interest in aviation would later reap some benefits. When the Ramsay MacDonald government refused to underwrite the research costs for the Supermarine S6, a new high-speed, single-engine airplane, she wrote a check for £100,000 herself. "Every true Briton would rather sell his last shirt than admit that England could not afford to defend herself." A few years later, the Supermarine Company would apply the know-how they had developed with the S6 on the prototype for an even more advanced high-speed fighter. Initially known as the Type 300, the Air Ministry was so impressed upon seeing the new plane at a series of test flights at an airfield outside of Southampton that it immediately ordered three hundred. By then it had a new name. It was called the Spitfire.

Back in London, meanwhile, Eric Shipton had reached a couple of conclusions.

The first regarded a career. On the way back to India from Mount Everest, he later wrote, "Wager and I left the main party and made our way across a small strip of unexplored country to the south and crossed into Sikkim by a new pass." The experience was exhilarating—and life changing. "Why not spend the rest of my life doing this sort of thing?" he asked himself, "There was no way of life that I liked more." But turning a passion into a career was a tall order, especially when it came to finances. Shipton was undeterred. There must be ways, he decided, that this could be solved. After all, others had done so before him. "No," he wrote, "lack of money must not be allowed to interfere." His second conclusion regarded the size and nature of mountaineering expeditions, especially in the Himalayas. Couldn't they be done on a much smaller scale, and for far less funds, and achieve the same or better results?

Halfway around the world, meanwhile, another mountaineering drama had played itself out. For while the attention of British climbers was very much focused on the 1933 Mount Everest Expedition, four unknown climbers had, in fact, tried exactly what Shipton was proposing. And when the word got out about what they did, the race to the roof of the world suddenly grew more crowded.

CHAPTER FOUR

The New Emersonians

New York smoldered like an oven.

As the late-August temperatures climbed into the nineties, steeplejacks and deliverymen stripped down to their undershirts, Fifth Avenue matrons dabbed their temples with silk handkerchiefs, and beat cops making their rounds in the Bowery found ways to keep on the shady side of the street. Manhole covers glowered like frying pans, the grass turned brown in Central Park, and lovers lingered along the rail at the Battery, hoping for a breeze off the Hudson. Even the bums at Union Square, roasting on park benches while soapbox orators droned on about class struggle and salvation, started to pray for rain.

But up on West 110th Street, on the second floor of a stately nine-story building set in the middle of the long block between Broadway and Amsterdam Avenue, the talk was of glaciers and ice falls, sheet ice and blizzards. It was hot there, too, but no one seemed to care. For in the member's lounge of the Explorers Club, while a fan buzzed somewhere nearby, a handful of American climbers and explorers weren't just talking about a proposed new expedition. They were also conspiring to turn the mountaineering world on its head.

At first, their talk centered upon making what would, in effect, be an end run at Mount Everest. Rather than trying to approach the mountain through British-controlled Sikkim, where the Brits would no doubt scotch any plans for such an expedition, the idea was to enter Tibet from the north, through China. Here, a group

57

of mountaineers might be able to travel all the way to the Tibetan frontier before the question of seeking permission to climb Mount Everest would even arise. This way, the reasoning went, a small American expedition might be able to launch an assault on Everest without having to deal with the British at all.

This was big thinking. But it was also quite risky. Breaking through the British stranglehold on Mount Everest, however desirable, might also have some momentous diplomatic consequences. Yet it also reflected the growing confidence that America's youthful climbers were starting to have in themselves and what they could accomplish. "There are quite a few people who believe I can climb Everest," Terris Moore, one of the climbers present at the late-August 1931 meeting at the Explorers Club, wrote to his soon-to-be fiancée. "I don't know whether I can or not." But he was willing to try. Soon, however, the discussion shifted to a more intriguing—and undoubtedly more feasible—possibility, one that had been slowly gaining traction for nearly two years.

In the fall of 1929, Kermit and Theodore Roosevelt III—Teddy's two eldest sons—published a book titled *Trailing the Giant Panda*. A gripping account of a hunting and scientific expedition to western China, the book was also a rare travelogue describing remote areas of Szechwan, Yunnan, and Sinkiang provinces. Not only did the Roosevelt brothers collect thousands of birds and animals for the Field Museum in Chicago, but they also pushed deep into areas that were essentially unknown to Westerners. And along the way, they made some surprising discoveries. "Early one morning we got our first glimpse of mysterious Mount Koonka, rising high in white majesty," the brothers wrote of passing near a spectacular, snow-covered peak located more than a hundred miles west of the Szechwan border. "The altitude of this mighty peak is unknown, but there are those who claim that it rises more than 30,000 feet and is the highest in the world. A geologist from Chengtu made a special expedition to establish Koonka's height, but after he had taken his observations he refused for some entirely unaccountable reason to divulge them."

In the map that accompanied the first edition of *Trailing the Giant Panda*, the mysterious mountain's height is listed as "30,000?" If true, it would be higher than Mount Everest.

Only the mystery did not end there. Four months later, an article titled "Seeking the Mountains of Mystery" appeared in the February 1930 issue of *National Geographic Magazine*. Authored by a legendary botanical collector named Joseph F. Rock, it described his visit to the same area where the Roosevelt brothers had been. "Twenty-eight thousand feet, or almost as high as Everest," he wrote of the towering peaks of the Anyi Machen range. But Rock also left open the possibility that the highest peak that he had seen, which he called Minya Konka, might "prove higher than Everest."

In fact, he already believed that it was. In the spring of 1928, Rock got his first view of Minya Konka, a bedazzling, pyramid-shaped peak that few Chinese, not to mention Americans or Europeans, had ever seen before. Not only did he extensively photograph the mountain, but from three different elevations he made three separate estimates of its height using an aneroid barometer, clinometer, and prismatic compass. His findings absolutely floored him. Waiting until the expedition was over and he was out of China, where he feared that news of his remarkable discovery might leak out, on February 27, 1930, Rock sent a cable from Haiphong, Indo-China, to National Geographic headquarters. It read:

MINYA KONKA HIGHEST PEAK ON GLOBE 30250 FEET ROCK

If true, this was stunning news. No longer would Mount Everest be the highest mountain on Earth.

At National Geographic Society headquarters on Sixteenth Street, NW, in Washington, however, caution ruled the hour. For one thing, Rock had used neither a theodolite nor a mercurial barometer, the then-standard instruments for measuring altitude, to estimate the height of Minya Konka. For another, even though he had few rivals as a collector or explorer in the wilds of western China and Tibet, he was also a notorious prima donna. On his expeditions, Rock traveled with a retinue that included fifteen armed guards and a cadre of servants. Absolutely refusing to eat the local Chinese cuisine, every evening he had his personal chef prepare *Wiener schnitzel*, potato-and-chive dumplings, delicate *Palatschinken* pancakes, and other dishes from his native Austria. And every morning, before donning one of his specially made silk robes, he insisted on taking a bath in a large folding canvas tub.

Put off by his thin-skinned histrionics whenever he was criticized, the leadership of the National Geographic Society refused to publish Rock's stunning height estimate for Minya Konka without an independent verification. When a second article by Rock appeared in the October 1930 issue of *National Geographic*, along with dazzling shots of Minya Konka itself, the editors lowered the estimate of Minya Konka's altitude to 25,600 feet.

Nonetheless, the *possibility* that an essentially unknown peak in China might be higher than Mount Everest was now in the air. And for the small group of mountaineers who gathered around the large globe in the Explorers Club in New York ten months after Joseph Rock's second article came out, the mystery of Minya Konka was simply too tempting. "Surely, we reasoned," wrote one of the members present, "there must be a very high peak there!" That was all it took, and plans for a Minya Konka expedition were quickly drawn up.

While the late summer traffic rumbled by on 110th Street, a handful of American climbers had rather casually decided to join the race to the roof of the world. Unlike their British and German counterparts, however, who brought huge caravans of men and supplies to the Himalayas, the American mountaineers could all comfortably fit into a single New York City taxicab.

Three months later, on November 24, 1931, a black-hulled freighter named the *Tai Ping Yang* slipped away from its moorings near the foot of Pioneer Street in Brooklyn, made a portside turn into

The World Beneath Their Feet

Buttermilk Channel, and, as the Manhattan skyline receded off the stern, began a twelve-thousand-mile voyage to the other side of the world. On board were the nine members—eight men and one woman—who made up the roster of the Lamb Tibetan Expedition. A largely scientific enterprise, with plans to collect the seeds of native plants as well as conduct medical and dental studies among the population of northern Tibet, the leader of the group, Gene Lamb, explained to reporters that they also hoped to reconcile some of the conflicting maps of the region. But the four mountaineers attached to the group, which included Terris Moore, had a different set of goals in mind. Not only did they intend to accurately measure the height of Minya Konka, possibly the highest mountain on earth, but they also planned to climb it.

A direct descendent of *Mayflower* pilgrims, Moore had grown up in a world of wealth and privilege. Summers were spent at the family cottage in Maine, while Thanksgiving and Christmas found him sitting in front of a roaring fireplace at his grandparents' towering stone mansion outside Philadelphia. He went to Europe before he was ten years old, and the first "mountain" that he ever climbed, a nineteen-hundred-foot granite outcropping, was on land owned by his family. But Moore also possessed an adventurous streak, one that was mirrored by a fierce determination to be a success. At age sixteen, he had taken off on a weeklong camping trip, alone, in the wilds of northern Maine, dodging thunderstorms and black bears, and living off bullheads, brook trout, and a bag of Aunt Jemima Pancake Flour. "Take featherweight oilskin poncho instead of cavalry poncho," he'd written to himself in a post-trip memorandum. "By no means use any 'Powdered Eggs.'" Of a wild canoe trip down the Allagash River that he took three years later, he described it as a "thrilling education, and the building of more self-confidence." Here was a young man on the move.

Now twenty-three years old, with sallow eyes and wiry, sunstreaked hair, Moore had already become a mountaineer of some note. During his senior year at Williams College, he made the first winter ascent,

61

on skis, of Mount Katahdin, the sixth-highest peak in New England. The following summer, as a member of a scientific expedition to South America, Moore led the second ascent of Chimborazo, the massive, 20,000-foot giant that Edward Whymper had written about in *Travels Amongst the Great Andes of the Equator*. But it would be at Harvard, where Moore enrolled as a graduate student in the fall of 1929, that his climbing skills would take on a crucial added dimension.

Though it had only been founded five years earlier, the Harvard Mountaineering Club was the only university-based climbing club in America. Yet what they lacked in age, the climbing enthusiasts of Harvard Yard—elevation 26 feet—more than made up for with their ardor and zeal. Offering regular weekend excursions to both the White Mountains in New Hampshire and the one-hundred-foot granite walls of the quarries in nearby Quincy, Massachusetts, club members largely mimicked the methods and equipment used by Britain's gentlemen climbers. But during the summers, when the Harvard climbers organized mountaineering expeditions out West, particularly among the little-visited peaks of the Canadian Rockies and in far-off Alaska Territory, they had to overcome challenges that were less familiar to their English cousins.

To begin with, unlike in the Alps, in Alaska and western Canada there were no guides, guidebooks, or mountain huts. And while the Harvard mountaineers could sometimes deduce likely climbing routes ahead of time from stray photographs or reports that might appear in outdoor magazines and newsletters, most of the time they had to figure out how to climb a peak the very first time they ever laid eyes on it. Nor was that all. Because, for the most part, not only were these Canadian and Alaskan mountains located far from any towns, villages, or railway lines, but also there weren't any locals they could hire to help haul their gear. Like their fellow Harvardian, Ralph Waldo Emerson, Class of 1821, the Harvard boys were all about self-reliance. They were going to have to do it themselves.

As a result, a new kind of mountaineering philosophy began to take shape among the small band of climbers whose paths crossed in Harvard Yard, an approach that soon found expression in their first expeditions beyond New England. "A new trend has become evident on these expeditions," wrote the editors of *Harvard Mountaineering*, "a trend which was largely developed in the Alaskan ranges. In contrast to the large unwieldy Himalayan expeditions with their complicated problems of transport, it places emphasis on lightness of equipment and mobility of organization. Whether such tactics could be effectively employed on the greater Himalayan peaks is an open question, as yet unanswered."

A couple of Harvard men were about to find out.

From New York City, the *Tai Ping Yang* steamed south into the bright blue waters of the Gulf Stream, stopping briefly at Newport News before skirting past Florida and Cuba and on through the Panama Canal and into the Pacific Ocean. The ship stopped again in Los Angeles in mid-December to take on supplies, mail, and newspapers—some featuring eyebrow-raising headlines.

Back in mid-September, following a trumped-up border incident, Japanese troops had invaded Manchuria, capturing the city of Mukden and defeating its garrison of Chinese troops. In the weeks that followed, more and more cities fell as the Japanese high command dispatched more than sixty thousand foot soldiers, accompanied by tanks and bombers, to China's northernmost province in a swift and brutal campaign of conquest. By the time the freighter carrying the American explorers and mountaineers set sail for Manila, Manchuria was well on its way to becoming Manchukuo, a Japanese puppet state. And while Manchuria was located a long ways from Minya Konka, there was growing concern that, because of the turmoil in the north, the Chinese government might be inclined to deny the expedition permission to travel to the country's interior.

The *Tai Ping Yang* arrived in Shanghai in late January 1932.

When they began unloading their supplies, however, the mountain climbers discovered, to their horror, that much of their equipment had either been stolen or lost. A few days later, while they were trying to figure out how to replace the missing items, the members of the expedition were suddenly caught up in a brand-new Asian crisis. "All nine of us were lunching in our hotel room on January 28 when the doors to our balcony, which by chance I had just latched, swung inward as though pushed by some giant unseen hand, accompanied by the sound of a vast detonation," Terris Moore later wrote. "We climbed to the roof of the hotel just in time to see the Japanese battleship *Idzumo*, anchored just off the Shanghai Bund, begin firing her shells at point blank range into Chapei, the Chinese part of Shanghai." A wave of Japanese fighter bombers appeared next, and by the end of the day thousands of Japanese soldiers had poured into the city. Moore and the other climbers were quickly armed and hustled into uniform to help defend the city's International Settlement. But when it became clear that the Japanese army only had designs on Chinese neighborhoods in Shanghai, the expedition could resume. Catching a coastal steamer north to Tientsin, the nine Americans then traveled by train to Peking.

Only now, the political situation had shifted. Convinced that the Chinese government would never grant them official permission to travel to the western interior, expedition leader Gene Lamb proposed that they proceed without it. But the mountain climbers wouldn't sign on to such a plan, and as a result, the Lamb Expedition to Tibet split apart. Lamb, his wife Corinne, and the expedition's second-in-command all decided to forge ahead without official permission. The expedition doctor and one of the climbers, meanwhile, chose to return to the United States.

Now, only three climbers were left—Moore and two others.

The grandson of a wealthy mining engineer and art collector, Arthur B. Emmons III was also a Harvard man and a member of the Harvard Mountaineering Club. A native Bostonian, Emmons had climbed in both the Dolomites and the Alps as a sixteen-year-old, and the summer after he graduated from St. Paul's he made the first successful ascent of the northeast face of Mount Hood in

Oregon. Now twenty-one, and with a lingering, boyish look about him, Emmons had put his undergraduate career on hold to join the expedition.

Dick Burdsall, on the other hand, might as well have been from another generation. Thirty-six years old, with rapidly thinning dark hair, he was a mechanical engineer in a family-owned nut and bolt manufacturing company located in Port Chester, New York. A Swarthmore graduate and a devout Quaker, Burdsall had done precious little mountaineering. But he was big and strong, as well as calm, tough, and filled with practical know-how.

Besides, the trio of climbers had also acquired a fourth member. And even though Jack Theodore Young hadn't done a lick of mountain climbing, he quickly became the proposed Minya Konka expedition's secret weapon. Nominally a twenty-one-year-old journalism student at New York University, Young was a Hawaii-born, Canton-raised Chinese American. The son of a family of wealthy traders who were on speaking terms with Sun Yat-sen, he was also a clotheshorse and a world-class hunter. Young had even talked himself onto the Roosevelt Brothers' 1928/1929 expedition to Szechwan, where, dressed in jodhpurs and a matching woolen driving cap and jacket, he served as a guide and translator. And even though his main interest, back in Manhattan, was courting Adelaide Chin Mow, a nineteen-year-old former cigarette girl at the China Doll Club, Young spoke flawless Mandarin and Cantonese and was a natural leader and negotiator. Because of Jack Young, the Americans were able to move back and forth across the line that separated Chinese ways from those of the Western world with relative ease, something that no European nation could match.

While they all waited for official permission to travel to the interior, Young had Moore, Emmons, and Burdsall enroll at the North China Union Language School in Peking, where, alongside dozens of newly arrived American missionaries, they took classes in conversational Mandarin. Five months later, they received some good news. The Chinese government would likely approve their request to travel to remote Sinkiang province. Abandoning the notion of making a back-door run at Everest, they instead sought permission to travel to Minya Konka, determine its height, and, if possible, climb it.

First, however, Terris Moore had to win the approval of Nelson T. Johnson, the head of the American Legation in China, who would then forward their plan to the Chinese authorities.

Johnson, as it turned out, was far from welcoming. "We understand your real objective is Mount Everest," he barked, and then added, in fluent bureaucratese, "but for such a destination in western Tibet the American Legation here in China does not have any authority to help anyone."

Eventually convincing Johnson that they were, indeed, going only to Minya Konka, Moore soon ran into other problems. For one thing, Johnson didn't at all cotton to the mountaineers' shoestring budget. Equally troubling to the career diplomat was the fact that no single individual was in command of the proposed expedition. But the climbers had their reasons.

"We had no leader," Dick Burdsall later recalled. "At first thought this might appear a weakness, but with our small and congenial group we found it a decided advantage. We were keen to accomplish all that we had set out to do, and with such a limited personnel this required that each give of his best at all times. In some instances decisions had to be made by the one or two who happened to be on hand, and were later ratified by the others. Important matters, however, were decided only after full discussion, with due consideration for the specialized knowledge of each member." The New England town meeting hadn't died. It was now a guiding philosophy of American mountaineering.

Johnson swallowed his skepticism and approved the application.

Finally, in June 1932, the four Americans received word from the Chinese that their travel request had been approved. It was time to solve the mystery of Minya Konka.

*　　*　　*

The World Beneath Their Feet

Dick Burdsall and Art Emmons left immediately.

In sweltering Shanghai, where Japanese gunboats still patrolled the harbor, they bought one-way tickets on the *Ichang*, a coal-powered river steamer, for a fifteen-hundred-mile journey up the Yangtze River, while Jack Young and Terris Moore stayed behind to collect the necessary supplies. On their river voyage, Burdsall and Emmons saw a China that they'd only read about in books—junks and rice paddies and ancient villages, forests of bamboo and a two-hundred-foot-tall stone Buddha. They observed gangs of coolies laboring along the shoreline, straw-hatted women working in the fields, and solitary old men, like a vision from another millenium, fishing with handmade dip nets. With the current swirling about them, they passed beneath the towering cliffs lining the Wushan and Wind Box Gorges, the mud-colored water churning in their wake.

But they also caught a glimpse of the simmering tensions then roiling the countryside. "We oppose the partition of China by foreign imperialists!" read one sign set along the north bank of the river, which an English-speaking Chinese Bible student translated for them. "Join the Red Army" read another. Indeed, the wheelhouse of the *Ichang* had been reinforced with steel armor to protect the crew from potshots fired by bandits and renegade soldiers.

Burdsall and Emmons made it to Chungking in nine and a half days, and spent the night in a dingy hotel, where the loud clacks of mah-jongg tiles kept them up late into the night. From the Yangtze, they traveled north, along the Min River, for two hundred miles. At Chengtu, the capital of Szechwan province, they caught a rickety bus made out of a wooden frame bolted to the chassis of a Chevrolet farm truck. "Twenty-one passengers with their baggage crowded into it," Burdsall recalled, "but in spite of this load some soldiers along the road held us up so that they could ride on the running-boards. Our driver stopped frequently at little streams to refill the leaky radiator." Their biggest worry, though, was the delicate, thirty-inch mercury barometer that had been loaned to the expedition by the American Geographical Society, which they would need to accurately measure the height of Minya Konka. "I had to hold it in vertically in my hands so that it would be eased gently over the little jolts," Burdsall wrote, "and yet not strike the floor or roof when we hit a big bump."

The roads, or at least those that could handle a car or a truck, ran out two days later in Yachow, a trading center along the old Peking-to-Lhasa diplomatic route. Here, with the help of two American missionaries, Burdsall and Emmons hired fifteen porters to help transport their nearly fourteen hundred pounds of supplies to Tatsienlu, some 140 miles to the west. As they were preparing to leave the American Baptist Mission the next morning, eight soldiers suddenly joined their caravan as well, explaining that the city magistrate had sent them along as protection from bandits. This was not an imaginary danger. During their journey, they passed the spot where thirteen bandits had been recently beheaded.

The walk to Tatsienlu took more than a week. They passed groves of apple and apricot trees, fields planted in peanuts and corn, and small wayside temples where the air was filled with the aroma of burning joss sticks. When they would stop to eat in the little tea shops in the villages along the way, crowds of people would suddenly materialize out of nowhere to stand and stare at the two Americans, the first round-eyed foreigners that the vast majority of them had ever seen. "Curiosity of the natives everywhere," Moore scribbled in his diary. "Want to feel my clothing. How much it costs, etc.; feel my hairy legs."

School-age boys were especially curious. Whenever one of the climbers started to write a letter or make a notation in his diary, a couple dozen young men would lean in and crane their necks in order to watch the strange, indecipherable characters that the two foreigners scratched on their paper. Back on the trail, they passed other travelers as well—traders with loads of tea, salt, coal, rice, straw sandals, and loads of medicinal bark. On one occasion they passed a lone man with a live pig tied to his back. On another it was three donkeys carrying a disassembled field gun. Fighting had broken out along the Tibetan border, and there were soldiers everywhere. The climbers were also rapidly gaining altitude. Some of the passes they crossed already topped 9,000 feet.

They reached Tatsienlu on the afternoon of the eighth day. A crossroads town set in the border country between Tibet and China, Tatsienlu amazed Burdsall with its polyglot local population. "What a variety of types they were!" he wrote. "Chinese officials, soldiers, and traders from many provinces; Tibetan lamas, nomads, and caravan-drivers, half-castes of every degree; and tribesmen, belonging to the several one-time independent little states and kingdoms." The town even boasted a small hydroelectric lighting plant, though its actual output was so low and the system was so overloaded that any lamps hooked up to it could only muster a "dull red glow."

Tatsienlu was also the jumping off place where Burdsall and Emmons would, for the most part, leave the modern world behind and begin the business of finding, measuring, and, they hoped, climbing the mysterious Minya Konka. With the help of two English-speaking missionaries, they again put together a small caravan and headed south. And while they were still technically in China, the countryside had the feel of Tibet. Gone were the rice paddies and pagodas, the water buffalo and the little shops. Now there were fields of barley, long strings of tattered prayer flags, black-haired yaks, and men wearing three-cornered hats and shoes with pointed, turned-up toes. But the mountains, though they were now quite near, remained shrouded in mist. Finally, on August 1, 1932, more than a month and a half after they had left Shanghai, they caught their first, fleeting glimpse of Minya Konka. "A stern and imposing sight," Burdsall wrote. "We had seen enough to satisfy us that this was one of the greatest mountain giants of our planet."

Over the next few weeks, after they had dismissed the porters and had set about triangulating and accurately measuring the height of Minya Konka, their awe of the mysterious, towering peak only increased. Of a brief look on the evening of August 18, when the curtain of mists surrounding the mountain momentarily parted, Burdsall wrote, "That forbidding face. The awful precipices, the snowy ridges, cold and gray in the evening dusk, appeared for an instant, to be concealed quickly by the swift curtain. Again and again the vision was unveiled by those moving rifts, until in the glowing darkness we could see it no more."

Emmons was no less awestruck. "There stood the resplendent Konka in the clear morning air, the very embodiment of majesty and awe, with a golden plume of sunlit snow streaming from its summit in the early dawn. It seemed so remote that it was almost ethereal in its aloof austerity," he wrote. "No wonder the Tibetans of this whole region worshipped it as a holy mountain!" Then, ominously, he added: "We stood silently and gazed in wonder. Climb it? There appeared not the remotest chance."

By early September, the two men had circumnavigated enough of Minya Konka to fully realize the immense defenses that this soaring peak would present to any attempt to climb it. Most of its faces were simply too steep. The only vague possibility, they concluded, was a daunting, windblown ridge that ran up toward the summit from the northwest. To further investigate, Burdsall and Emmons, hauling sixty-five pounds of equipment each, set up a camp at about 16,000 feet along the mountain's northern approach. From here they hoped to find a route to the northwest ridge.

Dubbing their perch "Cloud Camp" because of the late-monsoon clouds that normally blocked their view of the higher elevations, they were now close enough to hear the ice and snow falling off of Minya Konka's northern face. "At night the frequent rumble and roar of the avalanches falling from the heights above, thundering like a fast express train on an iron trestle, would startle us into wakefulness," Emmons wrote. "Sometimes they continued for several minutes at a stretch before they died away in a distant grumble."

Near dusk one evening, the two climbers learned why. Crawling out of their tent to brush away some six inches of snow that had fallen on their tent, they were shocked to discover that the clouds had lifted. "What a sight greeted our eyes!" Emmons wrote. "We were in a tremendous amphitheater hemmed in by all sides by jagged snow peaks which towered many thousands of feet above us." As thrilling as the sight was—along with offering an acoustical explanation for why they heard the avalanches so clearly—the scene before them was also a sobering reminder of the challenges that lay ahead. "Huge walls of blue-green ice menaced the lower slopes with the potential danger of mighty avalanches from their crumbling sides; razor-like ridges were fantastically capped by coxcombs and cornices," recalled the young Harvard grad. "We forgot our tent, supper, and everything else to stand by the magnificence of the scene. The Alps, the Canadian Rockies, even the great mountains of far Alaska would fade into the background before such glory and splendor."

Jack Young and Terris Moore, meanwhile, had finally gotten out of Shanghai. In large measure, they followed the route of their compatriots. But on their way from Yachow to Tatsienlu, they woke up one morning and discovered that one of their horses had been stolen, likely by a band of soldiers who had passed by during the night.

So they decided to get it back.

Armed with pistols and rifles, they set out after the soldiers, whom they finally overtook near Yachiagan pass. Jack Young, shouting in Mandarin, commanded them to halt. But the soldiers just kept walking. So Young fired over their heads. "Jack fired twice," Moore recalled. This time, the soldiers stopped, and while Moore covered him with a pistol, Young started questioning the men and began to look over their horses. When Young found the stolen animal, whose mane had been clipped, he disarmed the thief. Then he and Moore escorted him to the nearest magistrate. "Took back our prisoner, photographed him," Moore recorded, "and gave him hell."

A few days later, Young and Moore were reunited with Burdsall and Emmons. Yet despite the joy that the four-man expedition was finally back together, they had to cope with some less-than-spectacular news. After checking and rechecking their measurements, Burdsall and Emmons had determined that Minya Konka was 24,900 feet high. While it was still a formidable peak, and higher than any mountain in the Western Hemisphere, it was no Mount Everest. Regardless, however, there was no time to waste. "A cold drizzle was falling and leaden clouds clung to the mountainsides and filled the valley with their gloomy presence, but we could ill afford to wait for good weather," Emmons wrote. "It was now September, and winter was already on its way." Fully convinced that the northwest ridge offered the only hope of attaining the summit, with the help of six hired Tibetans, they stocked their Base Camp and got ready to begin their assault.

But another problem soon presented itself.

"Well," a long-faced Jack Young declared one evening, "maybe we'll go tomorrow, and maybe we won't." As it turned out, the leaders at the local lamasery had now turned against their project. Fearful that the proposed mountaineering expedition would anger the gods of the mountains, who would then punish the people with famine, the lamas were rescinding their approval. This was no hollow crisis. Without the consent of the head lamas, the climb was off. After a brief parley, the decision was reached that Young should try one more time, alone, to sway their thinking. Young wasted no time. Telling the lamas that the four Americans had traveled halfway around the world to "pay homage to their sacred mountain," Young asked them to burn juniper boughs and utter prayers for the climbers. He also made a liberal donation, in silver coins, to the lamasery.

It worked. The climb was on.

Though they faced a stream of challenges—pounding winds, crevasses that they were forced to leap across, and the ever-present danger of setting off a surface peel, a type of avalanche when a whole layer of new snow suddenly gives way—the four climbers made good progress. On the increasingly steep slopes, they fell into rhythmic, measured steps. "Rhythm was a god," Emmons gushed. "Rhythm was life!" With the incessant wind swirling about them, they made steady progress up the steep ridge.

In the evenings, crammed inside a seven-by-seven-foot tent, the four Americans didn't follow the standard protocol of cooking and eating dinner, grumbling about the lack of space, and trying to catch some uninterrupted sleep. Instead, they stayed up late, smoking, playing chess, and talking. They read *Vanity Fair* and a volume of Kipling's songs. And unlike their European counterparts, they often slept in. "We had got away to our usual late 9:00 a.m. start," Emmons wrote on October 10. And every time they pitched a new camp, they celebrated with a small bottle of Hennessy brandy. "High mountains are climbed on morale," Emmons observed. "This precarious mental condition must be maintained at all costs." By mid-October, they had established Camp Three at 20,700 feet.

But the higher they climbed, and the thinner the air became, the harder it became to do anything—and everything. "The slightest exertion in moving about the tent brought on a prolonged bout of panting," Emmons wrote. "It took fifteen minutes to put on and lace a pair of boots, five minutes to don a parka and mittens; all accomplished by much heavy breathing and pauses for rest. The cold as well as the rarified atmosphere slowed us down, until every action was done at one-third speed." Bringing up supplies was particularly taxing, and Young and Burdsall, in particular, were struggling with the effects of the altitude. Sleep grew increasingly difficult. Needing to regain some strength, and to collect more supplies to bring to the higher camps, the decision was made that all four climbers would briefly return to Camp One to collect new supplies, reorganize, and recuperate.

"*MAIL!*" Terris Moore wrote jubilantly in his diary, "Raw carrots!" But despite their joy at being at Camp One for a brief respite, another major decision needed to be taken. Though he had already become, in effect, the world's first Asian American mountain climber, Jack Young decided to take himself off of the summit team. For one thing, he'd had significant difficulty adjusting to the altitude. But more importantly, he could help resupply the camps while the others pushed toward the summit. And should an emergency arise, he would be the best candidate to seek help. The others agreed.

There would just be three of them now: Moore, Burdsall, and Emmons.

"It was now a case of risking everything in one last supreme effort, an effort requiring every atom of skill and strength we could master," Emmons wrote. "We were going the limit."

On October 22, the trio of climbers made it back up to Camp Three. Soon thereafter, Moore and Emmons established the next and final camp, Camp Four, on an impossibly tiny sliver of ridge at 22,000 feet. From here, they hoped to make a summit run. But more supplies still needed to be brought up, and the next day they hauled up the last of the food and fuel, making the exhausting journey in one trip instead of two. The truth of the matter, however, was that they were all nearly played out, Burdsall in particular. So, despite the very real worry about missing their window of opportunity, and the sudden onset of winter weather, the decision was made to rest the following day, which was spent cooking and playing chess. Emmons, using yak butter, yak cheese, and frozen eggs, prepared what was surely the world's highest soufflé.

Forty-eight hours later, on the afternoon of October 26, the three men hauled themselves, and the last of the supplies, into the tiny tent at Camp Four and collapsed on the floor. Icicles were hanging from their eyebrows and beards, while a layer of white rime covered their clothes and packs. For two days they had battled steely winds and piercing cold, and now were on the verge of climbing to the summit of Minya Konka. But the mountain had taken its toll. Despite his protests to the contrary, Dick Burdsall was clearly in poor condition, and it was a real question as to how much further he could go.

Terris Moore and Art Emmons were in better shape, but there was now a dangerous new concern. Emmons's feet had been growing colder and colder each day, and he had begun to worry that they were turning numb, an early sign of frostbite. While the walls of the tent shook in the wind, the trio held a war council. Burdsall would rest the next day, while Moore and Emmons, despite the growing concern over his feet, would begin to scout a route to the top. If all went well, they would all try for the summit one day later. It was a reasonable plan.

Then it happened.

While trying to cut a frozen biscuit in half, Emmons's hand slipped and he drove his knife into the palm of his hand, all the way to the bone. Working together, the three climbers were able to stanch the bleeding. But it was clear that Emmons could neither properly hold an ice axe nor grasp a rope on belay. Less than one day below the summit of Minya Konka, Emmons was done climbing. It was now an open question whether any of them would make it to the top.

But Dick Burdsall wouldn't hear of it.

Though he was the oldest and least experienced of the three—as well as the sickest—Burdsall insisted that he could push on. Again the three climbers put their heads together, and a new plan was hatched. Moore and Burdsall would make a run at the summit the next day. It was now or never. That night, working around his injured hand, Emmons precooked their oatmeal breakfast, while Moore packed two rucksacks loaded with cameras and film, emergency rations, and two flags, one American and one Chinese.

The climbers got up at 3:40 a.m.

As Emmons reheated the now frozen blocks of oatmeal, and made a pot of hot malted milk, the other two went about the long, slow business of getting dressed. Finally, a little after five o'clock, Moore and Burdsall stepped outside into the frigid early-morning air. There were no clouds, and above them in the crystal-clear atmosphere, the nighttime sky sparkled like a blanket studded with diamonds. Pulling on their crampons and adjusting the straps—no easy task with mittened hands—the two climbers then headed off.

"Moore took the lead and, with a perfunctory wave of his flashlight, was swallowed up in the frozen darkness, his only link to his companion a strand of flaxen rope paying out slowly through Burdsall's fingers," Emmons later wrote. "When fifty feet of it had slipped away, Burdsall drew his parka hood closer about his face and with a brief salute he too disappeared into the gloom." Emmons stood and watched for a while, his eyes following the conical beams of the two flashlights, growing ever smaller, as they worked their way upward. Then he crawled back into his sleeping bag and tried to rest. Nearly seven hours later, Emmons pulled on his own boots and parka, and stepped outside the Camp Four tent, hoping that he might be able to catch a glimpse of the two climbers. But he couldn't spot them, and he went back inside the tent. "I felt ill at ease," he wrote, "and a vague foreboding seized me."

Throughout the afternoon, Emmons's worries increased. Not only did the hour grow late, with sunset fast approaching, but the wind had picked up considerably and was now pounding the walls of the tent. But shortly after 6:00 p.m., he thought he heard a faint shout above the roar of the wind. Quickly unlacing the flaps of the tent, Emmons looked outside and saw Burdsall "stumbling down the slope, closely followed by Moore." Both men were sheathed in frost. They collapsed onto the floor of the tent, saying nothing.

Finally, Emmons couldn't stand the suspense any longer.

"Well," he said, "what luck?"

Moore looked up and smiled. "We made it."

Terris Moore's diary entry for October 28, 1932, was equally terse. "Away by 5 for ½ hour in total darkness," he scribbled in pencil inside a small pocket notebook. "22,500' by full sun. Bad part proved easy. Onto summit ridge. Clear day. Summit by 3 p.m. Ice hard going. Erect American and Chinese flags." It took the two men nine-and-one-half hours of slow but steady climbing to reach the top of Minya Konka. Despite the fact that they had to work their way over frost-covered rocks, broken ice, steep snow slopes, and more than one disheartening false summit, "our crampons held beautifully in the firm crust," Moore later wrote, and they were largely relieved of the tiring business of having to cut steps with their ice axes. And while the summit itself was cold and windblown, the sky was dazzlingly clear.

The World Beneath Their Feet

"The horizon surrounded us in one unbroken ring. No mountain massifs nor even clouds relieved the vast expanse of blue-black sky," Moore wrote, "and I fancied that I could see the curvature of the earth." Moore attached the American flag to his inverted ice axe and, kneeling briefly, posed for a photograph taken by Burdsall, a process they repeated with the flag of the Republic of China. They then took a series of photos of the entire horizon, and then packed up. On the way down, the wind had picked up so much that, Moore later wrote, his "parka hood beat about my ears with a noise not unlike gunfire, and the air was charged with a sand-blast of driven snow." His final entry for the day in his diary was "Return, and back to the tent by sunset."

What was missing was the magnificence of their achievement.

For not only had they climbed higher than any Americans had ever climbed before, but Dick Burdsall and Terris Moore had also climbed to the top of the second-highest mountain ever summitted, by anyone, in the world. Moreover, what the Americans had proven was that a small, lightweight expedition, with hardly any porters, could successfully tackle one of the great peaks of Asia. It would be a lesson that others would soon learn as well. The four college boys from the East Coast hadn't just announced America's entry in the Great Himalayan Race. For those who would listen, they were also changing the rules.

CHAPTER FIVE

Nanga Parbat

There was a new Germany now.

You could see it in the streets and at the railway stations, in the parks and in the schoolyards, in bars and in coffee houses. The unshaven men selling pencils and combs had all but disappeared, as had the long lines at the shelters and soup kitchens. For those who supported the new government, it was a time of rebirth and renewal, of pride in the nation, and in the coming settling of old scores. You could see it in their faces in the flickering torchlight of the rallies, and hear it in the tread of marching feet. *Deutschland über alles*—Germany above all others—was the new catchphrase, and "Heil Hitler" was the new all-purpose greeting. Here was a nation on the move.

In Munich, change came quickly. On March 9, 1933, less than six weeks after Adolf Hitler had been appointed chancellor, local Nazis seized control of the city government. Socialist members of the city council were arrested, and a huge swastika banner was unfurled from the tower atop the Neues Rathaus, Munich's landmark city hall. In the days that followed, trade union leaders were beaten up, while Michael Siegel, a prominent Jewish lawyer, was forced by the authorities to march through the streets, barefoot and with his trouser legs cut off, after he had sought the release of a client. Around his neck he was made to wear a sign that said: "I will no longer complain to the police."

Storm Troopers broke into the offices of the *Münchener Post*, a weekly newspaper that had opposed Hitler, smashing desks and chairs and throwing papers and typewriters out onto the street. In

April, Nazi authorities organized a one-day boycott of Jewish-owned shops and businesses, while on the evening of May 10, undergraduates at the University of Munich marched in a torchlit parade to the Königsplatz, where they tossed books by Albert Einstein, Sigmund Freud, Aldous Huxley, Helen Keller, and Ernest Hemingway as well as other authors considered to be "enemies of the German Reich" onto a wooden platform, ringed with logs, and doused them with kerosene. Then, as the cool spring air moved in, the students set the books ablaze.

On Easter Sunday, 1933, ministers across Bavaria praised the new Germany that was taking shape. "We can only plead with our fellow worshippers," read one such message, "to do all that they can to help these new productive forces in our land reach a complete and unimpeded victory." Some of their parishioners, meanwhile, had already taken matters in hand, and were reporting anti-Nazi statements and activities by neighbors and even family members to the police. And those who were judged to be enemies of the state soon had a new address. Eleven miles northwest of Munich's city center, a brand-new facility, called a "concentration camp," had been constructed just outside of the village of Dachau.

In Bavaria, and all across Germany, democracy wasn't dying. It was already dead.

More than a few cheered its demise. Now, a new kind of pride shone in the eyes of shopclerks and secretaries when they craned their neck to catch a glimpse of their *Führer*, and could be found in the proud bearing of old couples as they thrust out their arms in the Nazi salute. It was there, as well, in the beaming smiles of a mother and father as they dressed their child in a miniature Storm Trooper uniform, complete with armband, cap, and toy dagger. In 1932, the Nazi Party had claimed only around 100,000 members nationwide. The next year they had more than two million. So many membership applications poured into party headquarters in Munich that the clerks were forced to stack them along the walls in piles that were over six feet high.

Among them was an application from Paul Bauer.

Now making his living as an attorney and a *Notar*, a coveted government position, Bauer was living in Nabburg, a sleepy farm village located about fifty miles east of Nuremburg. But mountaineering was still at the center of his being. In 1931, he'd published *Im Kampf um den Himalaya*—"Struggle in the Himalayas"—a book-length account of his two campaigns on Kangchenjunga. Not only would there eventually be an English translation, but the book was awarded a Gold Medal for Literature in the arts competition at the 1932 Olympic Games in Los Angeles. Other books would follow, and in time Bauer would become one of the best-known mountaineers in Germany. More important, his well-publicized expeditions had also inspired other German climbers to look toward the Himalayas as well.

Bauer's plan had been to mount a third expedition to Kangchenjunga in 1934. Such an attempt would again require the cooperation of the British, who had some legitimate concerns over the impact of large-scale mountaineering expeditions on the fragile economies of nearby villages. Not only had the hiring of hundreds of local men as porters led to food shortages in the countryside along the way, but there were only so many Sherpas available who had high-altitude mountaineering experience. Accordingly, the British authorities in India tried to limit the number of Himalayan expeditions to only one or two per year. And in 1934, the German request did not go to Paul Bauer.

Instead it went to a thirty-four-year-old railway inspector named Willy Merkl. Stocky and handsome, with wavy blonde hair and blue eyes, Merkl had known many of the members of the Academic Climbing Club at the University of Munich, but he came from humbler blue-collar stock. A dazzling rock climber in his early twenties, he had gone on to tackle some of the most challenging climbs in the Alps and the Caucasus. But his focus now wasn't on Everest or Kangchenjunga or any of the other great peaks of the eastern Himalayas. Instead, it was firmly fixed on a mountain that would forever be etched into the German national consciousness.

Its name was Nanga Parbat.

The farthest west of the fourteen *Achttausenders*, Nanga Parbat was one of the most dramatic of all the Himalayan peaks. Rising up, alone, some fifteen thousand feet above the surrounding valleys, it was a truly colossal mountain, broad as well as high, with soaring ridgelines, impossibly steep cliffs, and monstrous walls of ice and snow. Runoff from its northern glaciers fed the Indus River, while its blindingly white icefalls stood out in sharp contrast to the barren hillsides and canyons below. Situated near the northernmost tip of British India, less than two hundred miles from the Afghan border, Nanga Parbat had long been a landmark in the era of the Great Game, the cloak-and-dagger struggle between Russia and Great Britain over control of Central Asia.

But India's northwestern frontier was also an increasingly troubled land. After pro-independence Indian activists were arrested during the spring of 1930, protests broke out in Peshawar, where government soldiers opened fire on the demonstrators. One Royal Tank Corps private was stoned to death, while an armored car was set on fire. "The troops behaved splendidly," claimed the *Times* back in London, "and fired only when necessary." A subsequent investigation, however, revealed that as many as one hundred and twenty-five of the protesters had either been run over, shot, or bayonetted to death by British and Gurkha troops. In the shadow of Nanga Parbat, the Britain Out Now movement already possessed an explosive undertone.

One year later, in July 1931, wholesale violence broke out in Kashmir, where tensions had long simmered between the impoverished Muslim majority and a powerful Hindu minority. After a spokesman for the Muhammadan Young Men's Association was arrested, crowds of Muslims gathered to protest—but were met with a hail of bullets, which killed nine and wounded scores of others. Enraged, the mob then dispersed to the Hindu quarter, smashing goods and attacking shopkeepers. Rioting continued for nearly a week, until the British authorities were able to regain control. And while Hindu–Muslim antagonism was at the heart of the violence, there was also plenty of anti-British resentment to go around, a sentiment that could be easily extended to other Europeans as well.

Indeed, Willy Merkl had already gotten a taste of it. In 1932, he had led the second-ever mountaineering expedition to Nanga Parbat. It had begun as an all-German affair until Merkl, short of funds, started looking for well-heeled climbers who could also provide financial support. He found them in Rand Herron, a wealthy twenty-nine-year-old American composer who had studied in Berlin, and Elizabeth Knowlton, a New Englander and Vassar graduate turned freelance journalist who had a talent for raising money. While the 1932 German–American Nanga Parbat Expedition had ended up falling well short of the summit, they did discover a promising route along the mountain's Rakhiot face. And for Merkl, the campaign had also been the bearer of some important lessons.

In 1932, Merkl had run into numerous problems with the local Balti, Astori, and Hunza men whom he had recruited and hired as porters. Twice the Kashmiri men had gone on strike, demanding higher wages and a reduction of duties. Even worse, more than one thousand silver rupees, as well as a half-dozen loads of badly needed equipment, had been stolen. In the aftermath of the expedition, Merkl vowed that the next time he came back to India and tried to climb Nanga Parbat, he would only do so if he could find a way to bring along some Sherpas from Darjeeling.

Two years later, he figured out how. Launching a fundraising campaign for a proposed second expedition, Merkl won the support of both the German State Railways and Transport Railway Workers Union, whose members nationwide had to contribute to the new attempt to climb Nanga Parbat. The German Association in Aid of Science, and the German and Austrian Alpine Club, also made significant contributions. He was so successful that, in time, Merkl created the best-funded mountaineering expedition in German history.

He also reached out to British authorities in India, and successfully arranged to hire a group of Sherpas and other high-altitude porters in Darjeeling, and then transport them more than two thousand miles to Nanga Parbat—thus solving his biggest headache from two years earlier. Merkl contacted journalists from across the country as well, and arranged to have motion-picture cameras record the early stages of the assault. The 1934 expedition was also going to be Germany's best-known mountaineering campaign, one that would capture the hearts and imaginations of citizens throughout the Reich.

Furthermore, Merkl also reached out to the new National Socialist government. Hans von Tschammer und Osten, the new director of sports for the Third Reich, immediately recognized the potential propaganda value of the expedition, and promised governmental support. But that approval also came with added pressure. "The conquest of the summit," the *Reischssportsführer* informed Merkl, "is expected for the glory of Germany." Merkl did not blink—at least in public. "We will fight for Germany and devote everything toward the conquest for Germany of the first *Achttausender*," he wrote, adding, "Heil Hitler!" But in truth, the expedition was a less than ideal representation of Nazi ideals. Most of the mountaineers had been opposed to Hitler, while Peter Misch, one of the scientists on the expedition, was Jewish. Despite all of the posturing and violence, the new laws and the ugly rhetoric, Germany did not become the Third Reich overnight.

On Palm Sunday, March 25, 1934, the advance party of Nanga Parbat climbers made their way through the boisterous crowd of well-wishers, family members, and newspapermen who had gathered in the Hauptbahnhof, Munich's central train station, to see them off. Young girls showered the mountaineers with flowers, while the dark interior of the railway terminal was crammed with giddy onlookers. "The train glided out of the station," remembered one who was present, "amid a roar of cheering and the waving of handkerchiefs."

*   *   *

Orchestrating an assault on Nanga Parbat was not a simple assignment.

From Venice, on board the *Victoria*, there first came the long sea voyage across the eastern Mediterranean, through the Suez Canal, and, finally, across the green waters of the Arabian Sea to India. In Bombay, there were forms and customs officers, Indian soldiers with waxed moustaches and Enfield Mk III rifles, baggage handlers and ragged groups of beggars and petty thieves, all amid the blazing heat of a pre-monsoon Indian spring. Willy Merkl took off for New Delhi to collect maps and to grease as many governmental wheels as possible—and to deliver a lecture about the expedition, in English, to the members of the United Service Club. Peter Aschenbrenner and Erwin Schneider, two Austrian climbers, took over guiding the first loads of baggage, by rail, more than two thousand miles to Kashmir, while Uli Wieland headed to Darjeeling to hire Sherpas and other high-altitude porters. Back in Munich, meanwhile, the second group of climbers departed for India on April 11. Two weeks later, the entire expedition gathered together for the first time in Srinagar, in the valley of Kashmir.

More storybook town than provincial capital, Srinagar was a city of lakes and poplars, thatched roofs and ancient gardens. Here the call for morning prayers echoed through intricate carved wooden screens, while turbaned men poled houseboats and lumber barges along the Jhelum River. Markets were filled with turnips and onions, eggplant and potatoes, wild apples and almonds, and jute bags filled with red and white Kashmiri rice. In the evening, as the night air rolled down off the Himalayas, sidewalk merchants fired up charcoal braziers, hawking bits of fish and bread and steaming cups of salted pink tea. Set in a rich valley ringed by forests of white birch and fir, Srinagar was at the end of the railway and nearly the end of the road, a final outpost of Indian civilization before the high walls of the greater Himalayas.

The expedition personnel were genuinely impressive. Merkl had organized a crack team of eight climbers, including Willo Welzenbach, a legendary Munich mountaineer, as well as a physician and a camp commandant. Three scientists—a cartographer, a geographer, and a geologist—also came along, as did two British transport officers. Ulie Wieland, meanwhile, had done a magnificent job in Darjeeling and had brought along a dozen Sherpas, each of whom was already a veteran of previous Himalayan expeditions. Kitar and Gaylay had been on Everest with Mallory, Nima Tashi had accompanied Bauer on Kangchenjunga, while Angtsering and several others had been on the 1933 Mount Everest Expedition.

Added to these were three hundred and fourteen local Kashmiri men who would serve as porters, carrying the expedition's supplies from Srinagar to Nanga Parbat. Farmers and day laborers, fishermen and woodcutters, wearing knit woolen caps and rope-soled sandals and carrying heavy walking sticks, they were a rugged lot— one whose brown and green and blue eyes told tales of armies and occupiers that spanned centuries.

By early May, the expedition was on the move. The long line of porters, Sherpas, and climbers, more than a quarter of a mile long, snaked its way past Bandipura, a way station along the old Silk Road, and then through forests of silver willow, Himalayan cedar, and blue pine. Once past Burzil Pass, still clogged with snow, the trees disappeared. Great brown hills rose up on either side of the gently winding trail to Astor, a sun-drenched village that was the last mail stop on the way to Nanga Parbat. For the eight climbers, however, the march in was merely prologue. For as they grew nearer and nearer to the awesomely stark and hypnotizing face of Nanga Parbat, their hoped-for destination was not just a mountain, but a lifetime of honor and glory, one that could be found in the narrow margin between earth and sky.

Come early June, the assault on Nanga Parbat was in full swing.

The tough Kashmiri porters had done their job splendidly, sleeping outside and hauling up crate after crate of supplies to more than 13,000 feet before being paid and sent home. Base Camp was a hive of activity, while Camps One, Two, and a temporary Camp Three had already been established. Willy Merkl, meanwhile, had worked out a careful yet audacious plan of attack.

Using Camp Four as an advanced Base Camp, two well-equipped teams would set out toward the summit, sometimes sharing the same camps, other times leapfrogging each other. But rather than burn up valuable time stocking and restocking the four camps that would likely have to be erected between Camp Four and the top of Nanga Parbat, the focus would be on quickly getting the two teams in position to make a run for the summit, and then getting them down as fast as possible. Merkl, being a railroad man, had drawn up precise timetables, and the necessary supplies had all been gathered together ahead of time. "Everything was provided for," Fritz Bechtold wrote, "and laid down as a result of careful calculation." It was time for the swastika to fly on top of Nanga Parbat. On June 22, the first assault party, consisting of six climbers and fourteen Sherpas, left Base Camp, singing and yodeling to each other as they moved up the mountain.

Once past Camp Four, their route would first take them up the face of Rakhiot Peak, a hard slog during which they would carve out Camp Five, digging their tents into the snow. The last part of the face was both the steepest and the most difficult, requiring considerable step-cutting and the placing of fixed-ropes. The summit teams would then take a sharp right turn and traverse along the edge of Rakhiot Ridge, whose sides were draped with immense hanging glaciers, some the size of city blocks. The climbers and Sherpas would build two more camps, Six and Seven, as they moved laterally along the long ridge, gaining altitude. Then it was sharply up again, toward the *Silbersattel*—"silver saddle"—a bow-shaped expanse of snow that led to the final approach to the summit. After that, only one more camp, Camp Eight, should be needed before they reached the summit.

By focusing on speed, mobility, and, above all, getting German climbers on the upper mountain as quickly as possible, Merkl hoped to overcome the final, high-altitude sluggishness that had doomed previous Himalayan expeditions. His climbers would get in, reach the summit, and quickly get out—rather than laboriously stock each camp with food, fuel, and supplies along the way. That meant that once they were past Camp Four, the summit teams would be on their own. No other climbers or Sherpas would be left behind to wait in any of the higher camps that they set up on their way to the summit, and it might be some time before the rest of the expedition, down at Base Camp, would learn of their progress.

The first report on the summit assault came toward midday on July 8.

"Hauptlager spricht! Wir können dich hören, aber bitte sprich lauter."

For nearly an hour, while the snow swirled about him, climber Fritz Bechtold had stood on a slight rise above Camp Four. Turning the dials on a wireless radio transceiver, and shouting into the built-in microphone, he was hoping to reach Base Camp. Finally, a response came crackling through the lightweight headset. "Base Camp speaking! We hear you but can you speak a little louder." Despite the fact that he was already shouting and that the weather at Camp Four was getting worse by the minute, Bechtold kept at it and relayed some incredible news.

Earlier that morning, through a break in the clouds, Bechtold and the others at Camp Four had briefly spotted a group of five climbers on the *Silbersattel*. But what was most important—and what Bechtold was trying to communicate to Base Camp—was that the climbers were coming *down* the mountain. "Our crystal was defective, and I roared into the microphone at the top of my voice," he later recalled. "After innumerable misunderstandings, I was able to report to him the main point, that probably the summit had fallen yesterday, while the advance party was now already on the way down." If true, these were magnificent tidings.

The message received, Bechtold grabbed the transceiver and made his way back to Camp Four, "stiff as a block of ice." But while the wind and snow beat against the sides of his tent, his heart was aglow. *I bet we did it*, he thought to himself. *I bet we did.*

Scott Ellsworth

*   *   *

Two days earlier. Wednesday, July 6, 1934.

As dawn broke along Rakhiot Ridge, sixteen men huddled inside the cluster of tents at Camp Seven. The five climbers and eleven Sherpas were all deeply fatigued. Over the previous two weeks, they had climbed nearly two miles into the sky, threading their way past yawning crevasses and monstrous seracs, heading ever upward while hauling as much as forty pounds of gear per man on their backs. Caked with dried sweat, their skin was tight and dry, and their hands and faces, save where they wore their snow goggles, were colored a deep reddish brown. Yet despite their growing exhaustion, sleep of any value had been hard to come by at 23,000 feet, and while they did not know it, their bodies were already beginning to deteriorate in the rarified atmosphere. But their spirits were still strong. No German, and few others of any nationality, had ever been this high before.

After a quick breakfast, two of the climbers, Erwin Schneider and Peter Aschenbrenner, set out alone, across the huge slabs of snow that topped the winding, rocky, and dazzling ridge that led to the *Silbersattel*. The morning was bright and sunny, while an ocean of clouds lingered below them. The two Austrians climbed with authority, their lungs and limbs moving together in tandem. On the way up the *Silbersattel* they cut steps for the Sherpas, their ice axes quickly piercing the outer layers of sun-hardened snow. After a short break along the crest of the saddle, the two climbers pushed on, pulled along by the welcome sight of the summit looming ahead of them. By then, the others had left Camp Seven as well.

Schneider and Aschenbrenner kept plowing ahead, past a wide spot on the final ridge, and onto the approach to the lower summit. Each of them carried a pair of short skis equipped with skins, which they could use on the less severe terrain. At about 25,000 feet, the two climbers stopped for a break—and to assess the situation. They were now only about 1,300 feet from the summit, not much more than the length of three soccer fields. And while every step had been getting harder, both Aschenbrenner and Schneider still had energy. There was no question that if they pushed on, they could easily reach the summit. Victory was at hand.

But as each of them sat and smoked one of the cigarettes that they had bummed off the Sherpas that morning, other concerns weighed in as well. Merkl, it was clear, wanted to get as many climbers up on the summit for the first time as possible. And as the only Austrians on what was, after all, a *German* expedition, it might not sit well for them to go on alone. Plus, looking down from their spot along the lower summit, they could now see that the Sherpas were busy setting up Camp Eight on the plateau below them. Tomorrow, they decided, would come soon enough. Schneider and Aschenbrenner got up and took one last look around them. Then they started walking down to join the others at the new camp.

At first, the wind was light, bellying out the sides of the tents, and swirling in little snow devils along the top of the saddle. But as night fell, gale-force winds ripped across the upper reaches of Nanga Parbat. At Camp Eight, the sides of the tents now snapped back and forth, straining the guy lines, while the windblown snow stung like sand on the face of anyone who stuck his head outside. Eventually the roar of the wind grew so loud that it was nearly impossible to talk inside the tents. All any of the climbers or Sherpas could do was try and sleep. Few succeeded. Luckily, storms on Nanga Parbat weren't thought to last long. But until this one abated, they were trapped.

The next morning, Thursday, July 7, was even worse.

"A tremendous snowstorm burst over the tents," one climber wrote, "The blizzard was so violent that it was almost impossible to breathe in the open." By then, enough wind was making its way through the seams and the secured opening of the tents that it became impossible to light any of the stoves, meaning that there was neither food nor water. And while Erwin Schneider and Peter Aschenbrenner, who were clearly in the best shape of all the mountaineers, gamely packed two rucksacks—containing cameras, a little food, and the new German flag with its bold black swastika—for what they hoped would be a summit attempt the next morning, that, of course, would all depend on the weather.

In the meantime, while the gale raged around them, there was little to do but wait. That, and to try and not think about the reality that not only were they stormbound at more than 23,000 feet, but also that none of the camps between them and Camp Four were stocked with either food or supplies. The five climbers and eleven Sherpas weren't just on their own. They were on their own in the middle of a monstrous storm so vast, with so much snow in the air, that it was pitch black outside even at noon.

By Friday morning, July 8, conditions inside the Camp Eight tents had grown unbearable. What food the climbers and Sherpas had was frozen, and they still could not melt snow for water. It was time to abandon the assault on the summit, and move down the mountain toward safety. Schneider and Aschenbrenner left first, taking three Sherpas—Pinzo Norbu, Nima Dorje, and Pasang—with them. With the windblown snow whipping their faces and clouding the lenses of their glacier goggles, the five men worked their way over the *Silbersattel* and down the treacherous drop to Rakhiot Ridge.

But the storm was already taking a toll. "An india-rubber mattress was torn off the back of a porter," Schneider wrote, "this was immediately followed by a heavy sleeping bag. The storm blew these horizontally into space—they vanished round a corner." And while Rakhiot Ridge offered some long stretches of relatively even terrain, there was no question now that their lives were in the balance. Dehydrated and constantly battered by the storm, the men found that visibility had grown so poor that even at only ten or fifteen feet away, another person became "but a greyish shadow."

Somewhere near Camp Seven, Schneider and Aschenbrenner unroped themselves. Then they strapped on their skis, and took off—leaving Pasang, Nima Dorje, and Pinzo Norbu behind. "We impressed on them that they should follow immediately in our track, to which they agreed absolutely," Aschenbrenner later claimed. But in conditions where even the deepest bootprints were soon obliterated by the raging snowstorm, the idea that the three Sherpas could follow any sort of trail was ridiculous. They would now have to fend for themselves.

Later that day, the two Austrian climbers arrived at Camp Four. Caked from head to toe with ice and snow, they were fatigued but physically sound. Warm tea and hot food followed, and both men were soon asleep, wrapped in sleeping bags. They had made it off the upper mountain all in one piece. But up on Rakhiot Ridge, the three Sherpas whom they had deserted were now fighting for their lives.

The others had left Camp Eight on the morning of July 8 as well.

This second group consisted of expedition leader Willy Merkl, climbers Uli Wieland and Willo Welzenbach, and eight Sherpas—Nima Tashi, Angtsering, Dakshi, Gaylay, Nima Norbu, Kikuli, Kitar, and Da Thundu. Determined to get down the mountain as quickly as possible, they did not pack any tents. Nor did they get very far. Pummeled by the storm, and physically and mentally weakened by altitude, Willy Merkl's resolve withered in the face of the blizzard and its terrible winds. Just below the *Silbersattel*, the expedition leader ordered a bivouac—that is, that they would all shelter themselves as best as they could, huddled together in the snow, and ride out the storm that day and night, hoping for better weather tomorrow. But without any tents, and with just three sleeping bags between eight people, the mountain took its portion. Twenty-year-old Nima Norbu, who had served as an assistant cook on the 1933 Mount Everest Expedition, died that night.

*   *   *

Saturday, July 9.

The storm had not lifted. Great plumes of snow were now being blown off the *Silbersattel*, while the wind tore at the backs of climber and Sherpa alike. There was no question that they could bivouac any longer. Merkl's right hand was frostbitten, as were both of Wieland's hands. They had to move down the mountain at once. But as they started to leave, three of the Sherpas—Angtsering, Gaylay, and Dakshi, all Everest veterans—decided to stay. "I was snow blind and the other two weak," Angtsering said. There was no choice but for the others to leave them. Gathering themselves together, the three Germans and the four other Sherpas started to move down the saddle toward Rakhiot Ridge, plunging through the powdery snow that sometimes reached above their waists. There were no songs now, no singing, no yodeling.

Uli Wieland began to lag behind.

Then he sat down in the snow. He died soon thereafter.

The four Sherpas made it first to the small, single tent that now comprised Camp Seven. "After we waited more than an hour," Kitar recalled, "Merkl and Welzenbach arrived. They told us we had better descend to Camp Six, owing to lack of sleeping room." Having no other choice, and desperately wanting to find shelter, the quartet of Sherpas left and began the long traverse toward the other end of Rakhiot Ridge. But high on the exposed ridge, with the wind screaming over the edge, forward progress ground to a halt. "During the descent of the ridge we sank in up to our chests in the snow," Kitar recalled. "The blizzard was so frightful that we could not reach Camp Six, and spent the night in a snow cave."

By nightfall on July 10, the unaccounted-for survivors of the summit attempt were divided into four different groups scattered across the upper reaches of Nanga Parbat. Angtsering, Gaylay, and Dakshi were still huddled together in a crude snow cave on the *Silbersattel*. Willy

The World Beneath Their Feet

Merkl and Willo Welzenbach were curled up inside the two-man tent at Camp Seven. Kitar, Nima Tashi, Kikuli, and Da Thundu were high up on Rakhiot Ridge in the pitch dark, with the wind shrieking just over their heads. And somewhere between the ridge and Rakhiot Peak, were the three Sherpas that Schneider and Aschenbrenner had abandoned.

None of them had any food or water.

Farther down the mountain at Camp Four, meanwhile, the mood had turned from joyful speculation over a successful summit attempt to a deepening dread over the fate of the climbers on the upper mountain. The storm had pounded the lower camps as well, burying tents and crates of food and supplies beneath several feet of snow. And despite their best efforts, every attempt to send a rescue team up to Camp Five had ended in failure. But near noon on Sunday, July 10, a wave of hope washed over the climbers who were still snowed in at Camp Four. Looking up through another break in the clouds, they saw something that immediately raised their spirits.

"At midday we caught sight of seven or eight men descending the ice-wall of Rakhiot Peak," Fritz Bechtold wrote. "The glasses, quick! No, they were not ghosts, they were really coming! I felt a gradual lifting of the load within me. Tea and food were at once got ready, tents and camp set in order, while Bernard brought out his medicine chest. Then we went out to meet them."

But as the two groups drew closer, the seven or eight men became only four. Bechtold immediately guessed that it was Merkl, Welzenbach, and Wieland, accompanied by one of the Sherpas—"Our three companions, we fancied, with one porter." Instead, the group turned out to be four Sherpas. They were all that were left of the three Sherpas that Schneider and Aschenbrenner had deserted and the four whom Merkl had sent on to Camp Six. Nima Dorje and Nima Tashi had perished along the fixed ropes on Rakhiot Peak, while Pinzo Norbu died ten feet away from the Camp Five tents.

The four survivors, Pasang, Kitar, Da Thundu, and Kikuli, were all at death's door themselves. "The wretched men were absolutely played out, at their last gasp," Bechtold recalled. "All four had their hands more or less severely frostbitten; Pasang had lost his snow-glasses and was snow blind." Brought inside the tents, the four exhausted Sherpas were given soup, while the other Sherpas and climbers at Camp Four worked furiously to restore circulation to their frostbitten hands and feet. "One man sat at each hand and each foot, and rubbed incessantly," Bechtold wrote. "When one's hands grew moist, a relief was exchanged. There was a battle over each single toe, over each finger."

The four survived.

Monday, July 11. Along the Silbersattel.

After spending three days and nights on bivouac, Angtsering could at last see again. The snow blindness had passed and he felt that he could move. So, too, could Gaylay. None of the three Sherpas had eaten any food for more than seventy-two hours, though Angtsering had chewed on and swallowed bits of ice. It had probably kept him alive. But if he was to keep on living, it was time to move. Only Dakshi wasn't going anywhere. Too weak to even sit up, he would die where he lay, probably that day.

Mercifully, the storm had finally broken. Through the deep, waist-high snow, Angtsering and Gaylay made their way down to Camp Seven. Inside the small tent, they found Merkl and Welzenbach. The two German climbers had no food or sleeping bags, just blankets and some rubber groundsheets. "Stay with us until food and help arrive," Merkl told them. They did. But no help came the next day, Tuesday, July 12, either. Angtsering wanted them all to move down the mountain, but Merkl again insisted that they wait until the others came up with food, fuel, and medicine.

Welzenbach died that night.

The next morning, Angtsering and Gaylay finally got Merkl to agree to move.

"We must go down now," Angtsering insisted. "No help will come."

Shouldering Merkl's rucksack, the rubber groundsheet, and his and Gaylay's sleeping bags, the mighty Angtsering led the way across Rakhiot Ridge. The two others followed behind, with Merkl supporting himself with an ice axe in each hand. But three quarters of the way along the ridge to Camp Six, the expedition leader could go no further. The two Sherpas then dug out an ice cave in which to spend the night. Merkl and Gaylay each slept in one of the sleeping bags, while Angtsering had only a groundsheet. The three men were spending what was at least their eighth night above 22,000 feet. They had not eaten anything for five days.

They survived the night.

Thursday morning, July 14.

The clouds had cleared enough that Angtsering could now look down the mountain. He could see three Germans and four Sherpas moving between two of the lower camps. But he could see no one coming up from Camp Four. Once again, they would have to move. If they didn't get down to where there was food and water and shelter, they would all die. But that was beyond what Willy Merkl could do. His feet and hands were now terribly frostbitten, as was his face. Gaylay was now too weak to move as well.

So Angtsering went.

All alone, he worked his way past the abandoned Camp Six and back up the side of Rakhiot Peak. Though his hands and feet were frostbitten as well, the thirty-year-old Sherpa navigated his way down the fixed ropes along the ice wall, where a single slip would cost him his life. This was where Nima Tashi and Pinzo Norbu had met their deaths four days earlier. When Angtsering reached Camp Five in the late afternoon, he yelled down for help, but his words were carried away by the wind. "It was a long time before anyone heard me," Angtsering later recalled. "At last Pasang Norji and Nurbu Sonam came out with tea laced with brandy, and assisted me in to Camp Four." Sick, exhausted, and in great pain, Angtsering would survive.

Gaylay and Willy Merkl did not.

The 1934 Nanga Parbat Expedition had taken ten lives.

It was the worst disaster in the history of mountaineering.

Four German climbers had died, among them some of the best mountaineers of their generation. The same could be said for the six Sherpas who perished, most of whom had already been on Everest and Kangchenjunga. That Pasang, Kitar, Kikuli, and Da Thundu had survived, after being stranded along Rakhiot Ridge during a blizzard, was miraculous. But even that could not compare to what Angtsering endured. At elevations above 22,000 feet, he had slept outside, during a raging storm, for six nights. He had also gone a week without food or water. His survival was one for the ages.

When news of the disaster reached the outside world, it hit the hardest in Munich, in Darjeeling, and especially in the villages of the Khumbu, in eastern Nepal, where many of the Sherpas were from. Brokenhearted wives and mothers buried their faces in their hands, and grown men wept openly. This was a disaster that would not soon be forgotten. But the deaths on Nanga Parbat touched climbers everywhere. This was especially true in rival England, where Willy Merkl was hailed as a fallen hero. "Willy Merkl, as leader of the Nanga Parbat 1934 attempt, displayed all the desperate gallantry we expected from him," ran one remembrance published by the Alpine Club.

But in Germany, there was an added twist in the post-disaster conversation.

For rather than discouraging another attempt on Nanga Parbat, the deaths on the mountain only guaranteed that another expedition would take place. Kangchenjunga and the other great peaks of the Himalayas were now of little interest. The Munich mountaineers, and Germany itself, had already lost too much on Nanga Parbat. Now, they *had* to climb it. Only next time it would be different. For while the nation mourned its losses in the Karakoram, Paul Bauer was already making plans.

CHAPTER SIX

Shangri-La

In a garden on the edge of London, a typewriter clicked and clacked. Whenever the young man who was doing the typing reached the end of a line of prose, a little bell went off. Automatically, as in a trance, he then pulled on the bright silver carriage return lever after which, with a near-silent but satisfying set of clunks, the black rubber platen advanced the sheet of paper in the machine to the next line, and the typing continued. Next to the machine, a cigarette burned lazily in an ashtray, while on one of the dining-room-table chairs set onto the grass in the yard behind a modest house, the pile of blank pages began to diminish as the number of typed pages grew. It was a routine with which the young man, whose name was James Hilton, was quite familiar.

The son of a schoolmaster and a schoolmaster's wife, Hilton had been "brought up in the English school world of the ablative absolute and toasted crumpets for tea, of Greek verses and cricket." Gregarious and athletic, with a thousand-watt smile, he loved to ride his bicycle in Epping Forest, especially after he became smitten with a young woman he'd met there one day. But Hilton also had a deep love for books and, blessed with keen eye for detail, he took to writing at an early age. He published his first newspaper article—in the *Manchester Guardian*, no less—at age seventeen. Three years later, while still an undergraduate at Christ's College, Cambridge, he published his first novel, a sentimental tale about a young piano student and her teacher. James Hilton was on his way.

The World Beneath Their Feet

Sort of.

Because writing two articles a week for an Irish newspaper, as well as penning occasional book reviews for the *Daily Telegraph*, barely provided a living wage. "I read twenty novels a week," he said, "reviewing eight out of the lot, wrote two special articles, and put in a few hours at night on a novel." Too young to have been a member of the Lost Generation—the closest that Hilton got to the war was watching a Zeppelin raid over London when he was in his teens—like many a writer before and since he had to find his own material and his own audience. And try he did. Over the next thirteen years, Hilton cranked out no fewer than eleven books, including thrillers and romance novels, spy stories and a murder mystery. And while he did garner dribs and drabs of critical praise—"Mr. Hilton must be commended for venturing an unusual if not totally new form within the genus of the novel," sniffed one review in the *Times*—his books weren't exactly flying off the shelves.

By the spring of 1933, when he was banging away at the typewriter he had set up in the backyard of his parents' home in Wofford Green, Hilton was trying something new. Three years earlier, he had read Joseph Rock's remarkable articles in *National Geographic* about the remote borderlands of western China, and of the unexplored mountains that were there. Rock's vivid descriptions had stuck with him, and in time Hilton begun to mix in bits and pieces drawn from the headlines of the day—the rioting in Peshawar, the development of new high-altitude aircraft, glimpses into mysterious Tibet, news blurbs about the Himalayas—and craft them into a novel. He would also add a dash of climbing as well. Hilton himself, it was said, was "a keen mountaineer." The book would be unlike anything that Hilton had ever written before. He titled it *Lost Horizon*.

At the heart of the story was a British consular official named Conway. As an undergraduate, with eyes that were colored "much more of a Cambridge blue than an Oxford," Conway had dazzled his fellow students and professors as a scholar and a debater, a pianist and an oarsman. "Our civilization doesn't often breed people like that nowadays," one classmate recalled. But Conway came home from the war a changed man, "clever, but rather slack." Joining His Majesty's Consular Service, he drifted from post to post, traveling the world but going nowhere—until he and two other British citizens and one American were kidnapped, at gunpoint, on an airplane flight that first took them past Nanga Parbat and the Karakoram, and then to an uninhabited land that was "far past the Frontier country." Running low on fuel and caught in a storm, the plane crash-landed in the Himalayas—"probably some part of Tibet"—fatally injuring the Chinese pilot. But before the pilot died, Conway told his fellow passengers, he'd whispered "something about a lamasery near here, along the valley, I gathered, where we could get food and shelter. Shangri-La, he called it."

Accessible only across a high, snow-covered ridge, for which the foursome has to rope up in order to cross, Shangri-La turns out to be a kind of paradise, one that appeared on no maps. At its heart is a mysterious monastery that is both ancient and up-to-date, and where time no longer operates by the normal rules. Equally remarkable is the setting itself—an Edenlike valley, lush and green, that is protected by virtually inaccessible mountain passes and is lorded over by a majestic, snow-shrouded, pyramid-shaped mountain, one said to be more than 28,000 feet high. By the book's closing chapter, Conway has left Shangri-La, only to want desperately to return. The novel ends with the narrator tracking down a final clue about whether Shangri-La really exists or not, a discovery that he makes while visiting Shanghai just as the Japanese attack the city in 1932.

Hilton finished writing the novel in April 1933. Five months later, *Lost Horizon* was published. And while the initial reviews were encouraging, sales remained sluggish until Christmas, when Hilton also published an "overly long" short story about an aged schoolmaster in a London magazine. Titled "Goodbye, Mr. Chips," and later made into both a best-selling book and hugely successful movie, it was the spark that finally lit James Hilton's literary career for good. Not only was *Goodbye, Mr. Chips* an instant best seller when it was issued in book form, but sales of *Lost Horizon* also exploded. Moreover, during the summer of 1934, James Hilton's novel of Shangri-La won the Hawthornden Prize, a British book award for "imaginative literature." But that was not the end of the story. For by then, *Lost Horizon* had taken on an eerily predictive quality all its own. Strange as it would seem, life had already begun to imitate art.

Eric Shipton was done.

He was done with committees.

He was through with gramophones and boxes of nerve tonic, and he was finished with photographers and journalists from the *Times*, the *Daily Telegraph*, and the *Daily Mail* clogging the gates at Victoria Station, shouting questions over the din of the crowd, and asking him to smile for the camera. Now twenty-six years old, Shipton had been the youngest climber on the 1933 Mount Everest Expedition. But since then he had had a change of heart and a change of mind on how mountaineering should be accomplished. He was frustrated with expeditions that required caravans consisting of hundreds of pack animals and scores of men. And he was finished with "the small town of tents that sprung up each evening, the noise and racket of each fresh start, the sight of a huge army invading the peaceful valleys." It was time to say goodbye to all that. There had to be a better way to run a Himalayan mountaineering campaign.

"I had become convinced that a small party, lightly equipped and shorn of supernumeraries and superfluous baggage, would not only be just as effective but would have several positive advantages," Shipton wrote. "Among these would be increased mobility and a greater sense of cohesion and purpose." From his mother's flat in London, he was already planning a Himalayan expedition all his own, one with a new and decidedly different set of operating principles. For rather than go big, Shipton intended to go small—something that ran directly counter to the accepted wisdom of the day, at least in Alpine Club circles.

Nor would he wait to try out his new ideas. "I had always rather deplored the notion that one must sacrifice the active years of one's life to the dignity of old age," he added. No, the trick, he decided, would be to begin by launching an expedition of his own, one whose ultimate goal would be attractive enough to draw outside financial support. Shipton then concluded that the Garhwal Himalaya, which straddled the India–Tibet border west of Nepal, offered the best possibilities, especially in the unexplored mountains off the left shoulder of Kamet.

But Tom Longstaff had other ideas.

A legendary British climber, now a fifty-eight-year-old physician with a winsome smile and a salt-and-pepper Van Dyke, Longstaff had been the first person to climb to the summit of a seven-thousand-meter peak. He'd also mountaineered in the Alps, the Caucasus, the Rockies, and in Greenland, and had served as the medical officer on the 1922 Everest expedition. More importantly, Longstaff's first Himalayan climbs had predated the days of the massive expeditions, and when he first caught wind of Shipton's plans for a small-scale approach in the Garhwal, he was eager to chat. But when the two mountaineers met, Longstaff steered Shipton not toward just any peak, but one that had vexed British climbers for half a century.

Rising up to more than 25,000 feet, Nanda Devi was one of Hinduism's most sacred mountains. Its name roughly translatable as "Blessed Goddess" or "Goddess of Bliss," it was said to have been the former home of the Seven Rishis, the sages who, before they became stars, were responsible for making the sun rise. Every year, thousands of devout pilgrims came from across northern India to pay homage to Nanda Devi, whose waters were one of the sources of the holy river Ganges. Buddhists revered the great mountain as well.

But Nanda Devi was also a geological marvel. The mountain itself, which looked like a broken tooth, was almost impossibly steep, something that was rare for a peak that was only six hundred feet shy of being an *Achttausender*. Even more remarkable, Nanda Devi was itself surrounded by a continuous ring of mountains, none lower than 17,000 feet, which were themselves equally formidable. Imagine, if you will, a sharp cone set inside a high-walled bowl, and you can get a sense of the unique topography of Nanda Devi. The only break in the circular wall protecting Nanda Devi was a deep gorge, known as the Rishi Nala, whose rock walls shot straight up for thousands of feet, and through which flowed the raging headwaters of the Rishi Ganga.

And there was something else as well.

Because lying between the base of Nanda Devi and the protective ring of mountains that surrounded it, was another wonder. Later known as the Sanctuary, it was a pristine, two hundred and fifty-square-mile amphitheater, a circular valley of grass and flowers, birds and mammals, that was completely cut off from the rest of the world. And while Tom Longstaff, hanging on to a 19,000-foot ridge, had gotten a brief glimpse of it in 1905, no human being had ever set foot inside the Nanda Devi Sanctuary. Others had tried, before and since, but no expedition had managed to pierce Nanda Devi's protective ring.

Longstaff, however, was convinced that it could be done. Meeting with Shipton at his home, he told the young climber that, as daunting as it seemed, the key to Nanda Devi was the Rishi Nala. Twenty-eight years earlier, Longstaff had led a party that had penetrated partway up the gorge. And while they had been defeated, he was convinced that another party could find success. Moreover, Longstaff's early Himalayan expeditions had been spartan affairs, carried off with only the barest handful of climbers and porters. Shipton found in the older man a kindred spirit, one who didn't have too hard of a time convincing his young protégé to alter his plans. Shipton was sold. He would be heading to Nanda Devi.

To do so, however, he would need at least one climbing partner—and here he ran into difficulties. For as fervently as Shipton believed in his new, less-is-more approach to Himalayan mountaineering, he was practically alone in his thinking. Most of his fellow climbers thought that without the requisite battalions of porters and pack animals, Shipton's effort would be doomed from the start. In truth, Shipton had planned on hiring a small number of Sherpas, two or three at most, to take part in the expedition. But when he couldn't find another British climber who was willing, able, and experienced enough to go, it looked as if his Nanda Devi plans might have to be scrapped. That, or he'd simply have to try it with only the Sherpas.

Providence, however, arrived via the Royal Mail. In January 1934, Shipton received a letter from an old climbing partner, one who had just returned to England after spending several years overseas. The former associate, whose name was Bill Tilman, had written to see if Shipton might be interested in doing some climbs in the Lake District. Shipton wrote back, proposing that Tilman come with him to the Himalayas instead.

Bill Tilman wasn't everyone's cup of tea.

A highly decorated World War veteran with bushy eyebrows, a steely gaze, and boot-brown hair, he was abrupt, taciturn, excessively formal, and did not by any means suffer fools gladly. Shipton had met him first in Kenya, where both of them had tried to launch careers as coffee farmers. Tilman had written Shipton for advice on how he might climb Mount Kilimanjaro—a letter that was to launch what turned out to be a two-year climbing partnership in East Africa. Even though Tilman was nearly a decade older than Shipton, and knew virtually nothing about mountaineering, he was an excellent student who quickly turned into a first-class climber. He was also tough as nails. Together, the two men put up some remarkable routes on Mount Kenya, the second-highest mountain in Africa, and climbed in the Ruwenzoris, the mysterious Mountains of the Moon. While in many ways they were as different as night and day, when they climbed together, Shipton and Tilman were a hard pair to beat.

Tilman was also game for adventures, and he had the gumption to carry them off. When he had finally given up on making a go of it as a coffee planter in East Africa, Tilman hadn't simply packed his bags and booked a one-way ticket on a steamship out of Mogadishu.

Instead, he purchased a black Raleigh bicycle—equipped with mud-guards and a bell—at a shop in Kampala, Uganda, and, armed with a crude map of Africa that he had torn out of a magazine, set off for the Atlantic coast. Living off a diet consisting largely of bananas—"A big, coarse variety which, when roasted in the ashes, was very excellent and satisfying," he wrote; "Two of these were enough to give one the sensation of having dined"—and sleeping outside, at night, beneath a mosquito net, Tilman rode, alone, for nearly three thousand miles across Uganda, the Belgian Congo, French Equatorial Africa, and the Cameroons. Carrying only a rucksack, and battling flat tires, lost pumps, blood-sucking flies, officious border guards and petty government functionaries, endless miscommunications, and throngs of villagers who would sometimes run alongside him for miles, he made the journey in an astonishing fifty-six days.

At Duala, a port town along the Wouri River, Tilman bought a coat and a pair of trousers, and then boarded a ship bound for England. "We dropped down the river whose muddy waters were soon to be lost in the clean, blue immensity of the sea, while the Cameroon mountains, showing faintly astern, waved to me Africa's last farewell." He was going home. But not for long.

The biggest problem with the Nanda Devi expedition was money.

Neither Shipton nor Tilman had much.

Still living in his mother's flat in a row of identical yet genteel town-houses in Lexham Gardens, London, Eric Shipton had still managed to avoid having been saddled with anything remotely resembling a career. While he had come home from Everest with big dreams and plans, none of them included getting a job and drawing a steady paycheck. Instead, to raise funds for the Nanda Devi adventure, Shipton had taken to the lecture circuit, delivering talks about his experiences on Everest. "I had managed to raise a little money by the distasteful business of lecturing," he wrote, but not enough to fund even the barest bones of an expedition. "Try as I would, I could not bring my estimates to below £150 each, if we were to allow ourselves the rather important luxury of three Sherpa porters, and spend the whole season in the field."

The largest single expense was for round-trip steamship passage from Great Britain to India, about fifty pounds per person. Tilman suggested that in order to cut costs, the two of them should, instead, ride bicycles all the way to India, a journey of about four thousand miles. But Shipton nixed the idea. As it turned out, however, while Shipton was making a quick lecture tour of Norway, Tilman found—and booked—round-trip passages, for £30 each, on a cargo steamer bound for India. And so, on April 6, 1934, beneath an iron-gray Liverpool sky, Eric Shipton and Bill Tilman boarded the *Mahsud*, a sturdy, Glasgow-built cargo ship, and began their seemingly preposterous shoestring expedition.

They reached Calcutta one month later, on Saturday, May 5.

The city was blisteringly hot and tense. While Gandhi had temporarily suspended his nonviolent civil disobedience campaign four weeks earlier, other independence advocates were fully prepared to take up armed struggle against the British. There had already been one assassination attempt against the governor-general of Bengal, who had been shot at by a female student in Convocation Hall at the University of Calcutta. Within a week there would come another attempt on his life.

But for Eric Shipton and Bill Tilman, the steamy provincial capital was merely a waystation. Early on Monday morning, they went to the Sealdah Railway Station to meet the train carrying the three Sherpas they had hired, sight unseen, from Darjeeling. But the Sherpas were nowhere to be found. Growing ever more depressed and desperate in the busy terminal, Shipton was ready to go to the police when he decided to first call their hotel to see if there might be a telegram.

"There is no telegram," the desk clerk said. "But can you throw any light on three very rum looking birds who drove up here in a taxi an hour ago?"

The three Sherpas were indeed quite the sight. "'Exotic' was a mild adjective," Shipton later wrote. "Clad in shirts and shorts, and crowned with billycock hats from under which glossy pigtails descended, the three were distinctive enough, but when one took into consideration that their shirts were a blinding purple in colour and that this crude shade was matched in their lips and teeth (the result of much betel-chewing), one understood how even the most myopic ticket-collector would notice them."

Despite never having been in a large city before, or having taken a long train journey, the Sherpas seemed unfazed by Calcutta and all of its urban distractions. "They greeted us very gravely," Shipton recalled, "apparently completely unconcerned." That continued when the party of five went down to the docks to assist in getting the expedition's supplies on shore, and then transferred to another train station. "The Sherpas went about their work in a matter-of-fact way, as little impressed by an eleven-thousand-ton ship and the busy traffic of the Hooghly as with a bullock-cart in the Darjeeling bazaar," Shipton added. That night, at a little after ten o'clock, the two English climbers and the three Sherpas boarded an overnight train to Bareilly, an ancient market town twelve hundred miles to the northwest.

The railway journey, into the ink-dark Indian night, was miserable. The heat was stifling, while one of the Sherpas, Shipton wrote, "insisted on sleeping on the floor of our compartment—much to the disgust of our fellow passengers." It wasn't until the party of five made it to Ranhiket, a hill station, on May 9 that spirits began to lift. "Jolting along the broad motor-road that winds its way among the steep, forest-clad foothills rising abruptly from the plains, we took great gulps of the pine-scented air, deliciously sweet after two days of travel in the appalling heat and dust of pre-monsoon India."

As Shipton and Tilman sorted through the expedition supplies, each of the Sherpas was presented with an Everest-style windproof suit, as well as a mix of undergarments, including mismatched pajamas, cast-off dress shirts, sweaters, and other miscellaneous clothing items that Shipton had cadged from friends or found buried in the back of his closet back home in London. One of the Sherpas "became firmly attached to a pair of my dress trousers," Shipton recalled, while another became so fond of an "ancient dinner jacket" that he kept it neatly folded inside his rucksack. Two days later, after a bone-jarring lorry ride to the temple town of Baijnath, and accompanied by a dozen local men hired as porters, the expedition set out on foot toward the great white wall of the Himalayas.

The Garhwal countryside was as spectacular as it was varied. Deep-green stands of cedar, oak, holly, and chestnut, as dense and dark as Sherwood Forest, rose up before them, the morning calm broken by the chattering of magpies and the tapping of woodpeckers. Then came tomblike villages and well-tilled fields of winter wheat, the grain heads bobbing in the spring wind. There were huge stands of pine and rhododendron, and vast, sun-drenched grasslands, dotted with islands of dwarf iris and bright red potentillas, right out of an impressionist painting. For nearly a fortnight they marched, heading north along the Pilgrim's Way, through vale and forest, grasslands and river bottoms. But as the two British climbers moved through the changing countryside, *they* began to change as well.

To begin, while they had brought along some provisions from home, including canned meats and thick rounds of English cheddar, Shipton and Tilman began to eat like the others. In the morning there would be steaming mugs of black tea and *tsampa*, and in the evening there were bowls of rice and fresh chapatis, cooked on an iron grill over a Primus stove. During the day, they would gather handfuls of wild chives and rhubarb along the trail, drink freely from the crystal-clear springs that dotted the landscape, and barter with the local villagers for eggs and onions and handfuls of flour. Even the nights were different. "We rarely bothered to pitch a tent, but lay, instead, on a luxurious bed of deep grass, beside a huge log fire," Shipton wrote. For this was a new kind of Himalayan expedition, one in which, as much as possible, Shipton and Tilman were determined to live simply and off the land. But what was equally remarkable was how their relationship changed with the trio of men whom, if all went well, they would spend the summer.

The World Beneath Their Feet

"The more we saw of the Sherpas," Shipton wrote, "the more we grew to like them."

Ang Tharkay, at age twenty-seven, was the eldest. With huge, brown eyes, a regal nose, and a calm exterior, his rather diminutive frame belied hidden reservoirs of strength. A veteran of the 1933 Mount Everest Expedition, he had been among the group who, despite howling winds and pounding snow, had established Camp Five at more than 25,000 feet. More worldly than the others, and possessed with a smattering of Hindi, he served as a spokesman and negotiator with the local porters and villagers. Steady and unwavering, he was particularly sound as a climber.

Tall and striking in his appearance, Passang was a superb climber as well—"quite brilliant on rocks," Shipton recalled. Deeply religious, he carried his own stock of prayer flags, built cairns at every campsite, and, "in order to propitiate the spirits," tossed bits of food in the air before eating. Kusang was the youngest and greenest. A hard worker, with firestarting and washing up as his particular specialties, he never had to be asked to pitch in. But Kusang also had a habit of moaning a dirge-like, three-word, two-note song whenever the group was on the move, one that nearly drove Shipton over the edge. "I confess to having suffered many moments when," he later wrote, "my one desire was to silence Kusang forever with an ice axe."

But what alternately floored and charmed the two British mountaineers was the Sherpas' robust sense of humor. "Any minor misfortune such as breaking a pipe or burning a hole in drying socks, would bring down the house," Shipton said, "and once when I sat on my snow-glasses and held up the result for Passang's inspection, I thought he would have hysterics." On another occasion, during a rest stop, Shipton accidentally nudged a thirty-pound sack full of rice and lentils over the edge of a cliff, where it "burst like a bomb" some two hundred feet below. "I recovered the sack, but not the contents, and the mangled remains, spilt in all directions, proved too much for them," he later wrote. "For a month afterwards, while it yet hung together, the sight of it always fetched a laugh." Not content to merely find humor along the way, the three Sherpas would also sneak rocks into each other's already heavy packs, and then, at the end of the day, they would all double up with fits of laughter when the ruse was uncovered.

But, below the surface, something deeper was happening.

For as the small party made its way toward Nanda Devi, the old, strict divisions between sahib and porter, European and native, and colonizer and colonized had begun to fray along the edges. Through belly laughs, shared pots of rice and *tsampa*, and sleeping bags laid in a circle around a pine-bough fire, Eric Shipton had already begun to regard the Sherpas not simply as porters, but also as "fellow mountaineers and companions." In a remote corner of the British Empire, around the glowing embers of untended campfires, a radical new vision of humanity was starting to stir.

At the end of May, the local porters were dismissed. The expedition was now down to five members: Shipton, Tilman, Ang Tharkay, Passang, and Kusang. They had made it to the edge of the Rishi Nala, the spectacular gorge through which they hoped to gain access to the Sanctuary. No human had ever made their way up the gorge, which the local villagers believed was possessed by demons. Now the two Brits and three Sherpas would give it a go. They had food for exactly thirty-one days.

The Rishi Nala quickly proved to be a true Gordian knot.

Usually unable to see more than a hundred yards or so up the narrow gorge, the climbers were never sure whether they should push ahead on one side or the other, to go high, along the near-vertical cliffs, or to stay low, by the raging river. "We were constantly toiling up some steep slope," Shipton wrote, "only to find that we had arrived at some impassible cut-off, which could only be avoided by making a long detour above or below." Even the occasional breaks in the sheer verticality of the gorge proved daunting. "I found myself being very nervous and shaky on the steep grass slopes and slabs on which we had to climb," Shipton added, while the river itself, colored nearly milk-white with all of the glacial silt it was carrying, proved to be a challenge all its own.

To increase their chances of success, and to reduce the amount of backtracking, the party split into two, with Shipton trying one route, Tilman another, and the Sherpas divided between them. At night they would try to find a cave or a sandbar along the river, where they would camp before heading out again the next day. Usually, they could rustle up some juniper branches for a fire, which should have revived their spirits. But the truth of the matter was that while they were making some progress, the Rishi Nala had proven to be far more difficult than any of them might have imagined—and they hadn't even gotten to the upper gorge yet. Shipton, in particular, started to have grave doubts about whether they'd find a way forward. "For a long time I lay awake," he wrote of one restless night, "weighing up in my mind our chance of success."

His worries increased a few days later when he and the others got their first look at "a huge dark buttress, which appeared to descend in an unbroken sweep from the great heights above to the water's edge, and looked to be utterly impassable." Nicknaming it Pisgah, after the Biblical mountain that God told Moses to climb in order to see the Promised Land, there was no question that it held the key to gaining access to the upper gorge. But just getting to it, along sloping, narrow terraces of rotten slab, was itself daunting. "Over and over again the terrace we were on would peter out into some deep cleft," Shipton wrote. As a result, the closer they got to the buttress, the lower they went into the gorge. By the time they were about a quarter-mile away, while reconnoitering a route one morning, they were less than three hundred feet above the river.

Then they saw it.

Just opposite of where the buttress came down to the river's edge, there was a narrow strip of shore. If they could ford the river and get to it, they reasoned, perhaps they could walk along the river past part of the buttress. But crossing the river would be no easy accomplishment. Not only did the frigid waters reach up to their thighs, but the current was so strong that all five of them had a devil of a time maintaining their balance. They made it across, only to discover that the strip of shore soon vanished. In the end, they had to cross the river five more times before they could begin to solve the problem of the great buttress.

It was, to say the least, a daunting prospect. On its upper reaches, the footing was either so narrow or so dubious that moving forward with fully loaded packs would be a challenge of the highest order, while a fall would likely result in a fatality. And the river itself would have to be crossed and recrossed, each time numbing and battering their legs. A slip here might be equally deadly, especially for the Sherpas, none of whom could swim. Still, they had found a route which led them to the upper canyons of the Rishi Nala.

There wasn't much discussion.

One by one, the five men started to make their way back to their last camp to start loading supplies for the way ahead.

By June 3, Shipton, Tilman, Ang Tharkay, Passang, and Kusang were well into the upper gorge. Carefully yet diligently, they had ferried all five hundred and fifty pounds of their supplies along the narrowest of ledges, through the bone-chilling river, and across riotous heaps of uneven slab. When crossing one snow-dusted gully, the footing was so dicey that the Sherpas took off their boots and felt their way in their bare feet. Other times, on even hairier pitches, each man's heart was in his throat. But day after day, the quintet of climbers plodded forward, turning corners that no one had ever turned before and, in so doing, making the Rishi Nala their own.

For a time, they tried to push their way entirely up the river itself, dodging from side to side, in search of a flat rock or a whisper of a sandbar. Once, they discovered a natural bridge across the rushing torrent. Another time, using birch branches that they wove together, they fashioned a makeshift—and barely functional—span across a stretch of rough water. But as they neared the head of the Rishi Nala, and the canyon narrowed, the milky white torrent became less and less fordable. "The force of the current was terrific," Shipton wrote of one crossing. "As I moved a foot forward, it would be swirled sideways, and it was only by shuffling along that I could make any headway. My legs were slashed by stones swept down by the force of the river, but soon the numbing cold robbed my lower limbs of all sensation." Midway across, with the raging water above his belt buckle, Shipton was nearly swept away. "I tried to turn around, but found that the current was impossible to face or turn my back upon, so I had to go on, and at length emerged with bleeding legs upon the opposite beach." The conclusion was inescapable. To make it through the last mile or so of the gorge, they would again have to go up.

On June 4, a dull gray morning, they split into two teams. Tilman and Ang Tharkay would take the southern side of the river, looking for any possible routes forward, while Shipton and Passang would take the northern side. "I confess that when we started out on our respective jobs," Shipton later wrote, "I thought that if anyone got through, it would be Passang and I; for to get past 'Pisgah' on the southern side appeared to be a hopeless task." But Shipton and Passang soon ran into plenty of difficulties all their own. They first tried to move along a sloping band of strata that they hoped would carry them beyond the buttress on the opposite shore. "But the corridor became more and more difficult to follow, and finally ended in a little platform five hundred feet above the river, completely isolated save for the way by which we had come," he added. "Further advance in any direction was impossible."

Passang and Shipton then returned to the river where, after a supreme effort, they were able to move ahead another two hundred yards before being brought to a dead halt by a box canyon where the current was far too strong to wade through. Backtracking, they then went over every inch of the sheer rock walls towering over the northern shore, looking for a set of stray knobs or a hidden crack—anything that might give them a way up. "We tried places that were obviously quite ridiculous; just as one searches under a teapot or in the coal-scuttle for a lost fountain pen when one has exhausted every likely place," Shipton wrote, "and I had a similar feeling of hopelessness." They had been licked. There was no way forward on the northern side of the Rishi Nala, and it was highly doubtful that Tilman and Ang Tharkay had found anything to the south. And when Shipton and Passang walked back to camp, it began to rain.

But as the afternoon bled into the evening, and the light began to dim at the bottom of the canyon, dejection was replaced with a growing concern. Tilman and Ang Tharkay had still not returned, and Shipton began to worry that they might have had an accident. "As the evening wore on, we began to scan the crags of the opposite side anxiously for any sign of the others," he wrote. "Then all at once we spotted them, descending through the mist at a seemingly reckless speed." Rushing to meet them at the river crossing, Shipton could see that Ang Tharkay was "in a state of great excitement." He was also shouting something that, at first, Shipton couldn't quite make out. Finally, the words rang loud and clear across the roar of the river.

"*Bahut achcha, sahib,*" Ang Tharkay thundered. "*Bahut achcha.*"

They had found a way. Twelve hundred feet above the river, Tilman and Ang Tharkay had discovered a stray sloping ledge, which, after a couple of nervous spots, led to a long gulley that flared down some eight hundred feet from a notch in the seemingly impregnable buttress. But there they found a "chimney," a narrow vertical crack where, by placing their backs against one wall, and their feet and hands against the other, they inchwormed their way to the crest of the ridge. From here, they could see that the way ahead was clear. Tomorrow, they would enter the Sanctuary.

And they did.

Past the ledge, up the gulley, and through the chimney, carrying full loads with the sweat soaking their backs and pouring off their brows and forearms, they crossed over their final barrier and made their way, one step at a time, toward the lost world of the Nanda Devi basin. And while the Blessed Goddess herself, and her surrounding peaks, were still shrouded in clouds, the land itself changed quickly.

The World Beneath Their Feet

Patches of wild rhubarb rose up to meet them, as did lush grass and gently flowing springs of crystal-clear water. Gone was the austere severity of the Rishi Nala, with its bare rock walls and endless shades of brown and gray. Gone was the deafening roar of the river.

Here there were choruses of birds—chattering pipits, blue and orange redstarts, and peeping rosefinches. Sturdy flocks of gray-capped snow pigeons winged by, while snowcocks and snow partridges nestled in the rocks. Mammals roamed the Sanctuary as well, including herds of bharal, or Himalayan blue sheep, with their heavy horns and two-toned forelegs. Calm and unafraid, they viewed the human intruders with a quiet curiosity. Smaller herds of goral could be found as well. They looked like a cross between a goat and an antelope, so Shipton mistook these for tahr, a kind of wild goat. And higher up, along the fog-shrouded glacial outcroppings, snow leopards patiently waited their turn.

But what delighted the men the most, after the long battle up the gorge, was the sudden riot of greenery they found in the Sanctuary. Here there were meadows upon meadows of bright green grass, fields of flowers, and hardy clumps of mountain juniper, stretching for miles. Gentians, with their light-blue flowers, grew out of the scree, while the Sherpas delighted in finding bunches of pungent wild onions. Some plants were small and spike-like, while others, to protect themselves from frost, would roll up their leaves at night. "It would be difficult," Shipton later remarked in a classic case of British understatement, "to give an adequate account of the loveliness of the country in which we found ourselves."

And once, as it was said, the mountains lifted their skirts and the clouds dissipated, the five men—the first humans ever to enter the Sanctuary—stared in awe at the terrible beauty that surrounded them. "First appeared the majestic head of Nanda Devi herself," Shipton wrote, "utterly detached from the earth. One by one the white giants of the unnamed ranges to the north followed suit; until at last it seemed as if the entire mountain realm stood before us bathed in the splendor of the dying sun."

James Hilton had written of a make-believe Shangri-La.

Shipton, Tilman, Ang Tharkay, Passang, and Kusang found the real one.

For the next twenty days, they explored the Sanctuary. They walked up moraines and glaciers, climbed to the top of some of the lower summits, and peered into the waters of an unnamed lake, its dark-blue waters hinting at a considerable but unknown depth. And while Shipton and Tilman spent dutiful hours at the plane table, mapping and charting this incredible amphitheater and its ring of mountain battlements, the urge to simply explore, especially when they were out walking about, was often overpowering.

"Every few hundred yards, some new feature would reveal itself—here a side valley to look up, and to speculate as to where it would lead, there some graceful ice-clad summit appearing from behind a buttress, and looking, in the newness of its form, lovelier than any of its neighbors," wrote Shipton. "In spite of the heavy load I was carrying, I frequently had difficulty in refraining from running in my eagerness to see round the next corner, or to get a better view of some fresh and slender spire which had just made its appearance." At night, they would often sleep in the open, around a juniper fire, beneath a blazing canopy of stars. Shipton, an eternal boy at heart, had found the playground of his soul.

With one asterisk.

Because despite his joy in entering the Sanctuary, Nanda Devi itself, in all of her icy splendor, called him as well. Viewed from inside the basin, the mountain looked even more majestic and even more terrifying, especially as they caught their first long look at its southern ridge. "As we looked at the mighty upward sweep of the ridge, all hope died," Shipton wrote, "for the thing appeared utterly unclimbable." Tilman felt it as well. Nonetheless, they began making plans for an assault on the mountain until they realized, much to the relief of the Sherpas, that they had neither the time nor the proper equipment to give it a go. "We spent the next day waiting for Mr.

Shipton . . . to make a decision about Nanda Devi," Ang Tharkay later reported. "For good reason, they abandoned the attempt."

It was now to time to leave.

With their food supplies running low, the first ranks of gray, woolly clouds rolled in from the south, announcing the arrival of the monsoon. Too much rain in the basin might make the river completely impassable, while Tilman had developed a painful carbuncle on his foot. "We were ordered to leave all superfluous utensils and food where we were," Ang Tharkay added, "and to make our loads as light as possible." By the twenty-fifth of June, the five men were on their way out of the Sanctuary.

When word hit the outside world of what they had accomplished, the mountaineering community was absolutely electrified. "The lists are now set for great deeds in the Himalayan snow-fields," wrote Hugh Ruttledge, the leader of the 1933 Mount Everest Expedition. "Messrs. Shipton and Tilman have shown the way; let us hope that many will follow." Shipton—and Longstaff—had been right after all. Not only could the Rishi Nala be breached, but a small Himalayan expedition could accomplish great things. Eric Shipton suddenly became the most famous living British mountaineer.

Shipton, for his part, was not one to brag. Writing about the expedition on the long ocean voyage back to England, his description of their last night in the Sanctuary perhaps best revealed his heart. "As we sat round our blazing fire of juniper wood in the gathering dusk, watching the heavy rain-clouds float lazily over the rolling moors of the basin, my content was marred by a feeling of sadness at having to leave so soon this country, which had provided us with a deep and lasting happiness, and whose beautiful secrets it had been our privilege to explore."

There was one other detail.

The 1933 Mount Everest Expedition had cost upward of £11,000.

Shipton and Tilman had each spent, in total, £143, 10s—a little less than six hundred American dollars.

CHAPTER SEVEN

Yogis and Yak Meat

Meanwhile, in another part of the Himalayas, another drama was unfolding.

At its center was an Englishman named Maurice Wilson. Tall and solidly built, with brown hair, a narrow chin, and large, inquisitive blue eyes, he had enlisted in the British Army in the spring of 1915, one day after his eighteenth birthday. Two years would pass before his West Yorkshire Regiment was sent to the Western Front, but when it was, Wilson was there in time to catch the full fury of the hellish campaigns near Ypres. As a second lieutenant, he had personally manned a machine gun on the front line and, while his battalion mates fell around him, helped to stave off a German attack, an action for which he was awarded the Military Cross.

But like many others in the so-called Lost Generation, Wilson came back from the war a changed man. Moody and restless, he grew deeply introspective, while satisfaction always seemed to just slip through his fingers. In 1922, he married a young woman named Beatrice Hardy Slater who, at age twenty, described herself on the parish register as a "spinster," though in fact she had already been married once before. The marriage didn't last, nor, for Wilson, did any kind of permanent or semi-permanent career. Though he was offered a steady job in the woolen trade, Wilson drifted, first to New York, and then on to San Francisco. In New Zealand, he sold patent medicine, tried farming, and, in Wellington, ran a women's clothing store that turned a steady profit. Despite his newfound success, however, something was missing.

Booking a one-way steamship passage on the long ocean voyage back to England, Wilson grew mesmerized by a group of Indian holy men who boarded the ship in Bombay. Interest in eastern religious philosophy had been on the rise in the West. A charismatic Hindu monk named Vivekananda had electrified audiences on a lecture tour of the United States and Great Britain, following up his presentations with classes on yoga and Vedanta, while authors like Rudyard Kipling and Hermann Hesse helped introduce some of the basic tenets of Buddhist thought to Western readers. Upon learning that the passengers from Bombay were yogis, Wilson paid special attention to their bearing and attitude, how they carried themselves and what their external appearance might reveal of their inner souls.

Back in England, he turned down pleas from his family to come home to Yorkshire, instead taking a flat in London. But satisfaction again eluded him and, worse, he grew seriously ill with a harsh, rasping cough that some thought might have been the first stages of tuberculosis. Though Maurice Wilson was physically worn down and unable to work, if he sought the advice of a regular physician, no record remains. Rather, what he seems to have done was to consult with some sort of amateur healer, a man who claimed that, some seventeen years earlier, he had been at death's door. Informed by every doctor that he had only weeks to live and that there was nothing that they could do, the mystery man then took matters into his own hands. He fasted for thirty-five days, drinking only small quantities of water, thus cleansing his body of the impurities that were killing him. He prayed as well, repeating over and over again from the Book of John, chapter 3, verse 5, that he might "be born again of water and of the Spirit." When the thirty-five days were up, he was restored to full health. It was, the man told Wilson, a "miracle cure."

Maurice Wilson wasted no time in trying it himself.

When he was finished, he was a changed man—mentally, physically, and spiritually. Elated, and convinced that his job on earth was to demonstrate to people how, through fasting and faith, human beings could accomplish seemingly impossible tasks, he started searching for the type of goal so difficult that, if he achieved it, he could spread the word about this amazing miracle cure. It didn't take long to find it. Only a few weeks or so later, Wilson went out to a celebratory dinner with a couple of friends in Mayfair, Leonard and Enid Evans. Still on fire about his spiritual discovery and its remarkable impact on his health, Wilson ended up talking well into the night.

"I haven't gone mad, and I haven't got religious mania," Wilson said. "But I've got a theory to prove, and I intend to prove it."

"And what," Enid asked, "are you going to do?"

Maurice Wilson told them.

"I'll climb Mount Everest alone."

Wilson's plan quickly took shape.

He read every book that he could find on Mount Everest and began to haunt mountaineering shops and expedition outfitters, asking questions about tents and boots, rations and supplemental oxygen. At his flat in Maida Vale, in northwest London, he spread out maps of India and Tibet and Nepal, following with his fingers the routes taken by the Mount Everest expeditions of 1921, 1922, and 1924. Convinced that a determined, physically fit individual could accomplish what large-scale campaigns, with their hundreds of porters and pack animals, could not, Wilson also believed that far too much time was spent on just getting to the mountain. The trick, he concluded, was really rather elementary. He would fly an airplane to Mount Everest, crash land on one of the glaciers, perhaps at around 14,000 feet, and, all alone, climb to the top of the highest peak on the planet.

In order to make his plan work, Wilson would, of course, have to learn how to fly an airplane first. Again taking to study, he read up on the various types of small planes that were available, taking note of their horsepower, fuel consumption, and air speed, and concluded that a de Havilland Gipsy Moth—an open-cockpit, two-seater touring airplane that had been flown by a number of well-known British aviators—would fit the bill nicely. A new model being a bit of a reach for his budget for the expedition, Wilson located a used Gipsy Moth for sale, which he promptly purchased. Then he set about taking flying lessons.

He was far from an ideal student. Dressed in an absurd getup that featured "huge hobnail boots, fawn-colored breeches tucked in at the calf by high gaiters, and a voluminous leather jerkin," Wilson would manhandle the controls, take off downwind, and nearly crash in a series of hair-raising landings. "No! No! No!" his flight instructor would scream. "Don't be so violent, man! Make your movements slowly and smoothly. Not like a butcher hacking up the scrag-end!" It took Wilson months to earn his pilot's license. His mountaineering training was equally shallow. Though he spent a few weeks in both the Lake District and in Wales, Britain's two most revered climbing locales, Wilson spent most of his time hiking and he apparently learned very little about basic mountaineering equipment and practice. His confidence in himself, and his mission, however, was still unshaken.

Others were less certain. As word of his quixotic quest reached the ears of Fleet Street reporters, Maurice Wilson began to be portrayed as someone who was either a lunatic or a dreamy-eyed buffoon, a sincere but misguided Englishman who innocently believed that he could accomplish what the nation's greatest climbers could not. But once news of Wilson's intentions reached His Majesty's government, the smiles promptly faded. Hoping to scotch Wilson's planned expedition before it got off the ground, the Air Ministry, in early May 1933, wrote to Wilson and informed him that it was "unlikely that the Nepalese Government would grant permission for you to fly over their territory to Mount Everest." Wilson fired back that "at this very moment that the Houston Expedition flyers are making daily flights over Nepalese territory." The frustrated government official responded, explaining that the Everest overflights had come about only "after elaborate negotiations with the Nepalese Government by the Government of India," further warning Wilson that he would not receive such permission. In the end, the Air Ministry was forced to send Wilson a telegram specifically forbidding his expedition.

Wilson tore up the telegram.

On Sunday morning, May 21, 1933, at the Stag Lane aerodrome outside of London, Maurice Wilson climbed into the cockpit of his Gipsy Moth G-ABJC, which he had named the "Ever-Wrest." Then he waved goodbye to the small crowd of friends, newspaper reporters, and onlookers, and began his journey. But, once again, he forgot a basic rule of aerodynamics and took off with the wind, clearing a hedgerow by only a couple of feet.

Flying a single-propeller, open-cockpit airplane from England to the Himalayas was no minor proposition. There were no radio beacons to guide fliers in 1933, and, unlike today, relatively few airports, almost all of which shut down at night. Armed with a compass, watch, altimeter, fuel gauge, and an incomplete set of aviation maps, Wilson would have to fly more than five thousand miles mainly by dead reckoning, looking for natural and man-made landmarks that would confirm he was on the right track. And when cloud cover cut down visibility, he would have to navigate by intuition as much as anything else.

From London, he flew to Germany, staying overnight with friends in Freiburg. The next day, from an airstrip in Bavaria, he'd planned on flying due south, crossing the Austrian Alps. But as he circled the plane and tried to gain altitude in the countryside east of Munich, he discovered that the Gipsy Moth was so overloaded that it couldn't climb to an elevation much more than 9,000 feet. Not wanting to crash-land in the wrong mountain range, Wilson then worked out a new route that skirted the Alps entirely, one which took him back to Freiburg, south to Marseille, and then along the shin of Italy, past Rome and Naples, and on to Sicily. The weather was gorgeous, and his spirits could not have been higher. "So far," Wilson wrote, "the trip is a piece of cake."

The World Beneath Their Feet

*   *   *

In Tunisia, however, he was arrested and briefly detained by the local police at an airfield in Bizerte. "You are not permitted to stay here," one of the *gendarmes* coldly informed him. "Suits me," Wilson replied. In Libya, with his engine starting to sputter, he almost crashed after he'd been sold a load of bad gasoline. "Your fuel had water in it," a mechanic told him. "You're lucky to be alive." But an entirely different kind of problem emerged once he made it to Egypt. Back in England, Wilson had dutifully applied for a permit to fly over Persia on his way to the Himalayas. It had been approved, he was informed, and the permit would be awaiting him in Cairo. Only it wasn't.

This was no small setback. Not only did Wilson suspect that the British government was behind the disappearance of the permit, but Persia served as the great buffer between the Arab states and the Indian subcontinent, and finding a way to fly to India without crossing Persian territory was a difficult, if not impossible, task. Pushing on to Baghdad, Wilson was able to scrounge up a beat-up school atlas and a survey map for part of the Persian Gulf. A working airfield existed at Bahrain, a British protectorate, some seven hundred miles to the south. And while that was near the limit of the flight range for the Gipsy Moth, Wilson pushed on, flying more than eight and a half hours straight before touching down on the sleepy island's windblown airstrip. For the last two hundred miles, Wilson had basically flown without any kind of map at all.

To make matters even more difficult, the mechanics at the Bahrain airfield—under the direct orders of the British Consul—refused to refill the now-bone-dry tanks of the Gipsy Moth. Going directly to the consulate, Wilson was informed why. To begin, he had no permit to fly over Persian territory. Secondly, aside from Baghdad, there were no other airports within the seven hundred and fifty mile range of his plane *except* for some in Persia, the government official informed him. Wilson's journey was over. Throwing up his arms in disgust,

Wilson then walked over to the large map of the Persian Gulf that hung on the office wall. But rather than focusing on Bahrain, his eyes instead wandered to the bottom right corner of the map, where something caught his eye: an airfield in Gwadar, a port city under control of Oman but surrounded by India, just across the Persian frontier. It was about eight hundred miles from Bahrain. But Wilson kept that to himself. Instead, feigning a crushing disappointment, Wilson asked the official what he should do.

"If I were in your shoes, I'd fly to Bushire—that's the nearest Persian drome," the government man said. "You could land and ask them for a permit there."

It was, of course, a trap.

Once he'd landed in Persia, Wilson would be arrested and his plane would be impounded. Wilson thanked the official for the suggestion, and said that he'd fly to Bushire the next day. The next morning, while the Gipsy Moth was being refilled, Wilson convinced one of the Arab mechanics to sell him an additional, small drum of gasoline, which was quietly loaded into the cargo hold of the plane. Then, he walked over to thank the official from the British Consulate, who had come to see him off. "Bye-bye, old man," the official shouted, undoubtedly pleased with himself that he had finally put this madness to rest. Maurice Wilson then taxied out onto the runway, gunned the engine, and took off into the bright midmorning sunlight of the Persian Gulf. Then he steered the Gipsy Moth east, toward Qatar, the Gulf of Oman, and, along the edge of the Arabian Sea, toward the sun-scorched coastline of India.

Already, it had been an astonishing performance.

Despite having precious little flying experience, Maurice Wilson had piloted a small plane, solo, for more than five thousand miles, almost a quarter of the way around the world, with only the crudest of maps. Even if he had done nothing else in his life, when he finally touched down in Gwadar, the tiny Oman protectorate in far western India, with his engine sputtering and his gas tanks nearly empty, he had successfully made the kind of airplane journey that was beyond the dreams of even the most accomplished aviators. But Wilson was far from done. And after a big meal and a good night's sleep, he again steered the Gipsy Moth into Indian skies and continued his journey westward.

He went slowly at first, stopping in Karachi and Hyderabad, Jodhpur and Allahabad. The press had found him—as had government officials. Twice he was barred from purchasing gasoline at airfields. But if nothing else, Wilson was inventive. Once he shared his petrol predicament with an Irish innkeeper, who casually showed Wilson where the gasoline was stored at a nearby airfield. Wilson then refueled the Gipsy Moth during the middle of the night, leaving the proper number of rupees as payment. But by the time he reached Lalbalu, an Indian village not far from the Nepalese border that was less than two hundred air miles from Mount Everest, the officials of the Raj had reached their limit.

"Mr. Maurice Wilson, an Englishman, who recently arrived in India in a light aeroplane," ran a small item in the *Times* on June 10, 1933, "has been refused permission to fly over Nepal." Even worse, British officials impounded his plane and began charging Wilson three rupees for every day that he kept it there. Adding to his difficulties were the facts that the monsoon had by now moved in, and that Wilson was running out of money. There would be no attempt on Everest this season. It didn't take a genius to figure out that his crazy dream was over. But Maurice Wilson didn't operate on any kind of predictable wavelength. He sold the Gipsy Moth to a British gentleman planter for five hundred rupees. Then he took off for Darjeeling.

All that summer, he lay low.

While the monsoon rains battered the fairy-tale town, Wilson took a room in Albert Hall, a small residential hotel catering to British citizens. He fasted and prayed, prowled the open-air markets, and lounged about the Planters Club, picking up stray bits of information about mountaineering expeditions. In October, after the monsoon passed and the white face of Kangchenjunga again showed itself, he was granted permission to take an extended hiking tour in the Sikkim foothills. While he was away, the Darjeeling police searched his lodgings to make sure his mountaineering equipment was still there, while the authorities in Sikkim kept close tabs on his whereabouts. They were wise to do so. Upon his return, Wilson adopted a strenuous exercise regimen, taking long walks in the hills surrounding Darjeeling, while alternating between fasting and consuming a strict vegetarian diet.

By January 1934, he had formulated a new plan.

He would walk to Mount Everest.

Then he would climb it.

Maurice Wilson slipped out of Darjeeling on the night of March 20, 1934.

Disguised as a Tibetan monk, he wore a brass-buttoned brocade waistcoat, dark trousers, a bright red silk sash, and an enormous cape. A fur cap was pulled down over his head, while he kept handy a pair of dark glasses and a large umbrella. The only off notes in his ensemble were his hobnail mountaineering boots. Avoiding the clock tower and the town square, Wilson threaded his way along the narrow side streets, his breath white in the cool night air.

Accompanying him was Tsering, a Sherpa who had been on the 1933 Mount Everest expedition. Two other Sherpas, Tewang and Rinzing, both carrying heavy packs filled with mountain climbing gear and supplies, were waiting for them at a pre-arranged, secluded spot in the forest. Wilson had also purchased a pony to haul the food and two Meade tents. Back in Darjeeling, to help avoid suspicion, he had paid up the rent on his room six months in advance. Traveling by night and sleeping in the forest by day, the four men made good progress as they moved north across Sikkim. Following the dirt path along the Tista River, they climbed through dense forests, thick with alder, oak, and bamboo. The Sherpas would go into the villages after dawn, or just before dusk, seeking to buy eggs or vegetables. If anyone wanted to meet with their monk, the Sherpas told them that he was sick. As they climbed higher, the trees and villages started to disappear, while snow flurries became more frequent. On Saturday, March 31, the three men and one pony pulled themselves past the barren slopes of the 16,000-foot pass at Kongra La, its prayer flags whipping back and forth in the wind, and crossed over into Tibet.

Speed, rather than subterfuge, now became the order of the day.

Abandoning his monk disguise and traveling by daylight, Wilson and the three Sherpas made record time across the bleak and barren Tibetan plateau, skirting past the dazzling hill town of Kampa Dzong and the white-walled monastery at Shekar Dzong. Despite punishing winds, high passes, and, for Wilson, restless, sleep-interrupted nights caused by not allowing enough time to properly acclimatize himself to the higher elevations, the party relentlessly pushed on. Wilson was both ecstatic and optimistic. "Maybe," he wrote in his diary on April 13, "in less than five weeks the world will be on fire." The next day, Wilson, Tsering, Tewang, Rinzing, and the little Sikkim pony made it to the Rongbuk Monastery. They had traveled more than three hundred miles, on foot, and gained nearly ten thousand feet in elevation, in less than twenty-five days.

Inside the stone-walled monastery, dimly lit by butter lamps, Wilson and the Sherpas were blessed by the head lama, who touched them with his sacred *dorje* while they chanted "*Om mani padme hum.*" Wilson was deeply moved by the ceremony. But what equally delighted him was being granted access to the leftover supplies from the 1933 expedition, held in one of the monastery storerooms, where he helped himself to a high-altitude tent and some other items. "Only another thirteen thousand feet to go!" he wrote in his diary. He was also deeply grateful for his Sherpas, and the job that they had done in helping him get to Rongbuk. "Boys all looking forward to me getting it over and back quickly," he added. "Chaps have been wonderful throughout."

The next morning, Maurice Wilson set out, alone, to climb Mount Everest.

It was a beautiful day, with crystal-clear skies and little wind. At first, Wilson could see practically the entire north face of the mountain, brilliantly white in the morning light, but as he worked his way along the sides of the Rongbuk Glacier, the mountain—and its summit, which was little more than ten miles away—slowly slipped from view. Still, he made good time, and as soon as he passed the remains of the 1933 base camp, Wilson knew that he was on the right track. Like previous expeditions, he planned on traveling up the Rongbuk Glacier to the mouth of the East Rongbuk Glacier, which he would then follow until its end, and then climb the icefall that led to the North Col. From there, he would work his way up to Everest's north-east ridge, which would lead him directly to the summit. His pack, which weighed some forty-five pounds, contained several days' worth of food, various supplies including a mountaineering stove, a camera, film, his tent and sleeping bag, plus a pennant signed by friends and well-wishers back in London. He didn't make it all the way to the 1933 expedition's Camp One that afternoon, but it had been a marvelous day. Not only had he climbed to more than 17,500 feet, but he felt strong and fit.

The next day, April 17, Wilson ran across the remains of Camp One early in the morning, confirming once again that he was on the right track. But as he moved deeper and deeper into the East Rongbuk Glacier, he now found himself having to contend with a virtual forest of ice pinnacles, blue and green and vivid white, some reaching a hundred feet into the sky. More than once he got lost trying to forge a path through this ragged maze. Moreover, in the blinding sunlight, it was exhausting work, and he soon began to discard superfluous items from his pack, including a second Tommy cooker, extra film and candles. Still, Wilson soldiered on. Once again, he didn't make it to that day's primary objective—the abandoned Camp Two—but he had made progress. He pitched his tent for the night at a little less than 19,000 feet. Yet he was also becoming increasingly exhausted. Before turning in, he scribbled in his pocket diary, "Had a hell of a day."

Wilson made it to Camp Two the next afternoon, Wednesday, April 18. But as he sat down for a quick break, and to eat some dates and a couple of slices of bread, it suddenly began to snow. Despite his fatigue, he quickly managed to pitch his tent, where he sat out the storm. The next two days were equally grueling. Uncertain of how to move across the incredibly challenging terrain of the upper end of the East Rongbuk Glacier, with its deadly crevasses and towering seracs, its ice towers and its vast moraines of loose rock and gravel, Wilson moved slowly, slipping and falling, taking one dead end after another, uncertain which was the best way to proceed. Worse, it had also begun to snow. By the night of April 20, he still hadn't made it to the North Col, or even to the site of Camp Three where, the Sherpas had told him, there were still food supplies left by the previous year's expedition. If only, he concluded, he had brought the Sherpas along with him, he would surely be much higher by now.

The next morning, Saturday, April 21, was Wilson's birthday. He was thirty-six years old. He was also at a crossroads. While he had now climbed to approximately 20,500 feet, he was nearly out of food, low on energy, and it was again snowing. Either he could try and make it to Camp Three, where it was said there was food, or he could head back down the mountain to the Rongbuk Monastery, where he could wait until the weather improved. He chose the latter.

And once again, Maurice Wilson showed what he was made of.

When he arrived at the monastery on Tuesday evening, April 24, his eyes were nearly swollen shut, his right ankle was badly sprained, and his mouth was so dry that he could barely speak. He had descended five thousand feet in less than twenty-four hours, the last four of which were in the dark. Overjoyed and amazed, the Sherpas fed him hot soup, rice, and tea. Then Wilson fell asleep. He slept for thirty-eight hours.

*   *   *

It took Wilson two and a half weeks to recover from his ordeal. His eyes remained stubbornly swollen, his muscles ached, and part of his face, which he described as looking like "a dried apricot," was temporarily paralyzed. The Sherpas made certain that he had plenty to eat, including ample portions of yak meat. But after a while, Wilson decided that the rich food was slowing his recovery, and, after fasting and going back to his simple, vegetarian diet, he soon felt better. He was determined to tackle the mountain again. Only this time it would be different.

And it was—but not in the way that Wilson had imagined. Two of the Sherpas, Tewang and Rinzing, accompanied him as far as the icefall leading up to the North Col, after which it was agreed that Wilson would make "a last dive for the sunmit" on his own. And despite the challenging terrain that they had passed, Wilson's spirits were soaring. "Summit and route to it can be seen quite clearly now," he wrote in his diary at Camp Three one night. "Only another 8,000 feet to go."

What followed, instead, was a lesson in humility.

With avalanches booming off the upper slopes of the mountain, Wilson plodded along, trying to make his way up the ice fall to the North Col. Time and again, he had to cut steps in the dense, almost rubbery ice, all the more difficult because he had no crampons. Pitches that might have taken an experienced mountaineer an hour or so to conquer took Wilson three, four, or five times as long. And while the days were sunny and bright, the nights were iron cold, a penetrating, teeth-rattling chill that was far, far colder than anything he had ever experienced. He spent the nights, alone, shivering in his tent.

Still, he soldiered on. At one point, he found himself blocked by a crevasse, its yawning depths colored a deep cerulean blue, across which spanned a solitary snowbridge. If it held, Wilson would make it safely to the other side. If it collapsed, he would perish in the crevasse, his cries unheard. He said a prayer and walked across. It held. But at around 23,000 feet, he was confronted with an obstacle that not even his faith could move him beyond: an ice chimney that ran straight up some one hundred–plus feet to the lip of the North Col. For seven hours he tried to climb it. But he just couldn't make any headway. The chimney was beyond his expertise. "Only one thing to do," he wrote in his diary. "No food, no water. Get back."

By the next morning, Wilson had a new plan.

With the Sherpas' help, he could surely master the chimney.

Once again, he started heading down the mountain.

Beaten and bruised by his nightmarish, five-hour descent down the icefall, where he'd continually slipped and fallen, Wilson spent three full days in bed at Camp Three. Rinzing tended to him, bringing hot tea and soup. Once he'd regained his composure, Wilson kept trying to convince the two others to accompany him only as far as Camp Five, but neither of the Sherpas would hear of it. No, no, and no, they told Wilson in their broken English, they would go no farther.

Once again, he would have to go it alone.

On Tuesday morning, May 29, 1934, Maurice Wilson hoisted his pack onto his back at Camp Three, and turned to his two Sherpas, Tewang and Rinzing. Wait for me here for ten days, he told them. If I don't come back by then, then return to Darjeeling on your own. Then he turned and, facing the growing wind coming off of the mountain, started to make his way back toward the icefall, the North Col, and his own patch of immortality. Two days later, he penciled in the last entry in his diary.

"Off again, gorgeous day."

One year later, Dr. Charles Warren, a member of a British reconnaissance expedition led by Eric Shipton, discovered Maurice Wilson's body. Dressed in gray flannel trousers, shirt, and Fairisle pullover, it was found curled up and lying on its left side, between Camp Three and the North Col. The members of the expedition also retrieved his diary, which they found in his rucksack buried nearby in the snow. One of the climbers then read the entries out loud. Afterward, they wrapped Wilson's body in his tent and, after a brief funeral service, Warren later wrote, "consigned it to the depths of a crevasse on the East Rongbuk Glacier." One of the Sherpas took Wilson's cork-lined boots, while some of the others built a cairn to mark the spot where he died.

As word of his demise reached England, Wilson would be dismissed as an eccentric, a madman, and a fool, and that his "stunt" amounted to little more than an elaborate form of suicide. "It is all very well to praise Wilson's sincerity, which, like fortitude, is not in question," came an assessment some years later in the *Alpine Journal*. "It is his motives and methods that invite criticism." Many climbers, however, saw it differently. For them, the Maurice Wilson saga brimmed with a far deeper resonance, one that spoke of dreams and dreamers, consciousness and idealism, boldness and action. "We cannot fail to admire his courage," Shipton later wrote.

But it was Frank Smythe who put it the best.

"It wasn't mountaineering," he said, "yet it was magnificent."

The summer of 1934 had been nothing short of astonishing.

A German expedition had come within a couple of hours, and one fleeting decision, of being the first to summit an *Achttausender*—only to be caught by a deadly storm that led to the greatest catastrophe in the history of mountaineering. Eric Shipton, Bill Tilman, Ang Tharkay, Passang, and Kusang had not only forced their way into the Nanda Devi Sanctuary, but they had irrefutably proven what small-scale expeditions were capable of, even in the most daunting mountain range on the planet. And a lone Englishman had defied government officials on three continents and pulled off an amazing aerial odyssey, only to discover, the hard way, the harsh realities of Mount Everest.

In Darjeeling, as the climbing season came to a close, and the first snap of autumn weather settled in off Kangchenjunga, the Sherpas retreated to their small bungalows on the backside of town. Some looked for work as rickshaw men, pulling the dwindling number of British tourists along the narrow streets for a few copper annas. Others retreated to their homes, tending smoky fires and looking at their chapbooks, wondering when the sahibs would come again.

They wouldn't have long to wait.

Book Two

It's been more than a week since Daniele Nardi and Tom Ballard were last in touch with the outside world, from 6,300 metres on Nanga Parbat, the ninth-highest mountain in the world.

"I see very little chance for the two climbers to be found alive. Heavy snowfall has significantly increased the avalanche risk, especially on the exposed *Mummery Rib*," says German mountaineering journalist and blogger, Stefan Nestler. "All signs point to the fact that Daniele Nardi and Tom Ballard were caught in an avalanche, and it's rather unlikely that the pair survived given the current conditions on the mountain."

To this very date, the rib has never been fully climbed.

— **Billi Bierling**
outdoorjournal.com
March 3, 2019

Got a message from brother Muhammad Ali Sadpara. The weather is bad at Nanga Parbat. It's windy and snowing with a low visibility. The Mummery spur where search-and-rescue operation is to be undertaken is prone to avalanches.

The team in leadership of Alex Txikon will use drones to search the area around Mummery spur and Kinshofer route. During the last helicopter flight a tent was spotted approximately 500m below the C3 where Daniele Nardi and Tom Ballard were spotted last time.

— **Rao Ahmad**
Skardu, Pakistan
Facebook Post
March 2, 2019, 1:05 p.m.

With great sadness I inform that the search for @NardiDaniele and Tom Ballard is over as @AlexTxikon and the search team have confirmed that the silhouettes spotted on Mummery at about 5900 meters are those of Daniele and Tom. R.I.P. #NangaParbat

— **Stefano Pontecorvo**
Italian Ambassador to Pakistan
Facebook Post
March 9, 2019, 4:56 p.m.

CHAPTER EIGHT

A Knock at the Door

The 1934 tragedy on Nanga Parbat hit Germany like a sledge-hammer.

Grown men fought back tears, while women caught their breaths while reading about the disaster in the morning paper. In Munich, city officials gathered beneath a gigantic swastika to pay tribute to the fallen, while newspaper editors and radio producers crafted stories that transformed the dead climbers into martyrs for the Reich. It didn't matter that most of the mountaineers had been opposed to Hitler. In the lower camps they had even placed their alpine caps on top of wooden poles bearing the new swastika flag—revealing, as it were, their higher allegiance to the mountains over nation—a detail that was cropped out of newspaper and magazine photographs. The official message now was one of national sacrifice. "What these heroes did," read one article, "was only for the honor of Germany." *Deutschland, Deutschland über alles.* Germany, Germany Above All. There was also no question that German climbers would return to Nanga Parbat, both to fight their way to the summit, and to honor the loss of their comrades.

The only question was who—and how.

Upon his return from India, Erwin Schneider, one of the two Austrian climbers who had come the closest to the summit, began to make noises about leading a return expedition to Nanga Parbat. Another name that was bandied about in climbing circles was Hermann Hoerlin, a legendary thirty-one-year-old mountaineer from

Württemberg. In 1930, as a member of the International Himalayan Expedition, Hoerlin had smashed a decades-old record by climbing to the top of Jongsong, a 24,000-foot peak along the borders of Tibet, Nepal, and Sikkim. Two years later, he made the first ascent of Huascarán, the highest peak in Peru. And while only Schneider had expressed interest in leading a return expedition to Nanga Parbat, both men had strong ties to the Alpenverein, the 250,000-strong organization of German and Austrian climbing clubs.

Paul Bauer had other ideas.

He, too, wanted his fellow Germans to succeed on Nanga Parbat. Equally important, he believed that the path to victory was through the leader-driven approach that he had developed in the Alps, the Caucasus, and Kangchenjunga. Only Bauer didn't bother to promote his candidacy as the leader of the next expedition to Nanga Parbat. Given some of the enemies he'd already made in the Alpenverein, that was far too uncertain a proposition. Instead, he set out to take over German mountaineering itself.

In December, 1934, Bauer wrote to Hans von Tschammer und Osten, a silver-haired Dresden patrician and ardent Nazi whom Hitler had appointed as *Reichssportsführer*, thus placing him in charge of all German sports and sporting activities. In his letters, Bauer's first goal was to destroy the competition, real or imagined, for the next Nanga Parbat expedition. After reminding the *Reichssportsführer* of Schneider and Aschenbrenner's desertion of the porters on Nanga Parbat, Bauer added, "It is very dangerous when people of such questionable conduct carry on as heroes; the bad example they set on Nanga Parbat could corrupt the younger generation of mountaineers. I could not bear responsibility for that." To taint Hoerlin, Bauer turned to anti-Semitism. For even though Hoerlin wasn't Jewish, he had taken part in the International Himalaya Expedition whose leader, "the sprig of a Jew Dyhrenfurth," was, according to Nazi racial classifications, half-Jewish.

Bauer sold himself as well. Despite the fact that he had been a Johnny-come-lately to the Nazi movement, and not joined the party itself until 1933, he presented himself as having been a true believer in both Hitler and national socialism for years. "I should say that I have for a long time felt myself to be an old soldier," Bauer wrote to Tschammer und Osten. He added that even when he was a member of the Academic Climbing Club as a student at the University of Munich, that he "consistently pursued a national and National Socialist course."

Bauer's gambit worked. Within a year and a half, Schneider had been found to be "without honor" by a court of inquiry convened by the *Reischssportsführer*, while Hoerlin had been effectively sidelined. And Bauer was well on his way to gaining control of mountaineering in the Third Reich. He had read the tea leaves well. In the old Germany, power had been shared by many different individuals and institutions—the church and the press, businesses and local officials. Not any longer. What counted now was one's connections within the Nazi Party, whose officials alone had the power to make things happen—or not happen—in the new Germany. And in the case of mountaineering, Paul Bauer had become the gatekeeper. Jews, of course, would not be allowed to take part in any mountaineering activities, and the once-independent climbing clubs would soon be put under his control. Any mountaineering expeditions outside of Germany would have to be personally approved by Bauer. Long jealous of the British, and troubled by their recent success on Nanda Devi, he was concerned that his old foes were on the verge of even more stunning achievements. But he was also determined to answer with equal, if not greater, German mountaineering victories.

The first order of business, of course, would be a return to Nanga Parbat.

But there was a snag.

By the middle of the 1930s, large-scale mountaineering was no longer the exclusive domain of the British. The Germans and the Swiss had sent well-organized expeditions to the Himalayas, while the Americans were itching to get in on more of the action. And decades earlier, a globe-hopping Italian nobleman, the Duke of the Abruzzi, had made the first serious attempt on K2, the second-highest mountain on earth. But as the various campaigns on Mount Everest, Kangchenjunga, Nanga Parbat, Kamet, and Nanda Devi had generated worldwide press coverage, other nations became determined to make their mark as well. High-altitude mountaineering was no longer just a matter of conquest. It had also become a bit player in global politics.

In 1933, a Russian climber named Yevgeniy Mikhaylovich Abalakov climbed to the summit of Pik Stalin, a 24,000-foot mountain in the Pamirs that was the highest mountain in the Soviet Union. A year later, an Italian professor made two unsuccessful summit attempts in the Karakoram. During the summer of 1936, the Japanese threw their hat into the ring as well, when an expedition led by a group of university students from Tokyo made the first ascent of Nanda Kot, a stunning 22,000-foot peak located southeast of Nanda Devi. While it was nowhere near an *Achttausender*, it gave the young Japanese climbers their first taste of a Himalayan campaign.

Then there were the French.

By the spring of 1934, French alpinists were determined not only to launch their nation's first large-scale expedition in the Himalayas, but to try, right off the bat, for an *Achttausender*. Not content to merely knock on the door of Himalayan mountaineering, they planned on kicking it off its hinges. An advisory committee was formed and, after long meetings held in a Paris townhouse in a haze of cigarette smoke, a decision was reached. French climbers would attempt to summit Hidden Peak, a 26,470-foot mountain located in the heart of the Karakoram. A broad, triangular-shaped peak with much exposed rock on its ridgelines, the committee had concluded, rather lukewarmly, that the mountain "appeared to offer a fair chance of success."

The timing of the expedition, however, proved to be something of a sticking point. Citing the stress and strain caused on the local villages near the Karakoram, the British authorities turned down the French request to launch their expedition in 1935. But they approved the request for one year later—thus postponing the next-earliest starting date for a German expedition to Nanga Parbat until 1937. *L'Expédition Français Himalaya* was on, then, for 1936. A nation that had consistently produced some of Europe's greatest climbers was now about to try its hand in the world's highest mountain range. At home, expectations accordingly ran high.

Nevertheless, the French Himalayan Expedition had an amateurish cast to it from the beginning. None of the seven climbers had ever been to India. Nor did the French believe in traveling light. For the expedition, they had purchased an eye-popping eight tons of supplies, including seventy-two *fillettes* of champagne, ninety-six bottles of Cointreau, Dubonnet, Médoc, and other aperitifs, and countless tins of foie gras. Indeed, to even get to Hidden Peak, the expedition had to employ, at times, as many as six hundred and seventy porters—and these were in addition to the thirty-six Sherpas and high-altitude porters who had been hired in Darjeeling on their behalf by a representative of the Himalayan Club.

Nonetheless, they pushed on. Base Camp was established in late May, and for three and a half weeks, the climbers and Sherpas carefully moved their way up Hidden Peak, battling rotten rock and treacherous stretches of sheet ice.

Then, in a flash, it was all over.

On June 22, the leading edge of the monsoon moved in, three weeks ahead of schedule. For ten solid days and nights, the higher camps were pounded with snow, stranding the Frenchmen and Sherpas inside their tents. Climbing any higher was impossible. By early July, the climbers and Sherpas were headed down Hidden Peak for good. "The first French Expedition has failed through unlooked-for bad luck," wrote Henry de Ségogne, the well-known Alpinist who directed the campaign. "But luck always turns and we still have the hope that the years to come will reserve for us a happier fate."

Time would tell.

* * *

Paul Bauer, meanwhile, had been grappling with two different kinds of problems.

The first was political. Despite the efforts of Nazi officials to convince the outside world that the Third Reich was a happy, peaceful land, filled with a contented citizenry, reports of Nazi thuggery, murder, and ever more virulent anti-Semitism had begun to appear regularly in newspapers, magazines, and books in Great Britain, the United States, and around the world. Even worse, in Bauer's eyes, such reporting threatened to undermine the long and cordial relations between British and German mountaineers. For in spite of the fact that there were plenty of well-connected Englishmen and Englishwomen—ranging from the Mitfords to Audrey Hepburn's father—who admired Hitler and the Nazis, many others were growing increasingly troubled by conditions in Germany. In practical terms, Bauer needed the support of the Alpine Club and British government officials, both in London and in India, in order to maintain German mountaineering operations in the Himalayas. Nazi violence had the potential to unravel that support.

His solution was organizational.

Instead of having official requests for German mountaineering expeditions in the Himalayas come through the office of the *Reichssportsführer*, or any official government body, Bauer instead created a front organization. Announcing its creation on May 15, 1934, the Deutsche Himalaya Foundation would in the future oversee all German mountaineering activities, with Bauer as its director. Rather than have it based in Berlin, the Nazi capital, the foundation's headquarters would instead be located in Munich, the traditional home of German alpinism. No swastikas would appear on its letterhead. And Bauer would never close a missive to a British citizen with his standard "Heil Hitler!"

The Deutsche Himalaya Foundation was Bauer's masterstroke. Not only did it help to solidify his now near-total control over mountaineering in the Third Reich, but it sent a reassuring—if false—message to the British. *We aren't Nazis or Storm Troopers. We are entirely separate from that. We are simply German mountaineers, heirs to a proud tradition, who simply want to help keep our climbing alive in such difficult times.* It was an ingenious plan.

And it worked.

Bauer's other challenge was equally worrisome. In order for the Germans to launch a strong expedition to Nanga Parbat in 1937, one with a good chance of success, he would need to stock it with a core group of highly accomplished mountaineers. And that was no small task. The loss of four veteran climbers on Nanga Parbat in 1934 had been a huge blow to German mountaineering. But Bauer himself had cut down the pool of potential climbers even further. He'd alienated a large number of mountaineers through his roughshod treatment of the local alpine clubs. Moreover, he'd also blackballed a number of experienced Himalayan climbers, like Schneider and Hoerlin, whom he undoubtedly—and also, probably, correctly—surmised would challenge his authority. The truth was, Bauer needed some new talent.

To redress this shortcoming, Bauer used the summer of 1936 to introduce a handpicked group of German climbers to the realities of Himalayan mountaineering. Their goal was Siniolchum, a magnificent unclimbed peak located less than ten miles east of Kangchenjunga in Sikkim. Though well shy of being an *Achttausender*, the 22,000-foot mountain was both exceptionally beautiful and challenging. Deeply fluted spurs, as fine as if they had been carved by a sculptor's knife, shot up toward an almost impossibly steep summit. Danger, in the form of hanging ice falls, active avalanche chutes, and untrustworthy rock, was everywhere. Siniolchum was to be a Himalayan boot camp for the German team.

Again, Bauer showed himself to be a master problem solver. Not only did the expedition members gain firsthand experience with Himalayan conditions, but a Nazi flag, tied to an ice axe, was proudly hoisted from the previously unclimbed summit of Siniolchum. Equally important, Bauer had found in Karl Wien—a crack Munich alpinist and son of a Nobel Prize–winning physicist—a leader for the next year's assault on Nanga Parbat. And while Paul Bauer might have basked in the triumph of Siniolchum, he instead got right back to work. For by the time the climbers returned to Munich, the leaves on the oaks and elms in the Englischer Garten had turned, while the cafés along the Tal and Neuhauser Strasse had packed up their folding tables and chairs and brought them inside. Already, there was a chill in the air.

The old Munich was also gone.

While waitresses in dirndls still served massive joints of Schweine-braten at the Augustiner, the city that had once charmed visitors as different as Mark Twain and Wassily Kandinsky was no more. It had been swept away by a tidal wave of hate-filled speeches and military parades, poison-pen editorials and spit-shined jackboots. It had gone up in smoke and kerosene, in piles of books set ablaze on ancient cobblestone streets, or with the click of a revolver behind a locked jailhouse door. And it had simply vanished, with a pink slip set upon one's desk, the neighbor who no longer said hello, or a knock upon the door in the middle of the night.

Near the Karolinenplatz, armed guards now stood around the clock, three hundred and sixty-five days a year, at the newly built Temples of Honor, two open-air memorials that held the remains of sixteen early Nazi martyrs. Citizens who failed to raise their arm in the Heil Hitler salute when passing by could be fined, arrested, or worse. Nearby, in the Maxvorstadt district, Nazi Party officials had taken over more than five dozen homes and buildings, turning the once-genteel neighborhood into the organizational center of national socialism. And a ten-minute stroll to the south, the synagogue on Herzog-Max-Strasse had been bulldozed by Munich city officials in early June 1938. It was said to have offended the sight of the *Führer*, who liked to hold post-opera gatherings at a fashionable restaurant next door.

There were other changes as well.

The concert repertoires for the Munich Philharmonic and the State

The World Beneath Their Feet

Theater were scrubbed to remove non-German composers. Catholic organizations and the Boy Scouts were banned, while young adults of approved racial stock were encouraged to procreate and help grow the German race. Brides-to-be could apply for special "Marriage Loans" at local department stores, and couples who tied the knot were presented with their very own copy of *Mein Kampf*. And all across town, in shop windows and in beauty parlors, on the glass doors of telephone booths and in restaurant widows, a wave of new signs had suddenly blossomed. *Juden Zutritt verboten!*—"Jews are forbidden access"—announced a metal plaque attached to the door to the library of the German Museum. So popular was a placard reading *Juden unerwünscht!*—"Jews Unwanted"—that a stationery manufacturer on Bayerstrasse offered a hanging version, complete with a black swastika, white lettering, and a braided cord, for only sixty pfennigs.

For Jewish families, the nightmare had become all too real. Going out at night became a thing of the past, while more and more bread-earners found themselves out of a job or unable to work. Despite the fact that Jews had lived in Munich for more than seven hundred years, many began to think of emigration. At Jewish schools, students would sometime play *Das Aliyah-Spiel*, a popular board game where players rolled the dice to move markers along a pathway that led from Germany to Palestine. For those who could, it was time to leave. For everyone else, the window was rapidly closing.

Peter Misch knew this better than most. A brilliant, Berlin-born geologist, Misch had been a member of the scientific team attached to the 1934 expedition to Nanga Parbat. "There are few places in the world where the earth's crust is open to a greater depth," wrote one of his colleagues, "and where it lies more freely exposed than in the Himalaya." An experienced and talented climber, Misch collected rock samples from high up on the mountain. And when the deadly blizzard trapped the summit team near the *Silbersattel*, he took an active part in the unsuccessful rescue efforts. Misch's work on Nanga Parbat was nothing short of exemplary.

His return to Germany was a rude awakening. Nazi officials demanded that Misch, who was Jewish, turn over all of his samples and field notes to an "approved scientist"—which he refused to do. But Misch could also read the writing on the wall. Not only were Jewish professors being fired from their jobs at universities across Germany, but anti-Semitism had crawled out of the gutter and had become an increasingly menacing feature of day-to-day life. A law was passed that forbade Jews from flying the national flag, while gangs of Storm Troopers began to rough up Jews on city streets and sidewalks. "When Jewish blood spurts from the knife," ran one Nazi chant, "things go twice as well."

Getting out of the Third Reich was by no means easy. Not only were there steep costs and dire financial consequences, but refugees also had to find a country willing to accept them. Still, in 1935 Misch found a job as professor of structural geology at Sun Yat-sen University in Canton, China. The next year, he slipped out of Germany with his wife, Susanne, and their two-year-old daughter, Hanna. In their luggage were Misch's notebooks and rock samples from Nanga Parbat.

There was, however, one other reverberation from the 1934 Nanga Parbat expedition. And, like the Peter Misch story, it was not fully reported in German newspapers at the time. It began, in Munich, with the ringing of a doorbell.

Sharp-witted but nearsighted, Willi Schmid worked as a music critic for the *Münchner Neueste Nachrichten*, the largest newspaper in Bavaria. Easily recognizable with his bald head and his steel-rimmed eyeglasses, he could often be found backstage at the Odeon or the National Theater, chatting up conductors and soloists. A master musician himself, and a sometime member of the Munich Viol Quintet, Schmid also sang baritone in the choir of the Frauenkirche, the city's distinctive, onion-domed cathedral. Bookish and pasty-faced, he looked the part of a scholar of early classical music, which he was as well. What was less obvious was that Schmid was also a decorated war veteran. Nearly killed by machine-gun fire in the Somme, bits of shrapnel kept painfully working their way to the surface of his stomach more than a half decade later.

Deeply Catholic, Schmid had two great loves. The first was his family—his pretty, flamboyant, and resourceful wife, Kate, and their three young children, daughters Duscha and Hedi, and a son, Thomi. The second was the cello. Willi Schmid practiced Bach's cello suites daily, the notes echoing across the wooden floors of the family's spacious apartment at Schackstrasse 3/III, between the Victory Gate and the city's famous Englischer Garten. But feeding a family of five, along with an ailing mother-in-law and Kate's sister, was difficult on a music critic's salary. So when Schmid was approached by Willy Merkl to see if he would, for hire, manage publicity for the 1934 Nanga Parbat Expedition, he leapt at the opportunity. Turning the back room of the family apartment into a mountaineering public relations office, all through the late spring and summer of 1934, Schmid—with Kate's help—kept German, Austrian, and the world's newspapers well supplied with press releases, stories, and photographs from the expedition, while carefully charting the progress of the climbers up the mountain. By late June 1934, both Willy and Kate held their breaths. For Merkl had by then launched the expedition's assault on the summit.

In Munich, of course, summer was by then in full blossom, with windows thrown open and the linden trees in bloom. Late on the afternoon of June 30, Willi was practicing one of the Bach cello suites while Kate was overseeing final preparation for dinner, which would include a strawberry tart, freshly baked by Anni, the family cook, that the two older children had been eyeing all afternoon. Duscha, the nine-year-old, was reading in her room with the door closed when the doorbell rang. "I did hear Anni going to answer it," Duscha later wrote. "Then I vaguely heard voices and heard Anni going to announce whoever it was to my father."

The visitors were three uniformed SS officers, accompanied by one man in civilian clothes. They had come for Willi. "No warrant for arrest was shown, nor did the arresting men present any identification," Kate Schmid wrote. "When I offered to give my husband his identity papers to take along, I was threatened with a revolver." Inside her room, Duscha heard her father ask if he could get his hat before the men took him away. "That was the last time," she recalled, "that I heard his voice." Schmid was taken to Dachau. Later that night he was shot in a detention room.

Willi Schmid was not alone. Some ninety other individuals across Germany were murdered that warm summer evening, and over the course of the next couple of days, in what would be later called the Night of the Long Knives. Most were snatched from their homes and then killed in jail cells or at police stations—most but not all. Kurt von Schleicher, a former German chancellor, and his wife Elisabeth were gunned down in their home in Berlin, while an ex-president of Bavaria was found hacked to death outside of Munich. Many were beaten before they were shot, while a few were given the opportunity to shoot themselves. The majority of the victims were part of the leadership of the SA, or *Sturmabteilung*, the brown-shirted thugs that had unleashed the first wave of Nazi terror on the streets of German cities and towns. But Hitler had grown worried that the SA might challenge his complete control of the Reich. And with help from Hermann Göring and Heinrich Himmler, two of his most trusted lieutenants, he unleashed a bloodbath to eliminate his rivals.

But why had Willi Schmid been killed?

Why had a mild-mannered music critic and mountaineering expedition publicist been murdered during the Night of the Long Knives? The answer appears to have been a case of mistaken identity. There had also been another Wilhelm Schmid, a prominent SA leader who had been elected to the Reichstag. Even though he, too, was murdered that night, many believed at the time that Willi had been mistaken for him. And while Nazi officials called Willi's death "an accident," nothing was the same anymore. After the Night of the Long Knives, it was clear that no one in Germany, including the nation's mountain climbers, was truly safe anymore.

The World Beneath Their Feet

*   *   *

Hermann Hoerlin was one of the most talented mountaineers in Germany. But with the rise of Paul Bauer, he knew that there was no longer any room for a voice like his. Hoerlin had resigned from the board of the Alpenverein, and while at age thirty-five he was easily still fit enough to join another Himalayan campaign, he wasn't expecting any invitations. For one thing, he had been close friends with Erwin Schneider, who had been condemned for his actions on Nanga Parbat in 1934. But he soon had another problem as well. For even though Hoerlin wasn't Jewish, the woman he had fallen in love with was. She was Willi Schmid's widow.

Katie Tietz Schmid had a magnetic effect on men. The illegitimate daughter of a Prussian aristocrat and a Jewish homemaker, she had been raised in a well-to-do, assimilated Jewish household in Schwerin, a lakeside town in northern Germany. A dark-haired beauty, with deep brown hair and eyes to match, she was also intelligent, strong-willed, colorful, and a lot of fun. At age nineteen, Kate's life took a sudden and dramatic turn. Accompanying a friend on a visit to a hospital in 1918, she was deeply struck by a wounded infantry officer that she met there, a twenty-five-year old Bavarian named Willi Schmid. One meeting led to another and another, as well as a flurry of letters, and Kate and Willi fell in love. Married soon thereafter, the couple settled in Munich. Children followed, and while they never had enough money, they nonetheless flourished. Music, theater, and the opera were a regular feature of their lives, while Kate's charming personality helped widen their circle of friends, especially in the world of music and books, including the likes of Pablo Casals and Oswald Spengler. Engaged and outgoing, they were living life as fully as they could on Willi's less-than-plentiful salary as a budding music critic.

June 30, 1934, ended all that.

When Willi Schmid was murdered by the SS, Kate's world should have shattered. Instead, she revealed a spine made of steel. Ignoring the growing dread with which the Nazi leadership was now regarded, she boldly pressed her case that the government of the Third Reich owed her and her children a pension for Willi's death. Rudolph Hess, Hitler's fearsome deputy, even made an unprecedented personal visit to the family apartment and all but apologized for the murder. Still, Kate pressed on. Traveling to Berlin, she eventually bedazzled the *Führer*'s personal adjutant, Fritz Wiedemann, who kept a photo of Kate in his wallet. Her persistence, and Wiedemann's help, paid off. Kate was granted the pension.

After her husband's murder, Kate had gamely carried on the work of publicizing the 1934 expedition to Nanga Parbat. But as the tragedy unfolded on the mountain, the Alpenverein asked Hermann Hoerlin to assist Kate, which he did. And, over time, they, too, fell in love—the blond, blue-eyed mountain climber and the petite, half-Jewish widow. But by 1937, their future was very much in doubt. Hoerlin had already concluded that they would have to leave Germany. It was simply too dangerous to remain. And to that end, he had already begun the process of securing a job with AGFA, the German film manufacturer, at their overseas plant in Binghamton, New York. The only way that Kate and her children could accompany him, however, was if Kate and Hermann were married. But since Kate was classified as being a *Mischling*, or half-Jew, under Nazi racial law, the marriage would have to be approved by the government, something which Nazi officials were increasingly reluctant to do. Once again, though, Kate's charm, determination, and connections won the day. On July 12, 1938, Kate Schmid and Hermann Hoerlin were married in a brief civil ceremony in Berlin.

Less than one month later, in the port city of Bremen, the newly-weds, Kate's three children, and a maid walked up the gangway of the SS *Columbus*, a refurbished ocean liner that had once been the pride of the Norddeutscher Lloyd steamship lines. In order to help prepare them for their new lives, the oldest daughter had read *The Adventures of Tom Sawyer*, while all three children had seen Mickey Mouse cartoons at a movie theater. Then the all-ashore horn blew, the lines were cast off, and the last of Germany slipped by the gunwales. They arrived in New York harbor on August 9, the late-summer sunshine glinting off the golden torch clasped in the right hand of the Statue of Liberty.

CHAPTER NINE

Murder Mountain

The Germans returned to Nanga Parbat in 1937.

Led by Karl Wien, the thirty-year-old mountaineer handpicked by Paul Bauer, the core group of seven climbers for the 1937 Nanga Parbat Expedition included two veterans of Siniolchum, four members of the Academic Climbing Club at the University of Munich, and one survivor of the tragic 1934 expedition. The Sherpas who had been recruited in Darjeeling were also able and experienced. Several had been to the high camps on Everest. Others had been with the French on Hidden Peak or the Japanese on Nanda Kot, while a few had even survived the 1934 disaster. Everyone knew what had to be done. It was time to climb to the top of Nanga Parbat and avenge the deaths that had occurred three years earlier.

Launching their assault from Base Camp in late May, the climbers repeatedly ran into one patch of bad weather after another, including rain, snow, hail, fog, and angry peals of thunder. So alarming was some of the weather that one climber at Camp One wrote, "From the porters' tent we could hear the chanting of Nepalese prayers for a long time." Near-daily accumulations of new powder snow obliterated their tracks from the day before, making it extremely difficult to navigate the jumbled terrain of the first icefalls. Avalanches roared down from above as well, as precarious seracs busted loose and came racing down the mountain.

One avalanche even made it all the way down to Camp Two. On

The World Beneath Their Feet

May 26, a group of climbers and Sherpas heard a loud crash and then looked up as an enormous cloud of snow came hurtling down upon them. "With one mighty sweep, men, tents, and loads were hurled to the ground," climber Günther Hepp later wrote in his diary. "I fell on top of two coolies and grasped their feet; my anorak was drawn over my head and for a half a minute I was unable to get my breath. I was forced to the ground as if by an icy fist." The avalanche had arrived with shocking speed.

Afterwards, nervous laughter broke out among both the climbers and the porters. "The Sherpas rubbed the snow from their hair, straightened their clothes and said: 'No good, Sahib!'" Hepp added. "The Baltis too joined in the grim humour and we all stood there, thirty men, and laughed." But on the inside, there was considerably less bravado. Two nights earlier, a holy man had suddenly appeared at Base Camp, having walked many miles with an urgent message. "We below had a visit from the Mohammedan village priest from Tato," wrote Ulricht Luft, one of the scientists attached to the expedition, "who described to us the devil who dwells upon the summit of Nanga Parbat; apparently he can call forth the storm wind simply by flapping his huge ears." In the local villages, others claimed that naked white women near the summit had lured the 1934 climbers and Sherpas to their deaths. The holy man wanted to continue further up the mountain, to warn the others. But when he was told that this wasn't possible, Luft wrote, he "said he would do what he could by prayer to influence him in our favor."

Despite the weather, and at a snail's pace, the expedition pressed its way up the mountain, establishing camps, stocking them with food and supplies, and moving the summit assault team higher and higher up the mountain. By the beginning of the second week of June, Camp Four, at 20,280 feet, had been set up and fully occupied, while the supplies for the next two camps had been laid out. Following the route taken by the 1934 expedition, the climbers were now working their way up Rakhiot Peak, after which they would traverse the long ridge which led toward the *Silbersattel* and the summit.

Finally, on Monday, June 14, the lousy weather lifted.

The morning had dawned raw and bitter, while brief but thick flurries again obliterated the tracks upward toward Camp Five. But in the afternoon, the sun finally broke through the clouds. "For the first time we could lie out warm in the sun," climber Martin Pfeffer wrote in his diary. "Morale grew high as the weather appeared to be improving at last and tomorrow Camp Five should be in order. Then the assault will progress and perhaps on Hartmann's birthday, June 22, the top itself will be conquered." Pfeffer and Hepp remained outside the longest, taking in the incredible view of the mountain ranges to the north, while the others climbed inside their tents. "I am indeed lucky," Pfeffer added, "to have seen all these glories."

Even though the wind began to kick up again that evening, rattling the sides of their tents, spirits remained high. With luck, they were a little more than a week away from the summit. Later that night, before turning in, Hartmann, Pfeffer, and Wien all made entries in their diaries.

Four days later, on the morning of July 18, Ulrich Luft, the physician and research physiologist attached to the expedition, made his way up from Camp Two accompanied by a half-dozen Balti porters. The weather was beautiful, and Luft was eager to reach the climbers at Camp Four. Not only was he anxious to see how the assault was progressing, but in his rucksack he was carrying a fresh load of mail—letters and postcards from loved ones back home in Germany—which had been forwarded by the British authorities at Astor village. By the time they reached Camp Three, however, the Baltis were complaining of headaches. So the doctor suggested that they take a break and make tea, while he moved on ahead toward Camps Four or Five, wherever his comrades might be. The porters could catch up later.

Pushing ahead alone, Luft crossed the smooth, snowy slopes that led toward Rakhiot Peak. "Breathing heavily I plodded upwards, expecting in a quarter of an hour to be able to hand my friends their eagerly awaited letters," he later wrote. But something wasn't right.

"An oppressive stillness reigned," Luft added. "An almost obliterated trail stretched away toward the ridge in the east as if into eternity." Then it hit him. There was no Camp Four. "With merciless force the truth dawned on me. Where I was standing an avalanche of terrific proportions had covered a surface of nearly fifteen acres with gigantic ice-blocks. There was not a single trace of the camp. It lay buried beneath thousands of cubic feet of ice."

The enormity of it all soon sank in. This wasn't just an avalanche trail. It was also a graveyard. Trapped in the ice and snow below were the corpses of sixteen men. When the Baltis arrived, they found a handful of tins and a couple of empty rucksacks farther down the mountain, confirming their worst fears. But armed with only ice axes, there was nothing else they could do. "The Silver Saddle glistened in the sun high above me," but, Luft added, "the team was no more." Together, he and the Baltis started to make their way down the mountain, trying to figure out what to do next.

Paul Bauer was in Munich when he heard the news.

"I was sitting in my office about noon on Sunday the 20th of June when I received a call on the telephone," he later recalled. "There was a journalist on the other end. Among the mass of indifferent agency communications he had come across one with the terrible news that seven climbers and nine porters had been killed on Nanga Parbat by an avalanche. It seemed so incredible that I could not believe it." Surpassing the 1934 tragedy, this new disaster was now the worst in the history of mountaineering. Five days later, a dispatch from Luft at Base Camp confirmed the news. Luft and one other scientist were the only German survivors of the expedition. By then, Bauer was already on his way to India.

Along with six porters and two other climbers, Bauer finally arrived at the site of Camp Four on July 13, nearly a month after the disaster. It did not take long to figure out what had happened. During the night of June 14/15, a huge serac had broken off of an ice terrace about a quarter mile above the camp, sending a mass of snow and blocks of ice, some as big as houses, hurtling down the mountain. Under normal conditions, the avalanche would have petered out maybe five hundred feet or so from the camp, along a long, level patch of terrain. But owing to both the extremely low temperatures and the thick top layer of powder snow, the mass of avalanche-borne ice and snow traveled even farther, coming to a rest and completely burying Camp Four, which now lay under tons of now compacted ice and snow, as dense as concrete. What under normal conditions was a good location for the camp became, under unusual ones, a death trap.

Finding the bodies was no easy task. Using nine-foot-long steel sounding rods, and digging slit trenches through the probable site of the camp, for three days they came up empty. Then on July 19, Dr. Luft uncovered an ice axe belonging to one of the porters. Two hours later they found the first body, that of a Sherpa. "A blanket, a woolen cap, and then the face of a porter was disclosed," Bauer wrote. "As far as they could tell from the curls and the rigid features, it was Pasang." But in accordance with Sherpa traditions, the remains were left where they fell, and no more efforts were made to recover the corpses of the other Sherpas.

After that, it did not take long to begin to find the bodies of the Germans. "Martin Pfeffer was the first to be extricated," Bauer wrote. "He lay peacefully at rest in his sleeping-sack, warmly clad in thick socks and breeches and a woolen vest; with his leather helmet on his head he looked like a medieval knight. His hands and face were composed, showing no signs of sudden fright. Next to him lay Hartmann, likewise peacefully sleeping." The wristwatches that the dead climbers wore had all stopped a few minutes after twelve. Hartmann's read 12:20.

Try as they might, Bauer and the other could only find the bodies of five of their countrymen, which, as the weather started to turn, they buried together in a common grave. "The Rakhiot Valley had filled with heavy clouds and snowflakes were fluttering in the air as Wien and Fankhauser were lowered into the grave," Bauer wrote. "Snow and ice were heaped upon them and two crossed ice axes and a rope marked our friends' last resting place. On a house-high ice-block at the head of the grave flew the German flag, the avalanche probes from the workshop of the British airmen in Lahore serving as a flag-mast. Luft and Bauer were the last to leave, and lightning whipped across the sky and thunder cracked as they descended. "It looked as if we should have to make a hurried retreat before an approaching storm." It was over.

Only it wasn't. Because Nanga Parbat now had the Germans even more tightly in her deadly embrace. The climbers had a new name for the peak—Murder Mountain. But they also knew that they would be back. National pride, now even stronger under the Nazis, demanded that German mountaineers return to Nanga Parbat, to climb it once and for all, and to do so soon. Paul Bauer knew this more than anyone else. But something else happened as well. On the way down the mountain, Hans Hartmann's watch, which Bauer had placed in his pocket, started ticking again.

Paul Bauer was no longer, however, the only Nazi official interested in the Himalayas. There had been some loose talk, among a handful of military planners, about the strategic value of Tibet—especially should war break out between the Reich and Great Britain. Tibet, ran the premise, was a place where a series of backdoor military actions could be launched against British India, draining troops and supplies that would otherwise be sent elsewhere. Others, in the Luftwaffe, also wondered whether German mountaineering expeditions in the Himalayas might provide opportunities for testing long-range, high-altitude aircraft.

But Heinrich Himmler had a whole other order of interest.

Now the head of the SS, the *Schutzstaffel* or "Protection Squadron"—the feared, black-uniformed Nazi paramilitary, security, and police division—Himmler had been a sickly and awkward agronomy student at a technical college in Munich in 1922. The next year, however, he joined the Nazi Party and rose quickly within the ranks. Appointed *Reichsführer* of the SS in 1929, he transformed it from a small, unimportant arm of the national socialist movement, one that was far overshadowed by the Storm Troopers, into one of the most powerful institutions in the Third Reich. One of Hitler's most trusted advisers, Himmler had helped to create both the Gestapo and the concentration camp at Dachau, and had been one of the architects of the Night of the Long Knives.

He was also a devotee of mysticism and the occult. Abandoning the Catholicism of his youth, Himmler had bought into a wide range of supernatural and pagan beliefs. He believed that the earth had once been populated by giants, and that the German people were the descendants of a blond-haired, blue-eyed super race known as the Aryans, who had originated in the icy lands of northernmost Europe—directly, some said, from the heavens. Himmler incorporated pagan symbolism into SS symbols and ceremonies and, aided by a compliant corps of pro-Nazi professors now teaching at German universities, he supported all manner of archaeological expeditions to uncover the supposed prehistory of the German *Volk*. Under his guidance, Nazi researchers made plaster of Paris casts of ancient rock inscriptions in Norway and Sweden, and planned archeological expeditions to Iceland, Finland, France, Greece, Libya, Iraq, and even South America. Himmler later gave Hitler a third-century iron spearhead covered with runes that had been stolen from a Warsaw museum.

But it was Asia that occupied a special place in the SS *Reichsführer's* pseudo-historical beliefs. Himmler often carried a copy of the *Bhagavad Gita* with him. He also believed that the caste system in India had been started by members of the Aryan race, and that the Buddha himself was of Aryan descent. More importantly, Himmler was convinced that there were still pockets of people with Aryan blood who could be found in the Himalayas. And when he read about a headstrong German explorer and scientist who had recently penetrated the remote highlands along the Tibetan–Chinese border, the *Reichsführer* of the SS believed that he had found the perfect candidate to lead an expedition to Tibet.

The World Beneath Their Feet

Twenty-seven-year-old Ernst Schäfer was both a crack shot and a university-trained zoologist. Teaming up with a wealthy American adventurer named Brooke Dolan II, a Main Line Philadelphian who sat on the board of the Academy of Natural Sciences, Schäfer had previously collected the carcasses of thousands of Tibetan birds and mammals, including some that were previously unknown in the West. Summoning the young zoologist in the fall of 1935 to his office in a Baroque palace on Prinz-Albrecht-Strasse in Berlin, Himmler likely quizzed Schäfer on his work, particularly any conclusions he may have reached regarding the Tibetan people. Schäfer had already informed others that he had been deeply struck by some of the Tibetans he had come across in remote areas, including those with "pure Aryan characteristics, strong hook noses, red-black hair, and almost gray-blue eyes." If he told this to Himmler, which he probably did, it was music to the *Reichsführer*'s ears. In the wake of the meeting, Schäfer's life took a dramatic turn. No longer was he a struggling graduate student who still needed to finish writing his doctoral dissertation. He was now the leader of an SS-sanctioned expedition to Tibet.

Some things, however, needed to be ironed out first. As much as he was grateful for Himmler's assistance, Schäfer was dubious of the so-called science that was being touted by some of Himmler's professors, and he immediately began to lobby to pick his own team. He also had some rather grand ideas about how much funding the expedition would require, and when Himmler balked at the proposed budget, the young scientist and adventurer, remarkably enough, was able to broker a compromise with the most-feared man in the Third Reich. Schäfer could pick his team, but they would all need to be members of the SS, while the funding would have to be secured from the outside. Neither proved to be much of an issue. Even Brooke Dolan sent along a check for four thousand American dollars.

But there was one problem that was not quite so easily dispatched. Because Germany had recently signed a defense pact with Japan, whose soldiers had already launched military actions in Manchuria and Shanghai, access to Tibet through China was now out of the question. The expedition would instead have to go through India. But there were significant difficulties here as well. The British Foreign Office, alarmed over the rise of Nazi militarism and Hitler's denunciation of the Treaty of Versailles, was in no mood to facilitate access to Tibet to a German expedition with a suspect scientific and political agenda. Traveling to London in order to obtain permission to enter Tibet through India, Schäfer's entreaties to the Foreign Office fell on deaf ears. The authorities in Lhasa, he was bluntly informed, were unlikely to allow the expedition to enter Tibet.

But Schäfer wasn't easily turned aside. In London he reached out to members of the so-called Cliveden Set, a loose coterie of English aristocrats widely felt to be pro-German. Led by Lady Astor, the American-born daughter of a Virginia tobacco auctioneer who had married into the British gentry, some of its members were merely pro-peace, while others were out-and-out admirers of Hitler. While in England, Schäfer also received the support of Sir Francis Younghusband, the legendary seventy-year-old former British Army officer and player in the Great Game who had led a military expedition to Lhasa some thirty-five years earlier. Younghusband, no fan of bureaucratic intrigue, also had some words of advice for the young German explorer. "Sneak over the border," he told Schäfer. "That's what I should do—sneak over the border. Then find a way around the regulations."

The DEUTSCHE TIBET EXPEDITION ERNST SCHÄFER, as its letterhead boldly proclaimed, departed Berlin on April 19, 1938. In addition to Schäfer, its four other members included a geophysicist who specialized in the study of the earth's core, an entomologist, and a logistics and transport officer. But the rising star of the group was Bruno Beger, a twenty-six-year-old anthropologist from Heidelberg. Tall, blond-haired, and blue-eyed, Beger not only looked like he walked out of a Nazi racial identification chart, but he enthusiastically subscribed to many of the racial theories so dear to Heinrich Himmler.

Yet despite its name, the Deutsche Tibet Expedition still lacked permission to enter Tibet, even as the members of the expedition boarded an India-bound steamer in Genoa.

Behind the scenes, however, wheels were turning.

After a story ran in a Berlin newspaper that the expedition was really an SS operation, Schäfer was deluged with negative press as soon as his party landed in India, and he angrily complained to the authorities in Berlin. In response, Himmler reached out to Sir Barry Domville, a former British naval intelligence officer and prominent pro-Nazi sympathizer, threatening reprisals if Schäfer and the others were treated as spies. Domville passed this information on to Prime Minister Neville Chamberlain, who at the time was keen on reducing tensions between Great Britain and Germany. Soon thereafter, Schäfer learned in Calcutta that his group had been granted permission to enter Sikkim, the diminutive Indian kingdom that was wedged between Nepal and Bhutan. It wasn't Tibet, which it also bordered, but it was a start. Schäfer graciously accepted the offer and, accompanied by the other four, set out from Darjeeling in June.

In Sikkim, the members of the expedition quickly got to work. Schäfer spent much of his time hunting in the Himalayan foothills, and eventually succeeded in bagging three *shapi*, exceedingly rare, dark-coated mountain goats, a kind then unknown to Western science. Beger, meanwhile, dove into his anthropometric research, using a steel measuring tape and a pair of giant calipers to gauge the length of skulls and lips and noses, shinbones and hips and feet of the startled but curious local Sikkimese. He also made face masks, a laborious process that involved applying a paste of crushed gypsum mixed with water to one's face, inserting two paper straws in the nose to allow the subject to breathe. The mixture then had to dry, and, very carefully, the hardened cast had to be pulled off. Yet, while the members of the expedition met with some Tibetans living in Sikkim, their ultimate destination still eluded them

In late July, Schäfer and his countrymen caught a break. Near the Tibet–Sikkim border, they met, by chance, a representative of a Tibetan village lord and, after an exchange of gifts, they were invited to visit the village itself. Slipping across the border into Tibet, Schäfer eventually then managed to wrangle permission, from the Tibetan authorities themselves, to visit Lhasa. And while the chief British diplomat in the Tibetan capital city was outraged, there was not much that he could do about it.

By the time they left Lhasa, the members of the Deutsche Tibet Expedition had accomplished some, but far from all, of what they had hoped to do. Just making it to Tibet was, on its own, a genuine achievement. And while they had not been able to conduct as much research as they had planned, among their newly acquired treasures on the way back home to the Reich were Beger's face masks, the skin and bones of an unknown mammal, and a set of Tibetan holy books.

There was one artifact, however, of particular interest. Nine and a half inches tall, but weighing more than twenty-three pounds, it was a statue of the Buddhist god Vaiśravaṇa, the guardian of the north. Thought to have been carved in the eleventh century, it was made from a single piece of a meteorite that fell to Earth some ten to twenty thousand years earlier. This wasn't just a statue. It was a statue from outer space. And carved right onto Vaiśravaṇa's breast plate on the statue was a familiar symbol. It was a swastika.

For Paul Bauer, none of this mattered.

What did matter was that the Germans return to Nanga Parbat. "Could we abandon the men who lay on the Silver Saddle and give up Nanga Parbat?" he asked. Luckily, for Bauer there would be no political problems with the British, and a new German climbing expedition to Nanga Parbat would be approved without delay. For Bauer's smoke and mirrors with the Deutsche Himalaya Foundation had worked. It represented German *mountaineers*, not German politics— or at least that seemed to be the case. At the Alpine Club in London, where Bauer himself had been made a member, the deaths on Nanga Parbat had been genuinely mourned. In November 1937, the *Alpine*

Journal ran an obituary of Karl Wien that had been written by Bauer. At the end of it, the editor added, "We would again associate the Club, *Journal*, and all British climbers with our member's tribute to a very great mountaineer and charming personality."

This time, Bauer himself would lead the expedition. Now forty-one years old, his plan had been to develop a core of talented younger climbers to carry the swastika to the roof of the world. But the twin disasters of 1934 and 1937 had cost the Reich eleven of its most experienced mountaineers, and Bauer felt that he needed to step in. Calling on the assistance of Fritz Bechtold and Ulricht Luft, both of whom were survivors of earlier Nanga Parbat expeditions, Bauer then put together a team of five younger mountaineers, whose enthusiasm helped to counterbalance some of the gaps in their experience. The expedition would also be assisted by a modified Junkers Ju 52 transport plane—the same model that the *Führer* himself traveled in—that would airdrop supplies to the climbers on the mountain. Finding experienced Sherpas to join the expedition, on the other hand, proved to be difficult. "There was much talk in Darjeeling about evil spirits and devils on Nanga Parbat," Bauer wrote, "and none of the surviving Sherpa porters were willing to go again." Arriving in Base Camp by June 1, the German climbers planned to follow the route taken by previous expeditions up the Rakhiot face.

In the end, the 1938 Nanga Parbat Expedition did not get very far. Hampered by illness, poor weather, and the arrival of the monsoon, Bauer called off the campaign even before the lead climbers reached the *Silbersattel*. It was a bitter pill to swallow. Nanga Parbat had defeated the Germans once more. But this time, as it turned out, there was a silver lining.

On the way back to Karachi, where they would catch the ship that would carry them home to Germany, Bauer and the other climbers were flown above Nanga Parbat in the modified Junkers airplane. Flying less than a thousand feet over the *Silbersattel*, they could easily pick out Camps Four and Five, now abandoned, and the long ridge leading to the summit. But what caught Bauer's eye were the rocky ribs and glaciers of the mountain's Diamir side. As he scanned this relatively unexplored face of Nanga Parbat, a new thought began to take shape. "When the rocks are free of snow a rapid and bold ascent to the summit ridge might succeed," he later wrote. "A new route will bring new surprises, fresh experience, and greater knowledge." And, he might have added, a victory for the Reich.

Paul Bauer returned to Munich in August 1938.

While he was disappointed that his expedition had not reached the summit of Nanga Parbat, he was proud of the fact that no lives had been lost. Still, there was little time to waste. There was no question that German mountaineers would return to Nanga Parbat in 1939. It was now a matter of national honor. What was less certain was who the climbers would be, and what route they would take. As it turned out, some new names had arisen while Bauer had been in India. And unlike Hermann Hoerlin and other politically dubious climbers, their allegiance to the Reich was unquestioned. One could never be too careful.

Soon, however, there would be other things to think about.

The first would arrive that September, when the eyes of the world were suddenly turned toward Munich. The second would come in November. It would begin with the sound of breaking glass.

CHAPTER TEN

Triumph — and Trouble

The applause was deafening.

For nearly an hour, Eric Shipton had held his audience spellbound. No longer were his listeners sitting inside the drafty assembly hall of the Royal Geographical Society on a drizzly London evening in February 1935. Instead, they were fighting their way up the Rishi Ganga, inching along treacherous ice-draped ledges, climbing thousand-foot rock walls, and, finally, feeling the soft grass of the Sanctuary beneath their feet. And no longer was Shipton the frightened, tongue-tied schoolboy. In his place stood a master speaker and a gifted writer, one who was on his way to becoming one of the most famous, and most admired, mountain climbers in all of Britain. A return to Nanda Devi, this time to try and summit the actual mountain itself, was clearly the next logical step, and Shipton and Bill Tilman were already plotting a new expedition for later in the year. But as events would have it, Shipton would, instead, soon have another shot at the biggest mountaineering prize of them all.

For nearly a year and a half, ever since the majestic failure that was the 1933 expedition, British climbers had been itching to have another crack at Mount Everest. Indeed, less than three months after Shipton and Smythe had made their last, lonely run at the summit, the British political officer in Sikkim had written to both the Dalai Lama and his chief minister in Lhasa, seeking permission for another expedition. The request was curtly refused. "The Kalon Lama was quite definite in maintaining that the expeditions caused offence to the gods and trouble in the country," the political officer reported. "When asked for specific instances he replied that we could not see these things, which were invisible." The door had been shut.

Then, in early 1935, the Tibetans suddenly reversed themselves.

The British would be allowed to return to Everest.

Only now there was a new problem. For as soon as the word hit the Alpine Club that another Everest expedition was to be launched, all of the old divisions and animosities over how to best climb the world's tallest mountain came rushing forth in a barrage of angry letters, heated arguments, broken friendships, and indignant resignations. One camp stood firmly by Hugh Ruttledge, the quiet but steady helmsman of the failed 1933 expedition, while another demanded a complete makeover, with newer, younger, and more aggressive leadership. Eventually, a compromise was brokered. In 1936 Ruttledge would lead a full-fledged assault on the mountain. But that very spring, a small reconnaissance expedition, led by Eric Shipton, and costing very little money, would be sent forthwith to Everest to assess snow conditions and to prepare for next year's big push.

In the end, the 1935 Reconnaissance Expedition turned out to be a quiet but influential episode in the British campaign on Everest. The climbers received no noisy send-off in London, there was precious little press coverage of their progress, and it was to be the first Everest expedition not made the subject of a book-length official report. On the mountain itself, the weather and snow conditions were uncooperative, and once they'd given up hope of climbing much higher than the North Col, the members of the expedition spent most of their time "peak bagging"—namely, climbing some twenty-six nearby mountains, all of them more than 20,000 feet high. But the reconnaissance also produced a couple of long-lasting effects—seemingly little things that might not seem all that important at the time.

One of them involved Shipton and a climber named Dan Bryant, a New Zealander. Up until then, and for some time thereafter, British expeditions had shown a marked preference for British mountaineers rather than those from the Commonwealth. But Bryant, who was a renowned ice climber, had the kind of skills that Shipton had been looking for. Bryant was also very tough, and very funny. "I have never had a more delightful companion—cheerful, humorous, and supremely confident," Shipton wrote. "He was certainly a wonderful ambassador for New Zealand climbers." Shipton would not forget this.

But something else happened as well.

In early August 1935, Shipton, Bryant, and a small group of Sherpas set out along the West Rongbuk Glacier toward Mount Everest's lesser-known western side. As with the mountain's eastern flank, here a long and dauntingly steep ridge ran off of the summit. What the terrain looked like on the other side of this great western ridge, however, was not at all certain—and Shipton simply could not resist trying to take a look. On August 9, they began to climb to the top of a high, unnamed col that connected two significant peaks, Lingtren and Pumori, about five miles west of Everest. From the top of the col, they believed, they should have a clear view of the little-known southerly approaches to Everest. When they got there, however, they were socked in with heavy clouds and mist and could see very little. But when they returned two days later, on August 11, the clouds broke.

What they saw amazed them.

Perhaps two miles away, near the head of the Khumbu Glacier, stood an icefall the likes of which neither they, nor few others, had ever seen before. A colossal jumble of impossibly huge, building-sized blocks of ice and snow, the Khumbu Icefall would be a deadly, constantly shifting barrier to any mountaineering expedition. But just on the other side of the treacherous icefall there lay a stable and seemingly placid snow-filled valley or cirque, beyond which potentially lay a new and unexplored approach to the summit of Mount Everest. Mallory, who had seen it, named it the Western Cwm, using a Welsh word for "valley." The sight was electrifying. While the Sherpas excitedly chattered about landmarks near their homes, Shipton pulled his camera out of his rucksack and took a haunting—and dramatic—

photograph of the Khumbu Icefall and the start of the Western Cwm before the clouds moved back in and again hid the view. Then he, Bryant, and the Sherpas all started back down the col.

But the brief view of the Western Cwm had gotten the wheels turning. It was all academic, of course. For everything that they had been looking at was in Nepal, which was closed to foreigners. Yet, at least in Shipton's mind, a door had cracked open. "As far as we could see the route up," he told the members of the Alpine Club on December 9, 1935, after he'd returned to London, "it did not look impossible, and I should very much like to have the opportunity of exploring it." For the time being, however, there would be one over-riding priority for both Eric Shipton and Britain's climbing elite, and that was to finally get to the top of Everest.

Plans for the 1936 Mount Everest Expedition, meanwhile, had done little to soothe the divide between the Old Guard and the Young Radicals at the Alpine Club. Not only did Hugh Ruttledge plan to hire an unprecedented number of Sherpas—sixty-one, all told—but, once again, the expedition would bring along a massive amount of provisions. Tensions between the older and younger climbers grew so ugly that, it was charged, even the voting on new member applications had been manipulated by opposing factions. Yet, despite the divide, there was solid hope that 1936 would be the year that British climbers would finally stand atop of Mount Everest once and for all.

The eight climbers who had been selected for the expedition, all of whom were judged capable of reaching the summit, had been tested under difficult conditions. For four long months, Ruttledge, Frank Smythe, his second-in-command, and Eric Shipton had carefully and tirelessly assembled all of the gear for the expedition, including new high-altitude tents, eiderdown jackets, new boots, and sleeping bags. Working with Royal Air Force experts, the expedition would also bring along artificial oxygen equipment, weighing thirty-five pounds and providing for six hours' worth of additional oxygen, for the attempts on the summit. The expedition made it to Darjeeling on March 4 and, after the long march across the plains of Tibet, to the Rongbuk Monastery by the twenty-fifth of April. Two and a half weeks later, on May 14, Camp Four had been established on the North Col. Spirits were high, and they were ahead of schedule. Nineteen thirty-six might be the year after all.

Eight days later, Shipton and Smythe led a group of forty-one porters up to Camp Four to begin preparations for an assault on the upper mountain when the weather suddenly changed. In his climbing diary, Smythe wrote that it was "the heaviest snowstorm I've ever experienced in the Himalayas." With the camp half buried and visibility reduced to near zero, "there was nothing to do but lie up for two whole days in our sleeping bags with the Primus stove between us cooking hot drinks to keep us warm." Even worse news came on May 25 when, over the wireless, Ruttledge informed them that, incredibly, the monsoon had already reached Darjeeling and "must be expected to reach Everest in two or three days' time." The monsoon had never come this early in living memory. The climbers lingered on for a couple of weeks, hoping for a break in the weather, but one never came. On June 14, the news reached London that the effort had been called off. "The 1936 Everest Expedition," Shipton later wrote, "was a bitter disappointment."

There was, however, one other expedition that summer.

Bill Tilman had desperately wanted to be on the 1936 Mount Everest Expedition. But he had acclimatized so poorly on the Reconnaissance Expedition the year before that he had been struck off the list of possible candidates. Afterward, with no plans for the 1936 climbing season in the Himalayas, and with his climbing partner Shipton tied up on Everest, Tilman started casting about for a new possibility. Instead, one came to him. It was from, of all places, the Harvard Mountaineering Club.

Since the triumph on Minya Konka, the boys from Boston had been busy. Blessed with both bravado and family money, members of the HMC had pulled off some impressive mountaineering expeditions, particularly to remote peaks in Canada and Alaska. In order to get to Mount Crillon, in the St. Elias Range, they'd had to charter a fishing boat to take them to Lituya Bay, one hundred miles north of Juneau, and then carry all their gear, including a canoe, across a glacier before they could even begin to approach the mountain itself, chasing off both bears and mosquitoes along the way. After their successful summit bid, they used dynamite to blow up their latrine at Base Camp. "A tremendous blast sent crap high into the air," expedition leader Bradford Washburn recalled. "It rained for an hour!" On Mount Foraker, a party led by Charlie Houston ate fresh caribou and had to contend with storms, bergschrunds, an earthquake, and a memorable case of skull-splitting hangovers, courtesy of a wrangler who brought them two bottles of red-eye whiskey.

Moreover, their climbs had also captured the attention of a slice of the American public. The Mount Foraker climb had even landed on the front page of the *New York Times*. As a result, some of the HMC members concluded that it was time to try their hand in the Himalayas—and, just like that, the Harvard Kangchenjunga Expedition was born. Not content to start with a less-daunting Himalayan giant, the members of the proposed expedition—Charlie Houston, Ad Carter, Farnie Loomis, and Art Emmons, who had lost all of his toes on Minya Konka—intended to take a shot at the third-highest mountain on the planet.

Reality, however, soon began to settle in. And as the planning for the expedition moved haphazardly forward near the end of 1935, the Harvard men decided to reach out to some experienced Himalayan climbers in England to see if they might be willing to come along. "It's hard to believe how naïve and presumptuous we were," Houston later recalled. "Four American college kids, Ad Carter, Art Emmons, Farnie Loomis, and I, inviting the best British climbers to join us on a major climb in the Himalayas." Even more remarkable, the English mountaineers said yes. And not just any climbers, but a top-notch group including Bill Tilman and Everest veteran Noel Odell.

The World Beneath Their Feet

Not surprisingly, a power shift soon followed. Convinced by their new climbing partners that it was too late to seek permission to climb Kangchenjunga, the four Harvard men agreed to follow Tilman's advice and select a less politically sensitive objective. But the mountain that Tilman had in mind was nothing less than Nanda Devi itself. Not only would they all have to fight their way into the Sanctuary for only the second time in human history, but they would then have to attempt to scale a dauntingly steep, 25,000-foot peak that no less a mountaineer than Eric Shipton himself had declared was likely unclimbable. The Americans agreed to the new destination and, overnight, the Harvard Kangchenjunga Expedition became, instead, the British–American Himalayan Expedition.

It was not until July 6, 1936, that the two groups of climbers met for the first time, at a forest hut in Ranikhet, United Provinces, India. Oddly enough, it was the normally gregarious Americans who suddenly grew reserved. "We were all quite shy," Houston recalled, while the more experienced Brits, for their part, were understandably wary of their new climbing partners. "I think," Houston added, "they were uncertain as to what these puppies were up to." And once Tilman began going over the supplies that the American climbers had brought, it soon became clear that the newcomers from across the pond had a considerable amount of learning to do. Over the protests of Houston, Tilman "with grunts and scowls ... ruthlessly bagged and scrapped half of our food." And once they set out for Nanda Devi, the Americans shocked the British by insisting on carrying their own packs, rather than leave them for the porters to carry.

On the route to Nanda Devi, however, the Americans proved to be both skilled mountaineers and worthy companions. "We were young, tough, strong," Houston recalled. A brief Independence Day celebration on July 4th was tolerated with quiet amusement by the British climbers, while Farnie Loomis surprised everyone, once they'd entered the Sanctuary, by producing a celebratory bottle of apricot brandy. "The Americans and ourselves do not always see eye to eye, but on those rare occasions when we come together to do a job of work," Tilman wrote, "we seem to pull together very well." They would need to.

By the third week in August, the assault on Nanda Devi had unfolded impressively. The climbers and Sherpas had overcome dangerous patches of rotten rock, dicey belays, forty-five-degree snow slopes, and had managed to set up a relatively safe Camp Three at about 21,200 feet. But the expedition was, in fact, holding on by barely a thread. Sickness had ravaged the ranks of the Sherpas. Nima Tsering, who had been on Everest in 1924, was down, while Pasang Kikuli, who had survived Nanga Parbat in 1934, had been stricken with snow blindness. Even Kitar, who had been to Everest three times, was dangerously ill. The remaining porters were either too old, or too young and inexperienced, to be of any help further up the mountain. The British and Americans were now on their own.

Nor was that all. The weather, which had thus far been tolerable, began to deteriorate. "It was cold and windy when we reached Camp Three in a flurry of snow," Tilman wrote. "There was a halo around the moon and two mock suns, and I have seldom seen a more ominous-looking sky." Late the next day, the weather looked even worse. "The sunset was again threatening, with greasy-looking cigar-shaped clouds hanging low over East Nanda Devi, a greenish watery haze to the west, and, to the south, black banks of cumulus ringed with copper." Before dawn, a blizzard was shaking the walls of their tents.

The expedition had reached its tipping point.

And the men knew it. Up until then, in a nod to the democratic impulses of the Americans, all major decisions had been made by consensus. But now, with the steadily increasing dangers of the upper mountain upon them, the climbers agreed to select a single leader for the rest of their efforts upward, however far those may last. And so, in a cramped tent four miles into the sky above India, secret ballots were jimmied up, a vote was held, and Bill Tilman was elected the leader of the first-ever attempt to climb Nanda Devi. "An obvious choice," Houston later recalled.

The World Beneath Their Feet

Once the storm stopped, which it did by the morning of August 24, the time had come to move. "It was imperative now to push on with all speed," Tilman wrote, "and surely after such a snorter we might expect several days of fine weather." Pushing on to Camp Four, from which a two- or three-day summit attempt could be launched, Tilman announced that a two-man summit team would leave the next morning. Once they returned, if time and weather allowed, another two-man team might also make a shot at the top. And the first team, Tilman added, would be made up of Noel Odell and Charlie Houston. It was, in many ways, a surprising choice. While Houston was climbing well, and was the likely candidate to represent the United States on what was, after all, a joint Anglo–American expedition, Tilman showed real leadership by leaving himself off the summit team, and instead selecting Odell, the thirty-five-year-old geologist, to represent mother England. The next morning, Odell and Houston were off.

The others heard nothing of them until Thursday, August 27.

It had, in fact, already been a busy morning. After breakfast, Farnie Loomis announced that he was taking his name off of any summit attempt. His feet, which had already been slightly frostbitten, were in no shape for an assault on the summit. Shortly thereafter, the climbers faintly heard Odell's voice calling—more of a yodel actually—from above. "It suddenly dawned on us that he was trying to send an SOS," Tilman later recalled. Ad Carter, the other American climber, who was blessed with an especially loud voice, then dashed outside the tent to try and communicate with Odell. A few minutes later, Carter returned to the tent, his face ashen.

"Charlie's been killed," he reported.

The news was crushing. How had Houston died? Equally important, how had Odell survived? Tilman and Loomis threw on their boots, grabbed their rucksacks, and started heading up the mountain, their hearts in their throats. Carter and T. Graham Brown would follow directly with some medical supplies. The summit was of no importance now. But when Tilman and Loomis finally made it up to Odell's tent, something remarkable happened. First, they heard *voices*. Then Odell popped his head out.

"Hullo, you blokes," he said. "Have some tea."

Carter had misheard the message. Odell hadn't yelled, "Charlie is killed." He had said, "Charlie is ill." And sitting inside the tent, pale, sleepy-eyed, but patently alive, was Charles Houston.

Odell promptly filled them in.

The day before, Houston and Odell had begun their attack on the summit. The weather couldn't have been better, and they made slow but steady progress up the final snow slope. By late afternoon, at around 25,000 feet, the altitude had begun to take its toll, especially as they were now having to push through waist-deep snow. So rather than take the risk of pushing on to the summit that day, and possibly having to retreat in the dark, they decided to make one final bivouac that night. They would climb to the summit the next morning, and then descend all the way to Camp Four that day.

It was a solid plan. And the two climbers, the seasoned Britisher and the young American, were ecstatic. For dinner that night, they opened a tin of bully beef—what the Yanks called corned beef. But neither of them had noticed that the can had been punctured on the bottom. Odell ate the uncontaminated portion on top and, unknowingly, Houston consumed the tainted meat in the bottom. "Two hours later," Houston's biographer, Bernadette McDonald, wrote, "he was violently ill, vomiting and wracked with diarrhea, crawling over Odell in order to get outside the tent. It was a long night for both of them."

Now, however, a decision had to be made. And it was Houston who stepped up. Rather than wait until he was well enough to climb again, he insisted that Tilman take his place on the summit team. "His plan was that he should go down that afternoon and that I should stay up with Odell, and thus no time would have been lost," Tilman recalled. Even though it was robbing himself of a chance to summit, Houston put the team first. Now it would be up to Tilman and Odell.

The World Beneath Their Feet

*   *   *

Few, if any, aspects of mountaineering are as disagreeable as a predawn start.

Not only are the climbers exhausted, not just from their exertions the day before, but also by not getting a decent amount of sleep. They are tired, their bodies are a catalog of aches and pains, it's cold, they can't see anything, and they have to get going. Murder seems infinitely preferable to going back outside, especially at 24,000 feet. But in the frozen blackness of Nanda Devi on Saturday, August 29, 1936, that's what Bill Tilman and Noel Odell had to do. Dreams of glory were nowhere to be found. This was all about getting the job done. "We were up at five o'clock to begin the grim business of cooking and the more revolting tasks of eating breakfast and getting dressed," Tilman wrote. An hour later, they were finally on their way.

"It was bitterly cold, for the sun had not risen yet over the shoulder of East Nanda Devi and there was a thin wind from the west," Tilman wrote. "What mugs we were to be fooling about on this infernal ridge at that hour of the morning!" But as the two men slogged their way up the ridge, their bodies started to warm up, and their mental equilibrium was soon restored. Thoughts of homicide blew away in the morning breeze, and their presence in the moment returned. "As the demands of the climbing became more insistent," Tilman later recalled, "grievances seemed less real, and that life was still worth living was a proposition that might conceivably be entertained." Their footing improved as well, as the rotten rock of the lower slopes was replaced with a rough quartzite schist that held together well and could be walked on with confidence.

But the Blessed Goddess wasn't finished with them yet.

A long snow slope, set at about a thirty-degree angle proved to be particularly challenging. "The snow was not good and soon became execrable," Tilman recalled. "We were going in over our knees at every step, and in places where the slope was steeper it was not easy to make any upward progress at all. One foot would be lifted and driven hard into the snow and then, on attempting to rise on it, one simply sank down through the snow to the previous level. It was like trying to climb up cotton wool." Their legs on fire, backs drenched in cold sweat, and needing to take as many as eight deep breaths for every step, Tilman added that, "Our hopes of the summit grew faint, but there was no way but to plug on and see how far we could get."

Plug on they did.

Step by step, raspy breath by raspy breath, with the white-hot Indian sun beating down upon them, the two men pushed slowly upward, taking more-and-more-frequent breaks. Once, after they had just successfully climbed to the top of a steep snow gully, a huge slab of snow, maybe four feet deep and over a hundred feet wide, suddenly hissed and peeled away nearly at their feet, the avalanche exploding into a cloud of powdered snow. But by one o'clock, as they stopped at the top of a snow rib that led to the skyline ridge, they noticed that they were now above the summit of East Nanda Devi, their peak's shorter twin. It gave them heart. "We had a long rest and tried to force some chocolate down our parched throats by eating snow at the same time," Tilman recalled. "Though neither of us said so, I think both felt that now it would take a lot to stop us."

Nothing did.

At three o'clock, Odell and Tilman stood on top of Nanda Devi.

The scene before them had never been regarded by human eyes. Trisul, which Longstaff had first climbed in 1907, lay below them, as did Nanda Devi East, the Sanctuary, and Nanda Devi's own barrier ring. There was not a higher mountain within two hundred miles. And while the peaks of Nepal were already cloaked in clouds, Tilman wrote, "Far to the north through a vista of white cloud the sun was colouring to a warm brown the bare and bleak Tibetan plateau." Three-quarters of an hour later, it was time to head down. Odell and Tilman were back in their tent by six o'clock, drinking jorum after jorum of tea. "There was but a pinch left and we squandered it recklessly," Tilman later wrote, "saving the leaves for the morning."

The news reached London on September 9.

In writing about the climb a few months later, Tom Longstaff, the grand old iconoclast of the Alpine Club, wrote that the Nanda Devi climb was "the finest mountain ascent yet made, either in the Himalaya or anywhere else." There was one additional detail. Nanda Devi was now the highest mountain climbed all the way to the top. It was, all told, a truly magnificent achievement, and despite its American presence, the expedition was also a clear triumph for British mountaineering.

But it wasn't Everest.

Nor was that the only problem.

London. Saturday evening, February 26, 1937.

Inside the Mercury Theatre, a tidy little playhouse in Notting Hill that had once served as a Congregationalist schoolhouse, a small crowd of poets, intellectuals, drama buffs, and mountaineers finished their coffee and chipolatas and took their seats. As the house lights dimmed, a pianist began to play the first rollicking, cacophonic notes of a score written—some of it the very night before—by a twenty-three-year-old composer named Benjamin Britten. And as the curtain rose, a mountain climber named Michael Ransom was seen sitting upon the summit of Pillar Rock, in the Lake District, reading aloud from a volume of Dante. Thus began the opening night of *The Ascent of F6*, perhaps the most remarkable mountaineering drama ever written.

A two-act play, co-authored by W. H. Auden and Christopher Isherwood, it told the story of the race between a British mountaineering expedition, led by Ransom, and one led by a made-up European power—read: Germany—to be the first to climb to the summit of F6, a remote Himalayan giant. "There's more than a mountain at stake!" shouts a character named Mrs. A at the end of the first act.

Mr A. England's honor is covered with rust.
Mrs A. Ransom must beat them! He must! He must!
Mr A. Or England falls. She has had her hour.
And must now decline to a second-class power.

Partially written in verse, and featuring high camps and wind-blown ridges, chanting monks and Primus stoves, ice axes and an avalanche, the play was brimming with accurate details about mountaineering that came from Auden's brother, John, a climber and cofounder of the Himalayan Club. Proudly eggheaded and intentionally provocative, *The Ascent of F6* also featured a grim chorus of "Nothing that matters will ever happen" along with its own roster of politically skewered stereotypes. "The fable is so good, the verse so stageworthy," noted the theater critic for the *Times*, "that the doctrinal purpose, if to provoke dissent, is a small gnat to swallow."

Indeed, the play did well enough in the small experimental theater that it even enjoyed a short run in the West End during the spring of 1937 before disappearing forever into the dimmer footlights of regional theaters and university productions. But as it slipped from view, Auden and Isherwood's play had, unintentionally, highlighted a darkening reality that the nation's mountaineering establishment could no longer wish away. For the fact was, the British were in trouble. It was true that, unlike the German climbs, the various post-Mallory British expeditions had not left a trail of dead bodies in their wake. And the twin successes on Nanda Devi, first on penetrating the Sanctuary and then on obtaining the summit, had been genuine mountaineering triumphs. But they weren't Everest.

"We ought not to treat the climbing of Mount Everest as a domestic issue," fumed G. Ingle Finch, a member of the 1922 expedition in the pages of the *Morning Post* in October 1936. "It is an issue of National and Imperial importance. The present position is that we are beginning to make ourselves look very ridiculous," he added. "The Germans and Americans have both wanted to make an attempt on Mount Everest, and unless we put up a better show, it will be difficult to argue that we are justified in keeping Mount Everest to ourselves."

Moreover, the British public had begun to lose interest. Part of this, of course, was due to the fact that they had plenty of other things to occupy their attention. During the second half of 1936, the nation's attention had been riveted by the saga of Edward VIII and his obsession with Wallis Simpson, a divorced Baltimore socialite who, it was whispered behind closed doors, had learned secret sexual techniques at a Chinese brothel. Most assumed that the king would simply retain Mrs. Simpson as his mistress, but when he announced his intention to marry her, a constitutional crisis erupted. In the end, Edward abdicated the throne in order to wed Wallis. There were other concerns as well, including the ongoing hard times, the rise of the independence movement in India, and the growing chorus of belligerence and saber rattling by Nazi Germany.

The truth was, the heady atmosphere that had enveloped British mountaineering in 1933 had all but dried up and disappeared. No longer did press photographers and crowds of well-wishers gather at Liverpool Street Station to see the climbers off. High-altitude tents and windproof clothing were no longer displayed in shop windows on Regent Street. And while the *Daily Telegraph*, the *Times*, the *Express*, and the *Daily Mirror* still ran stories on the expeditions, the stories had grown smaller. Anticipation and excitement had been replaced by stifled yawns and frustration. And there were other troubles as well, ones that the Mount Everest Committee could no longer ignore.

To begin with, the failed 1936 expedition had wiped out the committee's financial resources. And while they were again given permission to launch another expedition to Everest in 1938, permission they fully intended to take advantage of, they didn't have the funds to do so—at least not on the grand scale with which they were accustomed. As a result, and by no means out of its own preference, the committee suddenly found itself more favorably disposed to the small-scale expedition philosophy that had been championed by younger climbers, especially Eric Shipton. Even more remarkably, in February 1937, the gray-haired members of the Mount Everest Committee invited Shipton, Tilman, Frank Smythe, and Charles Warren to meet with them and discuss plans for a new attempt on Everest. The Old Guard had blinked. Youth would finally have its say. But there still remained one last, not insignificant hurdle—namely, how to pay for it all. By the late summer of 1937, the committee had a grand total of £335. It wasn't enough, even under the barest-boned scenario.

Tom Longstaff came to the rescue.

The grand old man of British mountaineering, Longstaff hadn't been enamored of the big-expedition approach to begin with. Indeed, back in 1905, he and two Italian alpine guides, without a tent and with only one piece of chocolate between them, almost climbed Gurla Mandhata, a 25,000-foot peak in Tibet. Longstaff wrote out a check for three thousand pounds to cover the expenses for the 1938 expedition, stipulating that either Shipton or Tilman needed to be selected as the leader. There were a couple of other conditions as well, including one that called for minimal publicity beforehand. In the end, everyone was satisfied. Tilman was chosen as the leader. More importantly, the climbers had finally won. No longer subservient to political pressures, marketing campaigns, or committee-think, this would be their show.

It was time to finish the job on the world's highest mountain.

The first thing to go was the wireless radio, which Tilman thought was unnecessary. He was all for ditching the oxygen equipment as well. Not only were the oxygen tanks and their harnesses and delivery apparatus bulky and heavy, weighing between twenty-five and thirty-five pounds, but the expedition leader was unconvinced of their value. In the end, four sets were taken, two of the older "open" type, where the climber breathed in oxygen through a tube placed in his mouth, and a pair of the newer "closed" type, which employed a face mask. Food was also a big sticking point for Tilman. A strong critic of the caviar and quails-in-aspic school of climbing, and being of the belief that at high altitudes, all tinned food basically tastes the same, Tilman opted for an exceedingly—if not excessively—bland expedition diet, one that met with less than universal acclaim.

Books, however, were a different matter.

Reading was part and parcel of the life blood of British climbers during the 1930s, and no climber was criticized for taking along his own private library, even to the highest camps of Mount Everest. Charles Warren carried in his rucksack a two-thousand-page physiology textbook, as well as a volume on tropical medicine. P. R. Oliver took Carl von Clausewitz's *On War*, Noel Odell brought along a book on geology, and Shipton took *Gone With the Wind*—"the longest and bulkiest novel that has appeared in recent years," groused Tilman. Even the highest wind-blown ridges of the Himalayas weren't safe from the intrigues of Scarlett and Rhett, Ashley Wilkes and, as Scarlett would have it, that mealy-mouthed little goody-goody Melanie Hamilton.

In fact, the tendrils connecting Great Britain's mountaineering and literary worlds were quite extensive. George Mallory had been connected to the Bloomsbury Set, while Eric Shipton liked to entertain poets and writers at his mother's flat in Lexham Gardens, Kensington. Novelist Graham Greene's older brother, Raymond, was an accomplished mountaineer and physician who served as the chief medical officer on the 1933 Mount Everest Expedition. And during the late spring and summer of 1937, Tilman and Shipton had explored the remote ranges of the Shaksgam region, along the Kashmiri–Sinkiang border, with poet W. H. Auden's brother, John, and Michael Spender, brother of the poet, essayist, and short-story writer Stephen Spender. One can only imagine the lines of Keats and Milton, Tennyson and Shakespeare that were recited alongside the campfires on the way to the Shaksgam, no doubt to the riotous amusement of the Sherpas.

The 1938 Mount Everest Expedition was not, however, as small as Tilman might have preferred. But the seven climbers and thirty porters were strong and fit. Indeed, Shipton and Frank Smythe, who were thought to be the best candidates for making the summit, were at the top of their game, while the Sherpa contingent included seasoned veterans such as Ang Tharkay and Pasang Bhotia. And in order to avoid the fate of the most recent Everest expedition, which was felled by an early monsoon, Tilman opted for an early start. Indeed, both Shipton and Tilman were in India by St. Valentine's Day, while the full party of climbers and Sherpas made it to the Rongbuk Monastery by April 6, a full ten days earlier than previous attempts.

It did not matter.

Hemmed in by bitter cold and wind that made climbing all but impossible, and racked by coughs, colds, and sore throats, the members of the expedition were forced to retreat to the Kharta Valley for three weeks of rest. When they returned to the mountain in mid-May, the monsoon had, once again, inexplicably arrived early. Despite the dangerous snow conditions, a determined effort was launched to reach the top. By June 9, 1938, Shipton and Smythe had made it all the way up to a scree slope just below the edge of the infamous Yellow Band, where they spent the night in a single tent pitched at about 27,000 feet. The weather conditions notwithstanding, literature would have its place in what was, that night, the highest human habitation in the world. Shipton had brought along in his rucksack a copy of Thornton Wilder's *The Bridge of San Luis Rey*, the best-selling novel about the collapse of a rope bridge in eighteenth-century Peru. "It was frightfully difficult to read," he wrote to his mother, "as all the words got muddled up with a sort of half-dream just like when one is falling asleep in bed." Much more importantly, if their luck held, Shipton and Tilman might have a shot at the summit the next day.

By the next morning, however, the conditions were hopeless. The steeply angled face of the Yellow Band was covered with a five-foot layer of loose, feathery, powdered snow. "The smallest movement even on the moderately steep rocks of the Yellow band was extremely dangerous," Shipton wrote. "Even if we had been able to reach the

Black Band, to have climbed its difficult rocks would have been as impossible as it would have been suicidal to attempt." Two days later, Tilman and a climber named Peter Lloyd, who had tried using an oxygen apparatus—which the Sherpas laughingly called "English air"—with mixed results the day before, also made a run at reaching the summit ridge. But they, too, fell short.

"Thus ended," Tilman later wrote, "the 1938 attempt."

But the 1938 expedition also registered one other notable impact.

For the Sherpas were changing.

Initially hired only to haul loads of equipment and supplies up the mountains, their roles had quietly but steadily expanded. In Tibet, they helped the climbers navigate cultural differences and resolve issues with local villagers. High on the great peaks, they were breaking and setting up camps, serving as messengers, and had begun to haul supplies on their own. And as their high-altitude experience continued to grow, so did their confidence. On the 1935 Everest Reconnaissance, the Sherpas threatened to quit when they were asked to serve as porters before reaching Base Camp, something which they felt was a breach of contract. And on the 1938 expedition, a Sherpa named Ang Karma got into such a heated shouting match with Tilman that he actually shoved him out of the way. Both situations were eventually—and amicably—resolved, but the message was clear. The wishes of the Sherpas were no longer to be brushed aside. And with the growing number of expeditions, a whole new generation of Sherpas was, by necessity, being brought in to work on the various climbing campaigns. Young men came in to replace those who had grown too old, had been killed, or had left mountaineering for good.

Among the newcomers was a young Sherpa named Tenzing.

The eleventh of thirteen children born to a family of poor, illiterate yak herders in Tibet, his name had originally been Namgyal Wangdi. But when his parents took him to see the head lama at the Rongbuk Monastery, the prelate informed them that their son was the reincarnation of a wealthy merchant who had recently died, and that his name needed to be changed.

The family left Tibet about the time that Tenzing was seven years old, hoping to find a better life in the Khumbu district in Nepal, home to many other Sherpa families. And while they were no longer under the thumb of a Tibetan overlord, their lives in the high valleys of eastern Nepal, with its rocky soil and bitter cold, continued to be both hard and poor. "Our house was small and crowded," Tenzing later recalled. "We ate only the simplest food. But there was always enough." They made their own clothes, including shoes, from yak wool and hides, and grew small patches of barley and potatoes. During the winter months, the yaks would gather on the lower level of their stone house, while the family lived on the upper floor. "All of us packed together in no space at all," he added, "with the noise and the stenches and the smoke from the cooking, but happy and contented because we did not know there was any other way to live."

There was no school for the poor Sherpa children in the villages of the Khumbu, so Tenzing would remain illiterate all of his life. But during the summer months, even as a young boy, he would help take the yaks to higher pastures, some as high as 18,000 feet. It was from these upper slopes that he got his first view of Chomolungma, "The Goddess Mother of the Wind" or "The Mountain So High That No Bird Can Fly over It"—what the *chilingna*, or foreigners, called Mount Everest. The view stirred his imagination and literally took his breath away. Something else did as well.

For by the time that Tenzing was ten years old, some of the men in the neighboring villages had come back to the Khumbu not only with unusual clothes, but also with incredible stories about the *chilingna* and their desire to climb to the top of Chomolungma. "Most of them wore big boots and strange clothes such as we had never seen before," Tenzing later recalled. "I was so fascinated that one day I paid money to use a pair of boots, but they were so heavy that I could not walk at all." The seed had been planted, though, and soon, so had another. While the other boys in the village would play games with mud and stones, he would often go off to sit alone and dream of other places.

At age thirteen, he ran away.

Without telling his parents or his brothers or sisters, Tenzing slipped out of the village and made what, in effect, was his walkabout. Some two weeks later, tired and hungry, he made his way into Kathmandu, the capital of Nepal. "It was the first city I had ever seen, and very strange and confusing," he later said. "For about two weeks I went all about the city and saw the crowds and bazaars and the big buildings and temples, and all sorts of things." He was equally fascinated by the people, "whose faces and clothes and ways of doing things were different from anything I had seen before." Here were high-stepping Ghurkha soldiers, newly-freed slaves, regal women carrying umbrellas to keep the sun off their heads, and Hindu shrines covered with strange and wondrous carvings. Though he stayed at night at a Buddhist monastery, he got homesick. When he got home, his overjoyed parents—who thought that he might be dead—wrapped him in their arms and hugged him.

"When they were through with the hugging," Tenzing added, "they spanked me."

But the urge to travel had taken root. And when he heard, five years later, that the *chilingna* were planning a return visit to what they called Mount Everest, Tenzing knew that he had to go to Darjeeling, where the porters were selected. It would be a difficult trip, nearly a month-long trek through the hills and forests of eastern Nepal. But this time, he was no longer traveling solo. Nearly a dozen other young people from the village, men and women alike, had planned to leave, and had been holding secret meetings and saving money. Among them was Dawa Thuti, the daughter of a more prosperous neighbor. Tenzing and Dawa Thuti had fallen in love. And one night in the fall of 1932, they slipped together out of the village with the others, with their minds set on a new life in a new world.

They ended up outside Darjeeling in a village called Alubari, where Tenzing took a job caring for a small herd of cows. He also began to dress like a Nepali, learning the local language and cutting his hair. "When I first came to Darjeeling I had long braided hair, like all the men in Solo Khumbu," he recalled, "but people laughed at me and called me a girl, so I had it cut short." He and Dawa Phuti even rode in an automobile, and soon began to familiarize themselves with Darjeeling's open-air markets and narrow, misty side streets, its clock tower and famous toy railway. But when the word came that the British would be hiring porters at the Planters Club, Tenzing anxiously lined up with the other applicants, ready to go to work.

It did not go well. Not only did he have no connections among the other Sherpas, but the British expedition members who were doing the hiring took one look at his short hair and Nepali clothes and quickly turned him away. "They thought I was a Nepali and they wanted only Sherpas," he recalled, "and I had no papers or a certificate from a previous expedition to help me. I suppose it is the same with many young people looking for work. They ask you, 'Have you done this before?' You say, 'No.' They say, 'We only want people with experience.' And you go away wondering if you will never get a job in your life, because you have not had one already." Tenzing wasn't hired. "When the expedition marched off from Darjeeling I stayed behind and was very miserable."

But two years later, in early 1935, his luck started to change.

Tenzing and Dawa Phuti were married now, and were lodging with Ang Tharkay in the Sherpa neighborhood on the back side of Darjeeling. Dawa Phuti was also pregnant. At the last moment, Eric Shipton had decided to hire a handful of additional porters for the Everest Reconnaissance Expedition. Tenzing still didn't have any expedition experience, and beyond the fact that he and his wife were renting a room from Ang Tharkay, he had no papers or connections. But he was young, he was strong, and he had a secret weapon— an amazing, utterly charming smile. "From a hundred applicants, we chose fifteen Sherpas to accompany the expedition from Darjeeling," Shipton wrote. "Nearly all of them were old friends, including, of course, Angtarkay, Pasang, and Kusang; but there was one Tibetan lad of nineteen, a newcomer, chosen largely because of his attractive grin. His name was Tensing."

He was on his way.

Tenzing served ably on the 1935 expedition, and upon its conclusion, generously gave Ang Tharkay the two-person sleeping bag that they'd been sharing. The next season, he was hired on a Survey of India trip to Nanda Devi. And in 1937, he helped out with a trekking expedition run out of the Doon School, a prestigious English-style school for Indian students located in Dehra Dun. The next year, he had little trouble getting hired on the 1938 Everest Expedition, where he particularly impressed Bill Tilman. "Young, keen, strong, and very likeable," the normally reserved Tilman later wrote. But Tenzing made his biggest impression on the expedition leader near the final days of the assault, when he and Pasang voluntarily went back down from Camp Five to pick up vital loads that had been abandoned by two sick Sherpas. "To descend and ascend with loads another seven hundred feet, on top of the toil they had already endured," Tilman wrote, "was a remarkable example of unwearying strength and vitality gallantly and unselfishly applied."

There was more. Tenzing himself recognized that he seemed to have "so little trouble at great heights." He didn't fall, and he didn't get frostbite—in part, he believed, because he didn't sweat when he climbed. Moreover, like Eric Shipton, he was very much a rhythmic climber. Plus, there was one other item of note. On their way up the north ridge, above the North Col, Tilman had let Tenzing *lead* part of the way. "In front we had the tireless Tensing to make things easier for us until we came to a steeper slope where the snow seemed very insecurely poised," Tilman wrote in his official report on the 1938 expedition. Tenzing wasn't just another porter. He was pushing the envelope of what a Sherpa could do.

When the British came back to Everest, he would be ready to join them.

* * *

Eric Shipton slipped back into London in the fall of 1938.

The last Everest expedition, of course, had already been deemed a failure, simply because the summit had yet again not been attained. But Shipton's thinking on mountaineering had continued to evolve. He had long been opposed to massive expeditions. But now he was starting to question the very ethos underlying the expeditions to begin with, be they big or small—and, with them, the very idea of the race to the roof of the world. By early October 1938, copies of his second book, *Blank on the Map*, an account of an expedition to the Shaksgam he'd taken with Bill Tilman one year before, had begun to appear in London bookstores. In the book's second chapter, titled "Of the Real Value of Climbing," he took direct aim at the comforts of the modern world: "With a wistfulness, perhaps a little tinged with sentimentality," he wrote, "I think of the leisurely days of a few hundred years ago, before life was so mad a rush, before the countryside was spoiled by droves of people, and beauty itself exploited as a commercial proposition. We have become so accustomed to having everyday life made easy for us, that our energies are not absorbed in the art of living, but run riot in a craving for sensation."

Turning to pursuits as varied as sailing and skiing, he threw arrows and darts at those who become consumed by competition "and care more for trophies, or record-breaking, or acclamation, than for a real understanding of their craft." Shipton quickly dismissed "the mountaineer who goes to the Alps for a season's climbing, with a desire to climb more peaks than other men, and by more difficult routes, misses the real value of the experience—the love of mountains for their own sake."

But he wasn't finished.

"Let us climb peaks by all means, because their beauty attracts us; not because others have failed, nor because the summits stand 28,000 feet above the sea, nor in patriotic fervour for the honour of the nation, nor for cheap publicity. Let us approach the peaks with humility, and, having found the way to them for ourselves, learn to solve their problems." Philosophical and impassioned, here were the beginnings of a new manifesto for mountaineering, and a bridge between New World thinkers like Thoreau and John Muir, and the aesthetic of a generation of climbers who were only just then being born. Eric Shipton wasn't just the most talented mountain climber of his own generation. He was also, in many ways, its most thoughtful.

But right then, and right there, this wasn't what the members of the Mount Everest Committee, nor his fellow climbers in the Alpine Club were looking for. It was not simply that British climbers had now failed, seven times in a row, to reach the summit of Mount Everest. Rather, the preeminence and invincibility of British mountaineering was no longer assured. And waiting in the wings were others who, in their own ways and their own time, were already scraping up against their own Himalayan stars. They had, in fact, been quite busy.

But there was something else as well.

It wasn't just the British who had been slipping further and further into trouble.

So, too, it seemed, was the entire world.

CHAPTER ELEVEN

An American Everest

Nanking, China. December 13th, 1937.

The city was collapsing. Thick clouds of smoke billowed out of the railway terminal and the post office, rifle fire could now be heard outside the International Safety Zone, while Chung San Road and Fukien Road were clogged with thousands of men, women, and children desperately trying to leave town. For most of the morning, Japanese soldiers had poured through the Ching Hua Gate, while to the east, near the Central Hospital, the last remnants of the Nanking Garrison Force had thrown away their weapons and uniforms and put on civilian clothes, hoping to blend in with the rest of the city's terrified population. Before the day was done, the new conquerors, dirty and grimy but drunk with pride, would begin their reign of terror. Teenaged girls and grandmothers alike were gang-raped and eight-year-olds were used for bayonet practice, while Japanese officers would hold competitions beheading old men with samurai swords. Humanity's dark hour had struck.

At the Academica Sinica, the city's natural history museum, Jack Young could read the writing on the wall. No longer a guide for the Roosevelt brothers, or a member of the 1932 Minya Konka expedition, he was now serving as an officer in the army of the Republic of China and, eventually if not already then, as a key set of eyes and ears for American military intelligence. As the Japanese troops drew nearer, Young finally ordered his squad of men to abandon the building. But before he left, the twenty-five-year-old American reached into a display case and grabbed the Chinese flag that his friends Dick Burdsall and Art Emmons had photographed on the summit of Minya Konka five years earlier. His climbing and hunting days behind him, Jack Young was already at war.

His compatriots back home, however, had not abandoned their Himalayan dreams, not by any stretch of the imagination. Save for a can of tainted meat, Charlie Houston had almost made it to the top of Nanda Devi in what had already been hailed as the most impressive climb ever undertaken in the Himalayas. Despite the troubles in Asia, and the growing uncertainty in Europe, a circle of young men with ties to the Harvard Mountaineering Club were determined to put American climbing firmly and decisively on the Himalayan map. Not content to settle for anything short of an eight-thousander, and wanting to avoid any peaks in politically sensitive areas, they decided to go for nothing less than the second-highest mountain on earth—K2.

It was, to say the least, an audacious choice.

Part of the great wall of the Karakoram, K2 was located less than fifty miles from the border with Sinkiang, the westernmost province of China. The mountain got its modern name during the early fall of 1856, when a British surveyor named Thomas Montgomerie jotted down the coordinates for a couple of unknown peaks in the Karakoram, which he called K1 and K2. And while the first mountain soon appeared on British maps as Masherbrum, the abbreviation K2 persisted for the second. Some urged that the peak be named Mount Montgomerie, while others suggested that it be named after Henry Haversham Godwin-Austen, an early Survey of India explorer who was also said to have been the first English convert to Buddhism. But it was K2, in all of its stark simplicity, that stuck.

Fittingly so. For, if anything, K2 provided a grim and austere challenge for any mountaineering expedition. Like most of the peaks in the Karakoram, it was difficult to reach. And while it was some eight hundred feet shorter than Everest, its defenses were arguably much greater. Rising up sharply for more than nine thousand feet above its surrounding glaciers, viewed from afar the overall shape of K2 was that of an intimidatingly steep yet near-perfect pyramid. But on closer inspection, it was a mountaineering nightmare. Huge seracs menaced K2's upper reaches, while its deeply angled ridge-lines were heavily corniced. Avalanche chutes and precarious icefalls abounded, while its skin of exposed rock was, more often than not, dangerously rotten and held together by a thin layer of verglas, or glaze ice. A jagged arrowhead splitting the sky, K2 wasn't just another *Achttausender*. It was a monster.

Not surprisingly, only a few had even attempted to climb it.

In the spring of 1902, a party of three Brits—including Aleister Crowley, England's notorious occultist mountaineer—plus two Austrians and one Swiss, the six of them armed with manila rope, ice axes, and thick woolen trousers, arrived in Srinagar, the capital of Kashmir. "Their light-hearted objective was to climb K2, which they imagined to be an easy mountain," mountaineer Günter Dyhrenfurth wrote. "In those days no one had any great idea of what an 'Eight Thousander'—let alone K2—involved." Battered by falling rocks, heavy snowfall, and a rash of medical problems, including a dangerous case of edema, the party was also hampered by bickering and a lack of inspired leadership. In the end, the climbers retired after making it little more than a few thousand feet above the head of the Baltoro Glacier.

The Italians, however, were made of far sterner stuff.

Especially His Royal Highness Prince Luigi Amedeo Giuseppe Maria Ferdinando Francesco di Savoia-Aosta, Duke of the Abruzzi. No milquetoast aristocrat who shuttled back and forth between costume balls and opera galas, he was a naval officer and an adventurer. As a twenty-five-year-old prince in 1899, he led a twenty-man expedition on a stripped-out whaling ship and sailed it to the barren islands of Franz Josef Land, less than six hundred miles from the North Pole. Wintering over on Rudolf Island, the duke lost two fingers to frostbite while other members took off for the North Pole by dogsled, where they set a new record for traveling the farthest north.

The World Beneath Their Feet

But it was mountains that were closest to the duke's heart. Two years earlier, he had led a successful expedition to the St. Elias Range in the Alaska Territory, where they became the first to climb Mount St. Elias, a legendary—and remote—peak that had been unknown to Europeans until the 1740s. In 1906, he commanded the first true mountaineering expedition to the Ruwenzori mountains near the equator in East Africa, where the tricolor Italian flag was unfurled on the summit of Mount Stanley. Not one to skimp on either comfort or ingenuity, the duke had an iron bed frame hauled from camp to camp in Alaska. Once in the Alps, when the party he was climbing with kept having trouble lassoing a rock spire, the duke had them tie a copper ball to the rope. When that didn't work, he attached the line to a rocket and fired it at the top.

But K2 would be his greatest challenge. In early 1909, when the alliances still held and Europe was at peace, the duke received permission from the British to launch an expedition to climb the greatest peak in the Karakoram. He assembled a party of twelve alpine guides and climbers, and as they traveled across the Kashmir the Italians were treated as royalty—which, in the duke's case, was of course true. In Srinagar, the reigning local British power couple, Sir Francis and Lady Younghusband, threw them an elaborate party. When the Italians left the city, by boat, they were serenaded by local musicians while locals cheered and showered them with flower petals. In dreamlike Skardu, a five-hundred-year-old town along the upper Indus River Valley, a polo match was held in their honor. Gracious and ever style-conscious, one of the Italians even wore a necktie all the way to Base Camp.

Nonetheless, the duke and his compatriots were all about the business at hand. He was deeply impressed with the more than two hundred local Balti men whom he hired to transport the expedition's five tons of supplies more than three hundred miles to the base of the mountain, which they reached by the end of May. And it was here that the truly formidable nature of the terrain became soberingly apparent. Their first view of K2, set among the great peaks and valleys of the Karakoram, literally took their breaths away.

"The impression made upon us was so strong, that no words can convey it to the reader," wrote expedition member Filippo De Filippi, though he did try. "All the landscape around K2 has the richest variety of design, the greatest majesty of form, and an infinite diversity of plane and perspective. The scale is far too vast for one to receive an impression of the whole at once." The Karakoram features the greatest concentration of high peaks on the face of the earth, peak after peak, pyramid after pyramid, jumbled together like monstrous dominoes. And lording above them all was K2.

Finding a route to the top was the first order of the day, and it was here that the duke and his team set a new standard for their careful and meticulous efforts. Not only did they circumnavigate nearly two-thirds of the mountain, but Vittorio Sella, the expedition photographer, with the help of a group of Balti porters, worked a kind of magic that would not be equaled for decades—if ever. Hauling different cameras, glass slides, and a complete darkroom-in-a-tent to various locations on the mountain, Sella created a photographic record of K2 and the surrounding peaks in the Karakoram that was without parallel.

But actually climbing to the summit proved to be a far more difficult asignment. A first attempt, along a rib of exposed rock on the southeastern face of K2, had to be called off at an altitude of about 21,000 feet, owing to the fact that the terrain would simply be too difficult for the Baltis. A second attempt was then launched, in late June, from the southwest. But once again, the climbers were stopped dead in their tracks, this time by the combination of both a deep crevasse and a near-vertical wall of ice. K2 had eluded them. Before leaving the Karakoram, the duke was convinced that the mountain was, in fact, unclimbable.

Nearly two decades later, in 1927, another Italian expedition to K2 was announced, once again with an aristocratic flair. This one, to be led by His Royal Highness Prince Aimone of Savoia-Aosta,

Duke of Spoleto, had been the brainchild of a group of mountaineers in Milan, working with members of the Italian Royal Geographical Society. But by the time the expedition finally and fully got off the ground, its purpose had shifted to a largely scientific and exploratory one. The Italians, however, weren't the only ones to have been enchanted by the Karakoram. The so-called International Expedition, led by German-Swiss mountaineer Günter Dyhrenfurth, came in 1934, as did the French two years later. And Eric Shipton passed through the region en route to the Shaksgam. But none of them, since the Duke of the Abruzzi, had attempted to climb K2.

Now it would be the Americans' turn.

Washington Heights, New York City. January 20, 1938.

Inside his small apartment in Bard Hall, a short walk from the endless traffic streaming across the George Washington Bridge, Charles Houston went over the list one more time, carefully making additions and deletions in his finely controlled and completely legible handwriting, the archetypal opposite of that of the medical doctor he one day hoped to become. In came more pencils, extra lightbulbs for the six flashlights, three match safes, a funnel, boot grease, four cakes of Brillo soap, and ten pounds each of cabbage and sweet potatoes. Out went four candle lanterns and forty-eight candles, a two-hundred-foot hank of clothesline, Rye Krisp, and ten pounds of ham. Beside each food item was listed both its total weight and the weight for a single day's portion for seven climbers. All told, one hundred and ninety-three items were on the list, neatly typed into single and double-spaced columns under subheads along that included Camp units, Floating Unit, Climbing kit, Base Camp, and PERSONAL.

Nor was that all. Additional pages, typed up on Houston's engraved letterhead, provide further details on specific items of clothing and equipment, drawn from both his personal observations and the writings of European climbers. For socks, those of Hertford brushed wool "in two different sizes to fit one over the other, marked with colored tape," were deemed best. Grenfell cloth parkas, silk handkerchiefs, Duraluminum pack frames, Meade tents, half-length air mattresses from Abercrombie & Fitch, and carabiners—"small tapered ones with small filed edge on opening jaw to facilitate quick use"—were all found to be up to standard.

Boots were of particular concern. Unlined Mark VIIIs, handcrafted by London bootmaker Robert Lawrie, were judged by Houston to be the "finest boots for alpine climbing made," with good-quality, non-freezing leather. Yet even these needed adjustments. "The toe is not deep enough, and the sole not wide enough to wear comfortably over socks needed at high altitude," he wrote. "If this is corrected, and if boot is fitted by Lawrie personally, or by cobbler here over desired number of socks, then this boot will be very good. We do not know any other boot as good even with these faults."

Lawrie would also be contracted to craft boots for the Sherpas on the expedition—"Make on Ghurka last to fit wide short Sherpa foot," Houston wrote, "Suggest 3 size 7, 3 size 8, and 1–2 size 9"—a relatively rare instance of providing porters with clothing and equipment equal to that of the climbers. While the American mountaineers would each sleep in a pair of sleeping bags, a soft, flannel-lined inner bag filled with eiderdown, and an outer bag of live goose down, both costing about eighty dollars, the Sherpas would be provided with lined or unlined down bags, each costing around fifteen or twenty dollars. "Our Sherpas never complained," Houston rationalized, referring to his experiences on Nanda Devi.

The lists kept coming.

Typed and carbon copied, or handwritten in Houston's precise and flowing hand, they were edited and amended, checked and double-checked. There were tabulations of the rations for the porters, inventories of the contents of each expedition box, including both individual and gross weights, and a checklist of activities each climber should have completed by April 1, 1938, including smallpox vaccinations, physical examinations, signed visa cards, and having as much of their personal gear sent, as possible, to Houston's parents' home in Great Neck, Long Island, where it was inventoried, weighed, and numbered. Finally, on the twelfth of April, a balmy Tuesday in New York, Houston typed up a final list of items still to be purchased for the expedition, including crampons in London, Toblerone chocolate bars in Paris, and cigarettes in Port Said, Egypt. But along with the final listing also came some general guidelines for both his and his fellow climbers' behavior on the way to K2.

"Remember that we are in a sense ambassadors," Houston wrote, "and Americans in general and American climbers in particular may well be judged on how we behave ourselves. Also some other countries who were discomfited by the fact that we got permission and they were refused will be only too glad to find some small lapse of etiquette or honesty in our party; we must therefore be doubly careful about what we do or say." Two nights later, Houston's father picked up the tab—for a party of twenty-two—for a farewell dinner at Lüchow's, the renowned German restaurant on East 14th Street near Union Square.

And then it was finished. While the other members of the expedition sailed first to Cherbourg, and then from Marseille to Bombay, Houston had to remain in New York to finish taking his medical school exams at Columbia. Finally, flying from London to India, he met up with the other climbers in Rawalpindi on May 9. Officially known as the 1938 American Alpine Club Karakoram Expedition, no one in the mountaineering world was at all fooled by what the real objective was. The Americans were aiming to conquer K2. And if they did, the race to the roof of the world would be effectively over. Charlie Houston's next great adventure was about to begin.

While still relatively new to the Himalayas proper, the American mountaineers were far from inexperienced. Houston, of course, had been one bad tin of bully beef away from summiting Nanda Devi two years earlier, while Dick Burdsall had been one of the two

Americans to climb to the top of Minya Konka. Bob Bates had made the first successful ascent of Mount Lucania in the Yukon, a remote 17,000-foot peak that was then the highest unclimbed mountain in North America, while Bill House had been one of the first two climbers to summit Mount Waddington in British Columbia. Moreover, with one exception, the 1938 American K2 climbers were cut from much the same social cloth. Bates, from Philadelphia, had prepped at Phillips Exeter Academy before enrolling at Harvard. Burdsall had attended Swarthmore, while House had graduated from both Choate and Yale. Superb climbers all, they were also the products of Northeastern elite society, and were as comfortable at a black-tie mixer or with a Latin passage to translate as they were on an exposed crag one thousand feet above an icy death somewhere in the White Mountains of New Hampshire.

The exception was Paul Petzoldt.

Part Woody Guthrie, part character out of Mark Twain, and part God-knows-what, he had already crammed several lifetimes into his thirty years. Born on a hardscrabble Iowa farm in 1908, his father died of influenza when Petzoldt was three years old. His German-born mother took over the farming herself, eventually moving Paul and his brothers and sisters to a patch of land outside of Twin Falls, Idaho. When he wasn't in school or helping out at home, Petzoldt loved to climb the five-hundred-foot rock walls of the nearby Snake River Canyon, or make forays into the Sawtooth Mountains, living off rainbow trout, camas roots, and wild huckleberries. But in 1922, his mother lost the farm and decided to head back east. Paul opted to stay in Twin Falls and live with an older brother and his wife. But the next summer, after he had completed the eighth grade, he decided to see the world. He was fourteen.

His mode of travel was hopping freight trains. He'd hide in a patch of woods or behind a switching shed, and once the locomotive had passed, he'd take off running, grab onto the side of an open box-car, and, like a pole-vaulter without a pole, swing himself up and inside. "He grabbed freights going east, and a few weeks later he'd be headed for California," wrote his future wife, Patricia. "He roamed through the Southern states and the Middle West. He picked fruit in California, and pitched hay in Kansas. He became an efficient dish-washer, cook's helper, and waiter. There was always too much to see, and none of the jobs lasted long." If he wasn't working, he'd spend his days in the nearest public library, reading.

But the mountains were still calling.

During the summer of 1924, when he was sixteen, he reconnected with Ralph Herron, an old friend from Twin Falls, and the pair of them hitchhiked to Jackson Hole, Wyoming. Overpowered by his first glimpse of the Grand Tetons, and told that the highest of the peaks had never been climbed, Petzoldt immediately decided to take on the project. He soon learned, however, that the Grand Teton had, in fact, been climbed back in 1898, and that one of the original climbers was still living in town. Petzold and Herron looked him up, and after first getting an earful of advice from the old-timer, they headed for the rocky, 13,000-foot peak. Their two-man expedition turned out to be a hair-raising adventure all of its own, not least due to the fact that they were wearing smooth-bottomed boots, and had to bivouac one night in a blizzard wearing little more than sweat-soaked cotton clothes. But in the end, they persevered and made it to the summit. Afterwards, every cowboy, shopkeeper, and panhandler in town wanted to shake the hands of the daring young men who had pulled off what most folks thought was little more than an invitation to suicide.

That notoriety, as it turned out, led to a business opportunity. For the next few years, Petzoldt would return to Jackson Hole every summer to lead guided climbs in the Tetons. During the winters he would leave Wyoming and scare up work wherever he could find it, some of it legal, other parts not so much. In Toledo, Ohio, where he graduated from high school, he became a good enough poker player that he was able to salt away two thousand dollars in winnings—a small fortune for a twenty-year-old. Then, in 1929, when Teton National Park was officially opened, Petzoldt won the climbing concession. He named his outfit the American School of Mountaineering.

Guiding everyone from New York bankers to Wyoming ranch hands on day hikes, overnighters, and easy-to-moderate climbs in the national park, Petzold was a hit—especially with well-heeled visitors from the East Coast and Europe. He would put them at ease in the wilderness, ask them questions about their lives and occupations, and entertain them with tales of his own adventures. Then, during the summer of 1933, Petzoldt had a client like no other he had ever had before. Sixty years old, a bit overweight, and forever carrying a walking stick, his name was Sir Albert Baillie.

An esteemed Anglican clergyman who had once been a favorite of Queen Victoria, Sir Albert was the Dean of Windsor and, as such, was the private chaplain to both the King and Queen of England. But Baillie had a very down-to-earth side to him as well. His first parishes had been along the rough-and-tumble docks of East London. Moreover, he took an immediate shine to Petzoldt. "Paul guided him on some of the lower trails of the Tetons," Patricia Petzoldt later recalled, "and, while at first they discussed the mountains and the country in general, gradually their conversations turned to history and world affairs. The dean was both amused and delighted by some of Paul's naïve observations, and also somewhat surprised that he was as well informed as he was. Although they disagreed on practically any subject they discussed, the dean gradually grew very fond of the young man." At the end of his visit in the Tetons, Baillie invited Petzoldt to spend the year at Windsor Castle as his guest.

Petzoldt was flabbergasted.

Then he said yes.

It was, to say the least, an eye-opening experience. Taking cues from Sir Albert on how to interact with the English upper class—saying "O.K." and "You bet" is fine, the dean told him, but never, ever, under any circumstances, shall you utter a coarse or vulgar word—Petzoldt discussed mountaineering with Edward, the Prince of Wales, and once had dinner in London with Sir Albert and Fred

Astaire. But he spent most of his time that year either reading in the castle library or improving his golf game. Sir Albert had hoped that his young American protégé might want to attend Cambridge, but, again the mountains called. Bidding farewell to England, he spent part of the summer of 1934 bicycling across Belgium, France, and Germany on the way to the Alps. In Switzerland, Petzold connected with a young New Zealand climber, Dan Bryant, and together, it was said, they pulled off the first double traverse of the Matterhorn in one day—first climbing up the Swiss side and down the Italian, and then up the Italian and down the Swiss.

Back in the United States, Petzoldt's fame as a mountaineer continued to grow. News of new routes that he pioneered in Wyoming—including a winter ascent of the Grand Teton, and a solo climb of Mount Owen by the east face of Granite Knob—appeared regularly in the pages of the *American Alpine Journal*, the house organ of the American Alpine Club, the nation's premier climbing organization. Significantly, he was also becoming an expert in the use of pitons, the iron spikes that some climbers would hammer into the rock face of a mountain for protection when climbing a particularly steep or exposed pitch. While a number of East Coast climbers looked down upon such contrivances as a form of cheating, Western climbers had no such reservations. In California, a new generation of young climbers was already pushing the envelope of what could and could not be climbed even further. A long way from Harvard Yard, in the Berkeley Hills, on Tahquitz Rock, and in the Sierra Nevada Mountains, a climbing revolution was already beginning to brew.

But Paul Petzoldt could also recognize a golden opportunity when he saw one.

In late March 1938, a telegram addressed to Petzoldt arrived in Jackson Hole. It was from Charles Houston, and it invited him to join the American expedition to K2 that would be leaving in three weeks. One of the other climbers on the expedition, a Harvard man named William Farnsworth Loomis, had had to drop out at the last moment, but would sponsor whoever would take his place. Would Petzold like to go? Houston didn't have to ask twice, and a little after midnight on April 14, 1938, the Wyoming mountain guide climbed on board the *Europa*, a German ocean liner docked at Pier 86, and watched the glittering Manhattan skyline slip by off the port side. One month later, he was in India.

The railroad ended in Rawalpindi.

A sun-scorched market town along the northernmost tip of the Punjab, where vendors in pointed-toe shoes hawked green corn and sugar cane, bushel baskets of grain and lumps of bright pink rock salt, it was where the hot plains ended and the foothills began. The next morning, May 10, the American climbers and their British transport officer, Captain Norman Streatfeild, took off for Srinagar by automobile, a ten-plus-hour, bone-rattling journey past steep gorges and barren hills, thundering streams and bright green patches of wheat and barley. A week later, now joined by six Sherpas from Darjeeling, twenty-five sturdy little Kashmiri ponies hauling their supplies, and a handful of wild-eyed drivers, they tramped through the soft snow at the top of the 11,000-foot pass at Zogi La, and dropped down into Baltistan—and into what felt like antiquity.

Gone were the grasslands and flowers of Kashmir, the gentle slopes covered with pine and fir. Here, the rough and arid countryside, with its treeless hills and silt-choked rivers, was all of the same dull palette—burnt umber mixed with cadmium white. "Instead of the fertile, green, water-soaked meadows of the vale, we found a dry, barren, and rocky country," Houston wrote, "whose heat and drought soon appalled us." The few-and-far-between villages that they passed were dingy collections of mud huts, with old men sitting quietly beneath a few scraggly trees. The modern world appeared again, briefly, in Skardu, which boasted a tennis court, but a day later they crossed the Indus River on an ancient barge, manned by six oarsmen and two helmsmen to steer, said to date to the time of Alexander the Great. Trading their ponies for some seventy-five porters, by early

June the expedition was well on its way to the foot of the Baltoro Glacier, which would carry them to K2.

Despite their prep-school diplomas, the American climbers were a strong, tough bunch. Lean and wiry, with sunburned noses and stubble turning into beards, the climbers had no trouble fording the ice-cold streams, nor covering as many as fifteen or twenty miles a day beneath the blazing sun of Baltistan. And they needed to be, for the march from Srinagar to K2 was a grueling three hundred and fifty miles. The Sherpas, whom Bill Tilman had handpicked in Darjeeling, were equally formidable. Pasang Kikuli, the head Sherpa, had survived Nanga Parbat in 1934. But all of them were eager, and they proudly wore their high-altitude jackets even in the heat. So, too, were the Balti porters, some barefoot and some blue-eyed, dressed in loose-fitting robes and headscarves, but always prepared to hoist their fifty-pound—or more—loads onto their backs each morning.

Paul Petzoldt, meanwhile, was quietly having an impact of his own. In Paris on the way over, he had purchased dozens of pitons at a mountaineering shop once he had learned that the expedition had hardly any. Now, on the long march to K2, he would teach the Sherpas climbing knots around the campfires at night. And when an unexpected chance to take a couple of days off came along near a village called Yuno, Petzoldt took the six Sherpas to some nearby cliffs and taught them how to rappel. Twelve-thousand miles from the Tetons, the self-taught Wyoming mountaineer was doing something no European or American climber had ever bothered to do before: teach the Sherpas what only the sahibs knew.

Base Camp was established on June 12.

Before sending their porters away, a plan was devised as to when they would come back. "We gave them forty-five stones," Houston recalled, "telling them to throw away one stone every day and return for us when all the stones were gone." The Americans now had a month and a half to climb the second-highest mountain on earth. For the first eleven days, they split up into groups and probed the west and northeast ridges of K2. But because of the extreme difficulties that each route presented—including knife-edged ridges and "green ice lying at an angle of over 50° and covered with a thin layer of loose snow"—none offered a viable route toward the summit. Everywhere they looked, K2 looked impossible. "A wet, heavy snowfall further added to our discouragement," Houston wrote of June 23, "and our spirits that evening were at a low point."

Gathering together in one of their tents at Base Camp, while the frigid night air rolled in off the mountain, the climbers held a war council. The Duke of the Abruzzi had been correct. Despite the possibly insurmountable problems that would have to be confronted near the summit, and numerous other difficulties along the way, the south ridge—which they renamed the Abruzzi Ridge—offered the best, and possibly the only, chance for success. Moreover, time was now a factor. Not only would their porters be back in a month, but the impact of the monsoon on K2 was still largely a mystery. "We had every reason to believe," Houston wrote, "that the weather would not improve but rather deteriorate during July." It was time to move.

And move they did. By the eighth of July, all of the climbers and Sherpas had made it to Camp Two, while the first loads of supplies had already been moved up to Camp Three, at 20,700 feet. But the climbing, which had not been easy, was growing progressively more and more difficult. Using Petzoldt's supply of Parisian pitons, long sections of fixed rope had to be put in place leading up to Camp Three—where a whole new set of unforeseen problems suddenly came literally crashing into view. Because the camp was built on a tiny platform of rock at the bottom of a long and slippery face, any rocks that were dislodged on the climb above would get funneled down toward Camp Three with uncanny accuracy. Each day, rock after rock tore through the camp, punching holes in the sides of the tents and threatening to knock their human occupants unconscious. As a result of this unavoidable barrage, a decision was reached to contract the size of the party. Burdsall, Captain Streatfeild, and three of the Sherpas would descend to Base Camp, while the others would continue the attack.

Petzoldt, in particular, was in his element. He loved the blue-black sky and the white-hot sunshine. Later singled out by Houston as the strongest and toughest of the climbers, he had done a brilliant job of leading the climb up to Camp Four, and he more than held his own on the steep slopes of the upper mountain. And despite a few off days of bad weather, by July 14 Petzoldt and Houston had fought their way up to over 23,000 feet, where they found a passable site for Camp Six. Pushing on two days later, they made it to the last one thousand feet of the Abruzzi Ridge. "This was the crux of the climb," Houston recalled. "Should we be able to surmount the difficulties which from below had seemed so formidable, and gain the 25,000-ft. shoulder, we were fairly confident that we could reach at least 26,000 ft." They persevered. At a little after three o'clock that afternoon, the two men shook hands at the top of the Abruzzi Ridge. They were, they believed, less than three-thousand feet from the summit of K2.

There was also no time to waste. Forcing a traverse toward the east across a steep slope of hard green ice, they used pitons and fixed rope to secure the passage upward, before turning around and heading back down to Camp Six before nightfall. There, the others were waiting for them. Houston shared the good news. "Abruzzi Ridge had been climbed and the summit cone seemed to lie clear before us," he wrote. "But grave decisions had to be made that evening."

Despite their unbridled joy at what they had accomplished, the clock was now ticking faster than ever. The key issue was supplies. While they had more than a week's worth of food and fuel in Camp Six, because of the difficulty of the route, they knew that they had to have good weather in order to descend safely. "How long storms could last was still a question," Houston recalled. While the storms they had faced thus far usually lasted only five or six days at the most, they also knew that much more prolonged bad weather could appear at any time. "It was clear then to all of us that we were nearly at the end of a safe advance," Houston wrote.

The question, then, was what to do next.

Err on the side of caution and come home with everyone alive and safe? Or gamble and make a run for the summit?

After what was later remembered as a spirited debate, a vote was taken and a decision was reached. Bob Bates, Bill House, and the Sherpa, Pasang Kikuli, would push ahead and establish a two-man Camp Seven for Houston and Petzoldt. They, in turn, would have one day to get as high as they could before returning. Safety, the majority had ruled, would come first.

Camp Seven. Late afternoon. July 20, 1938.

Tired and cold, Charles Houston and Paul Petzoldt bid the others goodbye and crawled into the small, two-man tent. While Houston gathered some snow to melt in one of the aluminum pots, Petzoldt assembled the stove. Digging around in the food bag, suddenly he stopped.

"My God," he said. "They forgot to pack the matches."

This was no idle matter. Without matches they could not light the stove, and without a lit stove, they could neither melt water to drink, nor cook food to eat. Luckily, Houston found a few beat-up matches in a coat pocket. The first two were duds, but the third one lit, and they soon got the stove going.

The next morning, it took three matches to light the stove.

They had three left.

Each man finished his breakfast and got ready. It was now or never.

The day dawned bright and sunny.

Roped together, the two climbers moved cautiously up the shoulder. Even at some 26,000 feet, Petzoldt climbed steadily and rhythmically, taking the same number of breaths between steps while moving upward, and decreasing the number when the ground was more even. And while they had been at elevations of more than

The World Beneath Their Feet

20,000 feet for more than two weeks, Petzoldt had shown little signs of altitude sickness. Over rock and snow, some of it soft and feathery, he slowly plodded ahead. Houston was not faring as well.

Around one o'clock, they stopped for a quick bite of food. They were nearing the end of a long snowfield. Above them lay a tricky pitch below a massive wall of compacted snow and ice. There would be avalanche danger there. But beyond it, as far as they could tell, lay the summit pyramid itself. After they had finished eating, and roped up, Petzoldt took the lead. But it was no good. "My progress was ludicrously slow," Houston later recalled. "Every inch I gained in altitude was an effort. My legs were so weak I was forced to rest every five or six steps." Finally, he stopped and slumped against a boulder.

"I've reached my limit," he called up to his partner.

Petzoldt did not argue.

"Why don't you rest there and I'll go on a bit further."

Petzoldt unroped and continued up a ways by himself. He could now see that the hard part of the mountain was behind him. The route to the summit wouldn't be difficult. Stopping to take a photograph, no American had ever stood on higher ground before. Then he turned around and went back to where Houston still lay, pale and breathing heavily. Petzoldt gave him a hug, and after roping back up, the two men then began to make their way back down to Camp Seven. "The whole world was deathly still," Houston recalled. "We trudged down to Camp Seven in a deepening twilight. About us the mountains turned first pink, the lavender, then purple. We reached camp safely." Back inside the tent, it took all three matches to light the stove.

They were back in Srinagar by August 10.

Despite their defeat, the Americans had found their mountain. The British had Mount Everest, the Germans had Nanga Parbat. Now the Americans had K2. And even before the first American attempt was over, a second expedition had already started to come together.

CHAPTER TWELVE

A Bit East of The Plaza

Fritz Wiessner was perpetually short.

He was short on time, short on money, and more often than not, short on patience. Small in stature, but solidly built, with huge hands, doe eyes, and nary a wisp of hair on top of his head, by the summer of 1938 he was not just the best rock climber in America. He was also a force to be reckoned with, a limestone and granite prophet who would revolutionize how generations of rock climbers would approach their craft—while living in a dumpy apartment in Brooklyn and working two jobs to finance climbing dreams that, more often than not, somehow had a way of working out.

Still a German citizen, Wiessner had grown up in Dresden. Born a year too late to take part in the Great War, at age seventeen he started to teach himself how to climb in the Elbsandsteingebirge, the haunting sandstone cliffs that rose up south of the city. But as he grew as a climber, he also became an advocate of free climbing— that is, rock climbing that was done, as much as possible, without the assistance of pitons. By the time he turned twenty-five, he had successfully completed some of the most difficult climbs ever attempted in his native Saxony. Two years later, Wiessner was putting up historic routes in the Dolomites, across the border in Italy. He was a wonder on rock, a baby-faced vertical ballet star, one of the best ever.

But the rest of his life was a cheap chapbook of busted dreams. Working as a pharmacist's aide while studying chemistry on his own,

Fritz Wiessner simply could not get ahead, especially during the tough economic times of the early Weimar Republic. So, in early 1929, he decided to give America a try. Buying one-way passage on the *St. Louis*, a workhorse steamship with the Hamburg America Line, he arrived in New York City in early April 1929 along with scores of other German immigrants, including clerks and housewives, cooks and tailors, seamstresses and upholsterers, all looking to gain a foothold in the New World.

This was no easy path. His English, spoken with a heavy German accent, was spotty at best, while six months after his arrival the nation was thrown into crisis with the stock market crash. But Wiessner had what he hoped was a way ahead. Building a makeshift laboratory at home, he had developed a new kind of ski wax, which he soon marketed as Wonderwax. He still had to work other jobs, including washing windows at the Empire State Building, where, armed with a wet sponge and a squeegee, he dangled a thousand feet above the traffic inching along West 33rd and 34th Streets. But his ski wax business helped get him to the mountains of America, and it was here that he not only began to meet fellow climbers and skiers, but also to make a name for himself in his adoptive new land. In 1935, he was the first climber to explore the possibilities of Shawangunk Ridge, a seven-and-a-half-mile-long, two-thousand-foot-tall wall of bedrock some eighty miles north of Manhattan.

But it was in the West where Wiessner carved his name into the annals of North American mountaineering. In 1936, he led the first successful ascent of Mount Waddington, a daunting 13,000-foot peak in British Columbia that had bedeviled Canadian and US climbers for years. The climb itself took twenty-three hours, and was so difficult near the summit that Wiessner took off his mountaineering boots and led the final pitches wearing rope-soled shoes. One year later, he led the first technical climb of Devils Tower, the soaring ribbed tower that punched a hole in the Wyoming sky. "He seemed to move with greater ease and confidence even as he wriggled up the what looked to us like the most difficult part," climbing partner Bill

House wrote of Wiessner's lead. "Incredibly he kept going, forcing himself up the crack with a power and rhythm that was beautiful to watch." Wiessner had become a climber to reckon with.

But his mind was on the Himalayas.

Like mountaineers everywhere, he had read with rapt attention the newspaper accounts of the British and German efforts in India and Tibet. But Wiessner also had some Himalayan experience of his own to draw upon. In 1932, he had been a member of the so-called German–American Expedition to Nanga Parbat, led by Willy Merkl. While they had been turned back by storms at 22,000 feet, Wiessner knew that it was in the Himalayas where true mountaineering glory would be found. And he wanted a piece of it. In the end, it was Wiessner who successfully lobbied the American Alpine Club to seek permission for an expedition—or two—to K2. And now that Charlie Houston's climbers had failed to reach the summit, it would be his turn. But he had two big problems.

The first was finding some American climbers who had the talent—and experience—to launch a successful assault on the world's second-highest mountain. Houston had assembled a strong team, but those climbers would be out of the loop for a 1939 effort. Other candidates had been put off by Wiessner's personality, which could be brusque and demanding, particularly at first. Still others, no doubt, might have been hesitant to sign on to an expedition whose leader was a German national.

The other problem was money.

Raising funds for his own passage to India was hard enough. But even with the support of the American Alpine Club, coming up with enough money to finance a major expedition to the Himalayas was a daunting prospect. He didn't just need climbers who were well-off enough to pay their own way on what was, by the standards of the day, a most costly project. He also needed someone he could rely on to freely tap into a hefty bank account and cover the costs of any additional expenses. And finding someone like that in Depression-era America was no easy task.

Or, at least, it should not have been.

But fate works by its own design. And in late 1938, just as his hopes for launching an expedition to K2 the next year were growing thin, Fritz Wiessner received an invitation in the mail from Alice Damrosch Wolfe, a well-to-do American ski racer. Would he be interested in attending a dinner party at her ex-husband's apartment? Her former spouse will be showing some slides, she added, from his recent mountaineering adventures in the Alps.

Dudley Wolfe hadn't done a lick of work in years.

Aged forty-two, with a high forehead, a yachtsman's tan, and a neatly trimmed, brown mustache hovering over a relaxed, gracious smile, Wolfe was an heir to a vast family fortune in mining, real estate, railroads, and cattle. Born in Irvington-on-Hudson, an exclusive enclave north of New York City, he had grown up in a world of butlers and golf outings, boarding schools and the *Social Register*. A lackluster student, his grades were so poor that Phillips Andover Academy finally refused to let him, at age twenty, continue his studies. Depressed, struggling with his weight, and uncertain what to do, Wolfe tried to enlist in the US Army, Navy, and Marine Corps, but was turned down by each due to his poor eyesight. Finally, like Ernest Hemingway and John Dos Passos, he was accepted into the Ambulance Corps run by the American Field Service. Dispatched to the Italian Front in the fall of 1917, he transported wounded soldiers from the front lines to military infirmaries and hospital tents. More than a few died in his arms.

Dudley Wolfe came back to America a changed man.

While he still wasn't a whiz in the classroom, he enrolled at Harvard, where he played football and graduated with the Class of 1929. Living comfortably off of a copious trust fund, he indulged himself in his boyhood love of sailing. He bought a series of larger and larger yachts and, in 1929, entered the *Mohawk*, his sixty-footer, in a transatlantic race from New York to Europe, winning second place. Wolfe was a skilled skier as well, and spent winter after winter hitting the slopes in Switzerland and Austria—particularly after he tied the knot with Alice Damrosch, the striking, six-foot-tall socialite daughter of Walter Damrosch, the well-known New York orchestra conductor. While the marriage didn't last, Alice and Dudley remained friends. And when Dudley decided to host a black-tie dinner party at his Manhattan apartment, where he would show color slides of his newest passion, mountaineering, Alice helped address the invitations, including one to the odd little German ski wax manufacturer and climber whom she had met.

As soon as he walked off the elevator, Fritz Wiessner's spirits began to rise.

Not only did the penthouse at 4 East 72nd Street, between Madison Avenue and Central Park, drip of wealth, but the apartment itself was a paragon of taste and refinement. "He liked what he saw," journalist Jennifer Jordan later wrote. "The room was utterly white: white walls, white curtains, white floors, white leather furniture, white roses on the piano. Even the wine was white. The scene was a masterpiece of simple elegance." In the heights of the Upper East Side, in a room as bright as a Himalayan snowfall, Wiessner had found what he was looking for. He got right to work.

After viewing Dudley Wolfe's slides of his recent climbs on the Matterhorn and Mont Blanc, Wiessner managed to have a private conversation with the host. He was planning a mountaineering expedition to K2, the second-highest mountain in the world, Wiessner said. The British and the Germans had been competing with each other for years, Wiessner told Wolfe, to see which nation could be the first to the top of one of the true Himalayan giants, the *Achttausenders*. Now, he said, it was the Americans' turn. A team from the United States had just returned from K2. Not only had they found a climbable route to the summit, including the locations of each high camp along the way, but they had gotten to within less than two thousand feet from the top—about the same distance as it was from Wolfe's apartment to the Plaza Hotel. What he needed,

The World Beneath Their Feet

Wiessner said, was a couple more good, strong, determined men to help complete the roster of climbers, and bring home this rare prize. It was, he added, the opportunity of a lifetime.

That was all it took. Wolfe was in.

In truth, Wiessner needed a lot more. The other members of the expedition were, if nothing else, a mixed lot. A talented rock climber, twenty-six-year-old Jack Durrance had climbed in the Alps, founded the Dartmouth Mountaineering Club, and put up new routes on both Devils Tower and the Grand Teton in Wyoming. Two other Dartmouth men, also in their twenties, Chappell Cramner and George Sheldon, had done some limited climbing in British Columbia and the Rockies. Forty-two-year-old Tony Cromwell, another extremely well-heeled New Yorker—Doris Duke was once his sister-in-law—had climbed scores of mountains, most of them in Canada, but all of them with a guide. None but Wiessner had been to the Himalayas.

That, of course, was all about to change.

And by early March 1939, team members were hurriedly making last-minute preparations for their departures for India. Fritz Wiessner had also attended to one other matter. On St. Valentine's Day, in District Court in Brooklyn, he had been sworn in as a naturalized US citizen.

The expedition got off to an auspicious start.

Meeting in Srinagar in mid-April, Wiessner concluded that a few days of skiing would help everyone acclimate, so for ten days the climbers took charge of the Ski Club of India's Khillanmarg Hut. And while there was nothing as much as a rope tow for getting up the mountain, the younger climbers, in particular, were in powder heaven. "We had all of our equipment carried three thousand feet up to the hut, we had a cook and two servants, and a general caretaker," George Sheldon wrote. Back in Srinagar, they were feted by a British Army officer at his home. "As a Dartmouth student would say," Sheldon added, "'Every night is party night.'" Dudley Wolfe, meanwhile, was enchanted by it all. Before leaving the lake and river town, he arranged to have most of his belongings—including his mono-grammed leather suitcases, gold cufflinks, gunmetal-gray Longines wristwatch, blue-and-white-checkered Brooks Brothers bath robe, and his wallet, with its Plaza Hotel and Hertz credit cards—safely stored until his return.

The march in also went smoothly. Averaging nearly fifteen miles a day, the climbers' spirits were high. "Blisters have all but dis-appeared," Tony Cromwell wrote from Baltistan on May 13, "and the entire party appear to walk easily." Nine Sherpas, hired out of Darjeeling, were also enthusiastic. Led by Pasang Kikuli, who had been on Kangchenjunga, Everest, Nanga Parbat, and Nanda Devi, they were a tough, campaign-hardened group. And while there were some tawdry annoyances along the way, including fleas and a brief round of porter troubles in Askole, the expedition pushed steadily onward. "Nothing calamitous has happened I can tell you," Sheldon wrote from Base Camp on June 14, Day 10 of their assault on K2. "Tony ripped the seat out of his pants the other day but that is as close to tragedy as we have come."

One month later, the expedition had a different feel.

Day 39. July 13, 1939.

Camp Six. 23,400 feet.

For five weeks they had battled their way up the Abruzzi Ridge, hauling up men and supplies, setting their camps up higher and higher, and fully taking part in that high-altitude perpetual-motion machine, so necessary for acclimatization, that saw climbers and Sherpas climbing high to stock camps, then to head down for rest before going up once more. During the third week of June they'd also been pummeled by what was for everyone but Fritz Wiessner their first true Himalayan storm, a week-long howler that pinned them inside their tents while one-hundred-mile-per-hour winds tore at the ice-draped ridges of K2. "We could do nothing," Sheldon wrote, "but lie in our sleeping bags and hope we wouldn't launch into a maiden flight into Tibet." Two more storms, each three days long, followed, further battering an already weakened team.

On June 1, Chappell Cramner started his day saying he didn't feel well. Within hours he was fighting for his life. Delirious, coughing up wet slime, and losing all control of his bodily functions, he had developed what Jack Durrance, then a first-year medical student, diagnosed as cardiac decompensation. While he would survive, Chappell would get no higher on the mountain than Camp One. Meanwhile, George Sheldon's toes had been frostbitten, and once his feet began to swell, he had been ordered to return to Base Camp. And it had been agreed from the start that Tony Cromwell would not climb above the higher camps. There were now three climbers left to tackle the summit—Wiessner, Wolfe, and Durrance.

And so, on the morning of July 13, this trio, along with two Sherpas, set out toward Camp Seven. But less than two hundred yards into the climb, Durrance began to have trouble breathing, and he returned to Camp Six on his own. Wiessner and Wolfe, and the two Sherpas, pushed on alone.

Day 43. July 17.

Dudley Wolfe had been going strong—remarkably so. Despite being a bit overweight, and more or less a mountaineering novice, he had more than held his own. "Dudley is up on the mountain and you can't get him to come down," George Sheldon had written back in June. "He's going darn well." And the higher he went, the stronger he got. "Wolfe doing actually better the higher we went," Wiessner wrote, "to my delight." No longer a walking bank account, or an Upper East Side dandy, Dudley Wolfe was climbing—truly *climbing*—the second-highest mountain on earth. The New Yorker was ecstatic.

The weather that day was perfect. "Dawned clear," Wiessner wrote.

"Staircase Peak to the E. was already below us, and behind Windy Gap we could see the Shaksgam Valley and the high snow summits of Turkestan." Pushing their way through hip-deep snow in the bright sunshine, Wiessner, Wolfe, and Pasang Kikuli had already made it above 25,000 feet. But about two hundred feet above Camp Eight, they had to cross a *bergschrund*, a deep crevasse that barred the way to a snow slope which led toward the mountain's southeast shoulder. The big problem, though, was in the approach. "As we approach the schrund the snow became deeper and deeper and finally apparently bottomless," Wiessner wrote. "After two hours of the hardest conceivable work I succeeded, almost by swimming, in getting up across a snow bridge and then treading out a firm belaying stance on the steep slope above the bridge." It then took Pasang Kikuli an hour to make it across.

But it was too much for Dudley Wolfe. The decision was then reached that he would return to Camp Eight, and stay there, alone, that night. He could then follow, with help from below, in a day or two. The camp was well-stocked with food and fuel, and Wolfe had his sleeping bag with him. Wiessner and Pasang Kikuli, meanwhile, continued to work their way slowly upward, breathing heavily in the thin air, until they reached a great ice-cliff that would need to be approached from either the left or the right. "This looked as if it were near at hand," Wiessner recalled, "but we had soon to realize that after our long spell of wallowing in the deep snow and with our heavy loads we could no longer make it." So, they made camp near a huge boulder and turned in for the night.

Day 45. July 19.

Camp Nine. 26,050 feet.

"After a quiet night and a warm hearty breakfast," Wiessner wrote, "we left camp on July 19 as late as 9 o'clock. Pasang carried our crampons and the reserve rope, 75 meters long and 9 mm. in diameter; I had the rucksack with food, pitons, carabiners, and warm extra clothing."

They were going for the summit.

Roped together, the two men climbed slowly but steadily. Over the course of two hours, they clambered over the rocks near the top of the southeast ridge, the worn-down nails of their hobnailed boots still finding adequate purchase. And despite the altitude, they were making good progress, gaining nearly eight hundred feet by eleven o'clock. But now, as they reached the foot of the buttress, the climbing changed radically. Opting to take the route to the left, Wiessner later wrote that they soon ran into a huge challenge—"a black verglaced couloir which soon became very steep and terminated in an over-hang." Setting pitons for protection, Wiessner brilliantly led several pitches of extremely difficult climbing. Now well above eight thousand meters, Wiessner figured that he and Pasang Kikuli only had about twenty-five more feet of steep climbing. Then they could take a short breather before moving on. But Pasang had other ideas.

"No, Sahib," he said, "tomorrow."

Wiessner attempted to make his case. "I now tried to make it clear to Pasang that the difficulties would be over in a few meters and that we could then have a long rest upon the ridge," he later recalled. "That in the clear night we could go to the summit over easier terrain and descend in sunshine the next morning."

Pasang held his ground, and refused to play out any more rope.

Finally, Wiessner gave in.

As it turned out, the descent back to Camp Nine was a nightmare. Darkness fell while they were still in the black couloir, and at one point while they were roping down, a rope got tangled in the two sets of crampons that Pasang was carrying on his back. The Sherpa was able to free the rope, but in so doing, the crampons broke free and were lost down the mountain. They did not make it to Camp Nine until two-thirty in the morning.

* * *

Day 47. July 21.

Camp Nine. 26,050 feet.

After a much-needed day of rest., Wiessner and Pasang decided to try for the summit again. This time, however, they would avoid the black couloir and try the route to the right. Leaving camp at six o'clock that morning, they ran into difficult climbing during the first couple of hours—verglaced slabs covered with scree, and handholds and footholds skinned with ice. But just past a difficult chimney, they discovered a snow gully that led all the way to the summit snowfield. It was clearly the way to the top, which lay only a little more than one thousand feet above them. The summit of K2 was theirs for the taking. But a new problem soon became evident. "The snow in the gully was hard as a rock, the lower portion was steep, and we had no crampons," Wiessner wrote. "With crampons one could have walked quickly up." Without them they would need to cut as many as four hundred steps in the ice, something that, at that elevation, would have taken more than a day to accomplish.

They had no choice but to return to Camp Nine. Hopefully some of the others would have come up by now. Surely, some of them would have crampons, which Weissner and Pasang could use to attain the summit. But when they made it back to camp, no one was there. Running low on food, Wiessner decided that the next morning, he and Pasang must go down to Camp Eight.

Day 48. June 22.

Camp Eight. 25,300 feet.

Dudley Wolfe had been alone at Camp Eight for five days. Though he still had food and fuel, he had run out of matches two days earlier. The only water he had to drink was melted snow that had gathered in one of the folds of his tent. Thank God that the weather had been good and sunny. "Wolfe was standing there and called to us," Wiessner recalled. "He was greatly pleased to see us again but considerably put out that no one had come up from below." After cooking and eating a warm lunch, a decision was made that the three men would all go down to Camp Seven, where a week's worth of supplies had been cached. They could then haul those up to Camp Nine, and from there make a successful assault on the summit.

But on the way down, along steep slope of hard snow, the three men—all roped together—took a fall. "We all plunged down the steep slope with the snow becoming harder and harder," Wiessner later wrote. "By means of my ice axe, and my boots scraping against the slope, I succeeded in obtaining a hold." He managed to check the fall, and all three men were safe. But in the process, Wolfe lost his sleeping bag. Because of the fall, it was already twilight by the time they finally reached Camp Seven. "Here," Wiessner recalled, "was the disappointment of our lives." Not only was the camp devoid of other humans, but one tent was full of snow, while the other was halfway collapsed. What food there was had been taken from the tents and scattered in the snow, while all of the sleeping bags and air mattresses were missing. Luckily, they found a can of fuel, so they were able to cook dinner. The night, with only one sleeping bag—Pasang's—to cover their knees and calves, was excruciating.

Day 49. July 23.

Camp Seven. 24,700 feet.

With only one sleeping bag between the three of them, two of the men had to go down to Camp Six, where they could collect more sleeping bags and other needed supplies. A decision was reached that Wolfe would remain at Camp Seven while Wiessner and Pasang headed down. But more than just getting supplies, Wiessner also wanted answers. Where was Jack Durrance? Where were the other Sherpas? And why was Camp Seven left in such an abominable condition? But the immediate plan was clear: to get the needed supplies at Camp Six, to bring them up to Camp Seven, and to resume the assault on the summit.

At eleven o'clock, after the wind had died down, Wiessner and Pasang said goodbye to Wolfe and started down. But when they made it to Camp Six, they found that there were no sleeping bags or mattresses there, either. "Our situation now became very serious," Wiessner wrote. "We could not go back to Camp Seven, since there was only one sleeping bag for Wolfe there, and this would have not been sufficient to keep the three of us from freezing." The only choice was to push down to the next camp that should have a cache of supplies, which was Camp Four. But when they got there, it, too, had been stripped. Now desperate, they had no choice but to keep going. "The fight for our lives," he added, "had begun." They needed to make it to Camp Two, and the supplies that were kept there.

They stumbled into Camp Two at nightfall. Two tents were still standing, one empty, the other half filled with food. But, once again, no sleeping bags. Exhausted, they pulled down one of the tents, and carried it inside the other, to be used as a kind of makeshift blanket. "The cold tent cloth however gave no warmth and we shivered miserably," Wiessner wrote, "our toes and fingers, frostbitten in the preceding night, became much worse."

Day 50. July 24.

Base Camp. 16,600 feet.

Physically and mentally wrecked, Fritz Wiessner and Pasang Kikuli stumbled into Base Camp. Wiessner could barely speak above a faint whisper, and had trouble making himself understood. But what he heard was nothing short of astonishing. The others had assumed that he and Pasang and Wolfe were dead. In fact, when Tony Cromwell and some of the Sherpas had spotted them just outside Base Camp, they had been searching for their bodies.

What had happened was this—

On July 17, when Wiessner, Pasang, and Wolfe had struggled with the *bergschrund*, four of the Sherpas were sent up toward Camp Eight, to check on everyone's condition. Getting to within shouting distance of the camp, they called out but heard no response. One of the Sherpas, Tendup, then began to spread the rumor that the trio had died in an avalanche. Whether he truly believed this or not, or simply wanted to get off the mountain, was unclear. But the idea took root. With Jack Durrance now in command of the expedition, an order was allegedly given by Durrance for the Sherpas to climb back up the mountain and recover all of the sleeping bags from Camp Seven down.

Wiessner couldn't believe his ears. Then he collapsed, utterly spent.

But he still planned on getting to the summit.

Day 55. July 29.

Camp Seven. 24,700 feet.

Dudley Wolfe was in trouble. He had now been at Camp Seven, alone, for nearly one week. His matches had run out three days earlier and, as a result, he had eaten no hot food or drink since the twenty-fifth. All he could do was to lie in his sleeping bag, and listen for the sounds of voices or footsteps that, so far, had never come.

Down at Base Camp, Jack Durrance and three Sherpas had started back up the mountain to rescue Wolfe the day after Wiessner and Pasang Kikuli had been found alive. They made it to Camp Four in two days, but Durrance and one of the Sherpas fell sick, and were unable to proceed.

On July 28, Pasang Kikuli and Tsering climbed from Base Camp to Camp Six in one day—an unprecedented, 6,800-foot climb and a truly magnificent feat. The next day, Pasang Kikuli and two other Sherpas finally made it up to Camp Seven. What they saw disturbed Pasang greatly. Dudley Wolfe was no longer the climber he had been with a week earlier. Not only was he morose and sluggish, but he had wet himself in his sleeping bag. Working together, the Sherpas woke Wolfe up, made tea, and prepared to escort him down the mountain, at least to Camp Six if not further. But Wolfe refused, saying that he wouldn't go until the next day. Despite their pleadings, the American climber held his ground. Because their sleeping bags were down at Camp Six, the Sherpas had to leave. They would be back, Pasang Kikuli told Wolfe, the next day.

Not long after they left, the flaps on Wolfe's tent began to flutter in the wind.

Day 57. July 31.

Camp Six. 23,400 feet.

The storm had come and gone, battering all the reaches of the mountain and making travel impossible for close to thirty hours. Even though the sky was still cloudy, the wind had finally died down and the snow had stopped. Now, one day after they had said that they would come, Pasang Kikuli and two other Sherpas, Kitar and Phinsoo, roped up and began the climb up to Camp Seven, their boots crunching through the new layer of snow. In his pocket, Pasang carried a pencil and a scrap of paper. If Wolfe again refused to come down, they would ask him to write a note, which they could show to Wiessner and the others, stating that this was his choice. Tsering, one of the Sherpas who remained at Camp Six, watched his three companions for a while, then he went back inside the tent.

Pasang Kikuli, Kitar, and Phinsoo were never seen alive again.

Nor was Dudley Wolfe.

Seven days later, on August 7, after another terrific storm, Fritz Wiessner called off the rescue efforts. By the ninth of the month, the last members of the expedition had begun their long walk back to Srinagar.

The World Beneath Their Feet

The Americans no longer had their Everest.

K2 was now their Nanga Parbat.

Up at Camp Seven, meanwhile, the wind continued to blow, bringing with it an early preview of the coming fall storms. By October, fresh snow would cover up the last bootprints, lie thickly on the abandoned food dumps, and snap the poles of the now-empty tents. In time it would bury not only the last traces of a failed expedition, but also the dreams that had once taken flight in the windy canyons of Manhattan, and in the fragile hearts of men who lived there.

CHAPTER THIRTEEN

The North Face

M unich was on edge.

While the ancient mechanical clock still tolled off the hours at Neues Rathaus, and the beer still flowed at the Hofbräuhaus, the city that Paul Bauer returned home to in the late summer of 1938 was now anxious and uncertain. Catholic church officials who had once welcomed the Nazis as a counterbalance to moral decay now found their shrines defaced and their priests and nuns sitting in courtrooms. Longtime neighbors quit looking each other in the eye, shopclerks gave only the briefest of answers to questions, while teenagers were told time and again to stick close to home. A handful of Nazi bigwigs and local businessmen, it was true, had reaped the benefits of having their city become celebrated as the birthplace of national socialism. But the average party member was now feeling fewer and fewer Reichsmarks in their purses and pocketbooks. Instead, German citizens were fed a steady diet of propaganda—both of Nazi triumphs and, even more powerfully, of the alleged mistreatment of Germany and Germans—all of which came to a head with the Sudetenland crisis that fall. Having snatched up Austria in the *Anschluss* back in March, Hitler was now demanding, more and more loudly and fervently, that the German-speaking regions of Czechoslovakia be incorporated into the Third Reich. And for several nervous weeks, while England and France tried to figure out what to do, war suddenly seemed just around the corner.

Paul Bauer, meanwhile, got back to work.

The World Beneath Their Feet

Soon to be remarried, and now living a short walk from his office just off the Marienplatz, the business at hand was, of course, to organize a return expedition to Nanga Parbat during the late spring and early summer of 1939. Not only did the glory and honor of the Reich demand that German climbers successfully attain the summit of this deadly giant, but Bauer's own reputation, unfairly or not, was increasingly at stake. The next expedition had to be carefully and precisely planned, for the margin for error had grown paper-thin. It was time for a victory, not another death march. The first step was to gain permission from the British. The second would be to find the right men.

A thousand kilometers to the northwest, Oxford, England was, in September 1938, awakening from its long summer nap. The baggage handlers at the railway station were doing a steady if rather tip-meager business, landlords could be seen pulling down handmade Room to Let signs, while the shop girls at Boffin's kept putting new cakes in the windows. There were plenty of visitors, too, who made their way in hushed awe to the Ashmolean Museum, the Bodleian Library, and the Sheldonian Theatre. If the world was going to hell in a handbasket, one might as well have a pint at the Eagle and Child first.

Among the out-of-towners visiting Oxford that month was a lanky Austrian, dressed in a conservative suit and tie, carrying a single suitcase. Though he was now a citizen of the Third Reich and had been a member of the Nazi Party for a number of years, Peter Aufschnaiter took care to present himself as nothing more than a mountaineer, one who had come to visit with English climbers about a planned expedition to the Himalayas.

Tall, thin, and thirty-nine, with long hands and perpetually smiling eyes, Aufschnaiter could have easily been mistaken for a vacationing blueblood—despite the fact that he was a carpenter's son from the Tyrol. After military service in the Great War, he'd drifted to Munich, where he studied agriculture and joined the Academic Climbing

Club at the University of Munich. When he had blossomed into a first-class climber, Paul Bauer had selected him as a member of both of his Kangchenjunga expeditions. Now, he was second-in-command at the Deutsche Himalayan Foundation. And as the Czechoslovakian crisis continued to bubble in the background, Aufschnaiter had come to smooth the way for a new German expedition to Nanga Parbat in 1939.

Aufschnaiter's host in Oxford was Kenneth Mason. Perhaps the most important unsung hero of British mountaineering, Mason had lived a life that alternated between high adventure and serious study. Thoroughly enchanted by Francis Younghusband's writings on the Himalayas, which he first read as a child, he moved to India in 1909 as a newly commissioned officer in the Royal Engineers, where he pioneered the use of new stereoplotting machines with the Survey of India. Teaching himself the rudiments of mountaineering, in 1912 he made the first ascent of Kolahoi, a remote 17,000-foot peak in Kashmir, along with a medical missionary and a local hunting guide. During the war, Mason was wounded in France, awarded the Military Cross for his actions in Mesopotamia, served as an intelligence officer in Baghdad, and drove the first automobile across the Syrian desert.

Disappointed not to be selected as a member of any of the British expeditions to Mount Everest in the 1920s, he instead founded the Himalayan Club, the first India-based mountaineering organization, and also served as the first editor of the esteemed *Himalayan Journal*. Not only did the club encourage and record the climbing efforts of British Army officers and other European nationals residing in India, but it also served as a vital go-between for international expeditions in the Himalayas, helped to secure permissions for travel to mountainous regions, provided information on local conditions, and assisted in recruiting porters in Darjeeling. As a result, Mason probably knew more high-altitude mountaineers than anyone else in the world.

In 1932, he returned to England to become the first Professor of Geography at Oxford, where he lived with his wife Dorothy in a charming white-trimmed, red-brick home at No. 1 Belbroughton Road, about a mile north of campus. But Mason's connection to both climbing and to the Himalayas hadn't missed a beat. Despite his age and position, he was a well-liked mentor to the lads in the Oxford Mountaineering Club—including a future Himalayan climber named Robin Hodgkin who, the night before the coronation of George VI, made the first known ascent of the Radcliffe Camera, planting the Union Jack on the summit. And Mason still served as the editor of the *Himalayan Journal* while mail from around the world still poured in. So respected was Mason that both Hugh Ruttledge and Paul Bauer had made pilgrimages to Oxford to pick his brain.

And thus did Peter Aufschnaiter.

Working over maps spread out in Mason's office, or on the dining-room table on Belbroughton Road—while the rest of Europe held its breath over the growing crisis in Czechoslovakia—the two men traded stories of climbing and India, and spoke of Everest and K2, the Karakoram and Tibet. Aufschnaiter also explained, to Mason's obvious interest, how the new expedition to Nanga Parbat would be different. When the visit ended, Mason offered to write some letters on behalf of the German climbers. Aufschnaiter was elated. Nanga Parbat was still theirs. As he began his journey back home, Peter Aufschnaiter felt confident he had gotten what he needed.

So, too, it seemed, had a traveler going in the opposite direction.

Returning from Munich on September 30, British prime minister Neville Chamberlain's airplane touched down at the Heston Aerodrome outside of London just before 6:00 p.m. Triumphantly waving a piece of paper before the crowd that had gathered to welcome him home from his summit with Hitler, Chamberlain said, "I want to say that the settlement of the Czechoslovak problem which has been achieved is, in my view, only a prelude to a larger settlement in which all Europe may find peace." The crowd burst into cheers and then started singing "For He's a Jolly Good Fellow." On the ride toward London, policemen had difficulty holding back the happy crowd, including the more than five score Eton students who had come to the airport on their own initiative. No one seemed to mind the rain.

In Munich, meanwhile, Paul Bauer was pleased with the results of Aufschnaiter's diplomatic visit to Oxford. Not only would his protégé lead the return to Nanga Parbat the next year, but the expedition itself would have a new objective. After the twin disasters of 1934 and 1937, and his own foreshortened attempt one year later, Bauer had decided to see if there was another route to the summit other than up the long and dangerous Rakhiot face. In particular, he wanted a team of mountaineers to carefully investigate the possibilities of the mountain's Diamir face, up which the intrepid British climber Alfred Mummery had reached an elevation of more than 20,000 feet before turning back. Rather than include a summit attempt, the 1939 expedition would purely be a reconnaissance. It was time to try something new.

But there was another change as well. For German mountaineering and the Deutsche Himalaya Foundation was no longer immune from the propaganda needs of the Third Reich. All of the climbers, of course, would have to be members of the Nazi Party. But beyond that, they would also need to serve as ideal representatives of the nation's highest aspirations. And there was one climber, in particular, who had caught not only the eye of Paul Bauer's boss, Hans von Tschammer und Osten, but even, it was said, that of the *Führer* himself.

A motorcycle tore through what used to be Austria, its single piston straining.

Sticking to the smaller roads, which took him well south of Salzburg, the lone rider pushed on, hour after hour, toward the west. By late-afternoon, he had skirted past Innsbruck, whose outdoor cafés were now filled with midsummer visitors, well-to-do families from Hamburg and Berlin in lederhosen and light cotton dresses, and uniformed regular army and SS officers in spit-shined jackboots, taking in the mountains and the gentle July weather. Come evening, the motorcyclist had left the Reich, crossing the frontier first at Liechtenstein, the tiny, postage-stamp duchy along the eastern shore of the Rhine, then into Switzerland, where the border guards took a bemused interest in the climbing rope, rock hammer, carabiners, and pitons stuffed into his canvas saddle bags and rucksack. And while the rider had been on the road for more than twelve hours straight, with dirt and dust caking his goggles, he pushed on, roaring along the two-lane highways, a ragged streamer of gray exhaust trailing off his tailpipe.

Twenty-six years old, with a shock of bright red hair, Heinrich Harrer was as rugged as the Julian Alps where he'd been born. The son of a housemaid and a postal worker, he had spent his first years with neither electricity nor running water in a grim mining town where children were born at home, herbal medicines took the place of doctor's visits, and poor families had to pay a fee in order to collect scraps of wood from a nearby forest just to heat their homes. But even as a youth, Harrer had sought further horizons. He hustled any jobs he could find—cleaning shoes, setting pins in a bowling alley, picking snowdrops and daffodils to sell—in order to buy, first, a crystal radio set, and then a pair of wooden skis. Excelling at school, he developed a deep love for geography and its maps and workbooks and stories of strange lands and exotic customs.

The mountains called as well. He made his first climb—alone—of Mangart, a steep, 8,000-foot limestone peak, when he was fifteen. A natural climber, he joined a local mountaineering club the next year, and by the time he was in his early twenties Harrer was tackling some of the hardest routes in the Dolomites, including the stomach-churning northwest face of Monte Civetta, which he and a young Austrian climbing star named Fritz Kasparek knocked off in a day. It was with skiing, however, that Harrer first made a name for himself. After winning some local and regional competitions, he was selected for the Austrian national team for the 1936 Winter Olympics. A year later, he won the downhill competition at the World University

Ski Championships, which he followed up by opening his own small, part-time ski school.

Heinrich Harrer was also a Nazi. At least on paper.

It has been claimed that he had joined the *Sturmabteilung*, or Storm Troopers, back in 1933, when the organization was outlawed in Austria. Hitler, of course, was of Austrian birth, and anti-Semitism had deep roots across the nation. Harrer later denied the accusation. But what is known is that right after the *Anschluss* took place, and Austria became absorbed in the Third Reich, his connection to Nazism was formalized. The day after German troops marched across the Austrian border, Harrer joined the SS. He later dismissed this as nothing more than a step required of him when he was asked to become a ski instructor for local SS men.

It would be in climbing, however, and not politics, where Heinrich Harrer would finally win genuine fame. While he was still a university student at Graz, studying both sport science and geography, he had been completely entranced by the newspaper coverage of all of the great mountaineering expeditions to the Himalayas. More importantly, he'd also determined that he wanted to join one. "So how was I going to get to the Himalaya? I hadn't the money and I was an unknown young climber," Harrer later recalled. "I had to do something to make the climbing world sit up and take notice." As it turned out, there was only one real answer. And so on July 9, 1938, Heinrich Harrer climbed onto his Puch 250 motorcycle, kicked the engine alive, and headed west out of Graz with the summer sun at his back. By the early hours of the next day, he would be in Grindelwald, ready for his date with destiny.

Rising up to an elevation of 13,000 feet above the posh hotels, family-style eateries, knick-knack shops, and endless postcard salesmen, the Eiger was a tourist magnet. School groups from Zurich, Bern, Lyon, Milan, and Freiburg marveled at the railway that coursed through tunnels cut through the mountain, while beaming honeymooners stood for snapshots with the dazzling peak as a backdrop.

The World Beneath Their Feet

And for a few Swiss rappens, you could gaze up at the imposing face of the mountain through a rented telescope. But for climbers, the Eiger, and its unclimbed North Face, meant something far different. For by the 1930s, it was the last, great, unsolved climbing problem in the Alps.

And for good reason.

Part of it was its sheer height and verticality. From its base to the summit, the North Face rose up some six thousand feet, much of it nearly straight up. Finding a ledge wide enough to sit upon, much less lie across, was a rarity, while some sections overhung—no small consideration for what would have to be a multi-day ascent. On the Eiger, you were usually either climbing or standing. Then there was the rock itself. While on a few sections of the climb, the strata was horizontal and offered a decent array of hand and foot holds, in others the rock was cantilevered out, like a chest of drawers tipped forward, making upward progress extremely difficult. But even worse was the quality of the rock itself. Nothing at all like the good, hard granite of Chamonix, the limestone on the Eiger was variable and often terrible. Entire chunks could break off in a mountaineer's hands, while pitons had to be placed with the utmost care—and more than a few whispered prayers.

But this was merely the beginning.

Battered by sudden snowstorms, even in summer, and often cloaked in clouds and mist, the walls of the North Face were often sheathed in ice or blanketed in wet snow, making finding any kind of reasonably safe grip a challenge of the highest order. On some sections, climbers would have to work their way across huge veins of ice, seemingly oblivious to summer temperatures, that snaked through the strata. At times, water would come cascading down the sides of the North Face, an icy chill running down a climber's shirtsleeves all the way down to their boots. With little warning, dense clouds could suddenly move in and reduce visibility to less than a rope length. On some days, the light was nothing more than variations of gray, while on others, thick black clouds would roll in, bringing thunder and lightning. On still others it might rain or hail. And temperatures on the North Face could suddenly plummet without warning, threatening climbers with hypothermia and, should they be exposed, certain death by freezing.

But probably the deadliest foes were the avalanches.

Shelves of snow that built up along the summit ridge would come crashing down without warning, dislodging rocks and ice, and creating great stone showers that would batter any climbers who were below. Equally dangerous was the avalanching snow itself, which, if it got between a climber and the wall, could push them off of their feet. With rocks and ice and snow raining down like artillery fire, climbing the North Face could be like crossing a vertical no-man's-land. Small wonder that hardly any birds or animals lived there.

While the Eiger itself had been climbed, up its western flank, for the first time in 1858, its northern face had so terrified the first generations of Alpine climbers that they stayed away from it completely. The first known attempt to climb the North Face in its entirety did not come until 1934, when two German climbers were forced to stop about one-third of the way up. One year later, two well-known Munich rock climbers died trying to climb the North Face, and in 1936, two German and two Austrian mountaineers perished in a similar attempt.

To some, the North Face was no longer the *Nordwand*.

Now it was the *Mordwand*. The Murder Face.

But the pressure for a successful first ascent continued to build. A book, *Der Kampf um die Eiger-Nordwand—The Struggle for the North Face*—had appeared the year before, while a documentary about the Eiger and the tragic attempts to climb the North Face was making its way through movie theaters in Germany, Austria, Switzerland, and Italy. There were no fatalities on the North Face during the summer of 1937. But no one made it to the top, either. A year later, it would be Heinrich Harrer's turn.

*　　*　　*

The World Beneath Their Feet

July 21, 1938.

They left at two o'clock in the morning. Moving first through the soft grass along the edge of the meadow, and then onto the rough cattle trails that led toward the base, Heinrich Harrer and Fritz Kasparek kept their own counsel. The summer climbing season had already opened with one tragedy. Two Italian mountaineers, Mario Menti and Bartolo Sandri, had been swept off the Eiger to their deaths by a fierce storm four weeks earlier. As the two Austrians had made their final preparations, they ran into two other sets of climbers who had designs on the North Face. One could not help but wonder what the mountain had in store for them all.

The first day, however, belonged to Harrer and Kasparek.

The weather was good, and while they both discovered how difficult it was to climb virtually anywhere on the North Face, with stones whizzing by their ears and water running down their arms, the Austrians made solid progress. Kasparek did a brilliant job of leading the first traverse, knocking away the sheets of ice covering the rock with his piton hammer in order to snake out handhold after handhold. Once past the "Swallow's Nest," they left a cache of carabiners, pitons, rope slings, food, and more than a hundred yards of rope as insurance, just in case they had to make a hasty retreat. Finally, upon reaching a huge ice knob, they decided to call it a day. Anchoring themselves and their gear with a couple of pitons, they then hacked out a rough seat on an ice ledge, covering it with their coiled rope. "The night was long, cold and uncomfortable," Harrer wrote. "We hadn't a dry stitch on us."

The next morning they heard voices.

They belonged to Anderl Heckmaier and Ludwig Vörg, two legendary rock climbers from Munich. Outfitted in the latest gear, including the new, twelve-point crampons, the two Bavarians were moving up the North Face at an incredible rate of speed. "They were two men running—and I mean running, not climbing," Harrer wrote. But what was equally astonishing was what happened next. Rather than fly on past the two Austrians, Heckmaier proposed that the two teams join together and work as one. Kasparek and Harrer immediately agreed, and a kind of mountaineering *Anschluss* was effected on the North Face. That night they bivouacked together along a thin ledge near the end of an ice field that had been dubbed "the Ramp." The two Austrians huddled beneath a Zdarsky sack, a lightweight canvas tent, their legs supported by rope slings, while the men from Munich, seemingly oblivious to the fact that they were stretched out above thousands of feet of Swiss air, lay down and went to sleep. Vörg even pulled on his fleece-lined slippers before retiring for the night.

The next day, Saturday, July 23, 1938, began at four o'clock, with breakfast and a difficult pitch up an ice-covered gully. A treacherous ice bulge followed. Then, along a brittle band of broken rocks, the quartet of mountaineers heard a strange humming. "It was neither a stone-fall nor an avalanche," Harrer wrote, "but an aeroplane flying quite close to us." The plane buzzed close enough that the climbers could see the faces of the passengers, one of whom was a news photographer from Bern.

While they didn't know it yet, the four climbers had already become international news. Crowds of onlookers, carrying binoculars, had flocked to Grindelwald, trying to catch a glimpse of the young daredevils high atop the North Face, while newspaper editors in Berlin, Munich, Bern, and Vienna, were running daily reports on the progress of the climb. For those who were not content to wait for the afternoon or morning editions, a radio network had begun to broadcast regular updates. Heckmair, Vörg, Kasparek, and Harrer weren't just trying to be the first to climb the North Face. They had become a news sensation.

Only now, it was the weather's turn.

As the climbers worked their way up "the Spider," a section of the face which was veined with long, ice-filled cracks, dark clouds began to roll in. The wind kicked up, blowing rock dust into the climbers' eyes and noses, and flattening the sleeves of their parkas against their arms. Then the hail came, pounding the upper reaches of the mountain, stinging the backs of the hands, and scattering across the thin ledges like deadly pearls. Roaring out of the north, the storm was suddenly upon them, cuffing their eardrums, clouding their vision, and making communication with each other nearly impossible.

But the worst were the avalanches that the storm set off, murderous cascades of rock and shards of ice falling on them from above. One of them caught Harrer on an ice shelf along the Spider, about sixty feet below Kasparek. "I snatched my rucksack over my head, holding it firmly with one hand, while the other gripped the rope which ran up to my companion. I jammed myself against the ice-cliff, just as the whole weight of the avalanche struck me," he wrote. "I was fighting for air, trying above all to prevent my rucksack being torn away and also to stop the endless stream of rushing snow from building up between me and the ice-slope and forcing me out of my footholds." Even worse was waiting for Kasparek to come flying off above him, and not knowing whether he could hold the fall. "I was only resisting," he added, "because one tries to resist so long as there is life in one." He was convinced that he was about to die. "All of these thoughts were calm, without any sense of fear or desperation. I had no time for things like that."

The avalanche stopped.

Then a second one began.

Finally, it also ended. The climbers got back to work. That night they bivouacked on a narrow ledge above the Spider. The closest level ground was five thousand feet below them.

The storm came back the next morning.

Sheets of snow had slid onto the tops of their tent-sacks, while flurries had begun to blow and swirl about them. Dawn was merely a slow brightening of the ocean of gray that surrounded them. "We could hear the gale shrieking across the ridges overhead," Harrer wrote. A decision had to be made. They could either wait on their narrow ledge until the weather improved, or forge ahead. "We decided to move on," he added. Wanting to lighten their loads, they tossed out every superfluous item in their rucksacks, including an entire loaf of bread. It was now or never.

Heckmaier again took the lead. Problems came at once. An over-hanging chimney proved impossible, so Heckmaier had to find a way up a steep, ice-lined gully, timing his forward motion against the small avalanches that came by like clockwork. He made it on the third try. But the biggest danger now was time. Wet snow was now falling heavily. They had to move quickly—and with speed came danger. Heckmaier slipped while trying to set a piton on a section of hard rock, and came off. Vörg caught him, but one of Heckmaier's crampon points was driven into his palm. Harrer quickly bandaged up the wounded hand, but the Munich man was now deathly pale.

"Do you feel bad?" Harrer asked.

"I'm not sure," Vörg replied. It was not a reassuring answer.

Harrer then dug into his rucksack and pulled out a vial of heart medication that a doctor in Grindelwald had insisted that he carry along with them, to be used only in the direst emergency. The directions indicated that the proper dose was ten drops. "I simply poured half of it into Wiggerl's mouth and drank the rest, as I happened to be thirsty," Harrer wrote. "We followed it up with a couple of glucose lozenges, and were soon in proper order again."

Onward they pushed, through the grayness and the swirling snow, up rock face and snow gully. They could faintly hear voices now, but they couldn't determine where they were coming from. Something else had happened as well. While there were still avalanches, they had lost their bite. Clearly, they were nearing the summit. "Minutes passed into hours," Harrer later remembered. "Up we went, yard by yard, rope by rope." The snow was now coming thick and heavy, blowing horizontally, and sticking to their gloves and eyebrows. Pushing ever upward, with Heckmaier in the lead, they climbed past the last great veins of ice and onto the final ice-field. Then it was over.

At half past three in the afternoon, on Sunday, July 24, 1938, the four climbers worked their way over the last ice-slope, and stood on the summit ridge of the Eiger, with only clouds and snowflakes above their heads. The last great problem of the Alps had been solved. The North Face had been conquered.

"CLIMBERS CONQUER DREAD EIGER PEAK" ran the headline in the *New York Times* two days later. "The amazement at seeing them come out from the storm," journalist Clarence Streit wrote, "was exceeded only by the amazement that they should have been able to complete the climb in such bitter weather." Similar stories appeared in newspapers in Paris, Milan, and Geneva, but in London, acknowledgement of the climb came with an Old School dig. "Their feat was certainly a daring one," sniffed the *Times*, "but it does not open a new road to ordinary climbers. While experience, training, and equipment, as well as dauntless energy, played an important part in their achievement, the ascent would have been impossible had they not made free use of *pitons* (screw footholds), which from the point of view of classic Alpinism is to be regretted." The German press, however, now under governmental control, unabashedly celebrated the triumph on the Eiger as not only a mountaineering milestone, but as a victory for the German people. One Nazi ghostwriter even claimed that Harrer had declared, "We have climbed the North Face of the Eiger to the summit and beyond for our *Führer!*"

Indeed, the ascent was such a big story that an audience was arranged with Hitler. The four climbers, with Vörg's right hand and arm still in a sling, were dispatched to Vienna. There, at the Hotel Monopol, which now served as the city's Gestapo headquarters, a smiling *Führer* greeted them with, "Boys, boys, what an achievement!" A group photo was then taken along with Reichssportsführer Tschammer und Osten and Nazi interior minister Wilhelm Frick. Harrer stood so close to Hitler that their jackets touched. Each of the climbers was presented with a signed declaration in a silver frame. Then they were whisked away. The audience was over. The *Führer* had other things to do.

One of them would come that November.

*   *   *

Across the Reich, the planning had gone on for months. Local party officers and trusted members had been quietly informed of their roles, while police officials had been instructed what they could and could not do. What would later be portrayed as a spontaneous public outcry against the Jews was, in fact a carefully designed operation. And late on the night of November 9/10, 1938, while sitting inside an office at Munich's city hall, Josef Goebbels, Hitler's handpicked minister of propaganda, gave the signal. Within minutes, in cities across Germany, party members were on the move, riding in cars or moving on foot, some armed with sledgehammers and crow bars, others with matches and cans of gasoline.

In Munich, the synagogue on Herzog-Rudolf-Strasse was set ablaze, its roof tiles crashing down into the sanctuary while members of the city's fire department stood by and watched. Storm Troopers busted down the wooden doors of the smaller synagogue on Reichenbachstrasse, splintering the altar and ripping the Torah from the holy ark. But the Nazi hit squads spent most of their time in the city center, smashing the windows of Jewish-owned shops and businesses and breaking inside. They shattered the plate-glass display windows at the J. Tauber ladies' hat shop on Rindermarkt, and the Speier shoe store on Kaufingerstrasse. Tables, chairs, and china were broken at the Schwarz restaurant, while in front of Sigmund Koch's music store, black shards of 78-rpm records littered the sidewalk along Neuhauser Strasse. But the greatest destruction was at Uhlfelder's, a long-beloved department store, where Nazi enthusiasts broke furniture and children's toys, trashed the cosmetics counters, and walked off with radios and winter coats. By morning, the cobblestones along the Tal sparkled with the glint of broken glass.

Walking to work the next day, from his home on the Amalienstrasse to his office at No. 4 Wienstrasse, Paul Bauer could not have missed what had happened the night before if he'd tried. Peter Aufschnaiter, on the other hand, likely didn't need any elucidation. For his mother, an ardent Nazi, had traveled to Munich from Austria to take part in what was soon called *Kristallnacht*, or the Night of the Broken Glass. One thing, however, was certain, especially as the two climbers went back to planning the upcoming expedition to Nanga Parbat.

They were all Nazis now.

CHAPTER FOURTEEN

The Summer at the End of the World

They did not share his enthusiasm.

Sitting inside the office of the Deutsche Himalaya Foundation at Wienstrasse 4, just around the corner from the Marienplatz, with the gray winter light leaking through the windows, Heinrich Harrer had not been greeted with the warm reception that he had been expecting. While both Paul Bauer and Peter Aufschnaiter acknowledged that the five thousand marks from the local government in Stygia had indeed been received, a payment that would allow Harrer to join the 1939 Nanga Parbat Expedition, they didn't seem particularly excited about his potential participation. Nor did they seem to share his enthusiasm for the new, twelve-point crampons that the climbers would be using. In fact, neither Bauer nor Aufschnaiter seemed excited about anything.

In truth, it had been an odd six months for Harrer since he and his three climbing comrades had stood on the summit of the Eiger. While there had been the brief audience with the *Führer*, and a triumphant appearance at the German Sport Festival in Breslau, where they were cheered by thousands, invitations to take part in more mountaineering activities had been as scarce as hen's teeth. Harrer had been asked to appear in a ski film, and he'd gotten married, wearing his black SS officer's uniform, to Lotte Wegener, the daughter of a well-known Austrian polar explorer. But the climbing world had not exactly been beating on his door. So, when the call came to come to meet Bauer and Aufschnaiter in Munich, he'd naturally been expecting a little more than dour expressions and reserved sentiments.

What Harrer did not know was that a bureaucratic fight was being waged, behind closed doors, over the control of the proposed up-coming expedition to Nanga Parbat—the very one that Harrer had risked his life climbing the North Face in order to join. There were those who wanted it to be an SS affair, like the so-called scientific expedition to Tibet. Bauer, however, had fought that, arguing that mountaineers, with their expertise, were the only ones who could successfully lead the way to the summit. The meeting with Harrer, more than anything else, was to give Bauer and Aufschnaiter a read on just what kind of person was this Austrian *wunderkind*. Having a climber who was also an SS man, it was clear, might also help their cause.

In the end—and only in the end—Harrer passed the test.

Invited to join the expedition at nearly the last minute, Harrer promptly dropped out of the film, kissed his bride goodbye, gathered his gear, and caught the train from Graz to Munich. The next day, he and the other climbers took the train to Antwerp, where a German freighter, the *Lindenfels*, sat in the black waters of the old Belgian harbor. On April 6, 1939, they set sail for India. Heinrich Harrer's epic Himalayan adventure was about to begin.

Bombay was a madhouse.

After two sluggish weeks on the Arabian Sea, oiling their boots and studying the maps that Peter Aufschnaiter kept locked up in a wooden box in his cabin, the members of the 1939 German Nanga Parbat Reconnaissance Expedition finally docked near the Gate of India on April 30, with the city rising up to meet them. Beat-up wooden ferries zigzagged in and out of the harbor, taking families on sightseeing cruises, while the crowded sidewalks thronged with bare-chested men and veiled Muslim women, Sikhs and soldiers, open-air vendors and ragged children calling for baksheesh. Mothers with infants at their sides cooked chapatis over charcoal fires, jerry-rigged buses and taxicabs rumbled by, mangy dogs sniffed around café entrances, and the air was a heady mixture of coffee and curry, human sweat and diesel smoke. Heinrich Harrer had never seen, heard, or smelled anything like it. This, he decided, was no place to linger.

What changed his mind were the city's Germans. Bankers and diplomats, matrons and businessmen, Bombay's small but vibrant community of German nationals had been notified of the arrival of the mountaineers ahead of time and now welcomed them with open arms. Instead of long hours spent waiting for visas and other governmental permissions, the climbers spent their afternoons playing tennis with pretty *Fräuleins* and drinking magnum bottles of ice-cold Beck's beer. Here, among their fellow Germans, they were already heroes.

Their papers in order—thanks to the assistance of Kenneth Mason back in Oxford, who had written to the India Office in London on their behalf—the climbers began a four-day railroad journey to Rawalpindi on May 3. Though they were served by turbaned waiters and ate their meals on white linen tablecloths in the dining car, the journey was a stark contrast to their ultimately enjoyable days in Bombay. The heat was oppressive, and expedition leader Peter Aufschnaiter was on a short fuse. *Tuck your shirt tail in*, he barked at Harrer one day. *Behave like a sahib and not an Indian.*

While Aufschnaiter had presented each of the climbers with a camera and a Rolex wristwatch, they were all reminded that everything, including any photographs that they took, belonged to the Deutsche Himalaya Foundation. He was grimly insistent about other matters as well. All fruit had to be carefully washed, and any water that they were to drink had to be first treated with a spoonful of deep-purple potassium permanganate crystals. The three other climbers, fully aware that the tall Austrian was in charge, avoided any hints of unwarranted familiarity and dutifully referred to him as "Herr Aufschnaiter."

Meeting up in Rawalpindi with two Bhotia porters—and a cook named Ramona—from Darjeeling, the expedition got right down to business, and on the long but uneventful march to Nanga Parbat, the climbers grew together. Aufschnaiter's stature improved as well, since he could converse fluently in Tibetan with the porters. And when they got their first good look at Nanga Parbat, between the villages of Bunar and Halala, there was no question as to just how challenging their assignment would be. Viewed from the west, with its hanging glaciers and steep pitches of ice and rock, Nanga Parbat looked even more daunting than its Rakhiot face. While the climb to the summit was much shorter than by the Rakhiot side—three miles as opposed to nine—it was also much, much steeper. By the first of June, the expedition had established their Base Camp on the north side of the Diamir Glacier. Then they got to work.

For the next eight weeks, the four German climbers, and their Sherpa and Bhotia support team, carefully and methodically explored the mountain's Diamir face. Well aware of Nanga Parbat's murderous past, they painstakingly eyeballed potential routes, and debated the hazards they might encounter at each step of the way. Usually working in pairs, and blessed by unusually good weather, two of the climbers—Hans Lobenhoffer, a bespectacled twenty-three-year-old Bavarian mountaineer who was also a soldier in a German army mountain regiment, and Lutz Chicken, a Munich-based climber and medical student—fought their way up the route attempted by British mountaineer Alfred Mummery and two Gurkha soldiers in 1895. Indeed, in a rock basin at around 18,000 feet, Lobenhoffer and Chicken discovered a ten-inch piece of charred wood that they believed had been from one of Mummery's camps. But this route was also prone to avalanche.

Harrer and Aufschnaiter had better luck. On June 15, battling their way up a different route, one that came off the middle rib extending down from the north peak, Harrer, who led much of the climb, was particularly in his element. "Exploring the steep ice-gullies between the various rock ribs was great fun with our twelve-point crampons," he later recalled. Climbing to an elevation of also about 18,000 feet, they had planned to go higher, but their two Bhotia porters had grown increasingly distressed about the steepness of the slope. Returning to Base Camp, they discovered that Lobenhoffer had turned dangerously ill, with a fever of more than 104 degrees Fahrenheit. The young soldier eventually pulled through, and the climbing resumed. Before the weather turned on July 25, Harrer and Aufschnaiter managed to make it up to 20,300 feet up the new route before they needed to turn back.

But the breakthrough had happened.

There was no question that, on the Diamir face, they had found a route to the summit of Nanga Parbat. While steep, it was nearly three times shorter, and much less exposed to avalanches, than the deadly route up the Rakhiot face. When they got back home to Munich, Aufschnaiter and Bauer would start the paperwork to request a new Nanga Parbat expedition for 1940. The Germans hadn't slain their dragon yet, but they were about to. A year from then, Nanga Parbat would become the first *Achttausender* to be summitted. They could all feel it in their bones.

The race to the roof of the world was about to end.

And the Third Reich was going to win it.

The expedition broke camp on July 26. Harrer and Lobenhoffer set out with the porters, and most of the gear, toward Bunar, while Aufschnaiter and Chicken went via the Rakhiot Valley, where they paid their respects at the memorial to the fallen Nanga Parbat climbers of 1934 and 1937. The plan was that they would all meet in Srinagar by mid-August. From there, they'd make it down to Karachi, where they were scheduled to catch a ship back home on the twenty-forth.

The Nanga Parbat reconnaissance hadn't been the only mountaineering expedition of note that year. The Americans, under Fritz Wiessner, had made their second tragic attempt at K2. And the very same Thursday in May 1939 that saw the German climbers depart Rawalpindi for Nanga Parbat, some five hundred miles to the east a group of four Polish mountain climbers, accompanied by four Sherpas and two Bhotias, left the hill station at Almora and began walking north through the pine-covered foothills toward the savage and foreboding ring of mountains encircling the Nanda Devi Sanctuary. But rather than try to enter the Sanctuary, their plan was to try and climb to the summit of Nanda Devi East, Nanda Devi's slightly shorter, but even steeper, 24,000-foot twin summit, from the eastern side of the ring itself.

What followed was an excruciating saga of sudden storms and near-deadly falls, treacherous slabs and fearsome overhangs, snow blindness and dystentery. But this was a determined, persistent bunch, and on July 2, 1939, two young Polish climbers stood upon the summit of Nanda Devi East. It had been, perhaps, the most difficult climb to date ever successfully tackled in the Himalayas. But outside of Poland, news of their triumph made very little splash in the newspapers. In London on July 29, 1939, the *Times* ran a short piece written by their Warsaw correspondent that credited the wrong climbers and the wrong peak. Both the writer and the editors back in England, however, would soon have far weightier matters on their minds.

There was also another mountaineering expedition that summer.

It received absolutely zero press attention, and rightly so. For it was neither a first ascent nor even a particularly difficult climb. But for one of the climbers involved, a gangly nineteen-year-old from New Zealand, it was the first step in a journey that would not only irrevocably change the course of his life, but, in time, would rewrite the very story of Himalayan mountaineering.

The family at 290 Remuera Road did not think like everyone else.

In buttoned-down Auckland, where roast lamb and baked kumaras, mince, and bangers and mash graced the weeknight dinner table, the Hillary family ate grated raw carrots and beetroots, apples and cabbage hearts, turnip tops and bright-green young dandelion leaves, and wholemeal biscuits. Unlike the architects, engineers, teachers, and merchants who lived nearby, the heads of this household, Percival Hillary and his wife, Gertrude, were beekeepers, with more than a thousand hives scattered about the fields and cow pastures outside the city.

There were other differences as well. Percival had come home from the Great War, where he'd been wounded at Gallipoli, a staunch pacifist. And both he and Gertrude and their eldest son had been deeply attracted to the teachings of Herbert Sutcliffe, a British-born Australian psychologist whose philosophy of "Radiant Living" promoted a mix of positive thinking, physical exercise, and spiritual awareness. Radical Christians in a world that was again tilting toward war, the Hillary family was bound together by attitudes that most of their neighbors would have considered to be sheer poppycock.

For Ed Hillary, the eldest of the three children, the most pressing matter at hand had been finding a path toward a career. Though he enjoyed reading, and had defied his father's strict bedtime rules by devouring *Tarzan of the Apes* and *Riders of the Purple Sage* by flashlight under the covers as a child, he had been lousy student. He managed to pass his matriculation examination, but after two frustrating years of study at Auckland University College he walked out of school forever, and he joined his father working full time in the family beekeeping business. But inside, he yearned for something else. And in the southern hemisphere summer of 1939, he found it.

On a vacation to the South Island, Ed and a friend stopped in for a couple of days at The Hermitage, a resort hotel set in the famed Southern Alps. Almost immediately, Ed found himself in awe of his surroundings—"the great rock walls, the hanging glaciers, and the avalanche-strewn slopes," he later recalled. He also went off on a walk by himself, and, in his tennis shoes, ended up climbing all the way up to a patch of old avalanche snow. "In an excess of enthusiasm I kicked steps up and down it, and then," he added, "with an astonishing sense of achievement, I climbed back down the long slopes to The Hermitage." But it was what happened that evening that saw his life angle off in a new direction.

Sitting in the lounge, Ed was, he later wrote, both excited and restless. "Then the hum of voices suddenly hushed, and I looked up to see two young men come into the room. They were fit and tanned; they had an unmistakable air of competence about them." He could hear someone nearby whisper, "They've just climbed Mount Cook." Soon, a number of the guests began to gather around the two climbers, whose names were Harry Stevenson and Doug Dick. Standing sheepishly nearby, Ed strained to hear what the two men were telling their admirers. Later, he learned that they'd just completed the first-ever, north-to-south traverse of Mount Cook, the highest peak in New Zealand. "I retreated to a corner of the lounge filled with a sense of futility at the dull, mundane nature of my existence," Ed later recalled. "Those chaps, now, were really getting a bit of excitement out of life. I decided there and then to take up mountaineering."

The next day, Ed and his friend hired a local guide to lead them to the top of Mount Ollivier, a rocky peak in the nearby Sealy Range. Ed was so excited that, on the climb, he raced ahead of the guide. And while Mount Ollivier was only 6,342 feet high, its summit could not have been any less important. "I returned to The Hermitage after the happiest day I had ever spent," he wrote. "And the next day I returned home. But my new enthusiasm for the mountains went home with me and gave me little rest in the years that followed." Edmund Hillary was on his way.

Some twelve thousand miles away, meanwhile, Heinrich Harrer had also been on the move. The four German climbers had reunited in Srinagar in mid-August, 1939. They had discussed next year's expedition, to the Diamir face on Nanga Parbat, with the resident British political officer, who was also a member of the Himalayan Club. They had also purchased bits of saffron and other souvenirs from the Kashmiri traders in the market, and taken their first hot baths in months. Then it was time to move—to Rawalpindi, Lahore, Karachi, and home to Germany. They would be back the next year, in 1940. And they would finish the job on Nanga Parbat.

In Karachi, their plans changed.

The *Uhlenfels*, the Hansa Line freighter on which they had booked their return passage to Germany, failed to show up in port on the appointed day. Nor was that all. By now, what bits of news that they could gather from the English-language Indian newspapers had grown increasingly grave. A crisis in Danzig, a port city along the German–Polish border that Hitler demanded be "returned" to the Reich, had led to open talk of war between Britain and France on one side, and Germany and Italy on the other. And as the four German mountaineers worked their way down to the docks each day from their hotel to see if there was any news of the *Uhlenfels*, they noticed that they were now being trailed.

Finally, Harrer had had enough. Convinced that a war was coming, and that they would be arrested as enemy aliens, he proposed that they make a break for it now, while they could. He also had a plan. There was an anti-British maharajah in Baluchistan, the next province over to the west. With his help, they should be able to slip across the border into Persia, and work their way home from there. Only Peter Aufschnaiter wouldn't go for it. A veteran of the fighting on the Western Front, he had seen all the war he needed to see. But Hans Lobenhoffer and Lutz Chicken were game, and that night, the three of them slipped quietly out of Karachi.

In Las Belas, they managed to gain an audience with the maharajah—"more boy than man," Harrer later grumbled—but nothing else. Instead, they were escorted by a group of soldiers back to Karachi, where the chief of police seemed surprisingly uninterested in their escapade. "Well, gentlemen, so you lost your way while hunting, did you?" he asked. He added that he would visit them later at their hotel.

And that was where they were sitting a couple of days later, drinking chilled English beer beneath the mango trees in the garden, when two dozen Indian soldiers, armed to the teeth, suddenly rushed in. The climbers were all under arrest. Great Britain had declared war on Germany.

Book Three

Descending quickly, I tried not to look at the warren of rocks around me where some of the bodies, blasted by storms down K2's slopes, were buried. Parts of some of the bodies were visible, and occasionally I glimpsed a piece of ripped climbing suit or an old boot, or smelled something sickly on the air.

The experience must have affected one of my Balti porters, Abbas. Later, around midnight, he ran barefoot over the dangerous crevasses back toward the memorial, my porters told me, screaming to the dead that he belonged with them. A couple of the other porters held him down and brought him back to the tent. Believing he was possessed, they read the Koran to soothe him, but he bolted again.

At 5:00 a.m. when I lifted the flap of the mess tent, Abbas was asleep on a mat on the cold, stony floor, his hands and feet trussed. When he awoke, he was untied, and he rubbed his wrists groggily. He shook his head no when I offered porridge and green tea. He staggered outside to the porters' shelter, a circle of blue-tarpaulin-covered stones where half a dozen porters were throwing down gasoline, lighting wisps of purple flames to warm themselves in the clear, freezing dawn.

I had finally realized my goal of reaching the base camp at

K2, in the heart of the Karakoram Mountain range in northern Pakistan.

—**Graham Bowley**
New York Times
January 13, 2010

If you are waiting, fear is growing. If you are acting, fear is getting less. You can fail. It is all the same. You cannot survive. The art of adventuring is not dying.

—**Reinhold Messner**
First mountaineer to
solo climb Mount Everest
National Geographic
YouTube Video
March 9, 2015

CHAPTER FIFTEEN

War

When the war came, the climbing largely stopped.

In then-neutral Bolivia, on Holy Saturday, March, 1940, three young German mountaineers climbed to the top of Illimani, the magnificent, 21,000-foot peak that hovered over the capital city of La Paz. At the summit, they planted an odd, hybrid banner. The bottom half consisted of the green, yellow, and red stripes of the Bolivian flag, while the top half featured a huge black swastika, framed by a white circle, set against a red background. "After planting this firmly on a stout pole and taking a photograph showing the party saluting it with outstretched hands," wrote an officer in the British Royal Marines, "which they were subsequently so incredibly foolish as to publish in a La Paz newspaper, they descended." Exactly sixteen days later, the officer, whose name was Edward S. G. de la Motte, and a Bolivian skier named Torres, returned to the summit and yanked down the offending flag, which they stowed in a rucksack. "The following day, April 8," de la Motte added, "saw the party back in La Paz, ready to lay a damper on virile, Nordic ardour." But aside from a few small climbs here and there, large-scale mountaineering, especially in the Himalayas, came to a standstill after the feverish summers of 1938 and 1939.

The war soon took its toll.

Norman R. Streatfeild, the British Army captain who had served as the liaison officer to Charlie Houston's 1938 expedition to K2, was killed at Dunkirk on May 29, 1940, when the destroyer he was on, the HMS *Grafton*, was torpedoed by a German U-boat.

Ludwig Vörg, who had climbed the North Face of the Eiger with Heinrich Harrer, became a corporal in the Wehrmacht. He was killed in action, in Poland, on June 22, 1941—the very first day of Operation Barbarossa, Hitler's invasion of Russia.

Others slipped by with the skin of their teeth.

Bill Tilman was also evacuated at Dunkirk. He then fought against Rommel with the British Eighth Army in North Africa, and, at age forty-five, he joined the special forces in order to parachute behind enemy lines. "He had volunteered for Albania, he informed us," one of his fellow officers later wrote, "in order to keep himself in practice for his next Himalayan attempt." He survived the mission, leading partisans in hit-and-run attacks against the Germans, but was again dropped behind the lines in northeastern Italy, on the Altoplano d'Asiago, along the edge of the Dolomites. Short on food, guns, and ammunition, this time leading a ragtag group largely comprised of communist guerilla fighters, Tilman fought a dangerous rearguard action against the Wehrmacht and SS, all the while carrying copies of the two-volume set of Carlyle's *French Revolution* in his rucksack. When the fighting ended, the grateful citizens of Belluno made him an honorary citizen.

Peter Misch, the German Jewish geologist on the 1934 Nanga Parbat Expedition, survived both the war and the Holocaust. Leaving the Third Reich in 1936 for China, where he took a position at Sun Yat-sen University in Canton, he then had to flee the onslaught of the Japanese army and moved to Beijing. But his wife longed to return to her homeland, which she did with their young daughter, Hanna. The mother did not survive Hitler's Germany, but Hanna, miraculously, did, and was later reunited with her father in Seattle, where he'd taken a professorship at the University of Washington.

Some left their imprints on world affairs. Others did what they were told.

Lady Houston, who had planned to land an airplane on Mount Everest in 1933 or, at the very least, have a weighted Union Jack dropped upon the summit, did not live to experience her nation again at war. She had been so troubled by the abdication of Edward VIII, it was said, that she stopped eating and died of a heart attack four days after Christmas in 1936. But the £100,000 that she donated to design and build a new, powerful aircraft engine helped to defend her beloved homeland during the Battle of Britain.

Eric Shipton enrolled in the British army officers' training school in Belgaum, in southern India, only to lead a protest when a fellow trainee, an Anglo-Indian, was denied an officership candidacy because of his race. Eight months later, in August 1940, despite having no diplomatic training whatsoever, nor any prior government service, Shipton was appointed the British consul-general in Sinkiang, the westernmost province in China. Posted to Kashgar, an old Silk Road town, his main job was to keep an eye on the Russians. Two years later, he was transferred to Persia. When the war ended, Shipton was an agricultural adviser with the British military mission in Hungary.

Frank Smythe spent the war in and out of uniform, writing books and pamphlets, giving talks to the troops about his experiences on Mount Everest, and eventually teaching mountaineering techniques to a unit of British Army Lovat Scouts in the Canadian Rockies. But one of his postings left a longer ripple. Asked to set up a new center for mountain warfare techniques in Wales, Smythe selected a Himalayan climber and regular army officer named John Hunt as his chief instructor. Hunt didn't think much of Smythe's abilities as a commanding officer. "He had no military experience and the direction of the courses lacked purpose and organization," the instructor later recalled. But the experience gave Hunt another skill to list on his résumé, one that would soon come in handy.

Paul Bauer began the war years as something of a minor celebrity. Assigned to a mountain infantry unit, he was filmed by a newsreel crew once the fighting broke out in France. He also spent time in Norway, before his unit was ordered to the Caucasus Mountains, his last training ground before heading to the Himalayas. "My return to Russia, and particularly to the Caucasus, turned out rather differently to what I had expected," he wrote some years later, "at the head of two thousand specially chosen alpine troops in 1943." He failed to add that the appearance of the German army was followed by the arrival of Gestapo agents and the systematic identification, deportation, and murder of members of the region's historic Jewish community. Bauer later ran a mountain warfare school in the Alps before surrendering to American GI's in the spring of 1945. Afterward, he dismissed the Nazi years as being "so troublesome."

Heinrich Harrer wouldn't stay put. On April 29, 1944, after spending more than four and a half years as a prisoner of war, he and Peter Aufschnaiter escaped from the Central Internment Camp in Dehra Dun, India, and began walking toward Tibet. A year and a half later, after walking some twelve hundred miles across some of the most foreboding terrain on the planet, they slipped through the western gate of Lhasa, the remote Tibetan capital. There they learned for the first time that the war was over, and that their side had lost.

The Americans followed their own paths.

Charlie Houston spent the war years in Florida as an officer in the US Navy, training pilots and performing research on high-altitude aviation. Paul Petzold served as an instructor in the Tenth Mountain Division, the United States Army's famous "ski troops," teaching them basic mountain rescue and survival skills.

The Minya Konka Four, however, cast the widest arc. Arthur B. Emmons III was on the staff of the American consulate in Seoul, Korea, on the day that Pearl Harbor was attacked. Arrested by the Japanese, he was interned in Tokyo during the Doolittle raid, and later sent home on the *Gripsholm*, the legendary Swedish-American liner that was used for repatriating Axis and Allied nationals. Dick Burdsall, a Quaker, sat out the war, while Terris Moore made the third ascent of Mount McKinley as part of the US Army's Alaska Test Expedition of 1942.

Jack Young outshone them all. He spent much of the war behind Japanese lines in China, helping guerilla units and radioing in reports of enemy troop strength and movements. Awarded two Silver Stars and three Bronze Stars, he served as General George Marshall's aide and interpreter when, in the late winter of 1946, Marshall met with Mao Zedong in the bleak mountain town of Yenan, in Shensi Province—site of the end of the Long March, the Red Army's epic five-thousand-mile journey from Kiangsi province in 1934/35.

For the Sherpas, the war was a bitter blow.

For nearly a decade, there would be no lining up outside the veranda of the Planters Club in Darjeeling, hoping to get selected for the next expedition, no special blessings at the monastery, no white silk scarves hung upon their necks, no more bags of silver rupees, down sleeping bags, and Grenfell cloth parkas to bring back home. With no mountaineering expeditions, the former high-altitude climbers and porters had to hustle up new work. Angtsering II worked as mess cook for a Gurkha regiment. Ang Tharkay tried to organize short treks in the foothills near Darjeeling. But the others simply got along as well as they could, working as common laborers and rickshaw men. Some returned to the Khumbu, but most stayed on in Darjeeling.

One Sherpa did neither.

By the beginning of 1939, Tenzing was no longer an anxious run-away from the mountains. Even though he was not yet twenty-five, he was now married, a father, and a veteran of three attempts on Mount Everest. Moreover, he had established a reputation as capable, energetic, and most reliable, one whose growing English language ability and winning personality made him an attractive candidate for getting hired on virtually any Himalayan climbing campaign. And that very spring, he did join an expedition. But instead of working for one of the attempts at an *Achttausender*, Tenzing was swept up by a human dynamo.

Her name was Beryl Smeeton.

The daughter of a British Army officer who had been killed during the First World War, she was dashing, adventurous, and utterly fearless during an era when women were expected to stay home, give birth to children, and serve their husbands dinner. When her first marriage, to a Royal Marine, started to fall apart, she took up with one of his fellow officers. Once she wandered, alone, across China for four months, traveling on the cheapest of boats and buses, crammed to the hilt with Chinese peasants, whose children stared in awe and wonder at this stranger with flax-colored hair. In time, Smeeton would ride the Trans-Siberian Railway, journey across Patagonia, sail the Atlantic and Pacific, and get pitchpoled by a rogue wave off the treacherous waters of Cape Horn. But in the spring of 1939, newly married to a British Army officer stationed in Baluchistan, in far northwestern India, she convinced her husband and a couple of Canadian friends to give mountaineering a try. Together, they decided to make an attempt on Tirich Mir, an unclimbed, 25,000-foot peak that was the highest mountain in the Hindu Kush. There were, however, a couple of roadblocks.

The first was that the province of Chitral, where Tirich Mir was located, did not allow Western women to visit. So Smeeton merely left anything identifying her as female off the application. The second was that neither Smeeton, her husband, nor their companions knew much about mountain climbing. So Smeeton drove a van, alone, more than fifteen hundred miles to Calcutta, where she borrowed equipment from the Himalayan Club. There, she also arranged for the hiring of Sherpas, one of whom turned out to be Tenzing, to accompany the expedition. Then she gassed up the tank and drove back another fifteen hundred miles to Baluchistan.

For Tenzing, the expedition proved to be another stepping stone of responsibility. "On Tirich Mir," he later recalled, "I was in charge of both the Sherpas and the local coolies." While he would not officially earn the distinction of being recognized as a sirdar, or head Sherpa, for several years, in practical terms he had become one. And while the expedition did not summit Tirich Mir, Smeeton and the other climbers did make it to 23,000 feet, which was close to an altitude record for a female climber. Moreover, Tenzing had made a deep impression on his British and Canadian clients. He "had something special about him," Smeeton's husband, Miles, later wrote. "We felt that he had been touched by some divine spirit which made him a little different from ordinary men." Tenzing was on his way, though not quite how he might have envisioned.

On the approach journey to Tirich Mir, at the British Army outpost at Drosh along the Afghan border, Tenzing had met the commander of the 9th Gurkha Rifles, who had offered him a job as an orderly. At first he gave it little thought, but after the attempt on Tirich Mir ended, and fighting broke out in Europe, Tenzing knew that there would be no more mountaineering expeditions until the war ended. So he took the job. And before the year was up, his wife and two daughters joined him, all the way at the opposite end of India.

Chitral proved to be an eye-opening experience. Tenzing eventually moved up to becoming a regimental cook, and a good one at that. He also took part in some small expeditions to the mountains, and helped to recruit local villagers to join the famed Chitral Scouts. And on a trip to Kashmir, he even learned how to ski. Grateful to have a steady paycheck, and happy to live with his wife and two young daughters, Tenzing had found what at first felt like an oasis of peace in a world at war. But it was his contact with others that taught him the most. An ancient trading town along the old Silk Road, Chitral wore its polyglot history on the faces of its citizenry. "I met Englishmen and Indians, Turkis and Afghans, Hindus and Moslems, Christians and Jews," he later recalled. "I learned to speak Hindustani, Chitrali, and Pasthu, and improved my English, of which I already knew a little. I became used to dealing with men and problems of many different kinds."

But also hovering over Chitral were clouds of unrest.

The Indian independence movement, which had mostly gone dark during the first years of the war, once again flickered to life. "Britain, Get Out of India!" now read the graffiti scrawled on the walls of the Government House. With the new wave of political activism also came the unleashing of ancient poisons. Because Chitral was mostly Muslim, the local Hindu minority felt increasingly embattled. "In those days, I knew little about politics or things of that sort," Tenzing said. "All I wanted was to live my life peacefully and do my work to the best of my ability."

When his wife suddenly died in the spring of 1944, leaving him to care for their two young daughters alone, Tenzing knew that he would have to return to Darjeeling. In early 1945, as the war was winding down, he decided that he could wait no longer. Loading his girls into twin saddlebags, he led them on horseback over the mountain pass to Dir, the nearest railway town. But the station there was mobbed with travelers trying to get home, and Tenzing could not buy tickets. Then he had an idea. Putting on a British Army officer's uniform that he'd been given in Chitral, he calmly walked on board the next military train. "No one objected," he later recalled.

When they finally arrived in Darjeeling, the other Sherpas regarded Tenzing with utter amazement. "To my old friends, I was almost a stranger. They stared at my strange clothes and laughed at my speaking." Good natured as always, Tenzing laughed along with them. But, inside, the wheels were turning. And without having planned it, he was no longer just another Sherpa. Instead, he was fast becoming a citizen of the world. But there was one thing that, regardless of his experiences, would forever bind him to his Sherpa brothers. And that was this: when the expeditions came again, he, too, would be ready.

CHAPTER SIXTEEN

A New World

The climbers had not forgotten, either.

The world, of course, had changed in almost unimaginable ways since September 1939. The Third Reich had been smashed, and Germany utterly defeated, its cities a wasteland of bombed-out buildings, starving children, and haunted, glassy-eyed widows. Millions of Jews, Russians, and Poles had been murdered by the Nazis—shot in the back of the head, starved in the ghettos, worked to death, or gassed in the concentration camps—along with thousands of Roma, Jehovah's Witnesses, communists, and homosexuals. Hitler, hiding in a bunker in Berlin as Soviet Army soldiers moved ever closer, had placed the muzzle of a pistol in his mouth and pulled the trigger, while his top advisers were either dead, imprisoned, or on the run. In the final months of the war, Germany had rained rockets onto the streets of London and launched jet-propelled fighters into the sky against the RAF. And in 1945, first in the New Mexico desert, then twice in Japan, the Americans had detonated atomic bombs, the most lethal weapon ever developed by humankind.

More changes lay just around the corner.

In 1947, the Indian independence movement finally prevailed, and the Jewel left the Crown. The British, drained by the war and, no doubt, cognizant of the writing on the wall, agreed to pull out. But the Raj was split into two nations: a larger, Hindu-majority India, and a smaller, Muslim-dominated Pakistan. And while the partition pleased some, it also left a trail of heartbreak and misery. Thousands were killed in anti-Muslim and anti-Hindu rioting, while millions of others lost their homes and businesses and were forced to leave their native soil. The traumatic birth of the new nations would, in the end, also claim the life of Gandhi, who was felled by an assassin's bullet the very next year.

Big changes were in store for Tibet as well.

"Here one must hold one's head," the American journalist John Gunther once wrote of the fabled, mystical land. "Tibet is without parallel." A purely theocratic state, ruled by the Dalai Lama, the status of Tibet vis-à-vis China had long been a question mark. Vast, remote, and sealed off from the outside, Tibetans had long run their own affairs despite Chinese assertions that Tibet was, in fact, a part of China. And during decades when the Chinese government was weak, or had larger worries to confront, the Tibetans were left alone.

That would end with the victory of Mao Zedong and the Red Army over Chiang Kai-shek's Nationalist forces in 1949. Now a communist state, and one that was determined to protect its borders against any potential foreign encroachment, the new Chinese government wasted little time asserting its power in Lhasa. When negotiations with the Tibetans over the status of Tibet broke down, the Chinese sent in troops and took over by force, and the Dalai Lama fled to India. By the end of 1950, Tibet was firmly under Chinese control.

For the first few years after the war, there was little talk of reviving the Great Himalayan Race. Europe, of course, was in shambles. Here, the top priorities were rebuilding the continent's ruined infrastructure, moving back toward a peacetime economy, and lifting nations on their feet again—not climbing to the top of distant mountains. And while the United States had been almost entirely spared the physical destruction of the war, Americans had their hands full with the Cold War, the Marshall Plan, and suddenly finding themselves to be the most powerful nation on earth. But dreams, especially hard-fought ones, rarely bother with practicalities. And in short order there was talk, at least among mountaineers, of returning to the Himalayas and picking up where they had left off.

But the map was different now.

For the Germans and the Americans, permission to mount an expedition to Nanga Parbat or K2 would no longer go through London. Instead, they would apply directly to the government of Pakistan. The British, however, now found themselves in a far different position. In the past, the only substantial roadblock that British mountaineers had needed to overcome was, in the case of Mount Everest, permission to enter Tibet. And while Bill Tilman once griped that gaining approval from Lhasa for an Everest expedition was "like asking the Dean and Chapter for permission to climb Westminster Abbey," the British track record had been largely successful. But with the Red Chinese now in charge in Lhasa, access to Tibet was cut off. If the British were to have another shot at Mount Everest, they would now have to climb up the Nepalese side—and Nepal had closed its borders to outsiders for decades. What the British needed was a miracle.

And that's exactly what they got. Unsettled by the political earthquakes happening in neighboring India and China, and concerned about the possibility of a communist revolution all their own, the government of Nepal decided to crack open its borders to a select number of outsiders. In 1948–49, an American scientific expedition, jointly sponsored by the National Geographic Society, the Smithsonian Institution, and Yale University, was allowed to do fieldwork in eastern Nepal. Later in 1949, two more expeditions, one British and one Swiss, gained entry into the kingdom. But it was not until 1950 that a purely mountaineering expedition was granted permission to come to Nepal.

It went to, of all nations, France.

The French, of course, had a long and proud mountaineering history. In the Alps, French climbers and guides had long been recognized as among the best, while the Groupe de Haute Montagne—the legendary GHM—was widely respected for its first-class alpinists.

But the résumés of French climbers outside of the Alps were notably thin, while the one major French expedition in the Himalayas, to Hidden Peak in 1936, had fallen noticeably short. In the race to the roof of the world, French climbers hadn't even been in the running.

Some climbers in postwar France, however, were determined to change that. Driven in part by the crushing defeat by the Germans in 1940 and the shame of the ensuing occupation, a group of French climbers boldly declared that, for the honor of their native land, they would be the first to climb an *Achttausender*. The leader of the expedition, a Chamonix-bred climber named Maurice Herzog, was, in fact, quite open about this being a do-or-die affair.

But the French climbers had done their homework, and the mistakes of 1936 were not to be repeated. Equipped with innovative new gear, including down parkas, rubber-soled boots, and nylon rope, which was much more durable and forgiving in the harsh Himalayan climate, the French expedition took aim at Annapurna, an *Achttausender* located in such a remote region in north-central Nepal that it had rarely been seen, much less accurately mapped. Blessed with good weather, a strong Sherpa support team, and the propitious discovery of a route around the mountain's deadly gorges, on June 3, 1950, Herzog and fellow climber Louis Lachenal stood on the summit of the tenth-highest mountain on earth. It was a stunning achievement.

Upon hearing the news, France erupted into joyous rapture. Crowds rushed the mountaineers' plane at Orly Airport when they returned on July 17, while Lachenal and Herzog, who'd lost toes and fingers, were awarded the Legion of Honor. *Paris Match* put out a special issue with Herzog holding aloft a tricolor flag along the summit, while Herzog's book about the expedition, *Annapurna*, which he dictated from a hospital bed, became the best-selling mountaineering book of all time.

Something else had happened as well. Because, technically, by climbing to the summit of the first *Achttausender*, Herzog and Lachenal had won the race to the roof of the world for France—

or, at least, its first iteration. But, in truth, the three nations whose climbers had fought the longest and hardest for Himalayan glory had their own prerogatives. For the Germans, it was Nanga Parbat. For the Americans, it had become K2. But for the British, it was, and always had been, Mount Everest. And they were now about to have another shot.

Despite the French triumph on Annapurna, careful preparation was still the name of the game at the Alpine Club in London. Precious little was known, really, about the southern, Nepalese side of Everest. There were some aerial photographs, and Bill Tilman had caught a glimpse of the south face while on a trek in Nepal with Charlie Houston, Betsy Cowles, and Anderson Blakewell on a trip that Houston's father had organized. "Our conclusions about the south face were that it presented much greater climbing difficulties than the north side," the group later reported. "The south face may well be impossible and we could see no practicable climbing route."

Michael Ward didn't believe it.

A young English physician attached to the Royal Army Medical Corps, Ward was also an accomplished climber. During the winter of 1950/51, he had been poking around in the archives of the Royal Geographical Society with a geography student named Ian Mumford when he made two important discoveries. The first was a series of photographs, taken covertly by an RAF Mosquito XIX, of the southern side of Mount Everest. The second was a hand-drawn map, completed in 1945 by a Royal Geographical Society cartographer and draftsman, of what was then known about the mountain's Nepalese flank. By carefully studying the two, Ward was convinced that he'd discovered a route to the summit. Members of the joint Alpine Club–Royal Geographical Society Himalayan Committee agreed, and a request was made to the Nepalese government for permission to send a reconnaissance expedition to the southern approaches to Mount Everest. In May 1951, the request was granted. The plan was to investigate whether the Western Cwm, the little-known, glaciated valley along the southern edge of the mountain, might be a gateway to the summit.

The British were going back to Everest.

Asked to lead the reconnaissance, Eric Shipton had wavered at first. Now forty-three years old, he had just slipped out of China, where he had been posted at the British Foreign Office in Kunming, and was looking forward to spending a peaceful English summer with his wife and family. "But the chance at last of looking into the mysterious Western Cwm was hard to resist," he later wrote, "while the prospect of visiting the Solu Khumbu, of seeing for myself the almost legendary home of the Sherpas was even more enthralling. So, with Diana's generous encouragement, I accepted the invitation."

Hamstrung by an incredibly tight schedule—they were to leave in six weeks—as well as a shortage of funds and dearth of equipment, the 1951 Mount Everest Reconnaissance Expedition would be, by necessity, a very Shiptonesque affair. Only four climbers would be involved. Two of them, a Scotsman named Bill Murray and the insightful doctor, Michael Ward, along with the expedition's supplies, would depart England by ship on August 2, bound for Bombay. Two weeks later, Shipton and Tom Bourdillon, a talented alpinist, would depart for Delhi by plane. But two days before Shipton left London, he received a telegram from the president of the New Zealand Alpine Club asking him if two New Zealand climbers, who had just finished a successful climb in the Garhwal and were still in India, might join the expedition. Shipton, with fond memories of Dan Bryant, the affable Kiwi whom he climbed with on Everest back in 1935, welcomed the idea. The names of the New Zealanders were Earle Riddiford and Ed Hillary.

The outbreak of the war in September 1939 had caused considerable stress among the members of the Hillary family on Remuera Road in Auckland. At first, Ed had wanted to join the Royal New Zealand Air Force, but his father had reminded him of the family's commitment to pacifism. "I was greatly troubled over the approach a Christian should have to killing," Ed later wrote. "I wasn't too impressed with the arguments put up by some clergymen and Christians to justify the support of the war, and I had no doubt that equally devout people in Germany were convinced that God was on their side." Ed withdrew his application to the RNZAF, registered as a conscientious objector, and was granted an exemption from military service. But when his younger brother tried to do the same, he was turned down—and sent to a squalid detention camp. Eventually, his brother's imprisonment proved to be too difficult of a burden to bear, and Ed convinced his father to allow him to enlist. Joining the air force, Ed was sent to the Solomon Islands as a navigator, but did not see combat.

After the war, mountaineering grew into a larger and larger part of Ed Hillary's life. Quickly growing into a first-rate climber, in 1947 and 1948 he helped put up a pair of demandingly difficult routes on Mount Cook. A year after that, on a family trip to Europe to attend the wedding of his sister, Ed managed to fit in some climbing in Austria and Switzerland. Then, in the late spring of 1951, after years of planning, he was a member of the four-man New Zealand Garhwal Expedition, a punishing slog that gave Ed his first experience with working with Sherpas. Three months later, in Ranikhet, they received at their hotel a telegram from Eric Shipton inviting them to join the Mount Everest reconnaissance. "ANY TWO CAN JOIN US," it read. "BRING THEIR OWN FOOD AND CATCH US UP." Hillary and Riddiford were soon on their way to Mount Everest.

Nearly two weeks later, on September 8, 1951, in a dank and dingy building in Dingla, a Nepalese village some fifty miles south of Everest, the two New Zealanders had their first meeting with Shipton and the others. "Feeling not a little like a couple of errant schoolboys going to visit the headmaster, we followed the Sherpa into a dark doorway and up some stairs into the upper room of a large building," Hillary later wrote. "As we came into the room, four figures rose to meet us. My first feeling was one of relief. I have rarely seen a more disreputable bunch, and my visions of changing for dinner faded away forever."

The Brits, for their part, were equally alarmed at first by the appearance of their new climbing partners with their "immense Victorian-looking ice axes" and ridiculous-looking sunhats. Any concerns, however, soon evaporated. "From the way they bounded up the hill and the ease with which they wolfed down a horrid meal of boiled rice and indeterminate green vegetables," Michael Ward later recalled, "they were both in training and used to the squalid aspects of Himalayan travel." Ed Hillary, in particular, with his long, lanky frame, his deep green eyes, and his seeming imperviousness to fatigue, soon made a deep impression on the British climbers.

The goals of the expedition were simple and direct. Assisted by a dozen Sherpas, including the redoubtable Ang Tharkay as sirdar— and, for the first time for most of those involved, a female Sherpa named Lhakpa—the members of the expedition would move past Namche Bazaar and the monastery at Thyangboche and establish a base camp along the western edge of the Khumbu Glacier. From there, different combinations of climbers and Sherpas would probe the possibilities on Everest's southern side, especially whether there was a way, via the Western Cwm, to access the South Col, a dip in a long ridge that led to the summit.

Here, there were two key questions. The first was whether the Western Cwm could be accessed via the Khumbu icefall, a daunting maze of broken seracs, some of them the size of ocean-going ships, that tumbled off the lower edge of the Western Cwm as it joined the Khumbu Glacier. The second was whether it could be possible to climb up the South Col from the Western Cwm, the long but generally flat glacial valley, surrounded by high ridges on either side, that skirted the southwestern side of the mountain. On September 30, the expedition began to find out.

Three of the climbers, plus two Sherpas, headed for the lower edge of the icefall.

Shipton and Hillary, as Ed was by then called, instead took off

The World Beneath Their Feet

for Pumori, a 23,500-foot peak that would give them a commanding view of both the icefall and the lower reaches of the Western Cwm. The climb itself was a ballbuster. "We were both fairly fit and climbed steadily upwards," Hillary later recalled. "But the height started taking its toll. In the rarefied air our lungs were working overtime and rapid movement was impossible." After a short rest at about 19,000 feet, Shipton urged them upward. "Then we pushed on up the last pitches," Hillary added. "We scrambled up a steep rock bluff, chipped a few steps over some firm snow, and collapsed with relief on a little edge at 20,000 feet."

The view was breathtaking.

Not only could they see the icefall in all of its terror and glory, but they could also see beyond it. "The most remarkable and unexpected aspect of the view," Shipton recalled, "was that we could see right up to the head of the West Cwm, the whole of the west face of Lhotse, the South Col and the slopes leading up to it. Indeed, a view from the interior of the Cwm itself could have hardly shown us more." And what they saw there was even more unforgettable. "We estimated that the floor of the Cwm at its head was nearly 23,000 feet, about 2,000 feet higher than we had expected," Shipton added. "From there we could see that there was a perfectly straightforward route up the face of Lhotse to about 25,000 feet, whence, it seemed, a traverse could be made to the South Col." Michael Ward had been right. There *was* a route to the summit of Everest from the south.

Only there was one big problem, namely, the icefall itself.

Viewed from their perch on Pumori, a quick study of the icefall, Shipton wrote, "soon sobered our spirits." That evening, back at Base Camp, Riddiford and the others gave a more promising assessment. There was no question that Shipton and Hillary had discovered a "practicable route" from the Western Cwm to the South Col. But the issue at hand was whether there was a safe route through the Khumbu icefall, especially with heavily laden porters. For the next month, the climbers and Sherpas tried to answer that question— but to no avail. While they eventually forced a way to the edge of the Cwm itself, and did so without any major mishap, there was no question that the inherent dangers of the icefall were a serious impediment, if not an actual roadblock, to a route up the Western Cwm. On a final push to find a safe route across the icefall on October 28, the Sherpas pushed back. "Pasang and I were firmly convinced that we should give up," Ang Tharkay later recalled. "We felt that it was inordinately dangerous to cross the icefall with heavy loads. Finally we refused to do so."

Hillary, however, had a different interpretation. "We returned to the Base with the strong feeling that the icefall was the key to any attempt on Everest on from the south. Our experience was that it was dangerous but that it could be climbed," he wrote. "In my heart, I knew that the only way to attempt this mountain was to modify the old standards of safety and justifiable risk and to meet the dangers as they came—to drive through regardless. Care and caution would never make a route through the icefall."

On the way home, a new plan was agreed upon.

Back in London, a new request would be made to the Nepalese government, seeking permission to launch a new Everest expedition, from the south, the following spring. It was time to see if the discoveries they had made that autumn could take them to the top in 1952. But when the climbers arrived in Kathmandu on November 17, they were in for an unhappy surprise. At the British embassy, where they were finally able to change their clothes and take a hot bath, they heard the news. The Nepalese had already granted permission for an Everest expedition in 1952. It had gone to the Swiss.

Although the war had prevented mountain climbers from neutral Switzerland, like everyone else, from launching mountaineering expeditions to India or Tibet, Swiss climbers were far from unacquainted with the Himalayas. Günter Dyhrenfurth had led expeditions to Kangchenjunga in 1930 and to the Karakoram in 1934—on the latter of which his wife, Hettie, set an altitude record for female mountaineers by climbing to the 23,861-foot summit of Queen Mary

Peak. Thirteen years later, the Swiss Foundation for Alpine Research sent two expeditions to India during the last months of the Raj, one to the Garhwal and the other to the Karakoram. And in 1949, two Swiss climbers led a small expedition to far eastern Nepal, along the border with Sikkim.

Now armed with the wealth of information created by Shipton's 1951 reconnaissance, the Swiss had every intention of conquering Everest. Convinced that additional oxygen was required at the highest elevations, they brought along their own oxygen equipment. But their two best weapons were human. The first was Raymond Lambert, an experience-toughened Genevois mountaineer who had once been caught in a crevasse for three days during a winter ascent of the Aiguilles Diables. Lambert survived the ordeal, but lost all of his toes and some of his fingers. Yet he continued to climb, in specially fitted boots. The Sherpas, in particular, took to Lambert immediately. Their second weapon was Tenzing. Having assisted on earlier expeditions with Swiss climbers, he had been named as the expedition's sirdar.

By the third week of April 1952, the expedition had set up its base camp along the western edge of the Khumbu Glacier and begun its assault on the icefall. Working quickly and diligently, and blessed with good weather, in less than a week they had made it through the treacherous, ever-shifting jumble of ice. By the middle of May, the expedition had worked its way up and across the Western Cwm, and were prepared to begin their attack on the South Col. By all measures, the Swiss team was performing magnificently.

The South Col brought them back down to earth.

It took them more than a week of hard, grueling work to fix a route, and once they ascended to the top of the col, they had to face the full wrath of its winds. "On the huge walls of the south face of Everest the wind blows almost continually, making a ceaseless noise like an express train," climber André Roch wrote. Building a windbreak with rocks would have undoubtedly helped, but by then, the energy reserves for most of the team had withered away, while three of the Sherpas had become sick. Moreover, the incessant wind had also revealed just how difficult the next obstacle, the southeast ridge leading to the summit, would be. "This infernal blast of air sweeps the snow from the couloirs, leaving nothing but bare ice," Roch added. "It caused us considerable anxiety to see the greenish mirror of the slopes increasing every day." The Swiss expedition, which had begun with such confidence and high hopes, was beginning to unravel.

In the end, their hopes would rest on two sets of shoulders.

Even though Raymond Lambert spoke no Asian languages, and knew only a few words of English, he had started climbing more and more with Tenzing, with whom he'd communicate with by hand signals. And Tenzing, for his part, had been deeply impressed with the huge, bear-like Swiss climber. "I was working mainly with Lambert," he later recalled. "There was nothing official about it; no one had ordered it that way. It had just seemed to happen." Even more significantly, Tenzing had crossed another barrier as well. No longer just the expedition's sirdar, he had, with the Swiss, finally walked across the line that had divided the Sherpas and the sahibs from the beginning. "As from the beginning, I was still sirdar of the Sherpas," he said. "But now I was also one of the climbing team and a real expedition member. It was an honor I was well aware of—the greatest honor that had ever been paid to me—and in my heart I swore that I would prove myself worthy."

In fact, he already had. It had largely been due to Tenzing's winning personality and superhuman efforts in both exhorting the other Sherpas to go higher and higher, and in making multiple trips to carry loads himself, that the expedition had gotten as far as it had. Soon there would come a chance to see how much farther they could go.

It began on Wednesday, May 27.

Concerned that the changes in the weather foreshadowed the imminent arrival of the monsoon, three Swiss climbers—Lambert, René Aubert, and Leon Flory—and Tenzing had surmounted the

The World Beneath Their Feet

South Col and spent a wild night in a hard-fought Camp Six, with the wind roaring about them. Low on supplies, and now without any Sherpas, the plan that day was to begin to work their way up the southeast ridge and establish a high camp with a small tent, before returning to Camp Six for the night—and to await the arrival of more supplies. But late on the afternoon of the twenty-seventh, probably at an altitude of around 27,200 feet, Tenzing had a revelation. "The weather was almost perfect," he remembered. "Lambert and I were not too tired. I saw a small, almost level place where the tent could be pitched." Motioning to Lambert, he pointed at the spot and said that they ought to stay there that night. "Lambert smiled at me," he added, "and I could tell he had been thinking the same thing." The other two climbers decided to return to Camp Six.

Tenzing and Lambert were now on their own.

They had no sleeping bags and no stove.

Inside the tent, they ate a little cheese, while Tenzing melted some snow with a candle. The weather was so mild, at first, that they were even able to sit outside, until the sun dipped below Pumori, some seven miles to the west. But once it did, the warmth disappeared in a flash, and they soon felt the iron wave of almost interstellar cold wash across the mountain, while the wind kicked up again with its ghastly howl. There would be no sleep. "Lying still, without any bags to protect us," Tenzing recalled, "we probably would have frozen to death." So all night long they huddled together, kneading and clapping together their arms and legs and, especially, their hands and feet, trying to keep the circulation going, trying to keep warm, trying to stay alive. "We just slapped and rubbed, rubbed and slapped, and slowly, slowly the hours passed, until at last there was a faint gray light in the tent. Stiff and cold, we crawled out and looked around: and what we saw was not good, for the weather had worsened," Tenzing said. "We hesitated a few moments, but, as usual, there was no need for words. Lambert jerked his thumb at the ridge with a wink, and I nodded, smiling."

Up they went.

Three steps. Then a breath. Then two. Sometimes one.

Each man wore a set of oxygen apparatus, the tanks on their backs connected to a rubber hose that led to a face mask. But the oxygen would only flow when were at a dead stop, and not when they were climbing. So they ditched the sets, happy to be relieved of the excess weight.

On they climbed. Every twenty yards or so, they would change places. Lambert would lead, then Tenzing. Three steps. Then stop to catch one's breath. Three more. Stop again. Up and up. On and on. The weather, meanwhile, was no longer on their side. "It was not wholly bad—there was no storm—but the clearness was gone," Tenzing remembered, "clouds filled the sky to the south and west, and the wind, rising, blew sharp grains of ice into our faces."

Three steps. Stop.

Three steps. Stop.

On and on they went. After four hours of steady climbing, Lambert suddenly stopped and turned around and looked at Tenzing. He was smiling.

"Ça va bien!" he said. It's going well.

"Ça va bien!" Tenzing replied.

"It was not true," Tenzing later said. Wracked with thirst, their throats now parched and sore, on some of the steeper spots they had been forced to crawl on all fours, with their shins and knees taking terrible punishment while their ice axes scraped uselessly against the rocks. Their thinking blurred as well, as stray thoughts and memories crowded upon the consciousness. After about five hours, they had climbed about six hundred and fifty feet, a bit more than the length of two football fields. "Then we stopped and did not move again," Tenzing remembered. They were still five hundred feet below the false South Summit. The real summit was another six hundred feet higher.

"I believe in God," Tenzing later told the American climber and mountaineer James Ramsey Ullman. "I believe that in men's hardest moments he sometimes tells them what to do, and that he did it then for Lambert and me. We could have gone on further. We could perhaps have gone to the top. But we could not have got down again. To go on would be to die." They turned around and headed back down. The next day, a second team of climbers and Sherpas also tried, but turned back as well. That fall, the Swiss attempted a post-monsoon assault on Everest, but it, too, failed.

The new Chinese government, meanwhile, was curtly dismissive of the events of that summer. In particular, the Ministry of the Interior condemned the use of the name Everest, claiming that it honored an "imperialist colonial administrator," and that its continued use was a form of "cultural aggression." From then on, the *Peking People's Daily* reported, the world's highest mountain was to be known as Chomolungma.

In London, the elation was palpable.

You could sense the relief in the broad smiles of Alpine Club members as they greeted each other, and hear it in their sighs of relief as they read newspaper reports on the final outcomes of the Swiss expeditions. "EVEREST INVIOLATE" crowed the *Times*. The British, who had been granted permission to launch an expedition to Mount Everest in 1953, would have another shot. But mixed with the genuine joy that the nation, and its mountaineers, had caught a break was a growing anxiety about the future. Things just weren't the same anymore.

It wasn't simply that the Swiss had failed. Nor that they had done so with such equanimity. "I think we've done some good work," René Dittert, one of the Swiss climbers remarked. "On Everest one expedition climbs upon the shoulders of the other. We climbed upon the shoulders of Shipton. He climbed on those of Houston. Those who will come after us will climb on ours." Rather, the British climbing establishment had to accept that their nation no longer had either a special claim or the inside track on mountaineering's greatest prize. Any schoolchild could see on a map that Mount Everest straddled the border between Tibet and Nepal, as it had for decades. But with the closing of Tibet, and the opening of Nepal, Everest was no longer a "British" mountain. Being the first to climb to the top of the world's tallest mountain was now fair game for any nation that could convince the Nepalese government to give it a shot.

But that wasn't the worst of it.

For while the British were given the go-ahead for 1953, the French had been awarded permission to attempt Everest in 1954. And following their success on Annapurna, there was every reason to think that they might succeed here as well. After that, it was anyone's guess. It could be the Americans or the Italians, or repeat efforts by the British and the Swiss. That would depend on the Nepalese. The only thing for certain was that 1953 was the only year that the British, and the British alone, would have for getting to the top of Everest before anyone else.

For the British, the stakes couldn't have been higher.

Nineteen fifty-three was to be the year.

It had to be.

CHAPTER SEVENTEEN

The Brightness of Their Rising

There was no question as to who should lead the expedition.

Eric Shipton wasn't simply the best-known climber in Great Britain. He had also spent more time on Everest than anyone else. In 1933, he had made it past Camp Six to within sixteen hundred feet of the summit. He had led the 1936 expedition and been a member of the 1938 effort. And on the reconnaissance expedition in 1951, which he'd also led, Shipton had discovered the route through the Khumbu icefall and the Western Cwm that led to the South Col. No other British climber of his era—neither Frank Smythe, who had tragically died of cerebral malaria in India in 1949, nor his longtime climbing partner, Bill Tilman, now fifty-five—could match his record of mountaineering achievement.

Accordingly, plans were soon put in place to establish Shipton as the leader of the 1953 expedition. On July 28, 1952, Shipton met with the members of what was now called the Joint Himalayan Committee to "consider plans for the organization of the attempt on Everest the following spring," as well as to discuss his recent visit to Nepal. "It was clear that the Committee assumed that I would lead the expedition," Shipton later wrote. At the end of the meeting, he added, "the Chairman informed me that they had reached the unanimous decision that I should be asked to lead."

Despite the vote, the meeting had raised more questions than it had answered. For while Shipton certainly had his supporters on the committee, there were others who would now begin to question, with growing urgency, whether the soon-to-be forty-five-year-old mountaineer was, in fact, the right man to lead the expedition. "It seemed clear to me, that Shipton's heart was not fully in the job," one committee member later wrote. "When the meeting broke up, he remarked to Colonel Lowndes, and I overheard it, that it would need a fanatic to get up Everest—and Shipton was in no sense a fanatic."

Others no doubt grew uneasy with a passage in Shipton's 1943 book, *Upon That Mountain*, where he had written that "there are some, even among those who have themselves attempted to reach the summit, who nurse a secret hope that Mount Everest will never be climbed. I must confess to such feelings myself." And there were lingering concerns over his performance on the Everest training expedition to Nepal earlier that year. The plan had been for Shipton to lead an assault on Cho Oyu, a dazzling eight-thousand-meter peak—and the sixth-highest mountain in the world—in order to both train, and weed out, a group of young climbers for an attempt on Everest. But once Shipton realized that he would have to cross the border into Chinese-controlled Tibet in order to launch a summit bid, he called off the attempt.

The whispers did not go away.

And as an English summer gave way to an English fall, a backstage drama of Shakespearean dimensions played itself out among the dissatisfied members of the Joint Himalayan Committee. Totally unaware of what he later described as "a great deal of backdoor diplomacy," Shipton was informed, out of the blue, at the September 11, 1952, meeting of the committee that Colonel John Hunt, an army officer and mountaineer, had been appointed co-leader of the expedition. When Shipton questioned the wisdom of dual leadership for such an important mission, he was asked to step out of the room. "I returned to be told," he later wrote, "that it had been decided to appoint John Hunt in my place."

The news did not go down well with some of the leading candidates for the expedition. Tom Bourdillon, a well-known English rock climber who, with his father, had designed a new type of oxygen equipment for the expedition, grew so incensed that he submitted a letter of resignation—one that Shipton was eventually able to convince him to retract. The news hit Hillary hard as well. "I feel thoroughly depressed about the whole thing," he wrote, "as Everest never will sound quite the same without Shipton." But it didn't matter. The deed was done.

Three months later, in a small story buried on page eight, the *Times* reported that Eric Shipton had taken a position as the warden at the Outward Bound Mountain School in Cumberland.

Born in India, John Hunt was a career British army officer who had served in Bengal, fought in Italy during the war, had been the chief instructor for the Commando Snow and Warfare School, and was currently on the planning staff for SHAEF, the Supreme Head-quarters Allied Expeditionary Force, under General Montgomery. An accomplished mountaineer and member of the Alpine Club, he was used to being given orders to fulfill a certain objective—and then getting the job done. Fair-minded, reasonable, and unopposed to winning personal acclaim, Hunt had also been, for a British officer of his generation, unusually sympathetic to the cause of Indian independence.

The expedition team itself was both impressive and, in a nod to the pre-Shipton era, far from small. All told, there would be eleven British climbers, including three rising stars of the postwar generation—Tom Bourdillon, Charles Evans, and Wilfrid Noyce. Two New Zealanders had also made the cut, Ed Hillary and his sometime mountaineering partner, a towering Hawke's Bay schoolteacher named George Lowe. But all of the members of the expedition, from the physician Michael Ward to cameraman Tom Stobart, had legitimate mountaineering experience. Also coming along was a special correspondent for the *Times*, which was helping to underwrite the expedition, a witty twenty-six-year-old journalist and former intelligence officer who would later become world renowned as the travel writer Jan Morris, but in 1953 she was James Morris

As with his recent Everest experience with the Swiss, Tenzing had been brought on board as the sirdar but would also be recognized as a climber. In Darjeeling, he'd hired twenty Sherpas, including two of his nephews. In addition, nearly four hundred porters, along with five Ghurkha NCOs, would be engaged to haul the nearly five tons of supplies to Base Camp. But when Tenzing and the Sherpas met most of the British members of the expedition at the British embassy in Kathmandu in early March 1953, trouble broke out almost immediately. While the British team members were all provided with rooms in the embassy proper, with its lush carpets, modern furniture, and billiards room, the Sherpas were told to sleep in a former stable, now a garage, on the grounds. "Our men didn't like it at all," Tenzing recalled, "so I presented their complaints to the English and for a time considered going myself to a hotel, as a form of protest." In the end, Tenzing tried diplomacy. "It is only for one night," he told the others. "Let's make the best of it." The next morning, the Sherpas let their true feelings be known by pissing on the low wall in front of the embassy entrance.

The incident, however, was not the end of the problems. On the march toward Namche Bazaar, some of the Sherpas began complaining about the fact that they were given different rations from those the British were eating. Moreover, they had not already been issued their expedition gear. "Why is this?" they wanted to know. "On other expeditions we have been given our things right away." But even more upsetting, and breaking longstanding tradition, when they were finally issued their clothing, sleeping bags, and other gear, the Sherpas were informed that "most of the things were not theirs to keep, but were only to be used on the mountain and then returned." This was the final straw. "The Sherpas did not like this at all," Tenzing remembered. "They considered the clothing and gear as part of their normal pay and were not going to go on unless they received it in that way." The expedition was on the verge of collapse.

The World Beneath Their Feet

The underlying issues, of course, went much deeper. And nobody knew that quite as well as Tenzing. "With the Swiss and the French I had been treated as a comrade, and equal, in a way that is not possible for the British," he said. The Raj was gone, and the Empire was soon to follow. But the mindset that had sustained it was still going strong. In the end, a compromise was reached, though two of the most vocal critics among the Sherpas, Pasang Phutar and Ang Dawa, quit and went home. Tenzing, caught between his identity as a Sherpa and his job as sirdar, was relieved. "I have always hated small bickerings and resentments while one is engaged on a great adventure," he added. "When people are going to a mountain they should forget the molehills. When they are involved in a big thing they should have big hearts to go with it."

On April 9, the first team of climbers and Sherpas set off from Thyangboche Monastery toward Everest, accompanied by thirty-nine Sherpa porters. Half of the porters were women. Each carried a sixty-pound load. As they departed, the long strands of tattered prayer flags suddenly grew still, a raven arced overhead, and a light snow began to fall.

They made it through the Khumbu icefall in six days.

Route-finding their way through unstable seracs and huge ice boulders, cutting steps, fixing ropes, and using ladders and long pieces of timber to span the crevasses at the upper end, this was a solid achievement. It had also been made easier by Hunt's decision to have the team spend six days climbing some nearby peaks before leaving Thyangboche. Not only did this help immensely with acclimatization, but it gave the climbers and Sherpas a chance to use, and familiarize themselves with, the new oxygen equipment that would be used on the upper reaches of Everest. Two types had been brought along—a closed-circuit system where the user breathed in pure oxygen, and an open-circuit system in which oxygen was mixed with fresh air. Moreover, the climbs also helped to bind the climbers and Sherpas together.

The lip of the Western Cwm was reached on April 17, and for the next two weeks it became the center of the expedition's activities. The climbers and Sherpas pushed on toward the South Col, establishing Camps Three, Four, and Five on the way, with people and supplies moving constantly back and forth between the camps. While the Cwm itself was nowhere near as dangerous as the icefall, with its weird subterranean creaks and groans, many found it to be haunting in its own right. "There was something inhuman about the place," Michael Ward later wrote. "The floor and sides of this extraordinary geological freak were a dazzling white," he said, adding that stepping onto the Cwm "was like being in the scoop of an electric fire." Moreover, because it was protected on either side by ridges that rose up more than 24,000 feet, the Western Cwm was often quiet and still.

But the days spent on the Cwm also produced some real consequences, particularly in how the likely pairings of summit teams began to emerge. Both Hillary and Tenzing had been keeping their eyes out for a potential climbing partner, and they were impressed by what they observed in each other. "From now on I was teamed with Hillary the whole time," Tenzing recalled. "We were not supposed to do the heaviest jobs and so wear ourselves out, but only to get ourselves in the best condition." Moreover, the two had clicked and worked together well.

"I suppose we made a funny-looking pair, he and I, with Hillary about six feet three inches tall and myself some seven inches shorter," Tenzing later recalled. "What was important was that, as we climbed together and became used to each other, we were becoming a strong and confident team." Once, when Hillary decided to leap across a crevasse and fell short, a quick-thinking Tenzing was able to arrest his fall and haul his much larger and much heavier partner back to the surface. And even though Tenzing jokingly dismissed the incident, it made a deep impression on Hillary. Later, in camp, Hillary told some of the other climbers, "Without Tenzing I would have been finished today." The outsiders on the nearly all-British climbing team had found each other.

The World Beneath Their Feet

Like a number of the other climbers, when team physician Michael Ward wasn't working, he was reading. "He caught up on Jane Austen and the Brontës," it was later reported, while Wilfrid Noyce knocked off *Nicholas Nickleby* and *The Brothers Karamazov*. James Morris, the *Times* correspondent, meanwhile, was not to be outdone. "I also acquired a handsome hurricane lamp, made in Czechoslovakia," the young journalist later wrote, "by the light of which I proposed to read the *Oxford Book of Greek Verse* in the authentic manner of the scholar-mountaineer."

But Ward also had a chance to study how the various climbers were faring physically. Hillary and George Lowe, the other New Zealand climber, impressed Ward considerably. They were, he later wrote, "both extremely fit and going like greyhounds." Wilfrid Noyce and Alfred Gregory were also doing quite well. But it was Tenzing who made the greatest impression on Ward. "None of the European members of the party had the same look of fitness and superb training that he did," Ward wrote. In the past, others had claimed that Tenzing must have a "third lung" to be able to climb so high and so easily, but what impressed the team doctor so much was the sirdar's natural grace and ease of movement. "It seemed," Ward wrote, "as if he were on oiled wheels." And while many of the other climbers were now suffering from headaches, insomnia, stomach problems, and other woes, for Tenzing, the further he went, the more fit he became. "The higher I got the better I felt," he recalled. "To keep busy, always busy: that was the secret of how I kept warm and healthy."

Following the Western Cwm, the next challenge faced by the expedition would be to make its way up to the South Col, the windswept pass between Everest and Lhotse, its neighbor to the south—and the fourth-highest mountain on earth. A steep and grueling three-thousand-foot climb, it would have been challenging enough at sea level. But at more than seven thousand meters, this was a formidable obstacle. To tackle this monster, Hunt gave the assignment of leading the way to George Lowe, who was already legendary for his work on ice in New Zealand, and Ang Nyima. The conditions were appalling. Day after day, through bone-cold mornings and snowy afternoons, the two men fought their way up the ice-sheathed face of Lhotse, chopping out handholds and footholds with their ice axes, the chips flying like diamonds, and setting fixed ropes, all at an elevation of more than 23,000 feet. But working without oxygen at such a height took its toll. On May 15, Wilfrid Noyce came up to spell Ang Nyima. But Lowe was finished as well. With one last tremendous push led by Noyce, the face was finally conquered.

One week later, Camp Seven was established on the South Col.

"A desolate, bare, and inhuman place," Ward wrote.

Swept by near-constant winds, which pounded one's back or chest, and rattled the hoods of the climbers' parkas, Ward described the South Col's surface as "irregular but polished ice—with stones stuck into it." Long enough and broad enough to house a city of tents, it nonetheless felt like death. "The col was cold and windy, and the camp was a terribly lonely place among the broken stones and ice," Tenzing recalled. "We had pitched it in the same place where the Swiss had been the year before, and around us were the old tent frames and packs and oxygen tanks that looked as if they had been left like ghosts." Like a vision out of a gothic novel, complete with a dim white sun hovering in a deathly gray sky, the South Col, Ward wrote, "had a primeval air of subdued ferocity as though anxious to be unmolested." But for the climbers and the Sherpas, many of whom had to be roused by Tenzing to make the push to Camp Seven, the col had one redeeming quality. For rising up off of its northern end, in all of its terrible and tantalizing glory, was the grand, rocky face of Everest itself, the dazzling edge of a sharp pyramid that led all the way to the South Summit. Here, they hoped, was the pathway to victory.

John Hunt laid out what would be two summit attempts.

Tom Bourdillon and Charles Evans would form the first team.

Hillary and Tenzing would comprise the second.

At about seven o'clock on the morning of Tuesday, May 26, the first attempt, by Bourdillon and Evans, got underway. A support team consisting of John Hunt and Da Namgyal stepped out of their tents and into the wind of the South Col and started to make their way upward, with each man carrying a forty-five-pound load. Bourdillon and Evans were supposed to have departed an hour earlier, but had been delayed by a problem with Evans's closed-circuit oxygen system. "The tap on the oxygen feed was broken in the closed position," Evans wrote. Once that had been fixed, the two climbers then began their ascent, and they soon passed Hunt and Da Namgyal.

A little after nine o'clock, Hunt and Da Namgyal had passed the site where Tenzing and Raymond Lambert had spent their last, fitful, and highest night on Mount Everest as members of the Swiss expedition of one year earlier. "Nothing remained but the bare poles," John Hunt later wrote, "to which were still attached shreds of yellow cloth." But the climb, especially since they were carrying so much extra weight, had been brutal. Some forty-five minutes later, Da Namgyal was overcome with exhaustion, while Hunt was near to being finished as well. Along a small gap in the ridge, they built a cairn and stashed the tent, food, and fuel they had been carrying, along with their own oxygen bottles, to be used by Hillary and Tenzing, if needed, the next day. Hunt and Da Namgyal then started their descent, without oxygen, back to the South Col. It had been a remarkable, unprecedented effort.

Tom Bourdillon and Charles Evans, meanwhile, continued their upward progress. The plan called for them to advance all the way to the South Summit, assessing the conditions on the way. Then, if they were able to, they could make a run at the actual summit, which sat another three hundred feet higher. It was an incredibly audacious goal for the two climbers, one that involved climbing up—and back down—more than three-thousand feet in a single day, all at extreme elevation. But Hunt's plan also gave the first shot at summiting Everest to two English-born climbers, the London native Bourdillon and the Liverpool-born but Welsh-bred Evans.

Bourdillon and Evans, meanwhile, were going well. "In spite of our load, which was over fifty pounds apiece, we made good progress," Evans later wrote. They started in on the southeast ridge, stepping gingerly over loose rock covered with a layer of soft snow. By eleven o'clock, they had climbed more than twenty-two hundred feet. Finding a small hollow that gave them some protection from the wind, they decided to change their oxygen tanks. They were also extremely thirsty, but when Evans pulled out an insulated bottle of lemon drink, he discovered that the glass liner had shattered and the shards were mixed in with the now frozen drink. "It was a sign of our fuddled state that we wondered for a moment if we could not suck the sweetened ice off the splintered glass," Evans recalled. "Instead we threw the flask down the South Face." Then they packed up and again got going.

Ten minutes later, Evans suddenly grew breathless.

They stopped and examined his oxygen set, but couldn't find anything obviously wrong. Perhaps, Bourdillon decided, the soda-lime canister had been damaged and carbon dioxide was entering the feed. Hoping for the best, they moved on. Step by step, breath by breath. First came a long snow slope, covered in deep, soft snow. Then came a firm, rocky rib. Then more snow. One hundred feet later, they were standing on the South Summit of Mount Everest. No human beings had ever climbed this high before.

The actual summit was now so close that they could almost taste it.

"At our feet the ridge fell very slightly, presenting no obstacle, and then swept up in a succession of steps to a great cornice which hid the true top," Evans wrote. "I guessed that it would need three hours' work to get it." But the time on their wristwatches wrote the end of their tale. "It was 1:15 p.m. Our oxygen was only good for two and a half hours more, enough to see us back to the South Col." Bourdillon and Evans might have reached the summit, but they would never have made it alive coming back down. Fifteen minutes later, after taking a few photographs, the heartbroken climbers began to make their way down to the South Col.

That night, at the col, once they had recovered, Bourdillon and Evans told Hillary and Tenzing everything they could about the route to the South Summit, where the problem areas were, and how best to navigate them. "They did everything they could to advise and help us," Tenzing recalled. "And I thought, 'Yes, that is how it is on a mountain. That is how a mountain makes men great.'" The plan was that Tenzing and Hillary would head out the next morning, May 27, for their summit attempt. But that night a storm blew in, and by morning, it was blowing so hard that the assault had to be postponed. When the wind eased up that afternoon, Bourdillon, Evans, and Hunt headed down the col, while the six men still in Camp Eight—George Lowe, Alfred Gregory, Ang Nyima, Pemba, Hillary, and Tenzing—stayed huddled in their tents trying not to think too much about tomorrow. Finally, that evening, the wind began to drop.

Hillary suffered through an uneasy night's sleep. It was so cold inside the tent that ice kept forming around the valve of his air mattress. And when it did, the plug popped out, the mattress deflated, and Hillary, with his body now pressed against the frozen tent floor, awoke with a start. He got so sick of waking up, reinflating the mattress, and trying to drift off to sleep that, finally, he jammed a pencil into the valve. It worked.

Tenzing had no such problems.

Sherpas believed that dreaming of animals was a good omen.

That night, Tenzing dreamt of a white horse.

And of yaks romping in a pasture.

May 28, 1953. 4:00 a.m.

"I awoke with the feeling that something went wrong," Hillary recalled.

It was the wind. There wasn't any.

It returned a short while later, again shrieking like a runaway train, but as the morning slowly unfolded on the South Col, the wind continued to drop and was no longer a major concern. Soon, the Primus stoves were all hissing flame and melting snow for coffee, tea, cocoa, and hot lemon drink. Pemba had been sick all night, and was in no condition to move. But the others tried to shake the grogginess out of their minds and bodies, and began the long, slow process of trying to eat a little something and get ready for the day ahead.

At a little after nine a.m., George Lowe, Alfred Gregory, and Ang Nyima stepped out of their tents and into a light breeze. Each carrying some forty pounds apiece, mainly cylinders of oxygen, they began to make their way toward the southeast ridge with Lowe in the lead, kicking some steps in the snow, cutting others with the blade of his ice axe. All three were using oxygen. About an hour later, Tenzing and Hillary started up behind them. They, too, were on oxygen, each using an open-circuit set. The going went well at first. George Lowe led brilliantly, rhythmically chopping steps with his ice axe. With Hillary and Tenzing slowly narrowing the gap between the two parties, they pushed up the southeast ridge, past a crevasse and couloir, and the sad remains of Tenzing and Lambert's tent from a year earlier. "One of the loneliest sights I have ever seen," Hillary said. But they were now over 27,000 feet, the oxygen sets were all working well, and they were going strong. "It was most encouraging to find how fit we were feeling."

Their first objective was to locate the supplies that John Hunt and Da Namgyal had left for them two days earlier, items that were vital to their attempt. Carefully searching the ridge as they climbed, they eventually spotted the stash along a steep section, covered with a light layer of loose snow. "We came upon the dump," Hillary recalled, "an impressive pile of oxygen bottles, a tent, food, and fuel, and all of it essential for our high camp." But it was also a sobering sight. "To add all this to our loads was going to give us burdens far heavier than it was thought possible to carry at this altitude, even using oxygen," he added. "We didn't even know if we *could* carry it." Nonetheless, they went about their business and divided the loads. Hillary, who took on the single-heaviest item, the fourteen-and-a-half-pound tent, was now shouldering more than sixty pounds of gear. All of the others had packs that weighed more than fifty pounds. No one had ever carried so much weight at such a high altitude before.

Off they went.

The going was crushingly hard now. Step by step, breath by breath, one cramponed boot in front of the other, they pushed up the ridge. Their backs aching and their calves on fire, up they went, breathing heavily into their oxygen masks. They needed to get as far as they possibly could, in order to set a new camp that was high enough to allow Hillary and Tenzing a real shot at the summit the next day. But as each block of minutes went by, their last reserves of energy dropped lower and lower. Now, when they stopped, they would bend over and rest their chests, still heaving for breath, onto the top of their bent legs, with their temples pounding and their vision starting to shimmer. Worse, they could find no place remotely suitable for a campsite. The ledge that George Lowe had spied from below turned out to be no ledge at all. On they went.

Another five minutes.

Rest.

Then five more.

From his climb with Lambert one year earlier, Tenzing thought he remembered a spot, off to the left, that was big enough for a tent. Again, off they went. But it, too, wouldn't work. Back up again. One step after another. Five minutes. Rest. Five more. Finally, at about two-thirty that afternoon, Lowe let out a muffled shout and pointed upwards with his ice axe. "About fifty feet up the slope there seemed to be a more promising ledge," Hillary recalled. "It certainly wasn't by any means flat, but it was extensive enough and sufficiently well protected to give us a chance."

That was all it took. They all removed their packs. Then Lowe, Gregory, and Ang Nyima descended the mountain, hoping to make it back to the South Col before their oxygen gave out and night fell. Wordlessly, Tenzing and Hillary began chipping away with their ice axes at the hard, compacted ice and rock that formed the ledge. But at nearly 28,000 feet, everything ran in slow motion. Two and a half hours later, they had managed to chop and scrape two somewhat level platforms, side by side, each of which could support a climber in a sleeping bag. An hour after that, as the sun began to disappear in the west, working slowly and deliberately, they managed to set up the tent and stow their gear inside.

"Far below us was the Western Cwm, already filling up with the gloom of night," Hillary wrote. "And on the South Col I could just pick out the tiny group of tents flapping furiously in the eternal South Col wind." He tried to take some photographs, but soon gave up in disgust. Inside the tent, the canvas walls flickered with a warm glow as Tenzing pumped the Primus to life.

They were alone.

"Rather astonishingly," Hillary wrote, "for this altitude, we were really hungry. Out came all our delicacies—we had sardines on biscuits, fresh dates, and pint after pint of hot lemon drink crammed with sugar. As a special treat I produced my tin of apricots and Tenzing opened it with his tin opener. He tipped it upside down, but instead of delicious fruit and tasty juice flowing out, all that emerged was a solid block of ice. However, a short dose of treatment in a saucepan over the primus soon made it highly edible, and we ate it slowly, lingering over the flavor."

Hillary had some real worries about whether they would have enough oxygen for the next day, so he set their "night oxygen" to run only from 9:00 to 11:00 p.m., and then again from 1:00 a.m. to 3:00 a.m. Both men woke up, cold and with a start, at eleven, so Tenzing fired up the stove again and started melting snow for more hot lemon drink. At one o'clock, with their oxygen switched back on again, they both began to drift off.

God is good to us, Tenzing thought to himself. *Chomolungma is good to us.*

Outside, the wind had stopped.

The only sound, Tenzing recalled, was that of their breathing.

The World Beneath Their Feet

*   *   *

May 29, 1953. High Camp, Mount Everest. 27,900 feet.

At 4:00 a.m., Hillary pulled back the flap to the tent and both he and Tenzing looked out at the world. The morning was cold—sixteen degrees below zero Fahrenheit—but clear. "The early morning light was already tinging the sky and clearly outlining the icy peaks which stretched from horizon to horizon," Hillary recalled. Then Tenzing nudged his shoulder and pointed below, to a darkish spot beyond the icefall. "Thyangboche," he said. Both men knew that the monks would have already begun their morning devotions—and hoped that they would say a prayer for them.

But, first, more-practical matters beckoned. There was snow to melt, and food and hot drinks to prepare. Hillary had also foolishly taken off his boots the night before, and left them outside of his sleeping bag. They were now frozen stiff, and he had to thaw them over the stove, filling the tent with the bitter smells of singed leather and burnt rubber. At a little after six, both men pulled on all of their clothes. Hillary wore "a string singlet, woolen shirt, Shetland wool pullover, woolen underclothes, thick down trousers and jackets, and over them all strong windproof trousers and jacket with a hood over the head." To this ensemble, Tenzing had added wool socks that had been knit by his wife, a sweater given to him by Mrs. Henderson of the Himalayan Club, and Raymond Lambert's red woolen scarf. Each of them wore three pairs of gloves—silk, wool, and, finally, windproof. Then they crawled out of the tent, looped and tied-off a forty-foot length of rope around their waists, and started up.

Tenzing took the first lead and, steadily plowing ahead, forced a way up and through the knee-high snow, the sun now hitting his right shoulder. When the ridge began to narrow, the two men changed places and Hillary took over. Luckily there was little wind, because the drop-offs on either side—to the Western Cwm on the left, and Kangshung Glacier on the right—were each more than three thousand feet. Keeping to the slightly steeper yet seemingly safer left side, where he figured that their crampons would easily grip into wind-hardened snow, Hillary stepped confidently forward. "Next moment I was almost thrown off balance as the wind-crust suddenly gave way and I sank through it up to my knee," he remembered. "It took me a little while to catch my breath. Then I gradually pulled my leg out of the hole. I was almost upright again when the wind-crust under the other foot gave way and I sank back with both legs enveloped in soft, loose snow to the knees. It was the mountaineer's curse—breakable crust."

There was no choice but to plunge ahead. But near a small crest came some good news: two oxygen bottles halfway buried in the snow. Left by Bourdillon and Evans, each was more than one-third full. Hillary and Tenzing's fears over not having enough oxygen were over, and with renewed vigor, they pushed forward. "All the way up and down we helped, and were helped by, each other," Tenzing recalled. "We were not leader and led. We were partners." And despite a nasty pitch on a snow slope up ahead, they made it to the top of the South Summit by nine o'clock. Chipping away a spot to sit on, they both sat down and removed their oxygen masks, breathing in fresh air at 28,700 feet. "The day was still remarkably fine, and we felt no discomfort through our thick layers of clothing from either wind or cold," Hillary recalled. After a short rest, they removed their near-empty oxygen tanks, and screwed in their last, full cylinders. Then they started off again.

There was only one true obstacle left—and it was a formidable one.

A great rock wall that rose up for nearly fifty feet, it presented a climbing challenge that would have been hard enough along a summit after a long climb in the Alps, but was almost unfathomably difficult at well above eight thousand meters. A frontal assault would have been nigh impossible, even with pitons, carabiners, and a rock hammer, none of which they possessed. There might be a way around it to the left, Hillary concluded, but that would involve dropping down nearly 150 feet over some dicey rock slabs before one could possibly begin to head up again, and even then, there was no guarantee of a climbable route to the summit.

But as they approached the far right edge of the wall, Hillary noticed something, in the form of a large cornice, that gave him an idea. "This cornice, in preparation for its inevitable crash down the mountainside, had started to lose its grip on the rock," he wrote, "and a long narrow vertical crack had been formed between the rock and the ice. The crack was large enough to take the human frame, and though it offered little security, it was at least a route. I quickly made up my mind—Tenzing had an excellent belay and we must be near the top—it was worth a try."

Squeezing his six-foot-two-inch frame into the fissure, facing the rock wall with his oxygen pack pressed against the cornice, Hillary inched his way up, grabbing whatever small holds he could find with his hands or ice axe on the rock face, while digging his crampons into the snow, taking baby steps as we went. "Slowly I forced my way up—wriggling and jambing and using every little hold," he later recalled. "And then I found a solid foothold in hollow in the ice, and the next moment I was reaching over the top of the rock and pulling myself to safety. The rope came tight—its forty feet had been barely enough." But he had made it. Tenzing then followed.

What they had left was a short walk, though at the time it seemed to go on forever. The summit, wherever it was, kept just out of sight, hidden beyond one snakelike rise in the final slope after another. They also had to cut steps and, now truly bone-tired, their pace slowed to a crawl. "Bump followed bump with maddening regularity," Hillary wrote. "A patch of shingle barred our way, and I climbed dully up it and started cutting steps around another bump. And then I realized that this was the last bump. For ahead of me the ridge dropped steeply away in a great corniced curve, and out in the distance I could see the pastel shades and fleecy clouds of the highlands of Tibet."

Tenzing later remembered what happened next.

"A little below the summit Hillary and I stopped. We looked up.

Then we went on. The rope that joined us was thirty feet long, but I held most of it in loops in my hand, so that there was only about six feet between us," he later said. "We went on slowly, steadily. And then we were there. Hillary stepped on top first. And I stepped up after him."

They had done it.

It was 11:30 in the morning on Friday, May 29, 1953.

"What we did first was what all climbers do when they reach the top of their mountain," Tenzing added. "We shook hands. But this was not enough for Everest. I waved my arms in the air and then threw them around Hillary, and we thumped each other on the back until, even with the oxygen, we were almost breathless. Then we looked around. It was eleven-thirty in the morning, the sun was shining, and the sky was the deepest blue I have ever seen."

They each turned off their oxygen, and shared a bit of Kendal Mint Cake.

Then Hillary pulled out his camera, and took a picture of Tenzing on the summit. His left leg was bent, while in his right hand, Tenzing held aloft his ice axe, off of which four flags were furiously snapping and whipping in the wind. From the top, they were the flags of the United Nations, Great Britain, Nepal, and India. "I am glad that the UN flag was on top. For I like to think that our victory was not only for ourselves—not only for our own nations—but for all men everywhere." Tenzing scooped a hole in the snow, and in it they buried a few things, including a pencil that Tenzing's daughter had given him, a crucifix, and a small black cloth cat that Hunt had given Hillary as a mascot for the expedition. Then they looked around a bit for any signs that George Mallory and Sandy Irvine had been to the top before them, but they found nothing.

A few minutes later, they switched their oxygen back on, and started back down.

Late that afternoon, George Lowe climbed up a ways from the South Col camp to meet Tenzing and Hillary as they came down.

Both men were dead tired, and Hillary had already slipped off his oxygen mask, as his last tank had already run out. Now that he could see that both men were all right, Lowe was dying to know whether they'd made it to the summit or not. Only neither said anything.

Finally, Hillary looked at his old climbing partner and smiled.

"Well, George," he said, "we knocked the bastard off."

CHAPTER EIGHTEEN

Glory, Strength, and Decency

James Morris, the reporter for the *Times*, had the scoop of a lifetime.

The twenty-six-year-old had been on the Western Cwm on the morning of May 30, 1953, when Hillary, Tenzing, George Lowe, Wilfrid Noyce, and Pasang Phutar were seen in the distance, walking toward Camp Four. Along with the other climbers and Sherpas gathered there, the *Times* correspondent too had watched them anxiously. "How were they walking?" Morris later wrote. "Jauntily, like men who have reached the summit? Or dragging their feet in the depression of failure." Finally, when they got close enough, George Lowe broke the news. Pointing up toward the summit of Everest with his ice axe, he gave a thumbs up sign with his other hand. They had done it. Camp Four erupted into a wild frenzy of screaming and shouting, laughter, smiles, and tears. The Sherpas greeted Tenzing with both joy and awe. "They stepped out, one by one, to congratulate him," Morris wrote. "Some bent their bodies forward, their hands clasped as if in prayer. Some shook hands lightly and delicately, the fingers scarcely touching. One old veteran, his black twisted pigtail flowing behind him, bowed gravely to touch Tenzing's hand with his forehead."

Then they all crammed into the big domed tent to laugh and talk and celebrate and ask questions. "Everest was climbed, and these two mortal men in front of us, sitting on old boxes, had stood upon the summit, the highest place on earth!" Morris added. "And nobody knew but us! The day was still dazzlingly bright—the snow so white, the sky so blue; and the air was so vibrant with excitement; and the news, however much we expected it, was still somehow such a wonderful surprise—shock waves of that moment must still linger there in the Western Cwm, so potent were they, and so gloriously charged with pleasure."

Writing like a madman, Morris shook himself back to work. "I scribbled it all down in a tattered old notebook." But now, at half past two on the afternoon of May 30, 1953, there was a hugeproblem. Morris needed to get the news back to the London office of the *Times* as quickly as possible. But the *Times* writer also needed to make sure that no other news organization caught wind of it first.

This was no small challenge.

For while the climbers had an exclusive contract with the *Times*, other newspapers had dispatched reporters to Nepal, hoping to sniff out what had happened. Ralph Izzard, of the *Daily Mail*, had been seen at Thyangboche, while Peter Jackson, a stringer for Reuters, had been hanging around Base Camp. Even more worrisome, there was a radio transmitter at Base Camp that could possibly be used by anyone to spread the news. The longer Morris waited, the greater the chance that the *Times* would get scooped by one of his competitors.

The young reporter wasted no time. That afternoon, Morris and Michael Westmacott, a former president of the Oxford University Mountaineering Club and the expedition's tent expert, took off for Base Camp, a grueling haul from Camp Four, one that would take them off the Cwm and all the way through the icefall. But, as Morris wrote, "Christmas angels were in the Cwm that day," and they stumbled into Base Camp that evening safe and sound. The next morning, Morris was met by one of his runners, who would then carry a message sealed in an envelope to Namche Bazaar. The runner would then deliver the envelope to a Mr. Tiwari, an Indian police officer who operated a wireless transmitter there and who would send a message to Christopher Summerhayes, the British consul in Kathmandu. Summerhayes would then relay the message over his Foreign Office radio transmitter to London, where it would be shared with the *Times*.

It was a good plan. But there was one aspect that had especially worried Morris. What if a competitor caught wind of the contents of the message, either in Namche Bazaar or somewhere else? A bribe could be easily offered just to take a peek at the message. Clearly, Morris needed some kind of a code. But if the message was obviously encoded—as in *The red fox is in the barn*—it wouldn't take another reporter long to figure out that there had been some big news on Everest. What was needed, Morris had concluded, was a code that didn't look like a code. So, he had cooked one up. It looked like this:

Snow Conditions Bad	Summit reached
South Col Untenable	George Band
Lhotse Face	Tom Bourdillon
Ridge Camp Untenable	Charles Evans
Withdrawal to West Basin	Alfred Gregory
Advanced Base Abandoned	Edmund Hillary
Camp Five Abandoned	John Hunt
Camp Six Abandoned	George Lowe
Camp Seven Abandoned	Wilfrid Noyce
Awaiting Improvement	Tensing
Further News Follows	Michael Ward
Assault Postponed	Michael Westmacott
Weather Deteriorating	Charles Wylie
Awaiting Oxygen Supplies	Sherpa

All the other words in the message would retain their regular meaning.

Morris then pulled out the typewriter at Base Camp, and pecked out the following words on a slip of paper: *Snow conditions bad stop advanced base abandoned yesterday stop awaiting improvement.* The message meant: *Summit reached. Edmund Hillary. Yesterday. Tenzing.*

Morris tucked the paper in an envelope, sealed it, and handed it to a runner. The young journalist then typed up his notes, ate an early lunch, and started off on the long walk toward Kathmandu. But a short bit past the monastery at Thyangboche, Morris ran into, of all people, Peter Jackson of Reuters. The two reporters had a brief exchange.

"Are you—er—leaving the mountain now?" Jackson asked.

"Oh, I've been up there so long, you know, I feel the need for a rest."

"Hmm. Things going all right?"

"Not too badly."

"Everybody all right?"

"More or less."

It was all a dance—a dance that journalists do when they don't want to share anything with a competitor. Morris said goodbye and hurried down the long trail toward Kathmandu, hoping that the carefully guarded news was already on its way to London.

Morris's plan worked. Barely.

On Monday, June 1, Mr. Tiwari, the Indian police officer stationed at Namche Bazaar, had sent the coded message over the wireless to the Indian Embassy in Kathmandu. But rather than send a word-for-word version of the message that the *Times* correspondent had written, the policeman and radio operator had instead sent *Snow condition bad hence expedition abandoned advance base on 29th and awaiting improvement being all well.* Luckily, it was close enough. The vice consul of the Indian diplomatic mission, one G. R Joshi, then forwarded the message to the British embassy, where Ambassador Summerhayes had it sent over his Foreign Office transmitter to London. Late that night at Buckingham Palace, on the very eve of her coronation, Queen Elizabeth II was informed of the triumph on Everest. The prime minister, Winston Churchill, was told as well, while over on Queen Victoria Street, the typesetters at the *Times* were busy preparing the mock-up for the next day's edition, complete with the exciting news from the Himalayas.

*　　*　　*

Tuesday, June 2, dawned wet and gray across London.

Drizzle seeped from a low bank of clouds, while gusts of wind mussed hairdos and rippled the dark waters of the Thames. No one cared. The Tube and the double-decker buses had been packed since the early hours with happy and excited citizens of the realm, all looking forward to witnessing some part of the coronation of Elizabeth II, their new but already beloved twenty-seven-year-old monarch. A lucky few had passes to attend the actual coronation service inside Westminster Abbey, with its ancient traditions of the anointing, the investing, and the crowning, but most would be aiming to find a good spot along the route of the procession. For nearly two hours, the queen, seated in a gilded coach drawn by eight gray horses, as well as hundreds of mounted escorts, soldiers, sailors, Royal Marines, military band members, equerries, marshals, and foreign heads of state would wend their way past Trafalgar Square, Hyde Park Corner, Marble Arch, Oxford Street, Piccadilly Circus, and St. James Park, before escorting the newly crowned monarch back inside the gates at Buckingham Palace. London hadn't experienced a day like this in years.

Even though the procession wasn't set to start until midafternoon, crowds had already started to line the parade route early that morning. There were families with children, old men and old women who had survived the Blitz, veterans wearing regimental badges and pins, East Londoners and Mayfair dowagers, bank presidents and housekeepers. Sidewalk entrepreneurs did a brisk business selling souvenir programs and sausage buns, paper periscopes and steaming cups of tea. Yet despite the mizzling rain, and the long hours that they would be on their feet, the mood of the people was cheery and upbeat.

Then, a little before eight o'clock, it suddenly got even better.

For over the loudspeakers came an announcement that three days earlier, British mountaineers had climbed to the top of Mount Everest. "The crowds waiting in the wet London Streets," it was reported, "cheered and danced to hear of it." It was a glorious, unforgettable moment, and a crowning touch to the coronation of the young queen. The word spread like wildfire. BBC announcers read the news over both radio and television, while editors at the *Daily Mail*, the *Express*, the *Daily Telegraph*, and the *News Chronicle* all scrambled to add the joyful tidings to their late editions.

Meanwhile, half the world away, another coronation was also about to commence.

And while it would feature no printed programs or state carriages, no jewelled crowns or gilded scepters, this enthronement was also very real. For when the news that a brown-skinned man who would soon be known to the world as Tenzing Norgay had climbed to the top of the highest mountain on earth, an explosion of joy swept across India and Nepal. Even before the members of the expedition reached Kathmandu, Tenzing was met by throngs of villagers who showered him with flowers and coins, and fistfuls of rice and bright red *holi* powder. In the Nepalese capital, there were banners and speeches, medals and receptions. Across the border in India, on the streets of Darjeeling and Calcutta, old and young alike would soon be singing along with a new 78-rpm recording of a song called *Hamro Tenzing Sherpa Le*—"Our Tenzing Sherpa."

Eventually, Tenzing's newfound fame would bring money and his first home of his own, but it would also bring some stubborn headaches as well, including one of the question of his nationality. From the start, an immense amount of pressure was brought to bear on Tenzing to choose. Was he an Indian, or a Nepali? But Tenzing swept the questions aside. "What difference does it make?" he told an American reporter. "We should all be the same—Hillary, myself, Indian, Nepali, everybody."

In an age of nationalism, here was a new kind of hero.

Back in London, Kenneth Mason had heard the news from Everest while sitting in a covered stand set up in Parliament Square, waiting for the queen's procession to begin. "It was during the very early morning of that day," he later wrote, "as we were making our way to our seats in the drizzling rain, that we heard the wonderful news that Everest had been climbed." Of all the thousands of people who had lined the city's sidewalks for the coronation that day, few felt the news as deeply as the sixty-five-year-old Oxford professor. A former member of the Royal Engineers, he had first gone to India in 1909, where he helped to plot and triangulate the peaks and foothills of Kashmir, learned how to mountain climb, and, in 1926, led the first-ever scientific expedition into the Shaksgam Valley, near K2. Three years later, he was the founding editor of the *Himalayan Journal*, which he edited until 1940. Mason had known practically every important Himalayan climber of the 1930s, as well as many of the Darjeeling Sherpas.

But he also knew that Hillary and Tenzing, and indeed the entire expedition that year, had not climbed to the top of Mount Everest alone. Rather they had walked in the footsteps of George Mallory and Sandy Irvine, Eric Shipton and Bill Tilman, Angtsering and Ang Tharkay, Charlie Houston and the Minya Konka Four, Paul Bauer and the rock-climbing pioneers of the Eastern Alps. For mountain climbers always rise on the shoulders of those that preceded them, including those whose earthly remains lay high on windswept ridges, or lay buried in the icy depths of tomblike crevasses. "So ended in triumph," Mason later wrote, "the efforts which started with the reconnaissance in 1921, more than thirty years earlier."

Later that afternoon, once the procession had ended, the crowds of onlookers began to make their way back to the Tube, their bus stops, and the train stations, or started to walk back home. The London rain had stopped, but the wind had begun to pick up once again. And as it did, sandwich wrappers and stray bits of trash began to blow through the now-empty parks and across the deserted sidewalks, wheeling and flying, like snowflakes on a mountainside that was far, far away.

There were two other Himalayan expeditions that year.

Both were haunted by ghosts of the past.

The World Beneath Their Feet

In mid-April 1953, a team of German and Austrian climbers once again stepped onto a southbound train in Munich's central railway terminal, the first leg of their journey to Nanga Parbat. But like the Hauptbahnhof itself, rebuilt after the war, everything was both old and new at the same time. American GI's were no longer such a common sight on the streets of Munich anymore, while the adults waiting for their trains, who had been born in Bavaria and survived the Third Reich, now lived in the Federal Republic of Germany, a four-year old nation with Bonn as its capital.

In Genoa, the mountaineers boarded the SS *Victoria*—not the old tub that carried the 1934 climbers to their ill-fated deaths on Nanga Parbat, but a beautiful, brand-new ocean liner, the pride of the Lloyd Triestino Line. Arriving in Karachi at the end of the month, they took the long, hot train ride north, but in Rawalpindi, the Pakistani government offered to fly them to Gilgit. By the end of May, the expedition had established its base camp, not along the Diamir side that Heinrich Harrer and Peter Aufschnaiter had probed in 1939, but again below the old, familiar, and murderous Rakhiot face.

A joint German and Austrian effort, the expedition was both well organized and up to date. The climbers were armed with walkie-talkies, rubber-soled boots, and modern altimeters, while soft music—along with a daily weather report from Radio Rawalpindi—floated out of the radio at Base Camp. Hans Ertl, who had served as the director of photography on Leni Riefenstahl's *Olympia*, her cinematic ode to the 1936 summer games in Berlin, had brought along an Arriflex camera, a state-of-the-art tripod, and a war chest of lenses. The team of climbers were directed by fifty-one-year-old Peter Aschenbrenner who, along with Erwin Schneider nearly two decades earlier, had infamously skied away from three Sherpas high on Nanga Parbat during the 1934 disaster.

But the key to the expedition was a twenty-nine-year-old Austrian with a shock of wiry brown hair and a faraway look in his eyes. His name was Hermann Buhl. A mountaineer with a single-minded, almost feverish dedication to climbing, the Innsbruck native had, beginning at age fourteen, already cut an impressive swath through the Alps, including climbing the North Face of the Eiger. But it was on Nanga Parbat where he would carve his name forever into mountaineering history. Ordered because of threatening weather to descend from the upper mountain, on July 3, 1953, Buhl instead took off from Camp Five all alone.

Aided by two tablets of Pervitin—a form of methamphetamine that had been used by Luftwaffe pilots during the war—Buhl climbed steadily for the next forty-one hours. Not only did he successfully climb up the four thousand feet that led to the summit, but he also survived a tentless bivouac where, as with other Himalayan mountaineers before him, he felt the mysterious presence of another climber. "During those hours of extreme tension I had an extraordinary feeling that I was not alone," he later wrote. "I had a partner with me, looking after me, taking care of me, belaying me." By the time he stumbled back down to Camp Five more than a day and a half later, Buhl could no longer speak. But Nanga Parbat had finally fallen. His ordeal, one writer observed a couple of years later, "set the seal on what must almost certainly remain the outstanding achievement by a single human being in the long as yet unfinished history of mountaineering."

Perhaps.

Only Buhl did not live long to enjoy his renown. For as the legendary Italian climber Reinhold Messner later wrote, "the bundle of energy that was Buhl was not destined for a long life." Hermann Buhl fell to his death, in the Karakoram, less than three years later.

The Americans had not forgotten either.

For years, they had tried to gain permission to return to K2. During the last days of the Raj, the time had not been right, they were told. The political situation in Kashmir was too delicate. Then came independence, partition, and the Indo-Pakistani War of 1947. Now there were miles of concertina wire strung across Kashmir, with nervous Indian and Pakistani artillery crews hunkered down on either side. This was no time for mountaineering in the Karakoram.

But Charlie Houston kept pushing, writing letters, making friends in the US Department of State, whatever it took. Part of it, of course, was personal. He wanted to finish the job on K2. But he was also keenly aware that the old international rivalries in the Himalayas had far from disappeared. "The Japanese are very definitely up to something this summer, but I know not what," he wrote to a friend in late February 1952. "The British are now publicizing their trip to Cho Oyu as a 'training climb' for Everest 1953."

The Great Himalayan Race wasn't dead after all.

Houston's persistence paid off. In May 1952, he got the green light for a return to K2 to take place the next summer. Like its two predecessors, the Third American Karakoram Expedition of 1953 planned to assault K2 along the Abruzzi Ridge. But there would also be some changes. Because no Sherpas were allowed to come to Pakistan, the expedition would lean toward a lightweight nature. Untrained local Hunza porters would be used to carry supplies up to Camp Three, but after that the climbers would have to haul everything themselves. Above 20,000 feet, Emersonian self-reliance would once again fully have its day. So, too, would American-made gear. No longer playing second fiddle to their counterparts overseas, American manufacturers had begun to produce high-quality, top-end mountaineering gear that was equal to European products, and the climbers would haul their gear in US-made packs and sleep in American-made tents.

There were other changes as well.

Originally, Houston had planned on filling the expedition's roster of climbers with members and former members of the Harvard and Dartmouth mountaineering clubs—the familiar Eastern elites that, like Houston himself, had dominated American efforts in the Himalayas before the war. Instead, as Houston and Bob Bates started to select the six other members of the climbing team, the expedition acquired a decidedly Western accent. Dee Molenaar and Pete Schoening were from Seattle, while a third climber, Bob Craig, was from Colorado. The unspoken truth was that the heart center of high-altitude American mountaineering was no longer located in the climbing clubs of the Ivy League, but had shifted to the Pacific Northwest. And unlike earlier expeditions, whose exploits would be shared with the public in newspapers, films shot by the K2 climbers would be aired on television by NBC.

Getting to the mountain changed as well. While the expedition's food and supplies still made the long, slow journey from New York to Karachi by sea, on the *City of Carlisle*, air transportation now played a larger role. On June 2, 1953, the climbers flew from Rawalpindi to Skardu—a flight that was nothing less than a wonder to Bates and Houston, the two veterans of the 1938 K2 expedition. "Fifteen years before," Bates wrote, "we had driven for a whole day to get from Rawalpindi to Srinagar and then had walked 241 miles over rough terrain to get to Skardu. Now in an hour and a half we had traveled the same distance!"

The expedition got off to a solid start. Determined to avoid the tragedy of 1939, which claimed the lives of Dudley Wolfe and the three Sherpas who set out to rescue him, Houston insisted that each camp along the way be well stocked with food, fuel, and supplies—something that took time. Nevertheless, by August 2, all eight climbers had fought their way up to Camp Eight, now stocked with provisions to last for at least ten days, and they had done so without any oxygen equipment. "We were all in extremely good condition and had acclimatized well," transport officer Tony Streather later wrote. "Our gear was in good shape and morale was high. Most of the difficult climbing was over and we were less than 3,000 feet from the summit. All we needed was a break in the weather."

That night a truly ferocious storm ripped across the mountain. "It is hard to describe the storm," Houston wrote. "The wind blew so hard that the flapping of the tents was like a fusillade and the wind had a personal malignant impact which made us all feel that the mountain was trying to kill us. It snowed, or blew snow, continuously." The wind was so savage, in fact, that the climbers were unable to either light their Primus stoves, or keep them lit for more than a couple of minutes at a time. On the second morning of the storm, Bob Bates heard Houston cry out, "Our tent's gone!" The wind had ripped it to shreds.

Nevertheless, morale remained high. Houston had gone out of the way to select a team of climbers who were easygoing and compatible, and their ability to adapt was now shining through. That day, they even held their own New England–style town meeting, four and a half miles in the Pakistani sky, and a plan for the summit was agreed upon. "On the first clear day we would all carry loads up to Camp Nine, which we hoped to establish at about 27,000 feet," Streather wrote. "The strongest two climbers would go ahead with light loads and reconnoiter the route. These two would remain at Camp Nine, with supplies for several days, and would make a bid for the summit on the next clear day." They also held a secret vote and selected the members of the first summit team, George Bell and Art Gilkey. But the storm showed no signs of abating.

Soon, that was not their only problem.

"On August 6 came our first disaster," Houston wrote. "Art complained of pain in his right leg and when I examined him there was unmistakable evidence of thromo phlebitis." Gilkey had a blood clot in his leg, and when he tried to stand up, he fainted. Two days later, a piece of the clot broke off and lodged in his lung. Gilkey was now in a desperate state. No longer did anyone talk about reaching the summit. Despite the dangerous conditions, they had to try and save the life of their fellow climber by somehow carrying him down the mountain. "There was nothing else to do," Houston added, "if we were to give Art any chance at all. His illness had spread by August 8 to involve both legs and his lung, and I felt he was almost certain to die, yet we had to try and bring him down before our supplies were exhausted."

Wrapping Gilkey up in his sleeping bag, they set out immediately. But they didn't get far.

"We had not estimated the depth of the new snow," Bates wrote.

"Only 120 yards from camp we stopped, for the whole slope was saturated with new snow and in danger of immediately avalanching. Our old route had become a trap." It took all of their strength to haul Gilkey and themselves back up to Camp Eight. Pete Schoening and Bob Craig, a climber and ski instructor from Aspen, then tried to see if they could find another route down, along a rock ridge, but clouds rolled in and they couldn't see enough of the possible route. Even worse news came over their walkie-talkies from Colonel Ullah Atta, the Pakistani army officer who was stationed at Base Camp: more storms were forecast. They had no choice but to wait until the weather improved.

But by August 10, they could wait no longer. Another clot had entered Gilkey's lungs, and getting him down to a lower elevation was now a clear matter of life or death. "We wrapped him again in a sleeping bag and tent and set out, in the raging storm, to get him down by the new route," Streather wrote. "This was a desperate attempt but we had no alternative." Not only did they have to try and move their friend down an uncertain route, during a storm, high up on the second-highest mountain on earth, but the other climbers were now feeling the effects of both dehydration and the bitter cold. Some were starting to lose sensation in their hands and feet. It took them hours to descend just a little over four hundred feet. "There was no chance now of reaching Camp Six as we had planned," Streather wrote. Somehow, they would have to spend the night along a nearby rock ledge.

And then it happened.

Right after they had lowered Gilkey over a steep rock cliff, one of the climbers suddenly slipped and fell. But even though they had largely been climbing in pairs, all of their ropes became entangled. And one by one, five climbers—Houston, Bates, Bell, Streather, and Molenaar—were all yanked off their feet and sent hurtling down a snow gully that would likely end in a fall of several thousand feet and their certain deaths. "Nothing, I knew, could stop us," Bates wrote. "This was the end." But, some way and somehow, Pete Schoening, who had wrapped his rope around both his ice axe and his shoulder, managed to arrest the fall of all five climbers—as well as hold onto Art Gilkey. Nothing, in the entire history of mountaineering, could quite compare with what the twenty-six-year-old climber and chemical engineer from Seattle had pulled off. It had been a miracle.

But the situation on the mountain had now grown even more desperate. Houston had been knocked unconscious, Molenaar was bleeding, and Bell had lost his gloves. "There was no time to waste," Bates recalled. "We must gain shelter." Anchoring Gilkey along the slope with two ice axes, the other climbers made their way to the cache of equipment that had been left at Camp Seven and began to set up tents, while the storm continued to howl around them. But when they returned to fetch Gilkey, their hearts sank. "As I crossed the rib of rock separating Camp Seven from the ice gully, I saw something I shall never forget," Bates wrote. "The slope was bare. An avalanche we never heard above the roar of the storm had swept the gully." Gilkey was gone. Later, Charles Houston came to believe that, using his last strength, the desperately ill climber might have found a way to loosen the grip of the ice axes that held him in place, and deliberately fell to his death. Instead of his comrades saving him, Gilkey chose to save them.

"Of the next week I won't say much," Houston later wrote.

Four days later, the battered climbers returned to Base Camp. Before they began the long march back to Skardu, they built a cairn on a spur of rock along the Savoia glacier. Next to it they placed Art Gilkey's ice axe, along with an aluminum box containing some mountain flowers and a copy of Art's favorite poem. George Bell's hands and feet were in such bad condition that the climbers and porters ended up carrying him on an improvised stretcher for the entire one hundred and fifty miles to Skardu from K2. "Someday soon it will be climbed," Tony Streather wrote a few months later. "Perhaps we should have tried earlier, perhaps oxygen is as necessary on K2 as it has proved to be on Everest. I think not. These questions will be answered before long." Streather was correct. An Italian team climbed to the summit of K2 the very next summer. The Americans hadn't just lost the Great Himalayan Race. They hadn't been the first to climb K2 either.

In an odd way, though, it did not matter. For while Houston and the others had been denied their prize, the 1953 American K2 expedition was a model of careful planning, teamwork, and sheer guts. "We entered the mountain as strangers," Houston later said, "but we left it as brothers." It was Reinhold Messner, the Italian mountaineer who in 1980 made the first solo ascent of Mount Everest—and who had climbed K2 the year before—who perhaps best understood the accomplishment of Houston's team on a deeper, almost spiritual level. "I have great respect for the Italians who summitted K2 for the first time in 1954, but even greater respect for the Americans and the way they failed in 1953," Messner said. "They were decent. They were strong. And they failed in the most beautiful way you can imagine. This is the inspiration for a lifetime."

EPILOGUE

To the Stars

During the closing years of the 1930s, a young John F. Kennedy had spent some time in both England and on the European mainland, drinking in the sights and sounds of a continent inexorably tilting toward war. On July 1, 1937, less than two weeks after the second disaster on Nanga Parbat, he and a college classmate embarked upon a two-month driving tour of France and England, Italy and Germany. And while they took time to visit museums and cathedrals, battlefields and other historic sites, they also threw themselves into the Europe of the day, "picking up young hitchikers who spoke English, interviewing Spanish refugees from the civil war," Kennedy biographer Nigel Hamilton later wrote, "motoring through Italy to Rome, attending an audience with the pope, listening to Mussolini rant." In Munich they booked a room with an energetically pro-Hitler innkeeper, while in Nuremberg, just before a Hitler rally, they experienced "the added attraction of being spitten on." JFK made another visit to Europe the following summer. And in early 1939, the Harvard undergraduate moved to London to work for his father, the US ambassador to Great Britain, staying in Europe until September. And while we have no way of knowing how much or how little attention he paid to the mountaineering news of the day, many years later he paid tribute to those who had struggled to climb to the top of the world in one of the most significant speeches of his presidency.

Speaking before a large crowd that had gathered in the Rice University football stadium in Houston, Texas on a warm and blustery day in September 1962, President Kennedy laid out what was nothing less than a stunningly ambitious program—to land an American astronaut on the surface of the moon before the end of the decade. The exploration of space, Kennedy told his audience, would be one of the great adventures of all time, one that would bring benefits to all humankind. "But why, some say, the moon? Why choose this as our goal?" he asked, "And they may well ask why climb the highest mountain?"

"We choose to go to the moon," Kennedy answered, "We choose to go to the moon in this decade and do the other things, not because they are easy, but because they are hard, because that goal will serve to organize and measure the best of our energies and skills, because that challenge is one that we are willing to accept, one we are unwilling to postpone, and one which we intend to win." It was an audacious and dangerous plan. Not only had the Soviets launched *Sputnik*, the world's first artificial satellite, in 1957, but Russian cosmonaut Yuri Gagarin had beaten the first American astronaut into space by three weeks. The Space Race was on and the Americans were losing.

Kennedy was undaunted. "It will be done," he said.

Then, in closing his speech, he turned to the past.

"Many years ago the great British explorer George Mallory, who was to die on Mount Everest, was asked why did he want to climb it. He said, 'Because it is there.' Well, space is there," Kennedy said, "and we're going to climb it, and the moon and the planets are there, and new hopes for knowledge and peace are there. And, therefore, as we set sail we ask God's blessing on the most hazardous and dangerous and greatest adventure on which man has ever embarked. Thank you."

The Great Himalayan Race hadn't ended after all.

It had merely moved on. Toward the stars.

ACKNOWLEDGMENTS

Books beget books.

My parents weren't big readers, and the corner bookshelf in the living room of the house I grew up in was primarily filled with a dusty and decidedly unread set of the *Harvard Classics*, a few volumes of Shakespeare, some religious tracts, *None Dare Call It Treason*, and the sturdy black and brown volumes of *Compton's Pictured Encyclopedia*, our family's Google search engine of the day. But one afternoon when I was about nine years old, a new book suddenly appeared. Unusually heavy for its size, it featured the embossed gold seal of the National Geographic Society on its front cover, and was printed on the kind of heavy, glossy paper that was usually reserved for high school yearbooks. Moreover, it had a solemn, reverential aura about it. This was no mere book, it seemed to announce, this was important.

Instead, I soon discovered that *Great Adventures with National Geographic: Exploring Land, Sea, and Sky*, with 583 illustrations—356 in full color—and nineteen maps, was nothing less than a passport to a world of epic journeys, momentous discoveries, and leaps into the unknown. Here were thrilling stories of deep-sea exploration, the discovery of Machu Picchu, and high-altitude ballooning; tales that would literally sweep me off my feet and on to the divan for an hour of uninterruptable reading pleasure.

It was then with a mixture of both surprise and nostalgia that, near the end of writing this book, I stumbled upon a copy of *Great Adventures*. Tenzing and Hillary, not surprisingly, were featured in

313

ACKNOWLEDGMENTS

the book. But what floored me was the fact that Joseph Rock and the Duke of the Abruzzi were there, too, as was a photograph of Terris Moore holding a forty-eight-star American flag on the summit of Minya Konka. If there is an urtext for the book you are holding in your hands, it is surely *Great Adventures with National Geographic*. Thanks, Mom and Dad, as always, for kicking things off.

Since then, of course, there have been lots of other helping hands.

In London, I am eternally grateful to the warm welcome and world-class professional assistance provided to me at the Alpine Club, especially by Nigel Buckley, the librarian, and by the redoubtable Barbara Grigor-Taylor, bibliophile, adventurer, and one-time California beachcomber, who graciously read my entire manuscript. Hats doffed to Susan Harp and Bernie Ingrams for their help as well. The Alpine Club is not merely the world's oldest mountaineering society. It is also a marvelous place to work. In the UK, thanks are also in order for the staffs of the Royal Geographical Society, especially Joy Wheeler, and that of the Bodleian Library at Oxford.

In Munich, a number of talented and hard-working individuals helped shape this book. Nicholas Mailänder, a climber and mountaineering writer of note, patiently answered my questions about Paul Bauer, Peter Aufschnaiter, and other leading figures of 1930s German and Austrian mountaineering. David Heath of the Bavarian International School provided me with the most incredible walking tour of 1930s Munich imaginable. Professor Karen Radner, a renowned Assyriologist, kindly connected me with two of her students at Ludwig-Maximilians Universitatät who provided me with translation assistance: Corinna Hendrich and Felix Haselsteiner, the latter a budding young author that the world will hear more from in the years to come. Stefan Ritter, the archivist at the Deutscher Alpenverein, produced boxes of period documents and photographs. History also lives in museum exhibitions as well. Here, sincere thanks are in order for those at the NS-Dokumentationszentrum, one of the world's most important historical museums, the Jüdisches Museum, and the Münchner Stadtmuseum. In Berlin, I was also assisted by Annegret

ACKNOWLEDGMENTS

Wilke of the Politisches Archiv des Auswärtigen Amts. Thanks as well to the staffs of Staatsarchiv München and Bundesarhiv Koblenz.

In Austria, Martin Achrainer not only scoured the collections of the Österreichischer Alpenverein for relevant documents and photographs, but also helped unlock the precarious history of Austrian mountaineers during the Nazi era. In Innsbruck, I am also grateful to Thomas Niedermeyer, who helped me to better understand his adopted home.

In India, where many of the key events in this book took place, my debts are many—and even predate my arrival in country. Dr. Kavita Luthra and Dr. Umesh Verma not only connected me with their India-based travel agents at MakeMyTrip.com, especially with Rohit Sharma and Harbant Singh, but also provided key contacts in Uttarakhand. In Mumbai, Deepa Balsavar, Nandini Purandare, and Harish Kapadia provided a warm welcome at the Himalayan Club and apprised me of the important work being done by the Sherpa Project. In helping me to better understand the German expatriate community in 1930s Bombay, sincere thanks are due to the kind efforts of Dr. Martin Wälde of the Goethe-Institut/Max Mulleller Bhavan Mumbai, and to Bhavika Vohra, Malte Kruse, and Jonas Stolze of the Deutsche-Indische Handelsman.

In Dehradun, I was blessed to have the assistance of Nalini Bhandari, a first-class scholar and guide, and to Raj Kanwar and his remarkable family, who brought the Doon of the war years vividly back to life. I am also indebted to Harish, who drove me from Dehradun to Uttarkashi, and the banks of the Ganges, and back. Despite the fact that we did not share a common language, with his assistance the 1944 escape by Heinrich Harrer from the Central Internment Camp in Dehradun came convincingly back into view.

In Darjeeling, I owe a special debt of gratitude to Gautham Shrestha and Catherine Canavan, and to Adventures Unlimited, top flight trekking outfitters, who served as my unofficial hosts in their magnificent home city, as did Amit Giri and Ranju Giri.

ACKNOWLEDGMENTS

Gautham kindly escorted me to Angtsering's former home, where I met with the legendary Sherpa's kind and gracious daughters, Phur Diki Sherpa, Pema Diki Sherpa, and Chamgy Sherpa. I am also grateful to the staff at the Planter's Club and the groundskeepers at St. Andrew's Church, both of whom helped gain me insight into the Darjeeling of the 1930s. Along the India/Nepal/Sikkim border, I am indebted not only to my trekking guides, Tenzi Tamang and Kumar Tamang, but also to the locals who welcomed me into their homes and their lives along the southern edges of the Himalayas, including Neela Gurung, Dawa Futti Sherpa, Kalpokhri, Uden Tamang, and Pem Diki Tamang.

In the United States, significant portions of this book took shape in the magnificent state of Colorado. In Golden, I owe a huge debt of gratitude to the American Alpine Club, especially to Katie Sauter—and Eric Reuth—at the club's archives and library, which comprise what is assuredly the greatest collection of mountaineering books, journals, and manuscripts in the world. I am also particularly grateful to the wonderful Delaney family, of Denver and Frisco, who have served as wonderful hosts to me for decades. Not only did Nan and Art Delaney, he of the legendary10th Mountain Division, raise a family of wonderful kids, but that now very accomplished Delaney generation encouraged this project from the start. Thanks to Cindy, Robin, Jay, and Tracy—you all are the tops. Ditto for Mira Ruder-Hook, Amy Hook, and Michel Ruder of Denver, and a special thank you to Rob Wesson, of Evergreen, Colorado, and McCarthy, Alaska. Rob is both an accomplished scientist and author—check out his *Darwin's First Theory*—and an old climbing buddy, who graciously read my manuscript.

Other mountaineering friends have directly impacted this book as well, both in the climbs we did together and what they taught us along the way. Thank you Bob Jacobs, founder of St. Elias Alpine Guides, Bob Horn, Owen McGeehon, and especially Craig Ryan, who reintroduced mountaineering into our lives. And while I've either forgotten or never knew any of their names, a sincere thanks

ACKNOWLEDGMENTS

goes out to the Argentine, Israeli, and Australian climbers I once spent a frigid night with in a cramped mountain hut in the Andes. While we didn't speak the same language, in the best of mountaineering tradition we shared food, equipment, and, accompanied by a beat-up flamenco guitar, perhaps the world's longest multilingual version of "House of the Rising Sun," our voices arcing upward into the pitch-black Patagonian night.

At the University of Michigan, assistance has been plentiful. Richard Salisbury, the longtime research and writing partner of Elizabeth Hawley, the legendary Kathmandu-based chronicler—and former Wolverine—of the Himalayan Database, encouraged this book at its very beginning. Donald S. Lopez, the Arthur E. Link Distinguished Professor of Buddhist and Tibetan Studies, provided both translation help and insight on Lhasa during the 1940s. In the Department of Afroamerican and African Studies, Wayne High and Arielle Chen provided both administrative and technical support, while Nyambura Mpesha helped me to better understand the Kenya that Eric Shipton lived and climbed in. Lynne Fellarton helped prepare me for my work in India and Nepal, as did Mandira Bannerjee, Ted Kolias, and Hakan Oral. Lastly, I am especially indebted to the remarkable University of Michigan library which, as I've attested previously, may well be the best library in the United States for a nonfiction writer to have at his or her side. Not only did the UM library have available an astonishing array of materials that I used to write this book, including daily weather reports from London in 1931 and a 1937 street map of Nanking, but if they didn't have what I needed, they got it for me. Special thanks here to Brenda Fischer and Ariel Ojibway at the circulation desk, to the wizards who run the Interlibrary Loan office, and to Karl Longstreth, map librarian at the Stephen S. Clark Library. Also in Ann Arbor, kudos to Annette Fraser, who was a great help in better understanding the New Zealand world that both she and Edmund Hillary grew up in.

No book worth its salt can progress without a good editor, and I've been blessed with two. John Parsley helped coax this book into

317

ACKNOWLEDGMENTS

being at Little, Brown, while Phil Marino seamlessly took over the reins after John's departure. I am indebted to them both. Thanks are also due to the incredible team at Little, Brown who have supported both this book and its author, including Reagan Arthur, Judy Clain, Amanda Orozco, Elizabeth Gassman, Michael Noon, and many others. It's an honor to work with all of you.

Special shout outs are also in order for my superb agents, David Larabell of CAA Literary, who has been all-in on this project from the beginning, and for Matthew Snyder at CAA in Los Angeles. The same applies to my brilliant friend and New York City writing buddy, Victoria Johnson, who helped to shape this book early on, and to my old pal and fellow amateur mountaineer, Craig Ryan of Portland, Oregon, both of whom are incredible writers.

Finally, a big thank you to Betsy, Will, and Johnny. Not only did you all put up with my seven-days-a-week writing schedule and trips abroad with grace and good humor, but you've rooted for this project from the start. Here's to another set of mountains behind us, and some new ones to climb ahead.

P.S.—Then there is Cameron, our very own Welsh Corgi alarm clock, who made sure that I got to work bright and early every day. On some mornings, however, she actually let me sleep in. Until six.

The Climbers

And Other Participants in the Great Himalayan Race

THE BRITISH

The Alpine Club, founded in 1857, the London-based mountaineering organization is the oldest in the world. Its members
have included the leading lights of British climbing for more
than one hundred and fifty years.

Tom Bourdillon, former president of the Oxford Mountaineering
Club, and a veteran of the 1951 Mount Everest Reconnaissance,
he helped to design the closed-circuit oxygen apparatus used on
Everest two years later.

James Hilton, author of *Lost Horizon,* a best-selling 1933 novel
that brought renewed interest in the Himalayas to readers
worldwide. Later made into a film directed by Frank Capra.

Lady Houston. Born Fanny Radmall, she was a former chorus
girl who, by the middle of the 1920s, was reputed to be the richest woman in Great Britain. Underwrote the successful 1933
flight over Mount Everest.

John Hunt, career army officer and mountaineer who replaced Eric Shipton as the leader of the 1953 British Mount
Everest Expedition.

Tom Longstaff, legendary British climber, whose 1907 ascent of
Trisul (23,406 feet) set an altitude record that stood for more

than two decades. A supporter of Eric Shipton's small-scale approach to mountaineering.

Kenneth Mason, civil servant in the Raj and founding editor of the *Himalayan Journal,* he was an invaluable source of information for climbers worldwide. He subsequently became the first Professor of Geography at Oxford.

Mount Everest Committee, joint creation of the Alpine Club and the Royal Geographical Society. It oversaw British mountaineering expeditions to Mount Everest from 1921 to 1953. Later renamed the Joint Himalayan Committee.

Noel Odell, veteran climber and geologist who was a member of the 1924 and 1938 Mount Everest expeditions. Summitted Nanda Devi with Bill Tilman on August 29, 1936.

Royal Geographical Society, founded in 1830 and a key supporter of British expeditions to Everest. It was in the Society's collections that Michael Ward discovered the photographs that would help solve the puzzle of the southern approach to the mountain.

Hugh Ruttledge, career civil servant in India and occasional mountaineer. A proponent of large-scale Himalayan mountaineering campaigns, he served as the leader of the 1933 and 1936 Mount Everest expeditions.

Eric Shipton, Ceylon-born climber, advocate of small-scale expeditions, and self-taught philosopher of mountaineering. With Bill Tilman, he led the first successful entry into the Nanda Devi Sanctuary. A member of the 1933, 1936, and 1938 Mount Everest expeditions, Shipton also led the reconnaissance expeditions in 1935 and 1951.

Beryl Smeeton, author and adventurer; with her husband Miles she organized an expedition to Tirich Mir in 1938, hiring a young Sherpa named Tenzing to serve as the de facto sirdar.

Frank Smythe, well-known climber, photographer, and mountaineering writer; he led the first successful ascent of Kamet in 1931, and was a member of the 1933, 1936, and 1938 Mount Everest expeditions.

The Climbers

Bill Tilman, world-class climber who got his start in mountaineering as a climber partner of Eric Shipton in Kenya in the early 1930s. Led the first successful ascent of Nanda Devi in 1936, as well as the 1938 Mount Everest Expedition.

Lawrence Wager, geologist and mountaineer, paired with Percy Wyn-Harris on their summit attempt on Mount Everest during the 1933 expedition.

Michael Ward, physician and climber who discovered a potential route to the summit of Mount Everest via the Western Cwm while looking at photographs at the Royal Geographical Society. Member of the 1951 Mount Everest Reconnaissance and the 1953 expedition.

Charles Warren, physician and mountaineer, he discovered the body of Maurice Wilson during the 1935 Mount Everest Reconnaissance Expedition. Also a member of the 1936 and 1938 expeditions.

Maurice Wilson, decorated war veteran and former clothing salesman, dismissed as an eccentric, who flew a single-engine biplane from England to India and snuck across the Tibetan border on foot in an effort to make the first ascent of Mount Everest.

Percy Wyn-Harris, colonial official in East Africa, where he made the first ascent of Mount Kenya's second summit with Eric Shipton. He was also a member of the 1933 and 1936 Mount Everest expeditions.

THE THIRD REICH

The Germans

Paul Bauer, first-rate climber and driving force in German mountaineering efforts in the Himalayas, who led expeditions to Kangchenjunga, Nanga Parbat, and Siniolchum. During the

Nazi era, Bauer was the chief of large-scale German mountaineering expeditions to the Himalayas.

Deutsche Alpenverein (DAV), mass-based association of German climbing and hiking clubs. After the *Anschluss* in 1938, the Austrian club was subsumed into the DAV.

Deutsche Himalaja Stiftung (Deutsche Himalaya Foundation), organization created by Paul Bauer in 1934. Based in Munich, it would help sell the idea to the British, who controlled access to the Himalayas, that German mountaineering efforts were completely separate from the Nazi state.

Hermann Hoerlin, veteran climber and physicist who resisted Paul Bauer's efforts to seize control of the DAV. Emigrated to the United States in 1938 after marrying Katie Tietz Schmid.

Willy Merkl, accomplished rock climber and railway inspector who led the disastrous 1934 Nanga Parbat Expedition.

Peter Misch, Berlin-born geologist and climber, member of the scientific team attached to the 1934 Nanga Parbat Expedition. Harassed by the Nazis due to his Jewish background, Misch fled to China in 1936, carrying rock samples from Nanga Parbat in his suitcase.

Willi Schmid, Munich-based musician and music critic who managed publicity for the 1934 Nanga Parbat Expedition. Mistakenly arrested and murdered by the Nazis on the Night of the Long Knives, June 30, 1934.

Ernst Schäfer, anthropologist and adventurer whose journeys to far western China caught the eye of Heinrich Himmler, who picked Schäfer to lead the SS expedition to Tibet in 1938/1939.

Kate Tietz, widow of Willi Schmid. Despite her status under Nazi racial laws as a *Mischling*, or person of half-Jewish ancestry, Tietz was successful in her efforts to get Nazi officials to pay her a pension for her husband's wrongful death.

Hans von Tschammer und Osten, the *Reichssportsführer* or director of German sport during the Nazi era. Paul Bauer's immediate boss.

Willo Welzenbach, legendary Munich climber and successful rival of Paul Bauer in the Academic Climbing Club at the University of Munich. Died on Nanga Parbat during the 1934 expedition.

Karl Wien, talented mountaineer and son of a Nobel Prize–winning physicist, he was a veteran of Paul Bauer's 1931 Kangchenjunga and 1936 Siniolchum expeditions. Leader of the 1937 Nanga Parbat Expedition.

The Austrians

Peter Aschenbrenner, climber and mountain guide in the Tyrol, who was a member of the 1930 German–American Himalayan Expedition, as well as the 1934 and 1953 expeditions to Nanga Parbat.

Peter Aufschnaiter, renowned climber and agricultural scientist; he was a member of the 1929 and 1931 Kangchenjunga expeditions, after which he learned the Tibetan language. Working with Paul Bauer at the Deutsche Himalayan Foundation, Aufschnaiter led the 1939 reconnaissance to Nanga Parbat, after which he was imprisoned by the British as a prisoner of war.

Hermann Buhl, innovative and immensely talented mountaineer; on July 3, 1953, climbing solo on the final summit push, he made the first ascent of Nanga Parbat. Less than three years later, he was killed by an avalanche in the Karakoram.

Heinrich Harrer, legendary climber, author, and teacher to the young Dalai Lama. His successful first ascent of the North Face of the Eiger in 1938 won him a spot on the 1939 Nanga Parbat Expedition. Five years later he escaped from a British POW camp in Dehra Dun, India, and, with Peter Aufschnaiter, walked all the way to Tibet.

Erwin Schneider, accomplished mountaineer and cartographer who had been a member of Günter Dyhrenfurth's 1930 International Expedition to the Himalayas. Schneider had also logged impressive ascents in the Pamirs and then the Andes, but his reputation was severely damaged during the 1934 Nanga Parbat Expedition when he and Peter Aschenbrenner skied away from Pasang, Nima Dorje, and Pinzo Norbu high on Rakhiot Ridge.

THE AMERICANS

American Alpine Club, established in 1902 and initially headquartered in New York City, the preeminent climbing organization in the United States.

Bob Bates, classical scholar and member of the "Harvard Five" climbers; in 1937, he and Bradford Washburn made the first ascent of Mount Lucania, then the highest unclimbed peak summitted in North America. Member of the 1938 and 1953 expeditions to K2.

Dick Burdsall, engineer, Swarthmore graduate, and devout Quaker who had done precious little mountaineering before heading to China—and Minya Konka. Member of the 1938 K2 expedition, he died on Aconcagua in 1953.

Arthur B. Emmons III, native Bostonian and Harvard man who, when still in his teens, made the first successful ascent of the northeast face of Mount Hood. Lost the front portions of both feet, including all of his toes, on Minya Konka.

Explorers Club, storied organization, headquartered on the Upper West Side of Manhattan, that combined exploration with scientific research.

Harvard Mountaineering Club, the oldest university-based climbing club in the United States and a powerful force in the development of American mountaineering.

Charles Houston, Harvard man and physician who came within

The Climbers

one bad tin of bully beef from being one of the first to stand on the summit of Nanda Devi. Later to find lasting fame as an expedition leader on K2.

Terris Moore, member of the so-called Harvard Five, an influential group of American climbers; he had notched important climbs in the Andes, Alaska, and the Canadian Rockies before joining the Minya Konka expedition

Paul Petzoldt, unbridled Westerner who crashed both Windsor Castle and the heavily East Coast–oriented American expedition scene; he was a last-minute replacement climber on the 1938 campaign on K2.

Joseph F. Rock, flamboyant Austrian-born botanist and explorer who, during an expedition to China, concluded that the mysterious peak known as Minya Konka was higher than Mount Everest.

Pete Schoening, Seattle-born-and-bred climber who arrested the fall of six fellow climbers on K2 in 1939 in a near-miraculous effort later known simply as "The Belay."

Fritz Wiessner, an immigrant from Germany, he was a brilliant rock climber whose legacy would be forever linked to his leadership of the doomed 1939 K2 expedition.

Dudley Wolfe, New York socialite and resident of a penthouse apartment on Fifth Avenue who had been invited on the 1939 K2 expedition mainly for his pocketbook. In the end, however, he revealed uncommon strength.

Jack Young, intrepid traveler, hunter, and perhaps the first Chinese-American mountaineer; his experience and resourcefulness proved to be key on Minya Konka.

THE SHERPAS

Ang Tharkay, giant among the Sherpa community despite his small stature; he assisted the Germans on Kangchenjunga in

1931, helped blaze a path into the Nanda Devi Sanctuary in 1932, was with the French on Annapurna, and accompanied Eric Shipton on the 1951 Everest Reconnaissance Expedition.

Angtsering, the most intrepid Sherpa of them all, who climbed with Mallory and Ruttledge on Everest, and with Bauer and Dyhrenfurth on Kangchenjunga. But it was on Nanga Parbat in 1934, when he slept outside for six nights at more than 22,000 feet, where Angtsering forever etched his name into mountaineering history.

Da Namgyal, member of the 1952 Swiss campaign on Mount Everest who played a vital role on the British expedition the following year when he and John Hunt carried a tent, food, fuel, and oxygen bottles above the South Col.

Gaylay, veteran of the 1924 British Mount Everest Expedition; he died—along with Nima Dorje, Nima Tashi, Pinzo Norbu, Dakshi, and Nima Norbu—on Nanga Parbat in 1934.

Kitar, one of the most experienced Sherpas; he had been on four early Everest expeditions, and three to Kangchenjunga. A survivor of the 1934 tragedy on Nanga Parbat.

Pasang Kikuli, veteran of both Kangchenjunga and the 1933 Mount Everest expeditions. He survived the 1934 disaster on Nanga Parbat but died, along with Kitar and Phinsoo, while trying to rescue Dudley Wolfe on K2 in 1939.

Tenzing, born Namgyal Wangdi, and later known as Tenzing Norgay. He was not selected for the 1933 Mount Everest Expedition, but after being chosen by Eric Shipton for the 1935 reconnaissance, he launched a climbing career that eventually made him into a figure of world renown—and the most famous Sherpa of all.

Tsering, along with Tewang and Rinzing, helped to sneak Maurice Wilson out of Darjeeling, and accompanied the lone Englishman all the way to the North Col on his ill-fated solo attempt to climb Mount Everest.

The Climbers

THE FRENCH

Maurice Herzog, former French resistance fighter and weekend climber who led the successful 1950 French Expedition to a remote *Achttausender* in north-central Nepal. His subsequent triumph on Annapurna made a deep and lasting impact on the French nation, and led to the best-selling mountaineering book of all time.

Louis Lachenal, climber who accompanied Herzog to the summit of Annapurna that day in 1950; but while Herzog became a national hero, Lachenal drifted into obscurity. He, too, lost all of his toes after the historic ascent.

THE ITALIANS

Luigi Amedeo Giuseppe Maria Fernando Ferdinando di Savoia-Aosta, Duke of the Abruzzi, soldier, sailor, grandson of the King of Italy, and also perhaps the most dazzling mountaineer of the late nineteenth and early twentieth centuries. In addition to making first ascents in both East Africa and Alaska, he also led the first well-equipped mountaineering expedition to K2.

Vittorio Sella, brilliant photographer whose images of the Karakoram, from the Duke of Abruzzi's 1909 expedition to K2 remain, to this day, a high-water mark of Himalayan photography.

THE SWISS

Günter Dyhrenfurth, German-born mountaineer, geologist, and alpine writer who led the International Himalayan Expedition to Kangchenjunga in 1930, and an expedition to the Karakoram Range four years later.

The Climbers

Hettie Dyhrenfurth, Polish-born expedition transport officer and climber. In 1934, she set the women's mountaineering altitude record by climbing to 7,315 meters in the Karakoram. Despite being half-Jewish, two years later she and her husband Günter received the gold medal for mountaineering at the 1936 Berlin Olympics, the last time the medal was awarded.

Raymond Lambert, Geneva-born-and-bred mountaineer whose 1936 winter ascent in the Alps resulted in the loss of all of his toes. Despite this handicap he continued to climb. On Everest in 1952, he and Tenzing climbed higher than any human being had ever done before.

THE NEW ZEALANDERS

Dan Bryant, schoolteacher and brilliant ice climber; the positive impression that he made as a member of the 1935 Mount Everest Reconnaissance opened the door to New Zealand climbers as members of postwar British mountaineering expeditions.

Edmund Hillary, lanky former beekeeper and one-time pacifist who, as a climber, was a model of grace and determination. On Everest on Friday morning, May 29, 1953, he and Tenzing tied a shared rope around their waists, picked up their ice axes, and began a slow walk to the top of the world.

George Lowe, Southern Alps mountaineer and climbing partner of Hillary. On the 1953 Mount Everest Expedition he helped to prepare the route up to the South Col and, alongside Alfred Gregory and Ang Nyima, hauled supplies for Tenzing and Hillary up to Camp Nine, the highest mountaineering camp ever established.

The Expeditions

1931

Kamet Expedition, 1931, April to August. British, led by Frank Smythe. Eric Shipton's first Himalayan climb. Sherpas included Passang, Nima Dorje.

Second German Kangchenjunga Expedition, May to September. Led by Paul Bauer. Climbing team featured Peter Aufschnaiter, Karl Wien.

1932

German–American Nanga Parbat Expedition, April to October. Willy Merkl led the expedition, while the mountaineering team included Fritz Wiessner, Peter Aschenbrenner, Fritz Bechtold, and Rand Herron. American journalist Elizabeth Knowlton climbed as well. "The men in charge of the climb," the *New York Times* later reported, "would not let her continue beyond the 20,000-ft. level."

Minya Konka Expedition, June to December. American. No leader. Dick Burdsall, Arthur B. Emmons III, Terris Moore, and Jack Theodore Young, team members. Also known as the Sikong Expedition.

The Expeditions

1933

1933 Mount Everest Expedition, January to July. British. Hugh Ruttledge, leader. The climbing team included Frank Smythe, Eric Shipton, Percy Wyn-Harris, and Lawrence R. Wager. Da Tsering, Nima Dorje, and Kipa among the Sherpas.

Houston-Mount Everest Expedition, February to April. British. Overflight of Mount Everest by Westland P.V. 3 aircraft. Underwritten by Lady Houston, née Fanny Lucy Radmall.

1934

1934 Nanga Parbat Expedition, March to August. German. Led by Willy Merkl. Peter Aschenbrenner, Fritz Bechtold, Erwin Schneider, Willo Welzenbach, and Uli Wieland were among the mountaineers, while Peter Misch served as the expedition's geologist.

Nanda Devi, April to August. British. Eric Shipton, Bill Tilman, Ang Tharkay, Passang, and Kusang enter the Nanda Devi Sanctuary for the first time.

Maurice Wilson, May 1933 to May 1934. Englishman Maurice Wilson attempted to climb Mount Everest alone. Tewang and Rinzing accompanied him as far as the icefall leading to the North Col.

1935

1935 Mount Everest Reconnaissance Expedition, May to August. British. Led by Eric Shipton, the climbers on this lightweight expedition included Bill Tilman, Charles Warren, Michael Spender, and New Zealander Dan Bryant, while the Sherpas included Ang Tharkay and, for the first time, Tenzing.

The Expeditions

Shipton got his first view of the Khumbu icefall and the Western Cwm.

1936

1936 Mount Everest Expedition, February to July. British. Hugh Ruttledge, leader. Cut short by the early arrival of the monsoon, the climbing party included Frank Smythe, Eric Shipton, Percy Wyn-Harris, Charles Warren, and Lawrence Wager.

French Himalayan Expedition, March to July. Leader, Henry de Ségogne. Attempt to summit Hidden Peak, cut short by the monsoon.

British–American Himalayan Expedition, to Nanda Devi, March to September. Led by Bill Tilman. The British climbers were T. Graham Brown, Noel Odell, and Peter Lloyd, while the Americans were Charles Houston, Arthur B. Emmons III, Farnie Loomis, and Ad Carter. Kitar, Nima Tsering were among the Sherpas.

1936 Japanese Expedition to Nanda Kot, July to October. Led by Y. Hotta, the climbing party featured four members of the Mountaineering Club from Tokyo's Rikkyo University, plus a former member of Japan's Olympic ski team. First Japanese mountaineering expedition in the Himalayas.

German Sikkim Expedition, 1936, July to October. Small-scale training expedition, led by Paul Bauer, whose intent was to climb Siniolchum. Karl Wien, Günther Hepp, and Adolf Göttner comprised the climbing party.

1937

1937 German Nanga Parbat Expedition, April to July. Karl Wien, Leader. Nine Sherpas and seven German mountaineers were killed when an avalanche swept onto Camp Four at a little after midnight on June 15.

1938

1938 Mount Everest Expedition, February to June. British. Led by Bill Tilman, the climbing team featured Eric Shipton, Frank Smythe, Noel Odell, and Charles Warren, while the Sherpa contingent included Tenzing, who made a deep impression on Tilman.

First American Alpine Club Karakoram Expedition, to K2, April to August. Charles Houston, leader. Climbers included Bob Bates, Dick Burdsall, Paul Petzoldt, and Bill House, while Pasang Kikuli and Kitar were among the Sherpas.

Deutsche Tibet Expedition / SS Expedition, April 1938 to July 1939. So-called scientific expedition to Tibet, led by zoologist adventurer Ernst Schäfer and partially underwritten by SS Reichsführer Heinrich Himmler. No shrinking violet when it came to self-promotion, Schäfer also called it the Deutsche Tibet Expedition Ernst Schäfer.

1938 German Nanga Parbat Expedition, May to August. Led by Paul Bauer, this effort featured airdrops of supplies from a Junkers aircraft, and new interest in a possible route to the summit from the mountain's Diamir face.

1939

1939 American Alpine Club Karakoram Expedition, to K2; March to August. With Fritz Wiessner as its leader, the climbing team included Jack Durrance, Chappell Cramner, George Sheldon, Tony Cromwell, and Dudley Wolfe, along with Pasang Kikuli, Tsering, Kitar, and Phinsoo.

Nanga Parbat Reconnaissance Expedition, April to August. Peter

The Expeditions

Aufschnaiter, leader. The climbers included Heinrich Harrer, Hans Lobenhoffer, and Lutz Chicken, all of whom were arrested by Indian troops in Karachi in September, and sent to POW camps.

Polish Expedition to Nanda Devi East, April to August. Led by Adam Karpiński, the other climbers, all members of the Polish Mountaineering Club, were Jakub Bujak, Stefan Bernadzikiewicz, and Janusz Klarner. The Sherpa and Bhotia support team was anchored by Dawa Tsering, Injung, Nima, and Booktay. Two and a half weeks after the successful ascent, Karpiński and Bernadzikiewicz were killed by an avalanche on Trisul.

1950

French Annapurna Expedition, March to July. Maurice Herzog, leader. The mountaineering team included Louis Lachenal, Lionel Terray, and Gaston Rébuffat. After summitting Annapurna—the first *Achttausender* to be successfully climbed—Herzog lost all of his fingers and toes, while Lachenal lost his toes.

1951

1951 Mount Everest Reconnaissance Expedition, August to November. British. Led by Eric Shipton, the climbing team featured Bill Murray, Michael Ward, and Tom Bourdillon, as well as a pair of New Zealanders, Ed Hillary and Earle Riddiford. The Sherpas included Ang Tharkay, and, notably, Lhakpa, a female Sherpa.

1952

Swiss Mount Everest Expedition, March to July. Edouard Wyss-Dunant, leader. Following the route envisioned and pioneered

The Expeditions

and by Shipton's reconnaissance expedition one year earlier, Raymond Lambert and Tenzing set a new altitude record by climbing to more than 28,000 feet on the mountain's southeast ridge. A second Swiss attempt occurred that fall.

1953

1953 British Mount Everest Expedition, March to June. Leader, John Hunt. The climbing team included Britons Tom Bourdillon, Charles Evans, Michael Ward, and Wilfrid Noyce, and New Zealanders Edmund Hillary and George Lowe. Tenzing, soon to be known as Tenzing Norgay, served as both a climber and the sirdar. Ang Nyima, Da Namgyal, and Pemba were all members of the large Sherpa contingent. The *Times* sent along correspondent James Morris. Hillary and Tenzing reached the summit at around 11:30 in the morning of May 29.

1953 Nanga Parbat Expedition, April to July. Karl Herrligkoffer, leader. The mountaineers were a mix of Austrians and Germans. No Sherpas were allowed to come to Pakistan, so local Hunza porters were employed. On July 3, Innsbruck native Hermann Buhl became the first person to stand on the summit of Nanga Parbat. He died on another Himalayan peak, Chogolisa, three years later.

Third American Karakoram Expedition, to K2, May to September. Led by Charles Houston, the climbing team included Bob Bates, Dee Molenaar, Peter Schoening, Bob Craig, George Bell, and Art Gilkey. Forced to retreat from a summit attempt in order to try and save the life of Gilkey, Schoening would forever enter the annals of climbing lore when he single-handedly arrested the fall of six of his fellow climbers in what was later known, simply, as "The Belay."

A Glossary of Mountaineering Terms

And other words from the Great Himalayan Race

Achttausender. A mountain that is eight thousand meters—26,246 feet—or more in height. There are fourteen such peaks on earth.

Alpinism. Mountain climbing or mountaineering.

altimeter. A device for measuring altitude.

arête. An especially sharp-angled mountain ridge.

avalanche chute. A trough or channel along the face of a mountain where ice and snow from avalanches is funneled.

balaclava. A knit cap covering the entire head and neck with a hole or holes for the eyes, nose, and, sometimes, mouth.

Balti. An ethnic group primarily located in Gilgit and Kashmir, near the Karakoram Range of the Himalayas. Though most Baltis practice forms of Islam, they are primarily of Tibetan lineage.

base camp. The first of a series of high camps established during a mountaineering campaign. Usually consisting of a group of tents, and stockpiles of an expedition's supplies, base camps can also serve as communication centers, as infirmaries, and as the last link between the outside world and the dangerous and forbidding terrain of the upper mountain.

belay. To protect a fellow climber, whom one is attached to by a rope, from a harmful or possibly fatal fall. This often involves establishing oneself in a strong position from which the belayer can arrest the fall of a climber by securing the rope around a natural feature, such as a large rock, or by wrapping the rope around an ice axe that has been firmly driven into ice or snow.

bergschrund. A large and often deep crevasse located at the upper limit of a glacier. Often a formidable barrier.

Bhotia. An ethnic group of Tibetan descent living in the Sikkim state of northern India, bordering Bhutan, Tibet, and Nepal. Related to but distinct from the Sherpas.

bivouac. An often forced, tentless, overnight stay on a mountainside.

butter tea. Traditional Tibetan hot beverage, made by churning together yak butter and salt with tea. Known as *po cha*, most Western climbers found it to be very much an acquired taste.

cairn. A tower or pile of stones used as a route marker or to mark a gravesite.

carabiner. An oval-shaped metal ring, with a moveable gate. In the 1930s, climbers primarily used carabiners to connect ropes to pitons.

chapbook. A pocket-sized booklet issued to Sherpas and other high-altitude porters that included their photograph, name and birthdate, the climbs they had been on, and any testimonials to their work. Invaluable in securing employment on mountaineering expeditions.

chimney. A vertical gap between two rock or ice walls that can be climbed by using one's hands, feet, and sometimes back to inch upward.

cirque. A steep, high-walled, hollowed-out basin on a mountain, often the terminus of a glacial valley.

col. The lowest part of a ridge connecting two peaks, often used as a way to gain access to the upper reaches of a mountain.

coolie. From the Hindi word *kulī*, a low-wage porter or laborer.

cornice. A windblown lip of snow formed on top of exposed mountain ridges. Often overhanging beyond the actual top of the ridge, cornices are prone to collapse—sometimes with deadly consequences. The challenge for climbers is finding a relatively safe line along a cornice to walk upon.

A Glossary of Mountaineering Terms

couloir. A steep gully, often covered with ice or snow, that can be used as a route up the side of a difficult, rocky ridge. Because they are often avalanche chutes, couloirs usually need to be climbed in early morning, before the sun has loosened nearby rocks and ice.

crampons. Attachable metal fangs that are strapped to the soles of mountaineering boots in order to help climbers gain better footholds on ice and hard snow. The invention of twelve-point crampons, with two of the fangs extending straight out from the toe of the boot, made previously impossible routes accessible.

crevasse. A deep crack or crevice in a glacier, sometimes extending for hundreds of feet. Crevasses are often covered by thin layers of snow, making them a hidden danger for mountaineering parties as they traverse a glacier.

cutting steps. On steep ice or snow-covered slopes, this is the process of chopping reliable footholds using the adze-like blade of an ice axe. A necessary but often exhausting process at high altitudes.

cwm. Pronounced "coom," this is a high glacial valley, often shaped like an amphitheater. (From the Welsh.)

face. A particular side of a mountain, usually defined by the predominant angle of its rock.

fixed rope. A rope that has been anchored along a particularly challenging slope or wall, where it will serve as a handhold for climbers and porters.

Fortnum & Mason. Established in 1707, London's best-known purveyor of high-end gastronomical delicacies.

glacier. A frozen river of ice and snow slowly moving down the sides of a mountain.

glacier goggles. Tinted goggles designed to prevent snow blindness and reduce glare while climbers stare at snow and ice for long periods. Also known as glacier glasses, between the 1930s and 1950s most featured colored glass lenses set in aluminum frames, and were held in place with cloth ribbons.

A Glossary of Mountaineering Terms

hobnailed boots. Leather boots with metal nails hammered or screwed into the soles for added traction on both rock and ice.

Hunza. Ethnic group largely residing in Chitral and Gilgit, near the Karakoram, in what today is northern Pakistan.

ice axe. The mountain climber's all-purpose tool. T-shaped, with an adze and a pick at the head, and a spike at the bottom, an ice axe can be used as a walking stick, as a belaying device, for cutting steps, and as a tool that climbers can use to arrest a fall. During the decades before and after World War II, most ice axes featured a steel head and a wooden shaft, and were roughly 32–34 inches in length.

icefall. Caused when a glacier drops over steep terrain, it is a mass of jumbled, broken pieces—some quite massive—of ice and snow. Writer Jan Morris memorably described the Khumbu icefall on Mount Everest as looking like a "squashed meringue."

Kendal Mint Cake. A sugar-and-glucose-based peppermint confection, shaped like a chocolate bar, favored by British climbers as a high-altitude treat.

lamasery. A monastery for lamas, or male monks. Prevalent in Tibetan Buddhism.

massif. A particularly large mountain or group of mountains, sometimes encompassing multiple summits.

monsoon. The annual season of rains and wind that moves across the Indian subcontinent beginning roughly in May and lasting until September. In the Himalayas, the onset of the monsoon is characterized by heavy snowfall, making high-altitude mountaineering extremely difficult if not impossible.

moraine. Mounds, ramparts, and heaps of rock and gravel deposited by glaciers, often at their farthest limits.

Om mani padme hum. A mantra or prayer common in Tibetan Buddhism that is often inscribed on rocks and prayer wheels. Its literal translation, "Praise to the jewel in the lotus," hints at deeper meanings.

A Glossary of Mountaineering Terms

oxygen equipment. Himalayan climbers during the first half of the twentieth century sometimes sought to supplement their oxygen intake at the highest elevations. The equipment that they used normally consisted of: oxygen cylinders; valves, pressure meters and other devices to regulate flow; rubber hoses; and a facemask. In an **open system,** the climbers breathed supplemental oxygen mixed with outside air. With a **closed system,** only bottled oxygen was breathed in. The equipment was both heavy, sometimes in excess of thirty-five pounds, and prone to breakdowns.

piton. An iron spike, usually with an eyelet, which climbers would hammer into cracks in a rock face, and then connect to a rope. Used for protecting climbers on steep or especially dangerous or difficult terrain.

porter. A local man or woman hired to carry an expedition's supplies to the mountain. Fifty or sixty pound loads—or more—were quite common, and sometimes porters would be on the road for weeks at a time. Most porters did not advance beyond Base Camp.

prayer flags. Rectangular cloth flags, often in primary colors, upon which are printed prayers and blessings. Prayer flags are common in Tibet and in those parts of India, Nepal, and Pakistan where Tibetan Buddhism is practiced.

Primus. Swedish designed and built brand of kerosene stove. Noted for their durability and general ease of operation, Primus stoves were extensively used by early twentieth-century climbers and Sherpas.

rappel. A form of rapid descent down a cliff or mountainside whereby a climber makes a controlled slide down a rope.

rope traverse. A method of moving laterally around a hazard while suspended from a rope.

rotten rock. Eroded and weathered rock of such poor quality that it is difficult to secure a firm handhold or foothold.

rucksack. A small, frameless pack or knapsack preferred by climbers.

A Glossary of Mountaineering Terms

Rucksacks during the era of the Great Himalayan Race were usually made from heavy canvas.

saddle. A ridge connecting two higher points on a mountain. Often gently arced, like the seat of a horse saddle.

sahib. A Hindi term, of Arabic origin, meaning boss or master. Sherpas often referred to their expedition employers as "the sahibs."

serac. A distinct tower or column of ice that has either broken free from a glacier, or is in the process thereof. Seracs can be quite massive—and quite dangerous.

scree. Fine, often pea-sized gravel. Can make for dangerous footing when scattered across solid rock.

Sherpa. Ethnic Tibetans who, some centuries ago, migrated to Nepal and came to live on the southern slopes of Mount Everest, where they raised yaks and grew barley at notably high elevations. Initially hired by European mountaineering expeditions as porters, the Sherpas grew into first-class climbers themselves.

sirdar. The head Sherpa on a mountaineering expedition. Part spokesman, part foreman, part diplomat, all leader.

slabs. Generally smooth and often lying at a downward-facing angle, these are substantial pieces of rock that, on the upper reaches of Everest, proved to be a daunting and treacherous challenge, especially when covered with a thin layer of loose, powdery snow.

snow blindness. Temporary blindness resulting from looking too long at bright snow without proper eye protection. Quite painful, snow blindness can last for several hours.

spur. A subsidiary ridge, often set at a right angle, coming off a more prominent ridge. Also used to describe one of the main ridges of a mountain.

theodolite. Surveying instrument used for measuring angles

Tommy cooker. A bare-bones cooking system using tins of solidified fuel. Notoriously ineffective at high altitudes.

tsampa. Ground, roasted barley flour, mixed with water or tea to a pastelike consistency. The essential food of the Sherpas.

A Glossary of Mountaineering Terms

verglacé, also **verglas**. Sheet ice, especially that adheres to rock. Extremely slippery and dangerous to climbers.

whiteout. A weather condition, usually caused by a dense, frozen fog or by blizzard conditions, resulting in near-zero visibility.

wind slab. Layer of wind-packed snow, often unstable and prone to avalanche.

wireless. Radio system, usually offering two-way communication.

Notes

CHAPTER ONE: *ICE AXES AND DINNER JACKETS*

The Times, May 25, 1931, p. 9.

Simon Thompson's *Unjustifiable Risk?* is a thoughtful overview of the history of British climbing, one that builds upon—and vastly updates—earlier works by Wilfrid Noyce, R. L. G. Irving, R. W. Clark, and others. For a revealing window into the sheer gumption and Victorian Era sensibilities of Great Britain's pioneering mountaineers, nothing quite compares with their own personal accounts and memoirs, including Edward Whymper's *Scrambles amongst the Alps in the Years 1860–69* (1871) and William Martin Conway's *The Alps from End to End* (1895).

The spirit of the Alpine Club, the oldest mountaineering society on the planet, is best revealed in the pages of the *Alpine Journal*, the club's primary publication, which has been in print since 1863. On the history of the club itself, see: George Band, *Summit: 150 Years of the Alpine Club* (2006).

For the story of the 1924 British Mount Everest Expedition and George Mallory, its ill-fated leader, the place to begin is Wade Davis's spectacular *Into the Silence: The Great War, Mallory, and the Conquest of Everest*, a triumph of research and writing, and one of the best mountaineering books ever.

For Paul Bauer's dispatches about his second Kangchenjunga expedition, see *The Times*, June 22, August 12, August 20, September 1, September 26, October 6, October 8, and October 26, 1931.

CHAPTER TWO: *A WIND FROM THE EAST*

Despite his relative fame as one of the pre-eminent German mountain climbers of the Twentieth century, Paul Bauer was highly circumspect in terms of what parts of his life he was willing to provide information on. Moreover, he carefully cultivated a certain image of himself abroad, particularly among the climbing community in England. As a result, most accounts of Bauer generally include a handful of the same facts—born in Kusel, fought in the First World War, captured by the British—and ignore those parts of his past, such as his allegiance to National Socialism, that are less palatable to modern readers.

Nonetheless, there are places where biographical information on Bauer can be found, foremost among them being his own books, most of which are available in English: *Himalayan Campaign: The German Attack on Kangchenjunga* (1937); *Himalayan Quest: The German Expeditions to Siniolchum and Nanga Parbat* (1938); *Kanchenjunga Challenge* (1955); and *The Siege of Nanga Parbat, 1856–1953* (1956). Selections from his books and expedition reports are also compiled in: Ingelies Zimmermann, *Paul Bauer: Wegbereiter für die Gipfelsiege von heute* (1987).

Peter Mierau's *Nationalsozialistische Expeditionspolitik: Deutsche Asien-Expeditionen, 1933–1945*, and Nicholas Mailänder's *Im Zeichen des Edelweiss: Die Gesschichte Münchens als Bergsteigerstadt*, both of which are superb works in their own right, also contains helpful biographical information on Bauer, while Harald Höbusch's *Mountain of Destiny: Nanga Parbat and Its Path into the German Imagination* offers penetrating insights into Bauer's thinking.

Other sources on Bauer include: "Paul Bauer Personenmappe" in the Deutscher Alpenverein archives, Munich; interview with Nicholas Mailänder, Munich, March 2, 2018; Paul Friederich, Peter Bauer, *Alpine Club, Qualification Papers, 1932–1935* and *Alpine Club Register, A–F, 1891–1957*, Alpine Club library, London; Edward L. Strutt, "Valedictory Address, Read before the Alpine Club, December 6, 1937," *Alpine Journal* 50, no. 256 (May 1938); "Paul Bauer, 1896–1990," *Alpine Journal*, 1991–1992; *Berg Heil! Alpenverein und Bergsteigen 1918–1945* (2011); and Helmuth Zebhauser, *Alpinismus im Hitlerstaat: Gedanken, Erinnerungen, Dokumente* (1998).

Information on Bauer's military service during World War I can be found in Bayerisches Hauptstaatarchiv: München: *Abteilung IV Kriegsarchiv, Kriegstammrollen, 1914–1918*, vol. 6851, *Kriegsrangliste: Bd.1*, which is available on Ancestry.com. Quote on the 18th Bavarian Infantry Regiment from US War Office, *Histories of Two Hundred and Fifty-One Divisions of the German Army Which Participated in the War (1914–1918).* Ian Passingham's *Pillars of Fire: The Battle of Messines Ridge, June 1917* is a captivating history of the battle where Bauer was taken prisoner. Also see: Frank Fox, *The Battles of the Ridges, Arras-Messines, March–June 1917* (1918). Hans Ernest Fried's *The Guilt of the German Army* (1942) is an interesting and largely forgotten work which connects the dots between the post–World War I experience of the German army, especially its officer corps, and the rise of National Socialism.

In reconstructing the atmosphere of Munich during the years that Bauer lived in the Bavarian capital, I found David Clay Large's *Where Ghosts Walked: Munich's Road to the Third Reich* to be essential. Equally important was the invaluable assistance—including a five-hour, 7.7-mile walking tour of National Socialist–era sights in Munich—given to me by David Heath, a brilliant Anglo-Canadian teacher at the Bavarian International School. Other key sources included: C. H. Beck, *Munich and National Socialism*, an extensive and heavily illustrated volume put out by the NS-Dokumentationszentrum, Munich's world-class museum on the history of National Socialism; Richard Bauer et al., eds., *München—'Hauptstadt der Bewegung': Bayerns Metropole und der Nationalsozialismus*, an extensive exhibition catalog from the München Stadtmuseum; Jutta Fleckenstein and Bernhard Purin, *Jüdisches Museum München* (2007); *Munich and the Royal Castles of Bavaria*, 5th ed., 1931; Georg Franz, "Munich: Birthplace and Center of the National Socialist German Workers' Party," *Journal of Modern History* 29, no. 4 (December 1957); Joseph Hergesheimer, *Berlin* (1932), which includes a chapter on Munich. See also: Maik Kopleck, *Past Finder: Munich, 1933–1945*, and *München baut auf: Ein Tatsachen- und Bildbericht über den nationalsozialstischen Aufbau in der Hauptstadt der Bewegung* (1939); and Adolf Dresler, *Das Braune Haus und die Verwaltungsgebäude der NSDAP* (1939), two Nazi-era books that, no doubt, found a place on the coffee tables of the party faithful just before all hell broke loose.

Finally, one must also tip one's hat to contemporary writers, of both fiction and nonfiction, who have shone their literary lights on the nightmare years of the Third Reich and Nazi-era Munich, thus keeping this history alive for readers whose connections to this period grow ever more distant and dim. Special thanks here to Erik Larson for *In the Garden of the Beasts* (2011), Jacqueline Winspear for *Journey to Munich* (2016), and Robert Harris for *Munich* (2018).

Notes

Historic water levels of the Isar River can be found in: O. Böhm and K.-F. Wetzel, "Flood History of the Danube Tributaries Lech and Isar in the Alpine Foreland of Germany," *Hydrological Sciences Journal* 51, no. 5 (October 2006). Philip Ball, "How 2 Pro-Nazi Nobelists Attacked Einstein's 'Jewish Science,'" *Scientific American*, February 13, 2015, is a revealing look at the pseudointellectual underpinnings of the assault on academic freedom at German universities in the 1930s. The deaths of Marie Sandemeier and the unnamed Munich waiter can be found in David Clay Large, *Where Ghosts Walked: Munich's Road to the Third Reich* (1997), p. 141.

The history of how German and Austrian climbers reinvented climbing in the late nineteenth and early twentieth centuries has yet to be written, at least in English. But their impact was so profound that traces of that history aren't difficult to find. Doug Scott's *Big Wall Climbing* (1974) is probably the best place to start. But Mike Parson and Mary B. Rose's *Invisible on Everest: Innovation and the Gear Makers* (2003) contains much useful information, as do the numerous biographical entries on German and Austrian climbers such as Hans Dülfer, Josef Enzensperger, Hans Fiechtl, Leo Maduschka, Paul Preuss, and Friedrich Rigele which can readily be found online on Wikipedia. Jean Moore Ireton and Caroline Schaumann's *Heights of Reflection: Mountains in the German Imagination from the Middle Ages to the Twenty-First Century* (2012) is also of value here. But the best current account in English of this true climbing revolution is: Lew Wallace Holt, "Mountains, Mountaineering, and Modernity: A Cultural History of German and Austrian Mountaineering," PhD dissertation, University of Texas, 2008.

The quotation on the passion and size of the Deutscher und Österreichischer Alpenverein is from A. Everard Gunther, "The Youth and the Alps of Europe," *Sierra Club Bulletin* 18, no. 1 (February 1933). See also: Guido Rey, *Alpinismo Acrobatico* (1914).

Paul Bauer wrote about his expedition to the Caucasus in *Kanchenjunga Challenge. On the Edge of Europe: Mountaineering in the Caucasus* (1993) by Audrey Salkeld and José Luis Bermúdez was also helpful, as were two contemporary accounts of travel in the Soviet Union during the 1920s— James Colquhoun's *Adventures in Red Russia* (1926) and Albert Rhys Williams's *The Russian Land* (1928).

Paul Bauer led two expeditions to Kangchenjunga, in 1929 and 1931.

Notes

For the sake of brevity, I have focused here on only the latter. For the history of both German expeditions to Kangchenjunga, Bauer is again the primary source: *Himalayan Campaign: The German Attack on Kanchenjunga* (1937); *Kanchenjunga Challenge* (1955); "Kanchenjunga, 1929: The Bavarian Attempt" and "The Fight for Kanchenjunga, 1929," *Alpine Journal* no. 42; and "Kanchenjunga, 1931: The Second Attempt," *Alpine Journal* no. 44. Also see: G. O. Dyhrenfurth, *To the Third Pole* (1955); Kenneth Mason, *Abode of Snow*, and "The Recent Assaults on Kanchenjunga," book review, *Geographical Journal* 80, no. 5 (1932); and "Science: A Pair of Skis," *Time* magazine, June 1, 1931.

CHAPTER THREE: *EVEREST, 1933*

Though it inevitably suffers, as most "official" reports do, from a perceived need for "objectivity" and a reluctance to publicly criticize the inevitable shortcomings of others, Hugh Ruttledge's *Everest 1933* (1934) is the single most noteworthy book about that year's British Mount Everest Expedition. Ruttledge also published a second account, *Attack On Everest*, in 1935. Other key accounts include Frank Smythe's *Camp Six* (1937) as well as the relevant sections in Eric Shipton's *Upon That Mountain* and *That Untravelled World*, and in Ang Tharkay's *Sherpa: The Memoir of Ang Tharkay* (1954/2016), which provides a brief but telling portrait of the 1933 expedition from a Sherpa's point of view. Also helpful are Tony Smythe's *My Father, Frank* and Jim Perrin's *Shipton & Tilman*. See also: Audrey Salkeld, "Hugh Ruttledge," *Oxford Dictionary of National Biography*, January 6, 2011, and J. L. Longland, "Caught in an Everest Blizzard," in Alan J. Cobham, et al., *Tight Corners: Tales of Adventure on Land, Sea, and Air* (1940).

The library and archives of the Alpine Club in London also contain numerous items either from or concerning the 1933 expedition, including: the second, handwritten volume of Frank Smythe's climbing diary; a bound photocopy of the "Memoirs of Percy Wyn-Harris"; various letters and medical records pertaining to members of the expedition; and a manuscript by Dr. Claude Wilson, a former Alpine Club president, who was involved with some of the medical tests. Four thousand miles to the east, in the archives of the American Alpine Club in Golden, Colorado, there rests a remarkable, 146-page scrapbook comprised of chronologically arranged clippings from London newspapers about both the 1933 Mount Everest

Notes

Expedition and Lady Houston's Everest overflight expedition. (*Note to future scrapbookers: please* date *all entries. Thanks.*)

Robert Lawrie's London mountaineering shop lived on for decades, and even made it into the pages of *Sports Illustrated* on October 13, 1969. A modern-day Renaissance man, Lawrie once drove an Aston Martin in the 24 Hours of Le Mans motor race, and was known to be "a keen pistol shot." His obituary can be found in the *Alpine Journal* no. 88 (1983).

The best sources on the life and times of Eric Shipton are twofold. The first are Shipton's own books. *Upon That Mountain* (1943) and *That Untravelled World* (1969) are key to reconstructing his early years, but the fact of the matter is that all of Shipton's books, six of which have been admirably republished by The Mountaineers as *The Six Mountain-Travel Books*, are well worth reading. The other key source on Shipton is Jim Perrin's magnificent *Shipton & Tilman: The Great Decade of Himalayan Exploration* (2014). Thoughtful, nuanced, carefully researched, bombastic, and unafraid to pick a fight, it is a most well-considered account—conceived over a lifetime of study of, and familiarity with, his two subjects: the lives and careers of Shipton and Tilman up until the outbreak of the Second World War. For Shipton's life post-1939, Peter Steele's *Eric Shipton: Everest & Beyond* is both uniquely valuable and the place to begin.

See also:

Board of Education, *Report of Inspection of Beaumont House School, Heronsgate, Hertfordshire*, March 27 & 28, 1930, National Archives, London.

Edward Whymper, *Travels amongst the Great Andes of the Equator* (1892).

For information on Nea Barnard, see: Nea Morin, *A Woman's Reach: Mountaineering Memoirs* (1968), including the foreword by Eric Shipton; Carol A. Osborne, "Morin [née Barnard], Nea Everilda," *Oxford Dictionary of National Biography*, 2004; and Bill Birkett and Bill Peascod, *Women Climbing: 200 Years of Achievement* (1989).

For the reports of Shipton's ascents in the *East African Standard*, see "New Conquest of the Twin Peaks of Mount Kenya," January 15, 1929, and "Both Peaks of Kenya Climbed," August 13, 1930. Shipton and Tilman's journey to the otherworldly Ruwenzori Mountains—now commonly spelled Rwenzori—is recounted in Tilman's *Snow on the Equator* (1937) and in Shipton's *Upon That Mountain* and, most briefly, in *That Untravelled World*. A revealing window into just how amazed Western scientists were by the biodiversity present in the range can be found in the multiple volumes published by the British Museum originating from the *Ruwenzori Expedition, 1934–35*, which were not published until 1939 and 1940, just as the Mountains of the Moon, once again, grew even more inaccessible.

Frank Smythe recounted the events of his 1931 expedition to Kamet in *The Times* ("The Conquest of Mount Kamet, July 6, 1931"), in "Explorations in Garhwal around Kamet," *Geographical Journal* 79, no. 1 (January 1932), and in detail in *Kamet Conquered* (1932). Eric Shipton includes brief but enlightening accounts of the expedition in both *Upon That Mountain* and *That Untravelled World*. Also see the two handwritten, bound volumes of Smythe's "Original Letters—Miscellaneous" and "Kamet Expedition Notes and Diary," both of which are held in the Alpine Club archives, London.

The key source on the Houston–Mount Everest Expedition is Air-Commodore P. F. M. Fellowes et al., *First Over Everest!* (1934), but the August 1933 edition of *National Geographic Magazine* is also of value. Lady Houston, née Fanny Lucy Radmall, is clearly in need of a movie. In the meantime, good places to begin include: Richard Davenport-Hines, "Dame Fanny Lucy Houston," *Oxford Dictionary of National Biography*, May 27, 2010; "Lady & Lion," November 27, 1933, and "Angel Repudiated," *Time* magazine, January 25, 1937; and Peter Almond, "Savior of the Spitfire," *The Telegraph*, September 15, 2010.

The literature of Mount Everest is both broad and a bit unwieldy. Jon Krakauer's *Into Thin Air* and Wade Davis's *Into the Silence* are superb introductions to the mountain and its often-tragic human interaction. Other recommendations include two magnificent photo-rich histories, both from 2013: Stephen Venables's *Everest: Summit of Achievement* and George Lowe and Huw Lewis-Jones's *The Conquest of Everest*. The National Geographic Society, in Washington, DC, has also spent decades educating its members on the importance and status of the world's highest peak. The Mount Everest Map that appeared in the November 1988 edition of *National Geographic* was a high-water mark of Himalayan cartography, while the May 2003 edition, commemorating the fiftieth anniversary of Hillary and Tenzing's successful summit attempt, was a detailed and clear-eyed snapshot of the mountain and its challenges.

Notes

CHAPTER FOUR: *THE NEW EMERSONIANS*

Men against the Clouds: The Conquest of Minya Konka (1935) by Richard L. Burdsall and Arthur B. Emmons III, with contributions by Terris Moore and Jack Theodore Young, remains the single most important source on the Minya Konka expedition. In the *New York Times*, see: "Two Americans Scale Huge Tibetan Peak Believed to Exceed 24,000-Foot Altitude," November 25, 1932; "Newly Scaled Peak Is in Remote Region," November 26, 1932; "Describe Ascent of Minya Konka," January 7, 1933; Terris Moore, "An American Climb into Tibetan Skies," May 28, 1933; and Henry E. Armstrong, "Scaling Minya Konka," May 5, 1935.

In some news reports about the expedition that appeared in newspapers in Southern California, Terris Moore is described as being in charge of the climb, a conceit that can surely be laid at the feet of Moore's father. See: "Pasadenan to Climb Tibet Peak," *Pasadena Post*, December 17, 1931; "Hardy Youth on Tibetan Exploit," *Pasadena Star-News*, December 17, 1931; and "Youth Conquers New Peak," *Pasadena Star-News*, December 12, 1932. For a more balanced view, see: "Tibetan Party Seeks Earth's Highest Peak," *Los Angeles Evening Herald and Express*, December 16, 1931.

Katrina Hincks Moore's *Borestone to Bering Strait: Glimpses of the Adventures of Terris Moore in the Mountains of Three Continents and Flights as a Seaplane Pilot Northward to the Frozen Ocean* (1999) is a loving biography put together by Terry Moore's widow and lifelong companion. But the best parts of the books are the period pieces written by Katrina herself. Full of verve and illuminating detail, they give us a glimpse into a talented writer that, in another era, we might have heard much more from. The Terris Moore and Katrina Hincks Moore Papers—which include Terry Moore's climbing diary from the Minya Konka expedition—are held in the archives at the Elmer E. Rasmuson Library at the University of Alaska-Fairbanks, where Terris served as the school's president from 1949–1953. In the *New York Times*, see: "Williams Harriers Name Moore," December 8, 1926; "Flies to Alaska for Hunting," April 4, 1931; "Terris Moore to Wed Miss Katrina Hincks," February 25, 1933; "Three Conquer Mount Fairweather," June 16, 1931; and "Terris Moore, Educator and an Adventurer," November 10, 1993.

On the Lamb Expedition to Tibet, see: "Explorer to Study Medicine of Tibet," April 22, 1931; "Denies Chinese Bar All Scientific Work," July 7, 1931; "Expedition to Tibet Leaves Today," November 28, 1931;

and "Chinese Demand End of Lamb Expedition," August 25, 1932, all in the *New York Times*.

Arthur B. Emmons III: Membership Proposal Form, American Alpine Club library, Golden, Colorado; "Arthur Brewster Emmons III, 1910–1962, *American Alpine Journal* 13, no. 2 (1963); *Who Was Who in America*, vol. 4: 1961–1968; "Evelyn Voorhees Becomes Engaged," *New York Times*, November 13, 1937; and "Arthur Emmons, Diplomatic Aide," *New York Times*, August 23, 1962.

Richard L. Burdsall: *By-Laws and Register of the American Alpine Club*, May 1940; "Richard L. Burdsall, 1895–1953," *American Alpine Journal*, 1953; "Elwood Burdsall, A Bank President," *New York Times*, March 11, 1939; and, "New York Man Dies on Argentine Climb," *New York Times*, February 27, 1953.

Jack Theodore Young (1910–2000) and Adelaide Min Chow "Su Lin" Young (1911–2008) are clearly in need of biographies. Information on both of them, including some basic family-tree information, city directory listings, passenger lists, and Federal Census information can be found on Ancestry.com. In Jack's case, a wealth of material regarding his military career should be available in federal archives. On Adelaide, also see: "Adelaide 'Su Lin' Young: Intrepid Traveller in China," *The Times*, June 16, 2008; Chris Treadway, "Life of 'Panda Lady' Celebrated," *Contra Costa Times*, May 16, 2008; and Patricia Sullivan, "Su-Lin Young, 96: Explorer Lent Her Name to Pandas," *Washington Post*, May 20, 2008. They just don't make 'em like that anymore.

Few American institutions will ever match the cachet of the Explorers Club, whose membership rolls have included the likes of Robert Peary, Matthew Henson, Charles Lindbergh, Neil Armstrong, and Buzz Aldrin. My mother's first boss, whom she worked for in the years leading up to World War II and during the first years of the war, was Laurence McKinley Gould, a geologist who was second-in-command on Admiral Byrd's first Antarctic expedition, was a member. "Explorers Club Has New Home," *New York Times*, April 14, 1929. *Explorers Journal* 8, no. 3 (July–September 1929). Alexander Gross, *The Complete Guide to New York City* (1940).

On the William V. Kelley-Roosevelt Asiatic Expedition of 1928–29, see: Theodore Roosevelt and Kermit Roosevelt, *Trailing the Giant Panda* (1929), and Ron Grossman, "Flashback: Love Pandas? Thank the Roosevelts and the Field Museum," *Chicago Tribune*, June 3, 2017.

Notes

The go-to source on the inimitable Joseph F. Rock is S. B. Sutton's *In China's Border Provinces: The Turbulent Career of Joseph Rock, Botanist-Explorer* (1974). Also of value is Jim Goodman, *Joseph F. Rock and His Shangri-La* (2006). Joseph F. Rock, "Seeking the Mountains of Mystery," *National Geographic Magazine* 57, no. 2 (February 1930), and "The Glories of the Minya Konka," 58, no. 4 (October 1930).

The North China Union Language School, undated pamphlet in the Columbia University libraries.

The forty-eight-star American flag that Terris Moore unfurled on the summit of Minya Konka rests in a light-protected map case in the library and archives of the American Alpine Club in Golden, Colorado. It is one of the true treasures of American mountaineering.

CHAPTER FIVE: *NANGA PARBAT*

The various German expeditions to Nanga Parbat, and their larger impact on the German national consciousness, have inspired a good deal of writing over the years.

For an overview of the pre–World War II expeditions, good places to begin are the relevant chapters in Kenneth Mason's *Abode of Snow*, G. O. Dyhrenfurth's *To the Third Pole*, and Paul Bauer's *The Siege of Nanga Parbat, 1856–1953* (1956). Horst Höfler's *Nanga Parbat: Expeditionen zum "Schicksalsberg der Deutschen," 1934–1962* (2002) is a stunning collection of photographs from mid-twentieth-century expeditions to the world's ninth-tallest mountain, while Harald Höbusch's *Mountain of Destiny: Nanga Parbat and Its Path into the German Imagination* (2016) is a creative and compelling literary study.

On the 1932 German–American Expedition, see: Elizabeth Knowlton's *The Naked Mountain* (1933), and Willy Merkl, "The Attack on Nanga Parbat, 1932," *Himalayan Journal* no. 7 (1935). Both Knowlton and her fellow American climber, Rand Herron, might make good characters in a novel. Knowlton, who became one of the first female mountaineers to climb to more than 20,000 feet, lived until the age of ninety-three. Herron tragically died on the way home from Nanga Parbat, when he slipped on a pebble while climbing the Second Pyramid at Giza. His remains were buried in a cemetery in Cairo.

For the 1934 expedition, key sources include: Franz Bechtold, *Nanga Parbat Adventure* (1936); Jonathan Neale, *Tigers of the Snow: How One*

Notes

Fateful Climb Made the Sherpas Mountaineering Legends (2002); Eric Roberts, *Welzenbach's Climbs* (1980); Erwin Schneider, "The Accident on Nanga Parbat," *Alpine Journal* no. 46 (November 1934); Erwin Schneider, "The German Assault on Nanga Parbat," *Alpine Journal* no. 47 (May 1935); "The Disaster on Nanga Parbat," *Geographical Journal* 85, no. 3 (March 1935); and the following articles, all of which appeared in the *Himalayan Journal* no. 7 (1935): Fritz Bechtold, "The German Himalayan Expedition to Nanga Parbat, 1934"; R. A. K. Sangster, "Diary Jottings: Nanga Parbat, 1934"; R. Finsterwalder, Walter Raechl, and Peter Misch, "The Scientific Work of the German Himalayan Expedition to Nanga Parbat, 1934"; "The Porters of the Nanga Parbat"; "The Porters Who Died on Nanga Parbat"; and "Willy Merkl, 1900–1934," "Ulrich Wieland, 1901–1934," and "Willo Welzenbach, 1900–1934." A British Pathé newsreel, "To the Roof of the World," contains a couple of minutes of footage shot on the expedition, while *Nanga Parbat: Ein Kampfbericht der Deutschen Himalaja Expedition 1934*, a documentary film directed by Frank Leberecht, was released in Germany in 1935.

On the coming of Nazi rule in Munich, see: Large, *Where Ghosts Walked*; Beck, *Munich and National Socialism*; Adolf Dresler, *Das Braune Haus und die Verwaltungsgebaüde der Reichsleitung der NSDAP* (1939); and Julius Schoeps and Werner Tress, *Orte der Bücherverbrennungen in Deutschland, 1933* (2008).

For Paul Bauer's activities between 1931 and 1934, much information was gleaned from his "Spruchkammerverfahren, SpkA, K 84," Bauer's 1948 de-Nazification file, the original of which is held in the Staatsarchiv München.

On Willy Merkl, see: Karl Herrligkoffer, *Willy Merkl: Ein Weg zum Nanga Parbat* (1936).

On the 1930 confrontation in Peshawar, see: Stephen Alan Rittenberg, *Ethnicity, Nationalism, and the Pakhtuns: The Independence Movement in India's North-West Frontier* (1988); and "Rioting at Peshawar," April 24, 1930, and "Peshawar Riots," April 25, 1930, both in *The Times*. For the 1931 violence in Srinagar, a good place to begin is Ian Copland, "Islam and Political Mobilization in Kashmir, 1931–1934," *Pacific Affairs* 54, no. 2 (Summer 1981).

On the relationship between the 1934 Nanga Parbat Expedition and the new Nazi state, as well as the political inclinations of the climbers,

Notes

see: Peter Mierau, *Nationalsozialistische Expeditionspolitik* (2005); Nicholas Mailänder, *Im Zeichen des Edelweiss* (2006); and Bettina Hoerlin, *Steps of Courage: My Parents' Journey from Nazi Germany to America* (2011).

Leaving Munich: "Science: All-Highest," *Time* magazine, July 30, 1934; and Bechtold, *Nanga Parbat Adventure*.

Srinagar and Kashmir: C. E. Tyndale, *Kashmir in Sunlight & Shade* (1922); Walter R. Lawrence, *The Valley of Kashmir* (1895); and Peter Fleming's magnificent *News from Tartary: A Journey from Peking to Kashmir* (1936).

As many, but not all, of the mountaineering Sherpas were illiterate, surviving statements by them—even though they were usually written down by Europeans—are of great value. Not only do they tend to be very specific in terms of describing the succession of events on an expedition, but they also can serve as a corrective to accounts written by expedition leaders who were oftentimes tasked with the unwelcome job of explaining why their summit attempt was unsuccessful.

Testimony by Kitar can be found in Bechtold, *Nanga Parbat Adventure*. "Statement made by Kitar and Parsang Ki Kuli, October 27, 1934," appears as a part of Erwin Schneider's "The German Assault on Nanga Parbat (1934)," *Alpine Journal* no. 47 (May 1935). Angtsering gave two contemporaneous statements. One can be found in Bechtold's book. The other, "Angtsering's Statement, October 27, 1934," also appears as part of Schhneider's 1934 account in the *Alpine Journal*. I am also indebted to Phurdiki Sherpa, Chamgy Sherpa, and Pema Diki Sherpa, three daughters of Angtsering, whom I interviewed in their family home in Darjeeling on May 29, 2018. They also generously allowed me to look at and photograph their father's passbook, medals, and other mountaineering items.

CHAPTER SIX: *SHANGRI-LA*

Like many popular writers, James Hilton has never received the critical and biographical attention that he deserves. A master storyteller, he was not only the author of *Lost Horizon*, *Random Harvest*, and *Goodbye, Mr. Chips*, but he was also one of the screenwriters for *Mrs. Miniver*, William Wyler's gracious and patriotic 1942 film that won six Academy Awards, and for *Foreign Correspondent*, Alfred Hitchcock's oft-neglected 1940 classic. There has never been either a popular or scholarly biography of Hilton, while his books have long fallen off high school reading lists. University-based literature professors have never given Hilton much thought—something he probably would have been thankful for. Even the plaque on his tombstone in a cemetery in Long Beach, California, has the year of his death wrong.

But during his heyday, Hilton was a literary tour de force. *Goodbye, Mr. Chips* was a mammoth bestseller, while *Lost Horizon*, which was published as Pocket Book No. 1, is widely recognized as launching the paperback book revolution. Both books have twice been made into movies, while *Mrs. Miniver* has found its own pixilated afterlife on cable networks, compact disc players, and living room TV sets from Tokyo to Tallahassee.

On Hilton: Biographical entries in *Current Biography, 1942* as well as Stanley J. Kunitz and Howard Haycraft, eds., *Twentieth Century Authors* (1942). Carroll Sibley's *Barrie and His Contemporaries*, published by the International Mark Twain Society in Webster Groves, Missouri, in 1936, contains a brief interview with Hilton. In the *Times*, see: "Books of the Day," September 6, 1932; "Some New Books," September 15, 1933"; "Novels of the Season," December 5, 1933; "The Hawthornden Prize," June 15, 1934; and "Mr. James Hilton, An Accomplished Story-Teller," obituary, December 22, 1954.

James Hilton, *Lost Horizon* (1933). Michael Buckley, *Shangri-La: A Practical Guide to the Himalayan Dream* (2008). George Stevens and Stanley Unwin, *Best-Sellers: Are They Born or Made?* (1939).

Much speculation has ensued over the years as to the "real" location of Shangri-La. On the various inspirations for Hilton's mythical valley and lamasery, see: "Clues to Real Shangri-La Point in China," *China Daily*, September 24, 2005; and Rasoul Sorkhabi, "James Hilton and Shangri-La," *Himalayan Journal*, no. 64 (2001). *N.B.—Do send word if you find it.*

Eric Shipton's *Nanda Devi* (1936) is the primary account of the 1934 expedition. Other key sources include: Shipton, "The Nanda Devi Basin," *Alpine Journal* no. 47 (1935), plus the relevant portions in *Upon That Mountain* and *That Untravelled World*; H. W. Tilman, *The Ascent of Nanda Devi* (1937); Ang Tharkay, *Sherpa*; Perrin, *Shipton & Tilman*; Hugh Ruttledge, "Nanda Devi," *Himalayan Journal* no. 5 (1933); and Ruttledge, "The Secret of Nanda Devi," August 22, 1932, and "In the Himalaya," November 2, 1934, both in the *Times*.

Bill Tilman recounts his bicycle ride across "Africa at its waist"— probably making him the first person to do so—in his first book, *Snow at the Equator* (1937).

Notes

Outward Passenger Lists for the *Mahsud*, Liverpool, April 4, 1934, Ancestry.com. Air Ministry, *Monthly Weather Report of the Meteorological Office* 51, no. 4 (April 1934).

Hugh Thomson's *Nanda Devi: A Journey to the Last Sanctuary* (2004) is a moving and thoughtfully written account that brings the Nanda Devi story into the twenty-first century. Also see: N. C. Shah, "A Botanical Survey of the Nanda Devi Sanctuary, 1974," and Lavkumar Khacher, "Nanda Devi Sanctuary—A Naturalist's Report," both in the *Himalayan Journal* no. 35 (1979).

Historical Currency Converter (Test Version 1.0), www.historicalstatistics .org/Currencyconverter.

CHAPTER SEVEN: *YOGIS AND YAK MEAT*

The single best introduction to the remarkable Himalayan journey of Maurice Wilson is Dennis Roberts's *I'll Climb Mount Everest Alone: The Story of Maurice Wilson*. First published in 1957, it's a superb and beautifully written volume, one that never got the initial attention that it deserved. In 2010, Faber & Faber issued a welcome reprint. Covering the same ground, Ruth Hanson's hard-to-find volume, *Maurice Wilson: A Yorkshireman on Everest* (2008) is also a well-considered take on the Wilson saga, one that included significant material that Roberts did not find or have access to. One cannot help feeling, however, that a bit more historical sleuthing about Wilson, particularly concerning his years abroad, might add considerably to his story.

The most compelling source on Wilson, however, is his own handwritten diary of his 1934 attempt on Mount Everest, the original of which is held in the archives of the Alpine Club in London. Discovered by the members of the 1935 Everest Reconnaissance Expedition, despite having endured a Himalayan winter, the book is in remarkably good shape. Written in pencil, in a pocket-sized notebook, now a faded green-gray, with "Present Time Book" and "Made in Japan" embossed on the cover, it is a humbling testament to both courage and obsession.

In the *Times*, see: Telegrams in Brief, June 10, 1933; "Single-Handed Attempt on Everest," July 18, 1934; "Mount Everest Climb," July 20, 1934; and "Attempt on Everest Single-Handed," September 5, 1935.

On the influence of Indian culture in Wilson's day, see: Ann Louise Bardach, "How Yoga Won the West," *New York Times*, October 1, 2011.

Notes

Around the time that Wilson was planning his expedition, yogis—both real and imagined—were creeping into British popular culture as well. In his best-selling 1930 autobiography, *The Lives of a Bengal Lancer*, Francis Yeats-Brown wrote glowingly of the *"yogis of the South"* (*The Times*, July 11, 1930), while at London's Regal Cinema in the fall of 1932, moviegoers could fall under the spell of *Chandu the Magician*, a British army officer "who has learnt the secrets of the Yogi" (*The Times*, November 14, 1932).

On the discovery of Wilson's body, see: Charles Wilson, Everest 1935 Diary, and E. G. H. Kempson, "Everest Reconnaissance Expedition, 1935," typescript, both in the Alpine Club library and archives, London; and, in the *Times*: Audrey Salkeld, "Victims of Everest," March 6, 1980, and Dr. Charles Warren, "A Lonely Victim of Everest," March 11, 1980.

T. S. Blakeney, "Maurice Wilson and Everest," *Alpine Journal* no. 70 (1965). Eric Shipton and Frank Smythe quotes from the latter's foreword to: Roberts, *I'll Climb Mount Everest Alone*.

One should add that Maurice Wilson and his incredible saga has had a persistent, if somewhat low-key, literary half-life for more than eight decades. The ghost of Wilson appears in Salman Rushdie's 1988 novel, *The Satanic Verses*, whose publication resulted in a *fatwa* issued by the Ayatollah Ruhollah Khomeni, calling for the author's death. In 1980, a one-act play about Wilson, *The Ice Chimney* by Barry Collins, premiered at the Edinburgh Fringe Festival, while every few years or so, Wilson's story will appear in various outdoor magazines, some hewing more closely than others to established facts. After a report later surfaced that a Chinese mountaineering team had found a woman's shoe on Everest in 1960, speculation blossomed in some climbing circles that Wilson was a cross-dresser. For a humorous rebuttal, see: Mike Harding, *Yorkshire Transvestite Found Dead on Everest* (2005).

Wilson was not the only one to connect Mount Everest with spiritual aspiration during the early 1930s. See: George S. Arundale, *Mount Everest: Its Spiritual Attainment* (1933).

CHAPTER EIGHT: *A KNOCK AT THE DOOR*

Interview with Nicholas Mailänder, Munich, March 2, 2018.

Excerpts from Paul Bauer's December 1934 letters to Reichssportsführer Hans von Tschammer und Osten can be found in: Isserman and Weaver,

Notes

Fallen Giants. Also see: Mierau, *Nationalsozialistische Expeditionspolitik*; Mailänder, *Im Zeichen des Edelweiss*; Höbusch, *Mountain of Destiny*; Paul Bauer, "Spruchkammerverfahren, SpkA, K 84," Staatsarchiv München.

Good overviews of pre–World War II international Himalayan mountaineering expeditions can be found in Mason, *Abode of Snow*, and Dyhrenfurth, *To the Third Pole*.

On the Japanese expedition, see: Y. Hotta, "The Ascent of Nanda Kot, 1936," *Himalayan Journal* no. 10 (1938).

Himalayan Assault: The French Himalayan Expedition 1936 (1938), translated by Nea Barnard Morin, is the English-language version of the official report of the 1936 expedition to Hidden Peak, which today is known as Gasherbrum I. See also N. R. Streatfeild, "The French Karakoram Expedition, 1936," *Himalayan Journal* no. 9 (1937).

Himalayan Quest: The German Expeditions to Siniolchum and Nanga Parbat (1938), edited by Paul Bauer, is a key source on both the 1936 expedition to Sikkim and the tragic 1937 campaign on Nanga Parbat. Also of value, and also by Bauer, are "The German Sikkim Expedition, 1936," *Alpine Journal* no. 49 (May 1937), and *The Siege of Nanga Parbat* (1956).

On Munich in the mid-to-late 1930s, see, especially: Winifred Nerdinger, ed., *Munich and National Socialism*, and Large, *Where Ghosts Walked*. Jutta Fleckenstein and Bernhard Purin, eds., *Jüdisches Museum München / Jewish Museum Munich* (2007), gives a brief but solid overview of the history of Munich's Jewish communities, and includes a photograph and description of *Das Aliyah-Spiel*. *Grieben's Guide Books*, vol. 130, *Munich and the Royal Castles of Bavaria* (1931).

R. Finsterwalder, Walter Raechl, and Peter Misch, "The Scientific Work of the German Himalayan Expedition to Nanga Parbat, 1934," *Himalayan Journal* no. 7 (1935). On Peter Misch, see: Dee Molenaar, "Hans Peter Misch, 1909–1987," *American Alpine Journal*, 1988, and "Peter Misch," University of Washington Alumni Column "Class Acts," September 1999; Guide to the Peter Misch Papers, 1930–1988, Special Collections, University of Washington Libraries; and, US Department of Justice, Petition for Naturalization for Hans Peter Misch, No. 44649, August 13, 1952, available at Ancestry.com.

There are two key sources on the saga of Kate Tietz, and her two husbands, Willi Schmid and Hermann Hoerlin, each written by one of her daughters. Duscha Schmid Weisskopf's *Willi Schmid: A Life in Germany* is a detailed and beautifully written account by Kate and Willi's eldest daughter, who was nine years old at the time of her father's murder. Bettina Hoerlin's *Steps of Courage: My Parents' Journey from Nazi Germany to America* (2011), also beautifully written, is a well-researched, unflinching, and heartfelt account, one that does a first-rate job of framing the larger struggles faced by German mountaineers during the bitter years of the Third Reich.

On Willi Schmid, also see: family-tree data for Wilhelm Eduard Schmid, and 1940 US Federal Census Schedule for Renate Schmid, Binghamton, New York, both available at Ancestry.com; and "Methods of Nazi Executioners: Victim Shot by Mistake," *The Times*, July 7, 1934.

On Kate and Hermann Hoerlin, also see: Passenger Lists of Vessels Arriving in New York, 1820–1957, SS *Columbus*, August 17, 1938, available at Ancestry.com; and Guide to the Papers of Kate and Hermann Hoerlin, 1932–1983, 2003–2013, Leo Baeck Institute, Center for Jewish History, New York City.

CHAPTER NINE: *MURDER MOUNTAIN*

Important sources on the 1937 German Expedition to Nanga Parbat include: "The Disaster on Nanga Parbat, 1937," *Alpine Journal* no. 49 (November 1937), which includes diary excerpts and other writings by expedition members Karl Wien, Martin Pfeffer, Hans Hartmann, Günther Hepp, and Ulricht Luft; Paul Bauer, "Nanga Parbat, 1937," *Himalayan Journal* no. 10 (1938); Bauer, *Himalayan Quest* and *The Siege of Nanga Parbat*; and "The German Expedition to Nanga Parbat," *Nature* 139 (June 26, 1937). On Wien, see: "Karl Wien, 1906–1937," *Alpine Journal* no. 49 (November 1937).

On the 1938–39 Ernst Schäfer / SS Expedition to Tibet, see: Christopher Hale, *Himmler's Crusade: The Nazi Expedition to Find the Origins of the Aryan Race* (2003); Heather Pringle, *The Master Plan: Himmler's Scholars and the Holocaust* (2006); and Isrun Engelhardt, ed., *Tibet in 1938–1939: Photographs from the Ernst Schäfer Expedition to Tibet* (2007). Gustav Must, "The Inscription on the Spearhead of Kovel," *Language* 31, no. 4 (October–December 1955).

The Nazi Statue: Nina Weber, "Scientists Say Buddha Statue Made of Meteorite," *SpiegelOnline*, September 27, 2012; Matt McGrath, "Ancient Statue Discovered by Nazis Is Made from Meteorite," BBC.com, September 27, 2012; and Elmar Buchner, et al., "Buddha from Space—

Notes

An Ancient Object of Art Made of a Chinga Iron Meteorite Fragment," *Meteoritics & Planetary Science* 47, no. 9 (2012).

Paul Bauer, "Nanga Parbat, 1938," *Himalayan Journal* no. 11 (1939). Dyhrenfurth, *To the Third Pole.*

CHAPTER TEN: *TRIUMPH—AND TROUBLE*

"The Nanda Devi Basin," *The Times*, February 5, 1935.

Copy of Letter No. 15 (1)-P/33, Lhasa, Tibet, October 2, 1933, from the Political Officer in Sikkim to the Foreign Secretary to the Government of India, New Delhi, in Alpine Club library and archives, London.

Walt Unsworth, in his *Everest: A Mountaineering History* (1981), does a fine job of illuminating the tensions within the Alpine Club and the Royal Geographical Society over the leadership of the 1935–36 Everest expeditions. "New Attempt on Everest," *The Times*, April 4, 1935.

On the 1935 Everest Reconnaissance Expedition, see: Tony Astill, *Mount Everest: The Reconnaissance, 1935* (2005); E. E. Shipton, "The Mount Everest Reconnaissance, 1935," *Alpine Journal* no. 48 (May 1936); Michael Spender, "Survey on the Mount Everest Reconnaissance, 1935," *Himalayan Journal* no. 9 (1937); Charles Warren, "Everest 1935: The Forgotten Adventure," *Alpine Journal* (1995); Shipton, *Upon That Mountain* and *That Untravelled World*; Ang Tharkay, *Sherpa*; and "Everest Reconnaisance Party," *The Times*, May 30, 1935. Charles Warren, Edwin Kempson, and Edmund Wigram, Everest 1935 climbing diaries, Alpine Club, London.

The writings of Hugh Ruttledge are the most exhaustive on the 1936 Mount Everest Expedition. See his: *Everest: The Unfinished Adventure* (1937); "The Mount Everest Expedition of 1936," *Geographical Journal* 88, no. 6 (December 1936), with appendices by C. J. Morris, W. R. Smith-Windham, F. S. Smythe, Noel Humphreys, and C. B. Warren; and "The Mount Everest Expedition, 1936," *Himalayan Journal* no. 9 (1937). Eric Shipton's *Upon That Mountain*, Ang Tharkay's *Sherpa*, Tony Smythe's *My Father, Frank*, and Jim Perrin's *Shipton & Tilman* also throw light on the 1936 effort, as do various volumes discussing Himalayan mountaineering during the 1930s that appear throughout these notes. "Mount Everest Expedition," February 3, 1936, "Everest Expedition," March 5, 1936, and "Attempt on Everest Abandoned," June 15, 1936, all in the *Times*. F. S. Smythe, J. N. L. Gavin, and C. B. Warren, Everest 1936 climbing diaries, Alpine Club, London.

Notes

Few American mountaineers have been as beloved, accomplished, and complex as physician-climber Charles Houston. Bernadette McDonald's impressive *Brotherhood of the Rope: The Biography of Charles Houston* (2007) is the place to begin. On the so-called Harvard Five and their place in the history of American mountaineering, also see Maurice Isserman's *Continental Divide*, a creative and much needed work of inspired climbing scholarship.

H. W. Tilman's *The Ascent of Nanda Devi* (1937) is the go-to account for the 1936 British–American Himalayan Expedition. And while Tilman is, of course, primarily known for his mountaineering achievements—usually asterisked by commentary about his alleged misogynistic attitudes, prickly personality, and so on—he was also a superb writer. Consider this Hemingwayesque gem from his Nanda Devi account: "The fifty miles of road between Ranikhet and Garul are carved for the most part out of abrupt hills and are as full of kinks as a wriggling eel." N. E. Odell correspondence, and "Nanda Devi, 1936, July–September," typescript expedition diary from the H. W. Tilman Collection, Alpine Club, London.

"Nanda Devi Scaled: An Anglo–American Success," *The Times*, September 9, 1936.

W. H. Auden and Christopher Isherwood, *The Ascent of F6* (1937). "The Mercury Theatre," January 23, 1937; "A Play in Verse," March 20, 1937; "Little Theatre," May 1, 1937; "Norwich Players' New Season," June 8, 1937; "Malvern Festival Director," December 30, 1937, all in the *Times*. Entries on the Mercury Theatre at londonremembers.com and ladbrokeassociation.info.

A recording Benjamin Britten's music for *The Ascent of F6*, titled *Britten to America: Music for Radio and Theatre*, was issued by NMC Recordings in 2014. Inventive yet deeply moody, it probably won't appear on any climber's playlist as they prep for their next ascent of El Capitan, Mont Blanc, or Fitz Roy. For a short but insightful analysis of the music, Lucy Walker's "Ascent of F6" podcast, brittenpears.org, is well worth a listen. With the notable exception of Patrick Meyers's *K2*, mountaineering has been a fairly untrod terrain for playwrights, though on January 30, 2015, Dallas Opera premiered *Everest*, a new opera by British composer Joby Talbot, libretto by Gene Scheer. Heidi Klein, "Peak Performance," *Dallas Hotel Magazine* 17 (Winter 2015).

Walt Unsworth, in his *Everest: A Mountaineering History* (1981), does

Notes

an excellent job of laying out the growing problems faced by the British climbing establishment in the mid to late 1930s.

For the 1938 Mount Everest Expedition, the place to begin with are the writings of H. W. Tilman. While his *Mount Everest 1938* (1948) wasn't published, on account of World War II, until a decade later, it still has a freshness about it. For more contemporaneous accounts by Tilman, see his "The Mount Everest Expedition of 1938," *Geographical Journal* 92, no. 6 (1938), and "Mount Everest, 1938," *Himalayan Journal* no. 11 (1939). Other helpful accounts can be found in Shipton's *Upon That Mountain* and Angtharkay's *Sherpa*. "Defences of Mount Everest," *The Times*, November 22, 1938. 1936 Everest Expedition correspondence, Alpine Club, London.

In a January 4, 1939, letter to Margaret Bradshaw, Shipton succinctly described the primary problems faced by Everest climbers as they neared the summit: "The trouble is that the last 2,000 feet is difficult even judged by alpine standards and it is impossible when there is a deposit of 5 feet of powder snow sitting on the rocks. Nothing seems to consolidate the snow and the only thing that removes it is the wind, which comes again in the winter. It is a silly problem in a way, and the only thing to do [is] to try each year until one strikes the right conditions, if ever." Jane Allen, ed., *A Walk through Blue Poppies: The Letters of Eric Shipton to Margaret Bradshaw, 1934–1974* (2004).

Key sources on the 1937 Shaksgam Expedition include: Eric Shipton, Michael Spender, and J. B. Auden, "The Shaksgam Expedition, 1937," *Geographical Journal* 91, no. 4 (April 1938); Eric Shipton, *Blank on the Map* (1938); and Michael Spender, "The Shaksgam Expedition, 1937," *Himalayan Journal* no. 10 (1938).

The balance of power between the Sherpas and the Europeans was always tilted in favor of the latter. After all, this was the British Raj. But despite the genuine warmth that often existed between the two groups, and the Sherpas' reliance upon the British and other outside groups for a significant portion of their livelihoods, as the decades of the 1930s, 1940s, and 1950s unfurled, the Sherpas moved from being mere employees to something akin to partners—second class, perhaps, but partners nonetheless—on the big Himalayan mountaineering expeditions. Traces of these subtle changes in activity and behaviors can be readily found in Ang Tharkay's oral memoir, *Sherpa*, one of the few more-or-less firsthand Sherpa accounts to survive from that era. But evidence of the evolving nature of Sherpa–climber relations can also be found in the books, climbing diaries, and official reports written by British, German, and other foreign climbers.

My own hunch is that while the growing assertiveness of the Sherpas stemmed largely from their experiences on the great peaks, they, like millions of other everyday people in British India, were likely also influenced by the Gandhian independence movement. Either way, however, we will all look forward to the forthcoming publications by the Sherpa Project, a multi-year oral history project—carried out by Nandini Purandare and Deepa Balsavar, with assistance from Harish Kapadia—about the lives of the high-altitude Sherpas who have been an integral part of Himalayan mountaineering for more than a century. Also see: Sherry B. Ortner, *Life and Death on Mount Everest: Sherpas and Himalayan Mountaineering* (1999).

Like many Sherpas of his era, Tenzing—or Tenzing Norgay, as he eventually became known—was illiterate, though he did eventually learn how to write his own name. As a result, the written accounts of his life have always been written by others, and, not surprisingly, discrepancies exist between the various versions. That said, some first-rate books exist which address Tenzing's early years and first expeditions, including: *Tiger of the Snows: The Autobiography of Tenzing of Everest* (1955), by Tenzing Norgay and James Ramsey Ullman, which introduced him to the world; Tashi Tenzing's *Tenzing Norgay and the Sherpas of Everest* (2001), a most careful account written by one of his grandsons; and Jamling Tenzing Norgay's heartfelt *Touching My Father's Soul: A Sherpa's Journey to the Top of Everest* (2001).

Eric Shipton, *Blank on the Map* (1938). Yvon Chouinard—climber, environmentalist, and founder of Patagonia, Inc.—was born in November 1938, one month after Shipton's second book was published. Rock climber Royal Robbins had been born three years earlier.

CHAPTER ELEVEN: *AN AMERICAN EVEREST*

For period reports of the bloody 1937 takeover of Nanking, see: H. J. Timperley, ed., *Japanese Terror in China* (1938); and Shuhsi Hsü, *The War Conduct of the Japanese* (1938) and *Documents of the Nanking Safety Zone* (1939). Shi Young and James Yin's *The Rape of Nanking: An Undeniable History in Photographs* (1997) is as advertised, while Iris Chang's *The Rape of Nanking* (1997) brought worldwide attention to the atrocities committed by Japanese soldiers. Deluged with hate mail, and spiraling into depression, the thirty-six-year-old Chang committed suicide in 2004.

On Jack Young and the second Minya Konka flag, that of the Republic of China, see: Terris Moore, "Epilogue: Last Search," in Richard L. Burdsall and Arthur B. Emmons III, *Men Against the Clouds: The Conquest of Minya Konka* (rev. ed. 1980).

Forever in the shadow of Mount Everest, its far younger but 778-feet-higher sister, K2 has not yet produced a best seller along the lines of *Into Thin Air*. Nevertheless, the world's second-highest peak has inspired a solid literature of its own, including Peter Zuckerman and Amanda Padoan's riveting *Buried in the Sky: The Extraordinary Story of the Sherpa Climbers on K2's Deadliest Day* (2012). Two other good introductions to the mountain are Dave Ohlson's award-winning documentary *K2: Siren of the Himalayas*, and "Why K2 Brings Out the Best and Worst of Those Who Climb It," nationalgeographic.com, December 13, 2015; see also: Simon Worrell's interview with Mick Conefrey, author of *The Ghosts of K2* (2015).

Mirella Tenderini and Michael Shandrick's *The Duke of Abruzzi: An Explorer's Life* (1997) is an admirable overview of the remarkable life and times of one of mountaineering's most singular practitioners. Born in Spain less than two years after the unification of Italy, the duke was also an admiral in the Italian navy. When he died in Italian Somaliland, in 1933, Mussolini had already been in power for more than a decade. Despite the duke's affection for adventure, the true love of his life was Katherine "Kitty" Elkins, the daughter of a coal baron and US senator from West Virginia. Though it was a case of love at first sight, love did not, in the end, however, conquer all. Kitty married, divorced, and remarried the son of an American diplomat, eventually living out her days raising dogs and horses in Middleburg, Virginia.

On the 1909 K2 Expedition, see Filippo De Filippi's *Karakoram and Western Himalaya, 1909: An Account of the the Expedition of H.R.H. Prince Luigi Amedeo of Savoy, Duke of the Abruzzi* (1912). One of the most beautiful mountaineering books ever published—with American and British first editions fetching more than one thousand dollars apiece—it features dozens of photographs, many in plate form, taken by Vittorio Sella. For the 1929 expedition, see: H.R.H. the Prince Aimone of Savoia-Aosta, Duke of Spoleto, "The Italian Expedition to the Karakoram in 1929," *Geographical Journal* 75, no. 5 (May 1930).

Notes

For the history of the 1938 American Karakoram Expedition, aka the 1938 K2 expedition, key sources include: Robert H. Bates, Richard Burdsall, Charles Houston, and Paul Petzoldt, *Five Miles High: The Story of an Attack on the Second-Highest Mountain in the World by the Members of the American Karakoram Expedition* (1939); Robert H. Bates, *The Love of Mountains Is Best: Climbs and Travels from K2 to Kathmandu* (1994); C. S. Houston, "The American Karakoram Expedition to K2, 1938," *Alpine Journal* 51, no. 258 (May 1939); William P. House, "K2—1938," *American Alpine Journal* 3, no. 3 (1939); Charles Houston, "A Reconnaissance of K2, 1938," *Himalayan Journal* no. 11 (1939); and N. R. Streatfeild, "The American Alpine Club Expedition to K2 in 1938," *Journal of the Royal Central Asian Society* 26, pt. II, April 1939. I have found, however, the collections at the American Alpine Club Library in Golden, Colorado, to be especially helpful, particularly the subject files on the expedition, Charles Houston's various lists of supplies and equipment, and a set of typewritten bulletins prepared by the climbers on the progress of the expedition. Finally, much insight about the expedition and its aftermath—including Petzoldt's bizarre 1938–1939 Indian postscript, complete with a cult and a manslaughter charge—can be found in Ed Viesturs' *K2: Life and Death on the World's Most Dangerous Mountain* (2009), written with the legendary mountaineering writer David Roberts.

Charles S. Houston, "William Farnsworth Loomis, 1914–1973," *American Alpine Journal* (1974). Wolfgang Saxon, "William P. House, 84; Blazed Trails to 2 Summits," *New York Times*, December 28, 1997. Robert H. Bates, "William P. House, 1913–1997," *American Alpine Journal* (1997). Erik Lambert, "A Tribute to Bob Bates," alpinist.com, September 19, 2007.

The larger-than-life Paul Petzoldt has been well served, thus far, by two biographical works: Patricia Petzoldt's *On Top of the World: My Adventures with My Climbing Husband* (1953), and Raye C. Ringholz's *On Belay! The Life of Legendary Mountaineer Paul Petzoldt* (1997). Also see Petzoldt's own *Teton Tales* (1995). A quick search at Ancestry.com will also turn up several interesting documents relating to Petzoldt's earlier years, including Federal Census schedules from 1910–1940, his World War II draft card, and brief mentions of him in the 1929 edition of *The Gem of the Mountains*, the yearbook of the University of Idaho. Nancy Wise Carson, "Paul Kiesow Petzoldt, 1908–1999," *American Alpine Journal* (2000).

Richard Ollard, "Albert Victor Baillie," *Oxford Dictionary of National Biography*.

Notes

The *American Alpine Journal* duly recorded Petzoldt's many break-through climbs in the Tetons. See, for example: "Mountaineering Notes From the Grand Teton National Park" (1931), "Various Notes" (1933), and "Wyoming Rockies" (1936 & 1937).

It is no secret that, during the 1950s, 1960s, and 1970s, rock climbers in California forever changed climbing not just in the United States, but worldwide. And while the incredible accomplishments of these pioneering climbers have been admirably documented, my own thinking is that the innovative spirit that first took hold in Yosemite Valley had far deeper roots in the American past. I once asked Gary Snyder, the Oregon-bred, Pulitzer Prize–winning poet and former US Forest Service employee, about why the West Coast of the United States had been such an incubator of creativity during the past century, encompassing everything from Fender electric guitars and souped-up dragsters to surfboards and Apple computers. His answer surprised me. Part of the reason, he said, came from the experiences that people had on the Oregon and California Trails, where the new emigrants to the West Coast had to be able to *make* or replace with their own hands anything that they needed. This self-sufficiency, in turn, helped to create what became a "garage culture" of creativity that, in the twentieth century, would lead to the founding of companies as different as Hewlett-Packard and Chouinard Equipment. I'm sure there are some holes here, including the role of immigrants, especially from Asia, in fueling this creativity. But the echoes from the past are clearly alive and well in the present.

CHAPTER TWELVE: *A BIT EAST OF THE PLAZA*

Few mountaineering expeditions have proven to be as controversial as the 1939 American K2 Expedition, whose fine details and assignments of blame are still being argued over today—and, one suspects, will be for some time to come. My goal has not been to put these differences to bed, nor have I discovered any shocking new evidence to transform the conversation. Rather, within the limits of a book whose larger focus is elsewhere, I've tried to present an interpretation that, as I can best determine, rests on a firm if incomplete evidentiary foundation.

For the 1939 expedition to K2, key published sources include: Andrew J. Kauffman and William L. Putnam, *K2: The 1939 Tragedy* (1992); Jennifer Jordan, *The Last Man on the Mountain: The Death of An American*

Notes

Adventurer on K2 (2010); Chappell Cranmer and Fritz Wiessner, "The Second American Expedition to K2," *American Alpine Journal* (1940); "The American Expedition to K2," *Himalayan Journal* no. 22 (1940); George C. Sheldon, "Lost Behind the Ranges," *Saturday Evening Post* 212, no. 38 (March 16, 1940); and Fritz Wiessner, *K2, Tragödien und Sieg am Zweithöchsten Berg der Erde* (1955), a portion of which was translated and published as Fritz H. Wiessner, "The K2 Expedition of 1939," *Appalachia* 22 (June 15, 1956). Over the decades, a number of mountaineering's leading lights have also weighed in on the controversies surrounding the expedition, including Charles Houston, Günter Dyhrenfurth, Kenneth Mason, and David Roberts, among others, and I highly commend and recommend their work.

A special shout-out is also given, as well, to T. C. Price Zimmermann, and his memoriam for William Lowell Putnam III, which appeared in the *American Alpine Journal* in 2015. A legendary professor at Reed College— later a dean at Davidson College—Zimmermann was that rare breed of teacher, like his historian colleagues Edward Segel and John Strawn, who had the ability not only to inspire their students with a love of history, but also to encourage them to aim for the highest standards of research.

For the purposes of this book however, I have primarily relied on the collection of documents relating to the 1939 expedition that are held in the archives of the American Alpine Club in Golden, Colorado, which is surely the most comprehensive collection of mountaineering books, manuscripts, and artifacts in the world. Of particular value were: "Report on the 1939 American Alpine Club Karakoram Expedition," July 10, 1940, a relatively brief but long-confidential analysis by the committee whose members included Joel Ellis Fisher, William P. House, Terris Moore, Bestor Robinson, and Walter A. Wood; typescript letters by members of the expedition to members of the American Alpine Club; "Movements of Climbers on K2, American Alpine Club Karakoram Expedition, 1939," a painstakingly detailed graph showing the movement of climbers and Sherpas on K2, July 4–September 10, 1939; an unsigned, handwritten four-page postmortem, titled "K2 Expedition"; Fritz Wiessner, "Wiessner Expedition to K2, 1939," nineteen-page typed manuscript, marked IMPORTANT; glass photographic slides from the expedition; and numerous telegrams and letters.

Fritz Wiessner is still awaiting his biographer. In the meantime, some places to begin include: Ed Webster, "A Man for All Mountains: The Life and Climbs of Fritz Wiessner," *Legends of North American Climbing*, December 1988; "Fritz Wiessner (1900–1988), bergfieber.de; John Rupley, "Fritz Wiessner," climbaz.com; Ed Webster, "Fritz Hermann Ernst Wiessner, 1900–1988," *Alpine Journal*, 1989; Hans Kraus, "Fritz Hermann Ernst Wiessner, 1900–1988," *American Alpine Journal*, 1989; and "Fritz Wiessner, 88; Career as a Climber Spanned 8 Decades," *New York Times*, July 6, 1988. Manifest of Alien Passengers, Arriving on the MS *St. Louis*, Sailing from Bremen, March 29, 1929, available at Ancestry.com. The *American Alpine Journal* duly recorded Wiessner's climbing accomplishments in the American and Trans-Canadian West. See, for example: Henry S. Hall Jr., "Mts. Monarch, Silverthorne, and the Klinaklini Glacier" (1937); William P. House, "Devils Tower" (1938); and Bestor Robinson, "Ascent of Mount Bell" (1938). Also in the *American Alpine Journal*, see Fritz Wiessner, "Nanga Parbat in Retrospect" (1933).

Jennifer Jordan's inspired research on Dudley Wolfe, the fruits of which can be seen in her *The Last Man on the Mountain*, swept away years of false impressions and gave us the first nuanced portrait of the doomed adventurer. Other sources on Wolfe include: "Report of the Death of an American Citizen, for Dudley F. Wolfe," by C. E. Macy, American Consul, Karachi, India, September 9, 1939; World War I Draft Registration Card, Rockland, Maine, June 5, 1917; US Passport Applications, October 8, 1917, and June 28, 1918; and Passenger List for the *Normandie*, Arriving in New York, May 2, 1938, all available at Ancestry.com. "Dudley Francis Wolfe, 1896–1939," *American Alpine Journal*, 1940. On Alice Damrosch Wolfe, see Nicholas Howe, "Alice Kiaer and Her Remarkable Red Stockings," *Skiing Heritage*, June 2006.

The *American Alpine Journal*, the unsurpassed chronicle of American mountaineering, diligently recorded the climbs of Jack Durrance, Eaton O. "Tony" Cromwell, and the other members of the 1939 K2 expedition over the years. They can be accessed at publications.americanalpineclub.org/search. "Dartmouth Mountaineering Club," *American Alpine Journal*, 1994.

"Pasang Kikuli, Phinsoo Sherpa, and Pasang Kitar," *Himalayan Journal* no. 12 (1940).

Members of the 1953 American K2 expedition ran across what remained of Camp Six. "We found two of the 1939 tents (blown to ribbons, of course), with sleeping bags, cooking utensils, stove, gas, and some food, all neatly stacked in the ruins," Tenth Expeditions Letter, September 11, 1953, American Alpine Club archives. These had all been carefully left by Tsering—in the unlikely event that his comrades were still alive—before he reluctantly abandoned the camp on August 2, 1939.

Dudley Wolfe's remains on K2 were discovered by Jennifer Jordan and Jeff Rhoads in July 2002. See Jordan, *The Last Man on the Mountain*, and Lindsay Griffin, "K2, Discovery of Dudley Wolfe's Body," *American Alpine Journal*, 2001. As in the case of the discovery of the remains of George Mallory, however, one cannot help but wish that some better guidelines can be developed that both answer the necessary historical questions while maintaining a proper respect for the dead. The remains of Pasang Kikuli, Kitar, and Phinsoo have never, to my knowledge, been found. Together, with Wolfe, they were the first four known fatalities on the world's second-highest mountain. But they weren't the last. As of December 2018, eighty-one climbers have died on K2.

CHAPTER THIRTEEN: *THE NORTH FACE*

Berg Heil! (2011). Large, *Where Ghosts Walked*.

Oxford: Official Handbook (Alden & Alden, 1936).

Nicholas Mailänder's long-awaited biography of Peter Aufschnaiter, *Er ging voraus nach Lhasa*, with contributions by Otto Kompatscher, was published as this book was going to press—one hopes that Mailänder's book will eventually be translated into English. Also see Martin Brauen, *Peter Aufschnaiter's Eight Years in Tibet* (2002), and Heinrich Harrer's obituary for his longtime friend, "Peter Aufschnaiter," *Himalayan Journal* no. 33 (1975).

A typescript copy of Kenneth Mason's unpublished autobiography is located in the Bodleian Library, Oxford University. A well-crafted memoir, Mason's manuscript also, from time to time, provides the reader with some revealing bits of social history. "The 'Thirties' seem today to be set in a different world," Mason wrote. "Dorothy and I always changed for dinner, and only on rare occasions in summer did I not put on a dinner jacket. At dinner parties when ladies were present, tail coats and stiff shirts were always worn; and at college dinner parties men were introduced to ladies and took them to dinner 'on their arm.'" Also see: Mason, *Abode of Snow*; Peter H. Hansen, "Kenneth Mason (1887–1976), geographer and moun-taineer," *Oxford Dictionary of National Biography* (1976); John Morris,

Notes

"Lieutenant-Colonel Kenneth Mason, M.C.," *Alpine Journal* 82, no. 326 (1977); "Lt-Col. Kenneth Mason: Notable Geographer," *The Times*, June 3, 1976; and 1939 England and Wales Register for Kenneth Mason, 1 Belbroughton Road, Oxford, available at Ancestry.com.

Mention of the first ascent of Oxford's Radcliffe Camera in 1937 can be found on p. 485 of Kenneth Mason's unpublished autobiography. "Robin Hodgkin," *The Telegraph*, August 27, 2003.

On the histories of the Himalayan Club and the *Himalayan Journal*, see: the Introduction by Nandini Purandare, and Harish Kapadia's "Journey of the Journal, 1929–2017," Special Volume (February 2017); Sir Geoffrey Corbett, "The Founding of the Himalayan Club," no. 1 (1929); and John Martyn, "The Story of the Himalayan Club, 1928–1978," and Trevor Braham, "Fifty Years Retrospect and Prospect"—all in the *Himalayan Journal* no. 35 (1979).

"Ovation in London: Mr. Chamberlain's Homecoming," *The Times*, October 1, 1938.

Despite all of his accomplishments and the not-inconsequential number of books that he authored, getting to the root of who Heinrich Harrer was during the Nazi era is no simple task. Like many Germans and Austrians who survived the war, he sought to minimize or trivialize any personal connections that he had with the Nazi state and its institutions. This does not by any means imply that the incredible personal transformation that Harrer experienced in Tibet was not genuine. I have no doubt that it was, and that he was a much different person in 1951 than he had been in, say, 1938. And it is this earlier version of himself that we are mainly concerned with here. Bearing that in mind, Harrer's own writings are still key, especially his autobiography, *Beyond Seven Years in Tibet* (2007).

On his connections with Nazism, some good places to begin include: Bernard Weinraub, "Dalai Lama's Tutor, Portrayed by Brad Pitt, Wasn't Just Roving through the Himalayas," *New York Times*, June 21, 1997; "Heinrich Harrer," *The Telegraph*, January 9, 2006; and Gerald Lehner, *Zwischen Hitler und Himalaya: Die Gedächtnislücken des Heinrich Harrer* (2007).

On the North Face of the Eiger, and the first successful ascent in 1938, see: Harrer, *The White Spider: The Story of the North Face of the Eiger* (1959); Ring, *How the English Made the Alps*; "An Irishman's Diary," *Irish Times*, April 23, 2004. In reconstructing Harrer's probable motorcycle route from

Notes

Graz to the Grindlewald on July 9/10, 1938, I relied on a Nazi-era road atlas, *V.B. Strassen-Atlas von Deutschland* (1936) which, prophetically or not, also included much of Austria and portions of western Poland. On better understanding the capabilities of a 1930s Puch 250 motorcycle, helmets off to two motorcyclist friends, Jon Lee of Portland, Oregon, and Kent Stull of Tulsa, Oklahoma, for lending their expertise.

Otto Zwahlen, *Der Kampf um die Eiger-Nordwand* (1936).

Zdarsky sacks were featured in the 1937 sporting goods catalog issued by Sporthaus Schuster in Munich, a copy of which can be viewed at verticalarchaeology.com.

Clarence K. Streit, "Climbers Conquer Dread Eiger Peak," *New York Times*, July 26, 1938. "The North Wall of the Eiger: Pitons Used in the Climb," *The Times*, July 26, 1938. See also the chapter titled "Miracle on the White Spider" in Harrer, *Beyond Seven Years in Tibet*.

On Kristallnacht in Munich, see: Large, *Where Ghosts Walked*; Nerdinger, *Munich and National Socialism*; and Fleckenstein and Purin, *Jüdisches Museum München*. The Online Multimedia Center at the Museum of Tolernace, Simon Wiesenthal Center, has published translations of the secret telegram sent from Munich at 1:20 a.m. by Gestapo chief Reinhard Heydrich instructing state police headquarters and SA officers on how to procede with anti-Jewish activities that night. See "Heydrich's Instructions, November 1938 Riots," Kristallnacht Documents at motlc.wiesenthal.com.

Interview with Nicholas Mailänder, Munich, March 2, 2018.

CHAPTER FOURTEEN: *THE SUMMER AT THE END OF THE WORLD*

Nicholas Mailänder, "Spitzenbergsport," in *Berg Heil!* Harrer, *Beyond Seven Years in Tibet*. Mierau, *Nationalsozialistische Politik*. Paul Bauer, *Spruchkammerverfahren*, April 19, 1948. Interview with Nicholas Mailänder, Munich, March 2, 2018.

Bombay, as it is still called by many despite its new official appellation, Mumbai, also has had a long and proud history of welcoming outsiders— from the Persians who ran the city's multi-caste restaurants, including the city's famous Leopold Café, to European Jews who came as refugees in the 1930s. On the latter, see: Anil Bhatti and Johannes Voigt, *Jewish Exile in India, 1933–1945* (1999), and Meylkh Viswanath, "From the Reich to the Raj: Uncovering the Story of German Refugees in India," *Jewish Standard*,

Notes

April 13, 2017. In uncovering the history of the German community in prewar Bombay, I'm indebted to the generous help given me in Mumbai by Dr. Martin Wälde, of the Goethe-Institut Max Mueller Bhavan, and by Jonas Stolze, Malte Kruse, and Bhavika Vohra of the Indo-German Chamber of Commerce.

For the 1939 German Nanga Parbat Reconnaissance expedition, see: Lutz Chicken, "Nanga Parbat Reconnaissance, 1939," and Peter Aufschnaiter, "Diamir Side of Nanga Parbat—Reconnaisance, 1939," *Himalayan Journal* no. 14 (1947); "German Overseas Expeditions," *Alpine Journal* 51, no. 259 (November 1939); Roger Croston, "Prisoners of the Raj," *Alpine Journal* (2006); Harrer, *Beyond Seven Years in Tibet*; "Hans Lobenhoffer," *The Telegraph*, October 15, 2014; "Lutz Chicken," *The Times*, May 12, 2012; and Lutz Chicken, *Durchs Jahrhundert: Mein Leben als Artz und Bergsteiger* (2004).

On the 1939 Polish Himalayan Expedition, see: "Polish Expedition to Nanda Devi," *Alpine Journal* 51, no. 259 (November 1939), and, S. B. Blake and Dr. Jakub Bujak, "The Polish Ascent of Nanda Devi East Peak, 1939," *Alpine Journal* 53, no. 262 (May 1941). "Polish Climbers Killed in the Himalayas," *The Times*, July 29, 1929. On the scrambling done by British journalists along the Polish–German frontier during the late summer of 1939, see Robert Fisk, "Clare Hollingworth: 104-Year-Old on Being First UK Correspondent to Report on Germans' Invasion of Poland," *The Independent*, March 19, 2016. "By far the hardest prewar climb in the Himalaya" is how Martin Moran, of the Alpine Club in London, described the 1939 Polish ascent. See his "Nanda Devi East, Northeast Ridge, Attempt," *American Alpine Journal*, 2016.

One cannot help but suspect that there was more to the life and times of Edmund Hillary than we are currently privy to. In the meantime, however, for learning more about New Zealand's most famous citizen, two superb places to begin include Alexa Johnston's superb authorized biography, *Sir Edmund Hillary: An Extraordinary Life* (2005), and Hillary's own writings, especially—as regards this book—*High Adventure: The True Story of the First Ascent of Everest* (1955).

Wise's New Zealand Post Office Directory, 1938 (1938). Also New Zealand Electoral Rolls for Percival Augustus Hillary, Auckland, available online at Ancestry.com. On the "Radiant Life" movement, see two articles by Hilary Stace: "Herbert Sutcliffe," *Dictionary of New Zealand Biography*, teara.govt.nz, and "School of Radiant Living," nzhistory.govt.nz. Dan Elish, *Edmund Hillary: First to the Top* (2006).

On the aborted escape attempt by Harrer, Loebenhoffer, and Chicken to Persia, see, especially: Harrer, *Beyond Seven Years in Tibet*; Croston, "Prisoners of the Raj"; and Aufschnaiter, "Diamir Side of Nanga Parbat."

CHAPTER FIFTEEN: *WAR*

E. S. G. De La Motte, "Illimani and the Nazis," *Alpine Journal* no. 53 (1940). *The Navy List: List of Ships, Establishments, and Officers of the Fleet*, April 1941, and Vol. III, October 1945. British Overseas Airways Corporation, Passenger List for Arrivals in Baltimore, Maryland, May 22, 1942, at Ancestry.com.

A British soldier who served for more than a decade along India's North-West Frontier, Norman Streatfeild also served as the transport officer for the 1936 French Himalayan expedition. See: C. S. Houston, "Norman R. Streatfeild, *Ob. 1940*," *Alpine Journal* 53, no. 262 (May 1941). Robert H. Bates, "Norman R. Streatfeild," *American Alpine Journal* (1941). "The Streatfeilds of Kent," streatfeild.info.

Volksbund Deutsche Kriegsgräberfürsorge, listing for Ludwig Vörg (1911–1941), volksbund.de.

H. W. Tilman, *When Men and Mountains Meet* (1946). Anderson, *High Mountains and Cold Seas*.

Dee Molenaar, "Hans Peter Misch, 1909–1987," *American Alpine Journal*, 1988. "Peter Misch," *Class Acts*, washington.edu/alumni/columns. "In Shanghai verstorben," *Aufbau*, May 3, 1946; Resident Alien's Border Crossing Identification Card, Peter H. Misch, Blaine, Washington, November 14, 1947; and Petition for Naturalization, Peter Hans Misch, Seattle, March 10, 1952, all at Ancestry.com.

Peter Almond, "Saviour of the Spitfire," *The Telegraph*, September 15, 2010.

Eric Shipton, *Mountains of Tartary* (1950) and *That Untravelled World*. Perrin, *Shipton & Tilman*.

Tony Smythe, *My Father, Frank*.

Paul Bauer, Personenmap, DAV Per 2 SG/9/0, DAV Archives, Munich. Spruchkammerverfahren for Paul Bauer, April 19, 1948. Bauer, *Kanchenjunga Challenge*. Interview with Nicholas Mailänder, Munich, March 2, 2018.

Notes

On the destruction of the so-called Mountain Jews on the Caucasus, two good places to begin are: Andrej Umansky, "The Mountain Jews and Their Fate During WWII," *Visions of Azerbaijan*, July–August 2012, visions.az; and Kiril Feferman, "Nazi Germany and the Mountain Jews: Was There a Policy?" *Holocaust and Genocide Studies* 21, no. 1 (Spring 2007), available online at Project Muse, jhu.edu.

In his 1953 application for readmission into the Alpine Club, Bauer wrote, "I feel obliged to apologize for the lack of details. The times were so troublesome. I have so few notes." Alpine Club, Qualification Papers, 1952–1954, Alpine Club library and archives, London.

Heinrich Harrer's *Seven Years in Tibet* and *Beyond Seven Years in Tibet* are the key sources on his escape from Dehra Dun. Other important sources include: Croston, "Prisoners of the Raj,"; Peter Aufschnaiter, "Escape to Lhasa, 1944–45," *Himalayan Journal* no. 14, (1947); Bettina von Reden and Roger Croston, "Turned Back from Tibet: Bruno Treipl's Wartime Adventures in Asia," *Tibet Journal* 32, no. 1 (Spring 2007); Rolf Magener, *Prisoner's Bluff* (1954), some of which are available online at gaebler.info/india/escape. Interview with Raj Kanwar, Dehra Dun, May 18, 2018. Martin Brauen, ed., *Peter Aufschnaiter's Eight Years in Tibet* (2002).

McDonald, *Brotherhood of the Rope: The Biography of Charles Houston.* Ringholz, *On Belay!: The Life of Legendary Mountaineer Paul Petzoldt.*

Burdsall, et al. *Men against the Clouds* (1980 revised edition). Terris Moore, "Arthur Brewster Emmons III, 1910–1962," *American Alpine Journal* 13, no. 2 (1963). "More than 1400 American Repatriates Arrive in New York Aboard Diplomatic Liner Gripsholm," *Santa Cruz Sentinel*, August 26, 1942. "Arthur Emmons, Diplomatic Aide," *New York Times*, August 23, 1962. Robert H. Bates, "Richard L. Burdsall, 1895–1953," *American Alpine Journal* (1953). Burdsall died in Argentina after reaching the summit of Aconcagua, at age fifty-seven, in 1953. See: Robert H. Bates, "Richard L. Burdsall, 1895–1953," *Alpine Journal* (1953). "Terris Moore, Educator and Adventurer, 85," *New York Times*, November 10, 1993. Robert H. Bates, "Terris Moore, 1908–1993," *American Alpine Journal* (1993). New York Chinese Exclusion Index, Jack Tai Young; 1930 US Federal Census, Brooklyn, for Jack Young, student at New York University; Passenger Manifest for the *Princess Marguerite*, Seattle, June 19, 1933, for Jack Theodore Young; and Major Jack T. Young, US Army, Masonic Membership Card, April 2, 1947, all at Ancestry.com. Chris

Notes

Treadway, "Life of 'Panda Lady' Celebrated," *Contra Costa Times*, May 16, 2008. Patricia Sullivan, "'Su-Lin' Young, 96; Explorer Lent Her Name to Pandas," *Washington Post*, May 20, 2008. Patricia Yollin, "China Explorer Adelaide 'Su-Lin' Young Dies," *SFGate*, May 18, 2008. "Adelaide 'Su Lin' Young: Intrepid Traveler in China," *The Times*, June 16, 2008. Jack Young is buried in Arlington National Cemetery, Section 66, Site 6024.

"Note on the Present Whereabouts and Occupation of Some of the Sherpa and Bhotia Porters," *Himalayan Journal* no. 14 (1947).

For Tenzing's experiences during the war years, see: *Tiger of the Snows*, Tenzing's 1955 autobiography as co-written by James Ramsey Ullman; and Ed Douglas, *Tenzing: Hero of Everest* (2003), a magnificent biography, beautifully researched and written with great insight and understanding.

Beryl Miles, *The Stars My Blanket* (1954). Beryl Smeeton, *Winter Shoes in Springtime* (1961). Miles Clark, *High Endeavors: The Extraordinary Life and Adventures of Miles & Beryl Smeeton* (1991).

CHAPTER SIXTEEN: *A NEW WORLD*

Alex von Tunzelmann, *Indian Summer: The Secret History of the End of an Empire* (2007). John Gunther, *Inside Asia* (1939).

Tilman quote is from Tony Smythe, *My Father, Frank*, p. 282.

Mason, *Abode of Snow*. S. Dillon Ripley, "Peerless Nepal—A Naturalist's Paradise," *National Geographic* 97, no. 1 (January 1950). Frances Leeson, "A Note on the U.S. Expedition to Nepal, 1949," *Himalayan Journal* no. 15 (1949). "Southern Face of Everest: American Expedition in Nepal," *The Times*, March 22, 1949. H. W. Tilman, "Exploring the Himalaya," *The Times*, November 18, 1950.

For the remarkable French expedition in 1950, the place to begin is Maurice Herzog's *Annapurna: First Conquest of an 8,000-Meter Peak* (1952) and Ang Tharkay's *Sherpa*, both of which should be followed by David Roberts' masterful investigation and analysis, *True Summit: What Really Happened on the Legendary Ascent of Annapurna* (2000). Also helpful are: Mason, *Abode of Snow*; Dyhrenfurth, *To the Third Pole*; and Maurice Herzog, "Annapurna," *Alpine Journal* 58, no. 283 (November 1951).

On the 1950 trek to Everest's south side, see: McDonald, *Brotherhood of the Rope*; and: Robert Trumbull, "U.S. Expedition Goes 18,000 Feet Up Unexplored Side of Mt. Everest," typescript of story for the *New York Times*, Bob Bates Papers, American Alpine Club Archives, Golden.

Notes

Colorado climber Elizabeth S. "Betsy" Cowles Partridge (1902–1977) is yet another prewar female American mountaineer in need of more biographical attention. For those interested, two places to begin are: Steven Yeager, "No Mountain Too High: The Climbs of Betsy Cowles Partridge," *American Heritage Center News*, ahcwyo.org; and Charles S. Houston, "Elizabeth Cowles Partridge," *American Alpine Journal*, 1977.

"Michael Ward," *The Telegraph*, October 18, 2005. Margalit Fox, "Michael Ward, 80, Doctor on '53 Everest Climb, Dies," *New York Times*, October 25, 2005. Michael Ward, "Exploration and Mapping of Everest," *Alpine Journal* (1994), and, "A New Map of the Everest Area," *Alpine Journal* (2003). George W. Rodway and Jeremy S. Windsor, "Pioneer of the High Realm: Michael Ward," *Himalayan Journal* no. 64 (2008). Bill Mumford, "Ian Mumford Obituary," *The Guardian*, June 8, 2015.

On the 1951 British Mount Everest Expedition, see: Eric Shipton, *Everest 1951: The Mount Everest Reconnaissance Expedition, 1951* (1951); Shipton, *That Untravelled World*; W. H. Murray, "The Reconnaissance of Mount Everest, 1951," *Alpine Journal* 58, no. 285 (November 1952); Hillary, *High Adventure*; Johnston, *Sir Edmund Hillary: An Extraordinary Life*; and Michael Ward, *In This Short Span: A Mountaineering Memoir* (1972). "Everest Expedition," July 3, 1951, and "Everest Expedition Plans," July 7, 1951, both in the *Times*.

The turmoil that the outbreak of World War II created in the Hillary household is well-documented in Johnston, *Sir Edmund Hillary*, and Hillary, *High Adventure*.

Eric Shipton also wrote an exclusive series of reports on the 1951 expedition for the *Times*, beginning with "Return to Everest: A New Reconnaissance from the South-West" on August 13, 1951. Moreover, Shipton created an international news sensation by publishing alleged photographs of footprints made by a Yeti or Abdominable Snowman. See: *The Times*, December 7, 1951; Shipton, *That Untravelled World*, pp. 195–200; and, most especially, Perrin, *Shipton & Tilman*, pp. 379–89. *Caveat emptor.*

Dyhrenfurth, *To the Third Pole*. Mason, *Abode of Snow*. Isserman and Weaver, *Fallen Giants*. A. Lohner, A Roch, A. Sutter, and Ernst Feuz, "The Swiss Garhwal Expedition of 1947," *Himalayan Journal* no. 15 (1949). H. W. Tilman, "Rakaposhi," *Alpine Journal* 56, no. 277 (November 1948). René Dittert, "Swiss Himalayan Expedition, 1949," *Himalayan Journal* no. 16 (1951).

Notes

On the two 1952 Swiss expeditions to Mount Everest, see: René Dittert, Gabriel Chevalley, and Raymond Lambert, *Forerunners to Everest: The Story of the Two Swiss Expeditions of 1952* (1954); André Roch, "The Swiss Everest Expedition—Spring, 1952," *Alpine Journal* 59, no. 286 (May 1953); and, Tenzing, *Tiger of the Snows*.

"Chinese Rename Everest," *The Times*, June 7, 1952.

"Everest Inviolate," *The Times*, July 25, 1952.

CHAPTER SEVENTEEN: *THE BRIGHTNESS OF THEIR RISING*

On the change in the leadership of the 1953 British Mount Everest Expedition by the members of the Himalayan Committee, see, especially, Jim Perrin's account in *Shipton & Tilman*. Shipton's own account, in *That Untravelled World*, is illuminating, while Maurice Isserman and Stewart Weaver do an excellent job of outlining the controversy in their *Fallen Giants*. The quote from the member of the committee is from a set of long typescript notes titled "Memo on the Everest Expedition Leadership for 1953," Everest History file folder, Box P5, Alpine Club archives, London. The Hillary letter is quoted in Johnston, *Sir Edmund Hillary*.

R. C. Evans, "The Cho Oyu Expedition, 1952," *Alpine Journal* 59, no. 286 (May 1953). Perrin, in *Shipton & Tilman*, provides an insightful and sobering analysis on why Shipton wanted to avoid entering Chinese territory.

"Mountain School Post for Mr. E. Shipton," *The Times*, December 8, 1952.

George Band, "John Hunt," *Oxford Dictionary of National Biography*, May 25, 2006. "Lord Hunt," *The Telegraph*, November 9, 1998.

Not surprisingly, the 1953 British Mount Everest Expedition has inspired more books than any other single episode in mountaineering history, a bibliography that now grows with every major anniversary of the historic climb. For the purposes of this book, I found those sources that were published closest to the actual date of the expedition to be the most useful. Among them are: Hillary, *High Adventure*; Tenzing, *Tiger of the Snows*; Wilfrid Noyce, *South Col* (1954); John Hunt, *The Ascent of Everest* (1953); and the extensive coverage in the *Alpine Journal* 59, no. 287 (November 1953), including John Hunt and Michael Westmacott's "Narrative of the Expedition" and "Sir John Hunt's Diary." Other valuable sources include: Michael Ward, *In This Short Span: Himalayan Mountaineering and*

Notes

Exploration (1972); Alfred Gregory, *Alfred Gregory's Everest* (1993); George Lowe and Huw Lewis-Jones, *The Conquest of Everest* (2013); Stephen Venables, *Everest: Summit of Achievement* (2013); Johnston, *Sir Edmund Hillary*; Douglas, *Tenzing*; as well as the most insightful writings of Chris Bonnington, Reinhold Messner, and Joe Simpson. Last, and far from least, is the incredible 1955 documentary film, *The Conquest of Everest*, which is in desperate need of a re-release by, and the caring attention of, the resident geniuses at the Criterion Collection.

The urination episode is detailed in Tenzing's *Tiger of the Snows*. Historic drawings, paintings, and photographs of the various British embassies in Kathmandu over the years can be found online at roomfordiplomacy.com.

Tenzing did not remember the crucifix, but did recall the cloth cat.

CHAPTER EIGHTEEN: *GLORY, STRENGTH, AND DECENCY*

Coronation Everest (1958),an account of James Morris' wherein he recounts his adventures as the official correspondent for *The Times* on the 1953 British Mount Everest Expedition, is a tru gem. Heartfelt, witty, and, methinks, an early influence on Eric Newby, it's a wonderful piece of travel writing from an era when the Raj was both gone and not gone at the same time. As Faulkner famously remarked, "The past isn't dead. It's not even past."

On how James Morris's coded message travelled from Namche Bazar to London, see: "How I Broke the News," in Venables, *Everest: Summit of Achievement*; and Morris, *Coronation Everest*. "Everest Conquered: Hilary and Tensing Reach the Summit," *The Times*, June 2, 1953.

King George's Jubilee Trust, *The Coronation of Her Majesty, Queen Elizabeth II: Approved Souvenir Programme* (1953). "The Coronation, 1953," *The Queen*, June 3, 1953 special edition. *The Conquest of Everest* (1953 documentary film).

Douglas, *Tenzing: Hero of Everest*. Tenzing and James Ramsey Ullman, *Tiger of the Snows*.

Kenneth Mason, Typescript Autobiography, dated April 1966, Bodleian Library, Oxford University.

On the 1953 German-Austrian expedition to Nanga Parbat, see: Hermann Buhl, *Nanga Parbat Pilgrimage* (1956), aka *Lonely Challenge* (1956); W. Frauenberger and Hermann Buhl, "The Ascent of Nanga Parbat," *Alpine Journal*, LIX, 289 (November 1954); Höfler, *Nanga Parbat*; and "Nanga Parbat, 1953," Hans Ertl's documentary film of the expedition,

Notes

available on YouTube. Reinhold Messner and Hirst Höfler's *Hermann Buhl: Climbing Without Compromise* (2000) is a superb introduction to the near-Homeric life and times of the Austrian climber. For the lingering impact of the not-yet-forgotten Paul Bauer on the 1953 Nanga Parbat expedition, see Mailänder, *Im Zeichen des Edelweiss*.

A wealth of helpful information on the Third American Karakoram Expedition, including letters and typescript reports, can be found among the Bob Bates Papers in the American Alpine Club Archives in Golden, Colorado. Other key sources on this 1953 American expedition to K2 include: Charles Houston and Robert H. Bates, *K2: The Savage Mountain* (1954); Curran, *K2: The Story of the Savage* Mountain; H. R. A. Streather, "K2; The Third American Karakoram Expedition," *Alpine Journal*, LIX, 289 (November 1954); Bates, "The Fight for K2," *American Alpine Journal*, 1954; McDonald, *Brotherhood of the Rope*; and Bates, *The Love of Mountains is Best*.

EPILOGUE: *TO THE STARS*

Nigel Hamilton, "The Influence of Europe on the Young JFK," *New England Journal of Public Policy*, IX, 1 (1993), and *JFK: Restless Youth* (1992). Robert Dallek, *An Unfinished Life* and Michael O'Brien, *John F. Kennedy*.

"John F. Kennedy Moon Speech—Rice Stadium, September 12, 1962," er.jsc.nasa.gov/she/ricetalk.htm. Eleven months after his speech in Houston, President Kennedy helped to present the Hubbard Medal from the National Geographic Society to the members of the American Mount Everest Expedition. They included expedition leader Norman Dyhrenfurth—the son of Günter and Hettie Dyhrenfurth, famed Swiss climbers of the 1930s—as well as the two climbers who made it first to the summit on May 1, 1963, Jim Whittaker from Seattle, and Nawang Gombu, Sherpa from Darjeeling. In a ceremony in the new flower garden at the White House, Nawang Gombu presented Kennedy with a *kata*, a friendship scarf. The President was also given the flag that three other members of the expedition placed on the summit on May 22. "Thank you," a smiling Kennedy replied. "We will hang this in the White House and then give it to the Archives. This is wonderful." Papers of John F. Kennedy, Presidential Papers, President's Office Files, Speech Files, "Remarks on presenting Hubbard Medal to leader of American Mount Everest Expedition, 5 July 1963." President Kennedy returned to Texas, for the last time, four and one half months later.

Index

Index

Index

Index

Index

Index

Index

Index

Index

Index

Index

Index

Index

ABOUT THE AUTHOR

Scott Ellsworth is the *New York Times* bestselling author of *The Secret Game*, which won the 2016 PEN/ESPN Award for Literary Sports Writing. He has written about American history for the *New York Times*, the *Washington Post*, and the *Los Angeles Times*. Formerly a historian at the Smithsonian Institution, he is also the author of *Death in a Promised Land*, a groundbreaking account of the 1921 Tulsa race massacre. He lives with his wife and twin sons in Ann Arbor, where he teaches at the University of Michigan.